Revised An Introduction Project Management Third Edition

With Brief Guides to Microsoft Project 2010 and @Task

By

Kathy Schwalbe

Professor, Augsburg College

Department of Business Administration

Minneapolis, Minnesota

Revised An Introduction to

Project Management, Third Edition

Reviewers/Editors
Ray Guidone
Carl Hixon
Cindy Dawson
Brian May

Cover Photo
Dan Schwalbe

Published by Kathy Schwalbe, LLC

Visit **www.kathyschwalbe.com** for more information on this and other books by Kathy Schwalbe.

Note: This text includes minor corrections from the first printing in August 2009 along with a new Appendix A based on Project 2010. It was created in April 2010.

For Dan, Anne, Bobby, and Scott

BRIEF TABLE OF CONTENTS

DETAILED TABLE OF CONTENTS

PREFACE

The recent recession has made organizations appreciate the need for good project, program, and portfolio management skills more than ever. Many organizations, including corporations, government agencies, non-profit organizations, colleges, and universities have responded to this need by establishing courses and programs in project management. Hundreds of books are now available on this topic.

After publishing the first two editions of this book, my publisher, Course Technology, now a branch of Cengage Learning, decided not to update it. They publish other books with higher sales, including my *Information Technology Project Managemen*t book, now in its sixth edition. I personally use this text, *An Introduction to Project Management*, in my project management courses at Augsburg College, and over 7,500 copies of the second edition were sold last year world-wide. I plan to keep updating and using this text for years to come. I thank Cengage Learning for giving me the rights to self-publish this third edition and permission to use some of the content from my other book.

What makes this book different from other project management books? First of all, people actually enjoy reading it. I get emails every week from readers like you who appreciate my straight-forward, organized writing style. They like the way that I explain concepts and then provide realistic examples to help them learn to apply those concepts. Since I use this text in my own classes, I get a lot of feedback from students and see first-hand what works and does not work in a classroom setting. Several people have commented that they like the cartoons, Jeopardy games on the companion Web site, and my honest, sometimes humorous style. Project management can be a boring subject, but I think it's one of the most exciting topics and careers, especially if you want to change the world for the better.

This text addresses the need for people in *all* majors and industries to understand and apply good project, program, and portfolio management. It includes many real-world examples in the "What Went Right," "What Went Wrong," "Media Snapshot," and "Best Practice" segments. People like to read about real projects to learn from the successes and failures of others. They also realize that there are projects in all aspects of life, from remodeling a house to running a political campaign to developing a new software application.

I'm most excited about the fact that this book provides comprehensive samples of applying various tools and techniques to a realistic project. Many people learn best by example, so I've provided detailed examples of applying project management to a project everyone can relate to. I have never come across a textbook that presents project management concepts and then brings them to life in a fully developed sample project. I also provide template files for creating the sample documents. I believe this approach helps many people truly understand and apply good project management.

NEW TO THE THIRD EDITION

Building on the success of the previous editions, *An Introduction to Project Management, Third Edition* introduces a uniquely effective combination of features. The main changes to the third edition include the following:

- The text is updated to reflect changes in the latest *PMBOK® Guide, Fourth Edition,* published by PMI in December, 2008.

- The text now includes nine chapters instead of eight. The previous chapter 8 included information on Closing and Best Practices. These two topics are now broken into two separate, shorter chapters.

- Appendix A, Brief Guide to Microsoft Project 2010, has been rewritten and provides an example based on performing a three-month class project. New exercises are provided as well based on my experience teaching students to use this powerful software.

- There is a new appendix, Appendix B, Brief Guide to @task, which provides information on using the number one online project management software, @task. It provides step-by-step instructions on creating a project in @task, importing a Project file, and using portfolio management features.

- Appendix C, Resources, includes information about the companion Web sites, a list of available template files, three running case studies, information about using the Fissure project management simulation software, and instructions for accessing information about the Project Management Professional (PMP) and related certifications. The Fissure simulation software is still available as a separate purchase from www.ichapters.com. Detailed instructions for using the simulation are available on the companion Web site.

- The Dilbert and other cartoons have been replaced with relevant (and funny) cartoons from xkcd.com.

- The companion Web site no longer requires a password. Simply go to www.intropm.com to access it. Instructors must contact me directly (schwalbe@augsburg.edu) to gain access to the instructor site.

- Updated Jeopardy games are included on the companion Web site for each chapter. You can use these as review games in a classroom setting, or you can go through them on your own to help reinforce your understanding of key terms and other concepts in each chapter. Sorry, but podcasts are no longer provided.

- Updated examples and references are provided throughout the text, and user feedback is incorporated.

APPROACH

This text provides up-to-date information on how good project, program, and portfolio management can help you achieve organizational as well as individual success. Distinct features of this text include its:

- relationship to the Project Management Body of Knowledge

- instructions on using Microsoft Project 2010 and @task software

- instructions on using project management simulation software developed by Fissure (purchased separately on CD/ROM for about $12 from www.ichapters.com)

- comprehensive samples of applying tools and techniques to a realistic project

- inclusion of templates and seamless integration of various software applications

- robust and free companion Web site

PMBOK® Guide Framework

The Project Management Institute (PMI) created the *Guide to the Project Management Body of Knowledge* (the *PMBOK® Guide*) as a framework for understanding project management. The *PMBOK® Guide* is, however, just that—a guide. This text uses the *PMBOK® Guide, Fourth Edition* as a foundation, but goes beyond it by providing more details, highlighting additional topics, and providing a real-world context for project, program, and portfolio management.

Instructions for using Microsoft Project 2010 and @task

Appendix A of the text includes basic information on project management software and detailed, step-by-step instructions on using the number one stand-alone product, Microsoft Project *2010*. You do not need to buy a separate book to learn how to use Project 2010 effectively. Appendix B includes instructions on using @task, the number one online project management tool. You can get free trials of both of these products from the vendor's Web sites (www.microsoft.com/project and www.attask.com).

Instructions for Using Simulation Software

You can also purchase a project management simulation tool developed by Fissure, a PMI Registered Education Provider, from www.ichapters.com and use the instructions on the companion Web site to use this powerful learning tool. Note that this simulation does not teach you how to use project management software; it teaches you how to manage a project.

Comprehensive Samples of Applying Tools and Techniques to a Realistic Project

After explaining basic concepts, tools, and techniques, this text shows the reader how an organization selected, initiated, planned, executed, monitored and controlled, and closed a realistic project, called the Just-In-Time Training project. It provides *over 50 sample project management deliverables* such as a business case, stakeholder register, project charter, project management plan, work breakdown structure, Gantt chart, cost baseline, Pareto chart, resource histogram, performance report, risk register, contract, lessons-learned report, and so on for this project. You can also access the template files used to create them from the free companion Web site for this text or from the author's personal Web site. As one reviewer stated:

> *It comprehensively communicates what it really takes to manage a large project, including required deliverables, work products, and documentation. I haven't seen either a text or documentation in industry which communicates this subject this comprehensively or this accurately.* (Gilbert S. Leonard, Adjunct Professor and retired project manager, Exxon Mobil Corporation)

Provides Templates and Seamless Integration of Various Software Applications

You do not have to reinvent the wheel when it comes to much of the documentation required for managing projects. This text uses over 50 free template files for creating various documents, spreadsheets, diagrams, and charts. Various software applications are used throughout the text in a seamless fashion. I purposely created the templates in a simple format. Feel free to modify them to meet your needs.

Includes a Free Companion Web Site (www.intropm.com)

A companion Web site provides you with a one-stop location to access informative links and tools to enhance your learning. This site will be a valuable resource as you access links mentioned in the text, take online quizzes, play Jeopardy games, and download templates and files for Project 2010. Instructors can access a protected instructor site, which includes the same information plus copyrighted lecture slides, solution files, sample syllabi, and other information. Instructors can also share information on how they use this text in their classes. You can also access the author's site to see real class syllabi, samples of student projects and presentations, and other helpful links.

ORGANIZATION AND CONTENT

An Introduction to Project Management, Third Edition, is organized into nine chapters and three appendices. The first two chapters introduce project, program, and portfolio management and discuss different approaches for their selection. You'll read about Global Construction, Inc. and how they decided to pursue the Just-In-Time Training project. The next six chapters follow the five process groups of project management: initiating, planning (broken down into two chapters), executing, monitoring and controlling, and closing. These six chapters apply various tools and techniques in each of these process groups to the Just-In-Time Training project. Chapter nine describes more information and research on best practices. Appendix A provides general information on project management software and a step-by-step guide to using Microsoft Project 2010. Appendix B includes information on using @task, and Appendix C provides resources information, such as a summary of information on the companion Web site, a list of templates, running case studies, advice on using the Fissure simulation software, and resources to help you learn more about project management certification.

PEDAGOGICAL FEATURES

Several pedagogical features are included in this text to enhance presentation of the materials so that you can more easily understand the concepts and apply them. Throughout the text, emphasis is placed on applying concepts to up-to-date, real-world project management.

Learning Objectives, Chapter Summaries, Quick Quizzes, Discussion Questions, Exercises, Team Projects, and Case Studies

Learning Objectives, Chapter Summaries, Quick Quizzes, Discussion Questions, Exercises, Team Projects, and Case Studies are designed to function as integrated study tools. Learning Objectives reflect what you should be able to accomplish after completing each chapter. Chapter Summaries highlight key concepts you should master. The Quick Quizzes help reinforce your understanding of important concepts in each chapter. The Discussion Questions help guide critical thinking about those key concepts. Exercises provide opportunities to practice important techniques, as do the Team Projects. The Case Studies in Appendix C provide a robust means to apply what you have learned from the text to realistic case studies, similar to the example used throughout the text.

Opening Case and Case Wrap-Up

To set the stage, each chapter begins with an opening case related to the materials in that chapter. These scenarios spark interest and introduce important concepts in a real-world context. As project management concepts and techniques are discussed, they are applied to the opening case and other similar scenarios. Each chapter then closes with a Case Wrap-Up—some problems are overcome and some problems require more effort—to further illustrate the real world of project management.

What Went Right? and What Went Wrong?

Failures, as much as successes, can be valuable learning experiences. Carl Hixson, a program manager at Oracle and adjunct instructor who uses this text, said he loves the anonymous quote, "We need to learn from people's mistakes because we'll never have time to make them all ourselves." Each chapter of the text includes one or more examples of real projects that went right as well as examples of projects that went wrong. These examples further illustrate the importance of mastering key concepts in each chapter.

Media Snapshots and Best Practice Features

The world is full of projects. Several television shows, movies, newspapers, Web sites, and other media highlight project results, good and bad. Relating project management concepts to all types of projects, as highlighted in the media, will help you understand and see the importance of this growing field. Why not get people excited about studying project management by showing them how to recognize project management concepts in popular television shows, movies, or other media? It is also important to study best practices so readers can learn how to implement project management in an optimum way.

Cartoons

Each chapter includes a new cartoon used with permission from the popular Web site xkcd.com. These cartoons use humor to illustrate concepts from the text.

Key Terms

The field of project management includes many unique terms that are vital to creating a common language and understanding of the field. Key terms are displayed in boldface and are defined the first time they appear. Definitions of key terms are provided in alphabetical order at the end of each chapter and in a glossary at the end of the text.

Application Software

Learning becomes much more dynamic with hands-on practice using the top project management software tools in the industry, Microsoft Project 2010 and @task, as well as other tools, such as spreadsheet software. Each chapter offers you many opportunities to get hands-on experience and build new software skills by applying concepts to problems posed for them. In this way, the text accommodates both those who learn by reading and those who learn by doing.

SUPPLEMENTS

The following supplemental materials are available when this text is used in a classroom setting. All of the teaching tools available with this text are provided to the instructor on a secure Web site. Instructors must contact me at schwalbe@augsburg.edu to gain access.

- **Instructor's Manual:** The Instructor's Manual that accompanies this textbook includes additional instructional material to assist in class preparation, including suggestions for lecture topics and additional discussion questions.

- **PowerPoint Presentations:** The instructor site for this text includes lecture slides for each chapter created with Microsoft PowerPoint. These slides provide a teaching aid for classroom presentation, and they can be made available to students on the organization's secure network for online review or they can be printed for classroom distribution. Instructors can modify slides or add their own slides for additional topics they introduce to the class. Remember that these slides are copyrighted materials.

- **Solution Files:** Solutions to end-of-chapter questions can be found on the instructor site.

- **Student Online Companion:** As mentioned earlier, the free student site includes links to sites mentioned in the text, template files, interactive quizzes, Jeopardy games, and other helpful resources.

ACKNOWLEDGEMENTS

I never would have taken on another major book project without the help of many people. I would like to thank the staff at Course Technology for their dedication and hard work in helping me produce the first two editions of this book and in providing me with the rights and permissions needed to produce to third edition. Tricia Coia,

Patricia Shogren, Cathie DiMassa, and many more people did a great job in planning and executing all of the work involved in producing the first two editions of this book. I'd like to thank Kate Mason, Charles McCormick, and Karen Lee of Cengage Learning for their help in getting rights and permissions for me to self publish this edition.

I thank my many colleagues and experts in the field who contributed information to this book. I especially thank Ray Guidone, a faculty member at New York City College of Technology, for providing a detailed review and edit of this edition. Carl Hixson, a program manager at Oracle and adjunct faculty member at Augsburg College, also provided valuable feedback. One of my favorite former students, Cindy Dawson, now a project manager at Express Scripts, agreed to do the final proofreading of this text. I thank Ty Kiisel and Josh Custer at @task for providing me with an evaluation copy of their software and helping to make it easier for readers of this book to download a free trial. I also thank Randall Munroe, creator of xkcd.com, for allowing me to use his great comics.

Several people contributed to earlier editions of this text. Paul Sundby provided information on the construction industry, Mike Vinje shared best practice information, Nick Matteucci provided software access and advice, Jesse Freese provided the Fissure simulation software, Angela Jaskowiak provided feedback on the New Business Venture case study, and many other people provided input and inspiration. I really enjoy the network of project managers, authors, and consultants in this field who are passionate about improving the theory and practice of project management. Four faculty reviewers provided excellent feedback. Gary Armstrong, Shippensburg University; Ray Guidone, New York City College of Technology; Gilbert S. Leonard, Cy-Fair College; and Tom Norris, State University of New York at Cobleskill provided outstanding suggestions for improving the first two editions of the text.

I also want to thank my students and colleagues at Augsburg College, the University of Minnesota, and corporate classes for providing input. I received many valuable comments from them on ways to improve my materials and courses. I am also grateful for the examples students provide and the questions they ask in classes. I learn new aspects of project management and teaching all the time by interacting with students, faculty, and staff.

Most of all, I am grateful to my family. Without their support, I never could have written this book. My wonderful husband, Dan, was very patient and supportive, as always. His expertise as a lead software developer for ComSquared Systems comes in handy, too. Our three children, Anne, Bobby, and Scott, continue to be very supportive of their mom's work. Our oldest, Anne, is now a Program Director for the Teach for America program in South Dakota. Bobby graduated from USC this year and is a software developer at Alelo Technology in Venice Beach, California. Scott will be a junior in high school this fall. He is glad that I can work at home a lot, and he likes seeing his name in print. Our children all understand the main reason why I write—I have a passion for educating future leaders of the world, including them.

As always, I am eager to receive your feedback on this book. Please send all feedback to me at schwalbe@augsburg.edu

Kathy Schwalbe, Ph.D., PMP

Professor, Department of Business Administration

Augsburg College

ABOUT THE AUTHOR

 Kathy Schwalbe is a Professor in the Department of Business Administration at Augsburg College in Minneapolis, where she primarily teaches courses in project management and problem solving for business. She has also taught systems analysis and design, information systems projects, and electronic commerce. Kathy was also an adjunct faculty member at the University of Minnesota, where she taught a graduate-level course in project management in the engineering department. She also provides training and consulting services to several organizations and speaks at numerous conferences. Kathy's first job out of college was as a project manager in the Air Force. Kathy worked for 10 years in industry before entering academia in 1991. She was an Air Force officer, project manager, systems analyst, senior engineer, and information technology consultant. Kathy is an active member of PMI, having served as the Student Chapter Liaison for the Minnesota chapter, VP of Education for the Minnesota chapter, Editor of the ISSIG Review, Director of Communications for PMI's Information Systems Specific Interest Group, member of PMI's test-writing team, and member of the OPM3 update team. Kathy earned her Ph.D. in Higher Education at the University of Minnesota, her MBA at Northeastern University's High Technology MBA program, and her B.S. in mathematics at the University of Notre Dame. Visit her personal Web site at www.kathyschwalbe.com.

Chapter 1

An Introduction to Project, Program, and Portfolio Management

> ## LEARNING OBJECTIVES
>
> **After reading this chapter, you will be able to:**
>
> - Understand the growing need for better project, program, and portfolio management
> - Explain what a project is, provide examples of projects, list various attributes of projects, and describe project constraints
> - Describe project management and discuss key elements of the project management framework, including project stakeholders, the project management knowledge areas, common tools and techniques, and project success factors
> - Discuss the relationship between project, program, and portfolio management and their contribution to enterprise success
> - Describe the project management profession, including suggested skills for project, program, and portfolio managers, the role of professional organizations like the Project Management Institute, the importance of certification and ethics, and the growth of project and portfolio management software

OPENING CASE

Doug Milis, the Chief Executive Officer (CEO) of Global Construction, Inc., was summarizing annual corporate highlights to the board of directors. Like many other large construction companies, they had a very difficult year. They had to scale down operations and let some employees go. When one of the board members asked what he was most proud of that year, Doug thought for a few seconds, and then replied,

"Excellent question, Gabe. Honestly, I think the main reason we survived this year was because we are truly a project-based organization. We have dramatically improved our ability to quickly select and implement projects that help our company succeed and cancel or redirect other projects. All of our projects align with our business strategies, and we have consistent processes in place for getting things done. We can also respond quickly to market changes, unlike many of our competitors. Marie Scott, our Director of the Project Management Office (PMO), has done an outstanding job in making this happen. And believe me, it was not easy. It's never easy to implement changes across an entire company. But with this new capability to manage projects across the organization, I am very confident that we will have continued success in years to come."

INTRODUCTION

Many people and organizations today have a new or renewed interest in project management. In the past, project management primarily focused on providing schedule and resource data to top management in just a few industries, such as the military and construction industries. Today's project management involves much more, and people in every industry and every country manage projects. New technologies have become a significant factor in many businesses, and the use of interdisciplinary and global work teams has radically changed the work environment.

The statistics below demonstrate the significance of project management in today's society:

- In 2007 the total compensation for the average senior project manager in U.S. dollars was $104,776 per year in the United States, $111,412 in Australia, and $120,364 in the United Kingdom. The average total compensation of a program manager was $122,825 in the United States, $133,718 in Australia, and $165,489 in the United Kingdom. The average total compensation for a Project Management Office (PMO) Director was $134,422 in the United States, $125,197 in Australia, and $210,392 in the United Kingdom. This survey was based on self-reported data from more than 5,500 practitioners in 19 countries.[1]
- Project management certification continues to be one of the most popular certifications throughout the world.
- The U.S. spends $2.3 trillion on projects every year, and the world as a whole spends nearly $10 trillion on projects of all kinds. Projects, therefore, account for about one fourth of the U.S. and the world's gross domestic product.[2]
- The Apprentice, a popular reality television show, portrays the important role project managers play in business. Each week of the show, teams select a project

manager to lead them in accomplishing that week's project. The project manager is held partly responsible for the team's success or failure. Whether you are trying to make money by selling lemonade, running a golf tournament, or developing a new product, project managers play a vital role to business success.

- Project management is also a vital skill for personal success. Managing a family budget, planning a wedding, remodeling a house, completing a college degree, and many other personal projects can benefit from good project management.

What Went Wrong?

In 1995, the Standish Group published an often-quoted study entitled "CHAOS". This prestigious consulting firm surveyed 365 information technology (IT) executive managers in the United States who managed more than 8,380 IT application projects. As the title of the study suggests, the projects were in a state of chaos. United States companies spent more than $250 billion each year in the early 1990s on approximately 175,000 IT application development projects. Examples of these projects included creating a new database for a state department of motor vehicles, developing a new system for car rental and hotel reservations, and implementing a client-server architecture for the banking industry. Their study reported that the overall success rate of IT projects was only 16.2 percent. The surveyors defined success as meeting project goals on time and on budget.

The study also found that more than 31 percent of IT projects were canceled before completion, costing U.S. companies and government agencies more than $81 billion. The authors of this study were adamant about the need for better project management in the IT industry. They explained, "Software development projects are in chaos, and we can no longer imitate the three monkeys—hear no failures, see no failures, speak no failures."[3]

In a more recent study, PricewaterhouseCoopers surveyed 200 companies from 30 different countries about their project management maturity and found that over half of all projects fail. They also found that only 2.5 percent of corporations consistently meet their targets for scope, time, and cost goals for all types of project.[4]

Although several researchers question the methodology of the CHAOS studies, their popularity has prompted organizations throughout the world to examine their practices in managing projects. Managers are recognizing that to be successful, they need to be conversant with and use modern project management techniques. People from all types of disciplines—science, liberal arts, education, business, etc.—can benefit from basic project management principles. Individuals are realizing that to remain competitive, they must develop skills to effectively manage the professional and personal projects they undertake. They also realize that many of the concepts of project management, especially interpersonal skills, will help them as they work with people on a day-to-day basis.

Many organizations claim that using project management provides advantages, such as:

- Better control of financial, physical, and human resources
- Improved customer relations
- Shorter development times
- Lower costs

An Introduction to Project Management, Third Edition

- Higher quality and increased reliability
- Higher profit margins
- Improved productivity
- Better internal coordination
- Higher worker morale

In addition to project management, organizations are embracing program and portfolio management to address enterprise-level needs. This chapter introduces projects and project management, describes the differences between project, program, and portfolio management, discusses the role of the project, program, and portfolio manager, and provides important background information on these growing professions.

WHAT IS A PROJECT?

To discuss project management, it is important to understand the concept of a project. A **project** is "a temporary endeavor undertaken to create a unique product, service, or result."[5] Operations, on the other hand, is work done in organizations to sustain the business. Projects are different from operations in that they end when their objectives have been reached or the project has been terminated.

Examples of Projects

Projects can be large or small and involve one person or thousands of people. They can be done in one day or take years to complete. Examples of projects include the following:

- A young couple hires a firm to design and build them a new house.
- A retail store manager works with employees to display a new clothing line.
- A college campus upgrades its technology infrastructure to provide wireless Internet access.
- A construction company designs and constructs a new office building for a client.
- A school implements new government standards for tracking student achievement
- A group of musicians starts a company to help children develop their musical talents
- A pharmaceutical company launches a new drug
- A television network develops a system to allow viewers to vote for contestants and provide other feedback on programs.
- The automobile industry develops standards to streamline procurement.
- A government group develops a program to track child immunizations.

Project Attributes

As you can see, projects come in all shapes and sizes. The following attributes help to define a project further:

- *A project has a unique purpose.* Every project should have a well-defined objective. For example, many people hire firms to design and build a new house, but each house, like each person, is unique.

- *A project is temporary.* A project has a definite beginning and a definite end. For a home construction project, owners usually have a date in mind when they'd like to move into their new homes.

- *A project is developed using progressive elaboration or in an iterative fashion.* Projects are often defined broadly when they begin, and as time passes, the specific details of the project become more clear. For example, there are many decisions that must be made in planning and building a new house. It works best to draft preliminary plans for owners to approve before more detailed plans are developed.

- *A project requires resources, often from various areas.* Resources include people, hardware, software, or other assets. Many different types of people, skill sets, and resources are needed to build a home.

- *A project should have a primary customer or sponsor.* Most projects have many interested parties or stakeholders, but someone must take the primary role of sponsorship. The **project sponsor** usually provides the direction and funding for the project.

- *A project involves uncertainty.* Because every project is unique, it is sometimes difficult to define the project's objectives clearly, estimate exactly how long it will take to complete, or determine how much it will cost. External factors also cause uncertainty, such as a supplier going out of business or a project team member needing unplanned time off. This uncertainty is one of the main reasons project management is so challenging.

It should not be difficult to explain the goals or purpose of a project. As described in the next chapter, it is important to work on projects for the right reasons. Unlike the characters in the comic in Figure 1-1, you should not work on projects just because you think they are cool; projects should add value to individuals or organizations in a cost-effective manner.

Figure 1-1. Not so practical projects (www.xkcd.com)

A good project manager contributes to a project's success. **Project managers** work with the project sponsors, the project team, and the other people involved in a project to define, communicate, and meet project goals.

Project Constraints

Every project is constrained in different ways. Some project managers focus on scope, time, and cost constraints. These limitations are sometimes referred to in project management as the **triple constraint**. To create a successful project, a project manager must consider scope, time, and cost and balance these three often-competing goals. He or she must consider the following:

- *Scope*: What work will be done as part of the project? What unique product, service, or result does the customer or sponsor expect from the project?
- *Time*: How long should it take to complete the project? What is the project's schedule?
- *Cost*: What should it cost to complete the project? What is the project's budget? What resources are needed?

Other people focus on the quaduple constraint, which adds quality as a fourth constraint.

- *Quality*: How good does the quality of the products or services need to be? What do we need to do to satisfy the customer?

The *PMBOK® Guide, Fourth Edition* suggests these four constraints plus risk.

- *Risk*: How much uncertainty are we willing to accept on the project?

Figure 1-2 shows these five constraints. The triple constraint goals—scope, time, and cost—often have a specific target at the beginning of the project. For example, a couple might initially plan to move into their new 2,000 square foot home in six months and spend $300,000 on the entire project. The couple will have to make many decisions along the way that may affect meeting those goals. They might need to increase the budget to meet scope and time goals or decrease the scope to meet time and budget goals. The other two constraints—quality and risk—affect the ability to meet scope, time, and cost goals. Projects by definition involve uncertainty, and the customer defines quality. No one can predict with one hundred percent accuracy what risks might occur on a project. Customers cannot define in detail their quality expecations for a project on day one. These two constraints often affect each other as well as the scope, time, and cost goals of a project.

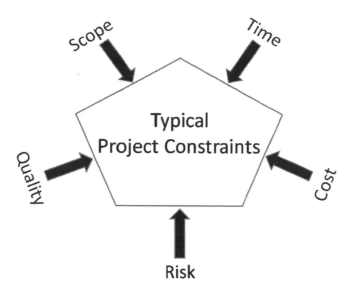

Figure 1-2. Typical project constraints

For example, the couple may have picked out a certain type of flooring for most of their home early in the design process, but that supplier may have run out of stock, forcing them to choose a different flooring to meet the schedule goal. This may affect the cost of the project. Projects rarely finish according to the discrete scope, time, and cost goals originally planned. Instead of discrete target goals for scope, time, and cost, it is often more realistic to set a range of goals that allow for uncertainties, such as spending between $275,000 and $325,000 and having the home completed within five to seven months. These goals allow for inevitable changes due to risk and quality considerations.

On some projects, other constraints may be more important than scope, time, cost, quality, or risk. Experienced project managers know that you must decide which constraints are most important on each particular project. If time is most important, you must often change the initial scope and/or cost goals to meet the schedule. You might have to accept more risk and lower quality expectations. If scope goals are most important, you may need to adjust time and/or cost goals, decrease risk, and increase quality expectations. If communications is most important, you must focus on that. If there are set procurement goals or constraints, that knowledge might be key to the project. In any case, sponsors must provide some type of target goals for a project's scope, time, and cost and define other key constraints for a project. The project manager should be communicating with the sponsor throughout the project to make sure the project meets his or her expectations.

How can you avoid the problems that occur when you meet scope, time, and cost goals, but lose sight of customer satisfaction? The answer is *good project management, which includes more than meeting project constraints.*

WHAT IS PROJECT MANAGEMENT?

Project management is "the application of knowledge, skills, tools and techniques to project activities to meet the project requirements."[6] Project managers must not only strive to meet specific scope, time, cost, and quality requirements of projects, they must also facilitate the entire process to meet the needs and expectations of the people involved in or affected by project activities.

Figure 1-3 illustrates a framework to help you understand project management. Key elements of this framework include the project stakeholders, project management knowledge areas, project management tools and techniques, project success, and the contribution of a portfolio of projects to the success of the entire enterprise. Each of these elements of project management is discussed in more detail in the following sections.

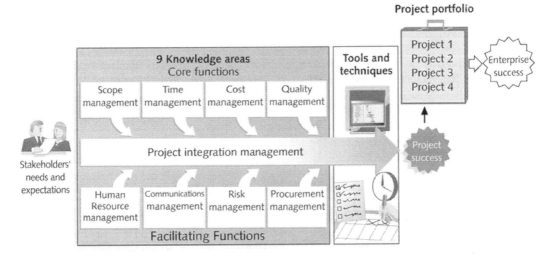

Figure 1-3. Project management framework (Schwalbe, Information Technology Project Management, Sixth Edition, 2010)

Project Stakeholders

Stakeholders are the people involved in or affected by project activities and include the project sponsor, project team, support staff, customers, users, suppliers, and even opponents to the project. These stakeholders often have very different needs and expectations. For example, there are several stakeholders involved in a home construction project.

- The project sponsors would be the potential new homeowners. They would be the people paying for the house and could be on a very tight budget, so they would expect the contractor to provide accurate estimates of the costs involved in building the house. They would also need a realistic idea of when they could move in and what type of home they could afford given their budget constraints. The new homeowners would have to make important decisions to keep the costs of the house within their budget. Can they afford to finish the basement right away? If they can afford to finish the basement, will it affect the projected move-in date? In this example, the project sponsors are also the customers and users for the product, which is the house.

- The project manager in this example would normally be the general contractor responsible for building the house. He or she needs to work with all the project stakeholders to meet their needs and expectations.

- The project team for building the house would include several construction workers, electricians, carpenters, and so on. These stakeholders would need to know exactly what work they must do and when they need to do it. They would need to know if the required materials and equipment will be at the construction site or if they are expected to provide the materials and equipment. Their work would need to be coordinated since there are many interrelated factors involved. For example, the carpenter cannot put in kitchen cabinets until the walls are completed.

- Support staff might include the employers of the homeowners, the general contractor's administrative assistant, and other people who support other stakeholders. The employers of the homeowners might expect their employees to complete their work but allow some flexibility so they can visit the building site or take phone calls related to building the house. The contractor's administrative assistant would support the project by coordinating meetings between the buyers, the contractor, suppliers, and other stakeholders.

- Building a house requires many suppliers. The suppliers would provide the wood, windows, flooring materials, appliances, and other items. Suppliers would expect exact details on what items they need to provide, where and when to deliver those items, and similar information.

- Additional stakeholders would include the city council and mayor, who would be interested in increasing revenues. They might suggest certain guidelines for the minimum value of the homes for providing adequate property taxes. The city may also have regulations to ensure the safety of the public in the area of the constuction site. The local housing inspector would also be a stakeholder, concerned with ensuring that everything meets specific codes and regulations.

- There may or may not be opponents to a project. In this example, there might be a neighbor who opposes the project because the workers are making so much noise that she cannot concentrate on her work at home, or the noise might awaken her sleeping children. She might interrupt the workers to voice her complaints or even file a formal complaint. Alternatively, the neighborhood might have association rules concerning new home design and construction. If the homeowners did not follow these rules, they might have to halt construction due to legal issues.

As you can see from this example, there are many different stakeholders on projects, and they all have different interests. Stakeholders' needs and expectations are important in the beginning and throughout the life of a project. Successful project managers develop good relationships with project stakeholders to understand and meet their needs and expectations.

Project Management Knowledge Areas

Project management knowledge areas describe the key competencies that project managers must develop. The center of Figure 1-3 shows the nine knowledge areas of project management. The four core knowledge areas of project management include project scope, time, cost, and quality management. These are core knowledge areas because they lead to specific project objectives. Brief descriptions of each core knowledge area are as follows:

- Project scope management involves working with all appropriate stakeholders to define, gain written agreement for, and manage all the work required to complete the project successfully.
- Project time management includes estimating how long it will take to complete the work, developing an acceptable project schedule given cost-effective use of available resources and ensuring timely completion of the project.
- Project cost management consists of preparing and managing the budget for the project.
- Project quality management ensures that the project will satisfy the stated or implied needs for which it was undertaken.

The four facilitating knowledge areas of project management are human resources, communications, risk, and procurement management. These are called facilitating areas because they are the processes through which the project objectives are achieved. Brief descriptions of each facilitating knowledge area are as follows:

- Project human resource management is concerned with making effective use of the people involved with the project.
- Project communications management involves generating, collecting, disseminating, and storing project information.
- Project risk management includes identifying, analyzing, and responding to risks related to the project.
- Project procurement management involves acquiring or procuring goods and services for a project from outside the performing organization.

Project integration management, the ninth knowledge area, is an overarching function that coordinates the work of all other knowledge areas. It affects and is affected by all of the other knowledge areas. Project managers must have knowledge and skills in all nine of these areas.

Project Management Tools and Techniques

Thomas Carlyle, a famous historian and author, stated, "Man is a tool-using animal. Without tools he is nothing, with tools he is all." As the world continues to become more complex, it is even more important for people to develop and use tools, especially for managing important projects. **Project management tools and techniques** assist project managers and their teams in carrying out work in all nine knowledge areas. For example, some popular time-management tools and techniques include Gantt charts, project network diagrams, and critical path analysis. Figure 1-4 lists some commonly used tools and techniques by knowledge area. You will learn more about these and other tools and techniques throughout this text.

A 2006 survey of 753 project and program managers was conducted to rate several project management tools. Respondents were asked to rate tools on a scale of 1–5 (low to high) based on the extent of their use and the potential of the tools to help improve project success. "Super tools" were defined as those that had high use and high potential for improving project success. These super tools included software for task scheduling (such as project management software), scope statements, requirement analyses, and lessons-learned reports. Tools that are already extensively used and have been found to improve project performance include progress reports, kick-off meetings, Gantt charts, and change requests.

These super tools are bolded in Figure 1-4.[7] Of course, different tools can be more effective in different situations. It is crucial for project managers and their team members to determine which tools will be most useful for their particular projects.

Knowledge Area/Category	Tools and Techniques
Integration management	Project selection methods, project management methodologies, stakeholder analyses, project charters, project management plans, **project management software, change requests**, change control boards, project review meetings, **lessons-learned reports**
Scope management	**Scope statements, work breakdown structures**, mind maps, statements of work, **requirements analyses**, scope management plans, scope verification techniques, and scope change controls
Time management	**Gantt charts**, project network diagrams, critical-path analyses, crashing, fast tracking, schedule performance measurements
Cost management	Net present value, return on investment, payback analyses, earned value management, project portfolio management, cost estimates, cost management plans, cost baselines
Quality management	Quality metrics, checklists, quality control charts, Pareto diagrams, fishbone diagrams, maturity models, statistical methods
Human resource management	Motivation techniques, empathic listening, responsibility assignment matrices, project organizational charts, resource histograms, team building exercises
Communications management	Communications management plans, **kickoff meetings**, conflict management, communications media selection, **status and progress reports**, virtual communications, templates, project Web sites
Risk management	Risk management plans, risk registers, probability/impact matrices, risk rankings
Procurement management	Make-or-buy analyses, contracts, requests for proposals or quotes, source selections, supplier evaluation matrices

Figure 1-4. Common project management tools and techniques by knowledge area (Schwalbe, Information Technology Project Management, Sixth Edition, 2010)

What Went Right?

Follow-up studies by the Standish Group (see the previously quoted "CHAOS" study in the What Went Wrong? passage) showed some improvement in the statistics for IT projects:

- The number of successful projects has doubled, from 16 percent in 1994 to 32 percent in 2008.

- The number of failed projects decreased from 31 percent in 1994 to 24 percent in 2008.[8]

    Even though there have been significant improvements in managing IT projects, there is still much room for improvement. The best news is that project managers are learning how to succeed more often. "The reasons for the increase in successful projects vary. First, the average cost of a project has been more than cut in half. Better tools have been created to monitor and control progress and better skilled project managers with better management processes are being used. The fact that there are processes is significant in itself."[9]

Despite its advantages, project management is not a silver bullet that guarantees success on all projects. Some projects, such as those involving new technologies, have a higher degree of uncertainty, so it is more difficult to meet their scope, time, and cost goals. Project management is a very broad, often complex discipline. What works on one project may not work on another, so it is essential for project managers to continue to develop their knowledge and skills in managing projects. It is also important to learn from the mistakes and successes of others.

Project Success

How do you define the success or failure of a project? There are several ways to define project success. The list that follows outlines a few common criteria for measuring project success as applied to the example project of building a new 2,000 square foot home within six months for $300,000:

- The project met scope, time, and cost goals. If the home was 2,000 square feet and met other scope requirements, was completed in six months, and cost $300,000, we could call it a successful project based on this criteria. Note that the CHAOS studies mentioned in the What Went Right? and What Went Wrong? examples used this definition of success.

- The project satisfied the customer/sponsor. Even if the project met initial scope, time, and cost goals, the couple paying for the house might not be satisfied. Perhaps the project manager never returned their calls and was rude to them or made important decisions without their approval. Perhaps the quality of some of the construction or materials was not acceptable. If the customers were not happy about important aspects of the project, it would be deemed a failure based on this criterion. Many organizations implement a customer satisfaction rating system for projects in order to measure project success.

- The results of the project met its main objective, such as making or saving a certain amount of money, providing a good return on investment, or simply making the sponsors happy. If the couple liked their new home and neighborhood after they lived there for a while, even if it cost more or took longer to build or the project manager was rude to them, it would be a successful project based on this criterion. As another example, suppose the owners really wanted to keep the house for just a few years and then sell it for a good return. If that happened, the couple would deem the project a success, regardless of other factors involved. Note that for many projects done to meet ROI objectives, financial success cannot be determined until some time after the project is completed.

Project managers play a vital role in helping projects succeed. Project managers work with the project sponsors, the project team, and the other people involved in a project to meet project goals. They also work with the sponsor to define success for that particular project. Good project managers do not assume that their definition of success is the same as the sponsors' definition. They take the time to understand their sponsors' expectations. For example, if you are building a home for someone, find out what is most important:

- meeting scope, time, and cost goals of the project to build the home
- satisfying other needs, such as communicating in a certain way
- being sure the project delivers a certain result, such as providing the home of the owners' dreams or a good return on investment.

The success criteria should help you to develop key performance indicators needed to track project progress. It is important to document this information in enough detail to eliminate ambiguity.

PROGRAM AND PROJECT PORTFOLIO MANAGEMENT

As mentioned earlier, about one-quarter of the world's gross domestic product is spent on projects. Projects make up a significant portion of work in most business organizations or enterprises, and successfully managing those projects is crucial to enterprise success. Two important concepts that help projects meet enterprise goals are the use of programs and project portfolio management.

Programs

A **program** is "a group of related projects managed in a coordinated way to obtain benefits and control not available from managing them individually."[10] As you can imagine, it is often more economical to group projects together to help streamline management, staffing, purchasing, and other work. The following are examples of programs (Figure 1-5 illustrates the first program in the list).

- A construction firm has programs for building single-family homes, apartment buildings, and office buildings, as shown in Figure 1-5. Each home, apartment building, and office building is a separate project for a specific sponsor, but each type of building is part of a program.. There would be several benefits to managing these projects under one program,. For example, for the single-family homes, the program manager could try to get planning approvals for all the homes at once, advertise them together, and purchase common materials in bulk to earn discounts.

- A clothing firm has a program to analyze customer-buying patterns. Projects under this program might include one to send out and analyze electronic surveys, one to conduct several focus groups in different geographic locations with different types of buyers, and a project to develop an information system to help collect and analyze current customers' buying patterns.

- A government agency has a program for children's services, which includes a project to provide pre-natal care for expectant mothers, a project to immunize newborns and young children, and a project for developmental testing for pre-school children., to name a few.

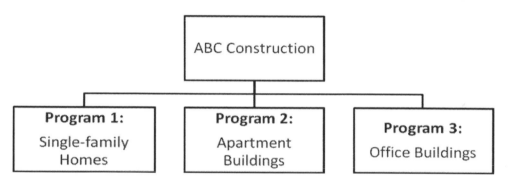

Figure 1-5. Example programs

A **program manager** provides leadership and direction for the project managers heading the projects within the program. Program managers also coordinate the efforts of project teams, functional groups, suppliers, and operations staff supporting the projects to ensure that project products and processes are implemented to maximize benefits. Program managers are responsible for more than the delivery of project results; they are change agents responsible for the success of products and processes produced by those projects.

Program managers often have review meetings with all their project managers to share important information and coordinate important aspects of each project. Many program managers worked as project managers earlier in their careers, and they enjoy sharing their wisdom and expertise with their project managers. Effective program managers recognize that managing a program is much more complex than managing a single project. They recognize that technical and project management skills are not enough. In addition to skills required for project managers, program managers must also possess strong business knowledge, leadership capability, and communication skills.

Project Portfolio Management

In many organizations, project managers also support an emerging business strategy of **project portfolio management** (also called just **portfolio management** in this text), in which organizations group and manage projects and programs as a portfolio of investments that contribute to the entire enterprise's success. Pacific Edge Software's product manager, Eric Burke, defines project portfolio management as "the continuous process of selecting and managing the optimum set of project initiatives that deliver maximum business value."[11]

PMI published the Standard for Portfolio Management, Second Edition, in 2008. Topics included in this standard include:

- Understanding the role of portfolio management in relation to an organization's structure and strategy

- Streamlining operations through portfolio management

- Improving the implemenation and maintenance of corporate governance initiatives

- Designing and implementing metrics to demonstrate and improve return on investment through portfolio management.

- Reporting information to make the most of an organization's projects and programs

PMI members can download this and other standards, such as the PMBOK® Guide, for free from www.pmi.org.

Portfolio managers need to understand how projects fit into the bigger picture of the organization, especially in terms of corporate strategy, finances, and business risks. They create portfolios based on meeting specific organizational goals, such as maximizing the value of the portfolio or making effective use of limited resources. Portfolio managers help their organizations make wise investment decisions by helping to select and analyze projects from a strategic perspective. Portfolio managers may or may not have previous experience as project or program managers. It is most important that they have strong financial and analytical skills and understand how projects and programs can contribute to meeting strategic goals.

The main distinction between project or program management and portfolio management is a focus on meeting tactical versus strategic goals. Tactical goals are generally more specific and short-term than strategic goals, which emphasize long-term goals for an organization. Individual projects and programs often address tactical goals, whereas portfolio management addresses strategic goals.

- Project and program management address questions like:
    o Are we carrying out projects well?
    o Are projects on time and budget?
    o Do project stakeholders know what they should be doing?
- Portfolio management addresses questions like:
    o Are we working on the right projects?
    o Are we investing in the right areas?
    o Do we have the right resources to be competitive?

There can be portfolios for all types of projects. The list that follows outlines a few examples:

- In a construction firm, strategic goals might include increasing profit margins on large projects, decreasing costs on supplies, and improving skill levels of key workers. Projects could be grouped into these three categories for portfolio management purposes.
- In a clothing firm, strategic goals might include improving the effectiveness of IT, introducing new clothing lines, reducing inventory costs, and increasing customer satisfaction. These might be the main categories for their portfolio of projects.
- A government agency for children's services could group projects into a portfolio based on key strategies such as improving health, providing education, and so on to help make decisions on the best way to use available funds and resources.

Organizations group projects into portfolios to help them make better investment decisions, such as increasing, decreasing, discontinuing, or changing specific projects or programs based on their financial performance, risks, resource utilization, and similar factors that affect business value and strategy. If a construction firm has much higher profit margins on apartment buildings than single-family homes, for example, it might choose to pursue more apartment building projects. The firm might also create a new project to investigate ways to increase profits for single-family home projects. On the other hand, if the company has too many projects focused on financial performance and not enough focused on improving its work force, the portfolio manager might suggest initiating more projects to support that strategic goal. Just like a personal financial portfolio, a businesses portfolio should be diversified to account for risk.

By grouping projects into portfolios, organizations can better tie their projects to meeting strategic goals. Portfolio management can also help organizations do a better job of managing its human resources by hiring, training, and retaining workers to support the projects in the organization's portfolio. For example, if the construction firm needs more people with experience in building apartment buildings, they can make necessary adjustments by hiring or training current workers in the necessary skills.

THE PROJECT MANAGEMENT PROFESSION

As you can imagine, good project managers should have a variety of skills. Good program and portfolio managers often need additional skills and experience in managing projects and understanding organizational strategies. This section describes some of the skills that help you manage projects, and you will learn many more throughout this text. If you are serious about considering a career in project management, you should consider becoming a certified Project Management Professional. You should also be familiar with some of the project management software products available on the market today.

Suggested Skills for Project, Program, and Portfolio Managers

Project managers and their teams must develop knowledge and skills in the following areas:

- All nine project management knowledge areas
- The application area (domain, industry, market, etc.)
- The project environment (politics, culture, change management, etc.)
- General management (financial management, strategic planning, etc.)
- Human relations (leadership, motivation, negotiations, etc.)

An earlier section of this chapter introduced the nine project management knowledge areas, as well as some tools and techniques that project managers use. The application area refers to the application to which project management is applied. For example, a project manager responsible for building houses or apartment buildings should understand the construction industry, including standards and regulations important to that industry and those types of construction projects. A project manager leading a large software development project must know a lot about that application area. A project manager in education, entertainment, the government, and other fields must understand those application areas.

The project environment differs from organization to organization and project to project, but there are some skills that will help in most project environments. These skills include understanding change, and understanding how organizations work within their social, political, and physical environments. Project managers must be comfortable leading and handling change, since most projects introduce changes in organizations and involve changes within the projects themselves. Project managers need to understand the organizations they work in and how products are developed and services are provided. For example, it takes different skills and behavior to manage a project for a Fortune 100 company in the United States than it does to manage a government project for a new business in Poland or India. It also takes different skills and behaviors to manage a project in the construction industry than one in the entertainment or pharmaceutical industry.

Project managers should also possess general management knowledge and skills. They should understand important topics related to financial management, accounting, procurement, sales, marketing, contracts, manufacturing, distribution, logistics, the supply chain, strategic planning, tactical planning, operations management, organizational structures and behavior, personnel administration, compensation, benefits, career paths, and health and safety practices. On some projects, it will be critical for the project manager to have substantial experience in one or several of these general management areas. On other projects, the project manager can delegate detailed responsibility for some of these areas to a team member, support staff, or even a supplier. Even so, the project manager must be intelligent and experienced enough to know which of these areas are most important and who is qualified to do the work. He or she must also make and/or take responsibility for all key project decisions.

Achieving high performance on projects requires human relations or soft skills. Some of these soft skills include effective communication, influencing the organization to get things done, leadership, motivation, negotiation, conflict management, and problem solving. Project managers must lead their project teams by providing vision, delegating work, creating an energetic and positive environment, and setting an example of appropriate and effective behavior. Project managers must focus on teamwork skills in order to use their people effectively. They need to be able to motivate different types of people and develop *esprit de corps* within the project team and with other project stakeholders.

Media Snapshot

In 2004, millions of people in the U.S. watched the first season of the reality show called *The Apprentice*, where contestants vied for a high-level position working for Donald Trump. Each week, Trump fired one contestant and told everyone bluntly why they were fired. Trump's reasons provide insight into improving project management skills, as follows:

- Leadership and professionalism are crucial. No matter how smart you are (the first candidate fired had degrees in medicine and business), you must be professional in how you deal with people and display some leadership potential.
- Know what your sponsor expects from the project, and learn from your mistakes. Jason, the second person and first project manager fired, decided not to take the time to meet with his project sponsors, causing his team to fail their assignment. Mr. Trump wanted everyone to remember that crucial mistake.
- Trust your team and delegate decisions. Sam had several problems as a team member and project manager, but his lack of trust in and respect for and from his teammates led to his downfall.
- Know the business. Restaurants often have the highest profit margins on certain items, like drinks. Find out what's most important to your business when running projects. One team focused on increasing bar sales, which generated the most profit, and easily won the competition that week.
- Stand up for yourself. When Trump fired Kristi over two other candidates, he explained his decision by saying that Kristi didn't fight for herself, while the other two women did.
- Be a team player. Tammy clearly did not get along with her team, and no one supported her in the boardroom when her team lost. *continued*

- Don't be overly emotional and stay organized. Erika had a difficult time leading her team in selling Trump Ice, and she became flustered when they did not get credit for sales because paperwork was not done correctly. Her emotions were evident in the boardroom when she was fired.
- Work on projects and for people you believe in. Kwame's team selected an artist based on her profit potential, even though he and other teammates disliked her work. The other team picked an artist they liked, and they easily outsold Kwame's team.
- Think outside the box. Troy led his team in trying to make the most money selling rickshaw rides using traditional methods. The other team brainstormed ideas and decided to sell advertising space on the rickshaws, which was a huge success.
- There is some luck involved in project management, and you should always aim high. Nick and Amy were teamed against Bill, Troy, and Kwame to rent out a party room for the highest price. Troy's team seemed very organized and did get a couple of good bids, but Nick and Amy didn't seem to have any real prospects. They got lucky when one potential client came back at the last minute and agreed to a much higher than normal price.

The show continues to run in 2009 with celebrities as contestants with money raised being donated to charity. In the 2008 celebrity season, the last two contestants were Trace Adkins, a popular country music star and wonderful person to work with and for, and Piers Morgan, a former British tabloid editor and judge on America's Got Talent. An important lesson from that season was that the key stakeholder, Donald Trump, believed it was more important to focus on how much money the winner raised than what his teammates thought of him. In the 2009 season, comedian Joan Rivers beat poker player Annie Duke. See the companion Web site for links related to this show.

Importance of Leadership Skills

In a popular study, one hundred project managers listed the characteristics they believed were critical for effective project management and the characteristics that made project managers ineffective. Figure 1-6 lists the results. The study found that effective project managers provide leadership by example, are visionary, technically competent, decisive, good communicators, and good motivators. They also stand up to top management when necessary, support team members, and encourage new ideas. The study also found that respondents believed *positive leadership contributes the most to project success*. The most important characteristics and behaviors of positive leaders include being a team builder and communicator, having high self-esteem, focusing on results, demonstrating trust and respect, and setting goals.

Effective Project Managers	Ineffective Project Managers
Lead by example	Set bad examples
Are visionaries	Are not self-assured
Are technically competent	Lack technical expertise
Are decisive	Avoid or delay making decisions
Are good communicators	Are poor communicators
Are good motivators	Are poor motivators

Zimmerer, Thomas W. and Mahmoud M. Yasin, "A Leadership Profile of American Project Managers," Project Management Journal (March 1998), 31-38.

Figure 1-6. Most significant characteristics of effective and ineffective project managers

Leadership and *management* are terms often used interchangeably, although there are differences. Generally, a **leader** focuses on long-term goals and big-picture objectives, while inspiring people to reach those goals. A **manager** often deals with the day-to-day details of meeting specific goals. Some people say that, "Managers do things right, and leaders do the right things." "Leaders determine the vision, and managers achieve the vision." "You lead people and manage things."

Project managers often take on the role of both leader and manager. Good project managers know that people make or break projects, so they must set a good example to lead their team to success. They are aware of the greater needs of their stakeholders and organizations, so they are visionary in guiding their current projects and in suggesting future ones.

In a recent study, project management experts from various industries were asked to identify the ten most important skills and competencies for effective project managers. Figure 1-7 shows the results.

Top Ten Skills and Competencies for Effective Project Managers	
1. People skills	6. Verbal communication
2. Leadership	7. Strong at building teams
3. Listening	8. Conflict resolution/management
4. Integrity, ethical behavior, consistent	9. Critical thinking/problem solving
5. Strong at building trust	10. Understands and balances priorities

Jennifer Krahn, "Effective Project Leadership: A Combination of Project Manager Skills and Competencies in Context," PMI Research Conference Proceedings (July 2006).

Figure 1-7. Ten most important skills and competencies for project managers

Respondents were also asked what skills and competencies were most important in various project situations:

- *Large projects*: Leadership, relevant prior experience, planning, people skills, verbal communication, and team-building skills were most important.

- *High uncertainty projects*: Risk management, expectation management, leadership, people skills, and planning skills were most important.

- *Very novel projects:* Leadership, people skills, having vision and goals, self confidence, expectations management, and listening skills were most important.[12]

Notice that a few additional skills and competencies not cited in the top 10 list were mentioned when people thought about the context of a project. To be the most effective, project managers require a changing mix of skills and competencies depending on the project being delivered.

As mentioned earlier, program managers need the same skills as project managers. They often rely on their past experience as project managers, strong business knowledge, leadership capability, and communication skills to handle the responsibility of overseeing the multiple projects that make up their programs. It is most important that portfolio managers have strong financial and analytical skills and understand how projects and programs can contribute to meeting strategic goals.

Companies that excel in project, program, and portfolio management grow project leaders, emphasizing development of business and communication skills. Instead of thinking of leaders and managers as specific people, it is better to think of people as having leadership skills, such as being visionary and inspiring, and management skills, such as being organized and effective. Therefore, the best project, program, and portfolio managers have leadership and management characteristics; they are visionary yet focused on the bottom line. Above all else, they focus on achieving positive results!

Best Practice

A **best practice** is "an optimal way recognized by industry to achieve a stated goal or objective."[13] Robert Butrick, author of *The Project Workout*, wrote an article on best practices in project management for the *Ultimate Business Library's Best Practice* book. He suggests that organizations need to follow basic principles of project management, including these two mentioned earlier in this chapter:

- Make sure your projects are driven by your strategy. Be able to demonstrate how each project you undertake fits your business strategy, and screen out unwanted projects as soon as possible.

- Engage your stakeholders. Ignoring stakeholders often leads to project failure. Be sure to engage stakeholders at all stages of a project, and encourage teamwork and commitment at all times. Use leadership and open communications to make things happen.[14]

Project Management Certification

Professional certification is an important factor in recognizing and ensuring quality in a profession. The **Project Management Institute (PMI)** is a global professional society for project and program managers. PMI provides certification as a **Project Management Professional (PMP)**—someone who has documented sufficient project experience, agreed to follow the PMI code of professional conduct, and demonstrated knowledge of the field of project management by passing a comprehensive examination. As a student, you can join PMI for a reduced fee. Consult PMI's Web site (www.pmi.org) or the Information Systems SIG site (www.pmi-issig.org) for more information. You can also network with other students studying project management by joining the Students of Project Management SIG at www.studentsofpm.org.

The number of people earning PMP certification continues to increase. In 1993, there were about 1,000 certified project management professionals. By the end of May, 2009 there were 346,053 active certified project management professionals. There were also 8,139 CAPMs (Certified Associate in Project Management.[15] See Appendx C of this text for more information on certification. Figure 1-8 shows the rapid growth in the number of people earning project management professional certification from 1993 to the end of May 2009. Although most PMPs are in the U.S. and Canada, the PMP credential is growing in popularity in several countries, such as Japan, China, and India.

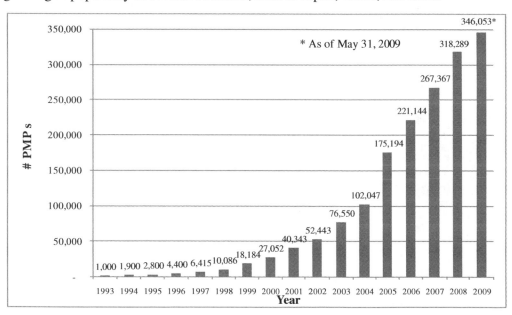

Figure 1-8. Growth in PMP certification, 1993–2009

Some companies are requiring that all project managers be PMP certified. Project management certification is also enabling professionals throughout the world to share a common base of knowledge. For example, any person with PMP certification can list, describe, and use the nine project management knowledge areas, as described in PMI's Guide to the Project Management Body of Knowledge (PMBOK® Guide). Sharing a common base of knowledge is important because it helps advance the theory and practice of project management. Consult PMI''s Web site at *www.pmi.org* for detailed information on their certification programs. Also, see Appendix C of this text for resource information.

Many colleges, universities, and companies around the world now offer courses related to various aspects of project management. You can even earn bachelor's, master's, and doctoral degrees in project management. PMI reported in 2008 that of the 280 institutions it has identified that offer degrees in project management, 103 are in mainland China. "When Western companies come into China they are more likely to hire individuals who have PMP certification as an additional verification of their skills. In our salary survey, the salary differences in IT, for example, was dramatic. A person with certification could make five to six times as much salary, so there is a terrific incentive to get certified and work for these Western companies." [16]

Ethics in Project Management

Ethics, loosely defined, is a set of principles that guide our decision making based on personal values of what is "right" and "wrong." Making ethical decisions is an important part of our personal and professional lives because it generates trust and respect with other people. Project managers often face ethical dilemmas. For example, several projects involve different payment methods. If a project manager can make more money by doing a job poorly, should he or she do the job poorly? No! If a project manager is personally opposed to the development of nuclear weapons, should he or she refuse to manage a project that helps produce them? Yes! Ethics guide us in making these types of decisions.

PMI approved a new Code of Ethics and Professional Conduct effective January 1, 2007. This new code applies not only to PMPs, but to all PMI members and individuals who hold a PMI certification, apply for a PMI certification, or serve PMI in a volunteer capacity. It is vital for project management practitioners to conduct their work in an ethical manner. Even if you are not affiliated with PMI, these guidelines can help you conduct your work in an ethical manner, which helps the profession earn the confidence of the public, employers, employees, and all project stakeholders. The PMI Code of Ethics and Professional Conduct includes short chapters addressing vision and applicability, responsibility, respect, fairness, and honesty. A few excerpts from this document include the following:

"As <u>practitioners</u> in the global project management community:

2.2.1	We make decisions and take actions based on the best interests of society, public safety, and the environment.
2.2.2	We accept only those assignments that are consistent with our background, experience, skills, and qualifications.
2.2.3.	We fulfill the commitments that we undertake—we do what we say we will do.
3.2.1	We inform ourselves about the norms and customs of others and avoid engaging in behaviors they might consider disrespectful.
3.2.2	We listen to others' points of view, seeking to understand them.

3.2.3	We approach directly those persons with whom we have a conflict or disagreement.
4.2.1	We demonstrate transparency in our decision-making process.
4.2.2	We constantly reexamine our impartiality and objectivity, taking corrective action as appropriate.
4.3.1	We proactively and fully disclose any real or potential conflicts of interest to appropriate stakeholders.
5.2.1	We earnestly seek to understand the truth.
5.2.2	We are truthful in our communications and in our conduct."[17]

In addition, PMI added a new series of questions to the PMP certification exam in March 2002 to emphasize the importance of ethics and professional responsibility.

Project Management Software

The project management and software development communities have definitely responded to the need to provide more software to assist in managing projects. The Project Management Center, a Web site for people involved in project management, provides an alphabetical directory of more than 300 project management software solutions (*www.infogoal.com/pmc*). This site and others demonstrate the growth in available project management software products, especially Web-based tools. Deciding which project management software to use has become a project in itself. This section provides a summary of the basic types of project management software available and references for finding more information. In Appendix A, you will learn how to use Microsoft Project 2010, the most widely used project management software tool today. You will also learn how to use the most popular online tool, @task.

Free Trial Software and Guides to Using Project 2010 and @task

A 60-day evaluation copy of Microsoft Project is available from Microsoft's Web site at www.microsoft.com/project. You can also download a free trial of @task from www.attask.com. Appendix A and Appendix B include basic information on project management software and brief guides to both of these tools so you can develop hands-on skills using these popular project management software tools.

Many people still use basic productivity software such as Microsoft Word and Excel to perform many project management functions, including determining project scope, time, and cost, assigning resources, preparing project documentation, and other tasks. People often use productivity software instead of specialized project management software because they already have it and know how to use it. However, there are hundreds of project management software tools that provide specific functionality for managing projects. These project management software tools can be divided into three general categories based on functionality and price:

- *Low-end tools*: These tools provide basic project management features and generally cost less than $200 per user. They are often recommended for small projects and single users. Most of these tools allow users to create Gantt charts, which cannot be done easily using current productivity software. Some of these tools are available online while others are stand-along desktop applications

- *Midrange tools*: A step up from low-end tools, midrange tools are designed to handle larger projects, multiple users, and multiple projects. All of these tools can produce Gantt charts and network diagrams, and can assist in critical path analysis, resource allocation, project tracking, status reporting, and other tasks. Prices range from about $200 to $600 per user, and several tools require additional server software for using workgroup features. Microsoft Project is still the most widely used project management software today in this category and in general. Figure 1-9 provides a screen shot from Microsoft Project showing a Gantt chart for a project that you can create by following the steps in Appendix A. There is also an enterprise version of Microsoft Project, as described briefly below.

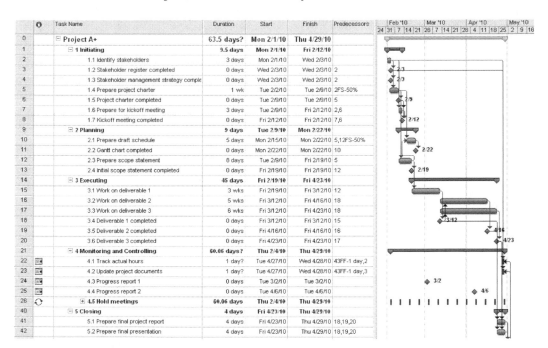

Figure 1-9. Screen shot from Microsoft Project

- *High-end tools*: Another category of project management software is high-end tools, sometimes referred to as enterprise project management software. These tools provide robust capabilities to handle very large projects, dispersed workgroups, and enterprise and portfolio management functions that summarize and combine individual project information to provide an enterprise view of all projects. These products are generally licensed on a per-user basis, integrate with enterprise database management software, and are accessible via the Internet. In mid-2002, Microsoft introduced the first version of their Enterprise Project Management software, and in 2003, they introduced the Microsoft Enterprise Project Management solution, which was updated in 2007 to include Microsoft Office Project Server 2007 and Microsoft Office Project Portfolio Server 2007. In 2008, Oracle acquired Primavera Software, Inc., another popular tool for project-intensive industries.

Several totally Web-based products that provide basic as well as enterprise and portfolio management capabilities are now on the market. For example, TopTenReviews listed @task (www.attask.com) as their number one pick for online project management software available for a monthly fee per user. Figure 1-10 provides a screen shot from @task. See Appendix B for more information on using @task. See the Project Management Center Web site *(www.infogoal.com/pmc)* or *TopTenReviews.com (http://project-management-software-review.toptenreviews.com)* for links to many companies that provide project management software.

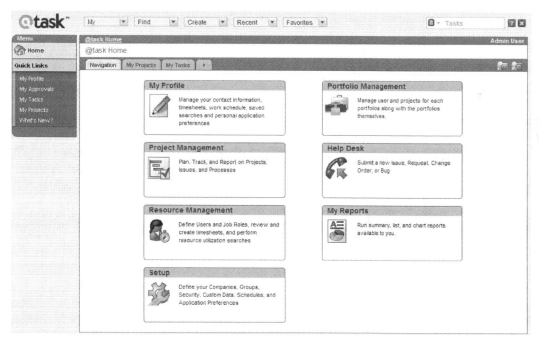

Figure 1-10. Screen shot from @task

There are also several free or open-source tools available. For example, many people are familiar with Zoho, which provides online applications accessible from their

Web site. They have a tool called Zoho Project (www.projects.zoho.com), which is free for users running just one project, and plans are available for a fee for more projects and users. OpenProj (recently purchased by Serena Software, www.openproj.org), Open Workbench (*www.openworkbench.org*), dotProject (*www.dotproject.net*), and TaskJuggler (*www.taskjuggler.org*) are all free open-source online project management tools. Remember, however, that open-source tools are developed, managed, and maintained by volunteers. They also often run on limited platforms and may not be well supported.

By the end of the twentieth century, people in virtually every industry around the globe began to investigate and apply different aspects of project, program, and portfolio management. The sophistication and effectiveness with which organizations use these concepts and tools today is influencing the way companies do business, use resources, and respond to market needs with speed and accuracy. As mentioned earlier, there are many reasons to study project, program, and portfolio management. The number of projects continues to grow, the complexity of these projects continues to increase, and the profession of project management continues to expand and mature. Many colleges, universities, and companies now offer courses related to various aspects of project, program, and portfolio management. The growing number of projects and the evidence that good project management really can make a difference continue to contribute to the growth of this field.

CASE WRAP-UP

Another board member asked the CEO to describe more about what the PMO Director did to help the company become more successful at managing projects. He explained how Marie Scott worked with him and all the VPs to reorganize several parts of the company to support their new emphasis on project, program, and project portfolio management. They formed a project team to implement a web-based project management software tool across the enterprise. They formed another team to develop project-based reward systems for all employees. They also authorized funds for a project to educate all employees in project management and to develop a mentoring program for project, program, and project portfolio managers. Doug and Marie had successfully convinced everyone that effectively selecting and managing projects was crucial to their company's future. The board and the company's shareholders were very pleased with the results.

CHAPTER SUMMARY

There is a new or renewed interest in project management today as the number of projects continues to grow and their complexity continues to increase. The success rate of IT projects has more than doubled since 1995, but still only about a third are successful in meeting scope, time, and cost goals. Using a more disciplined approach to managing all types of projects can help organizations succeed.

A project is a temporary endeavor undertaken to create a unique product, service, or result. Projects are developed incrementally; they require resources, have a sponsor, and involve uncertainty. The triple constraint of project management refers to managing the scope, time, and cost dimensions of a project.

Project management is the application of knowledge, skills, tools, and techniques to project activities to meet project requirements. Stakeholders are the people involved in or affected by project activities. A framework for project management includes the project stakeholders, project management knowledge areas, and project management tools and techniques. The nine knowledge areas are project integration management, scope, time, cost, quality, human resource, communications, risk, and procurement management.

A program is a group of related projects managed in a coordinated way to obtain benefits and control not available from managing them individually. Project portfolio management involves organizing and managing projects and programs as a portfolio of investments that contribute to the entire enterprise's success. Portfolio management emphasizes meeting strategic goals while project management focuses on tactical goals.

The profession of project management continues to grow and mature. Project, program, and portfolio managers play key roles in helping projects and organizations succeed. They must perform various duties, possess many skills, and continue to develop skills in project management, general management, and their application area, such as IT. Soft skills, especially leadership, are particularly important for project, program, and portfolio managers.The Project Management Institute (PMI) is an international professional society that provides certification as a Project Management Professional (PMP) and upholds a code of ethics. Today, hundreds of project management software products are available to assist people in managing projects.

QUICK QUIZ

1. Approximately what percentage of the world's gross domestic product is spent on projects?
   A. 10%
   B. 25%
   C. 50%
   D. 75%

2. Which of the following is a not a potential advantage of using good project management?
   A. Shorter development times
   B. Higher worker morale
   C. Lower cost of capital
   D. Higher profit margins

3. A _____ is a temporary endeavor undertaken to create a unique product, service, or result.
   A. program
   B. process
   C. project
   D. portfolio

4. Which of the following is not an attribute of a project?
   A. projects are unique
   B. projects are developed using progressive elaboration
   C. projects have a primary customer or sponsor
   D. projects involve no uncertainty

5. Which of the following is not part of the triple constraint of project management?
   A. meeting scope goals
   B. meeting time goals
   C. meeting communications goals
   D. meeting cost goals

6. _____ is the application of knowledge, skills, tools and techniques to project activities to meet project requirements.
   A. Project management
   B. Program management
   C. Project portfolio management
   D. Requirements management

7. Project portfolio management addresses _____ goals of an organization, while project management addresses _____ goals..
   A. strategic, tactical
   B. tactical, strategic
   C. internal, external
   D. external, internal

8. Several individual housing projects done in the same area by the same firm might best be managed as part of a _____.
   A. portfolio
   B. program
   C. investment
   D. collaborative

9. What is the most significant characteristic or attribute of an effective project manager?
   A. is a strong communicator
   B. is decisive
   C. is visionary
   D. leads by example

10. What is the certification program called that the Project Management Institute provides?
   A. Microsoft Certified Project Manager (MCPM)
   B. Project Management Professional (PMP)
   C. Project Management Expert (PME)
   D. Project Management Mentor (PMM)

Quick Quiz Anwers
1.B, 2. C 3. C, 4. D, 5. C, 6. A, 7. A, 8. B, 9. D, 10. B

DISCUSSION QUESTIONS

1. Why is there a new or renewed interest in the field of project management?
2. What is a project, and what are its main attributes? How is a project different from what most people do in their day-to-day jobs? What is the triple constraint?
3. What is project management? Briefly describe the project management framework, providing examples of stakeholders, knowledge areas, tools and techniques, and project success factors.
4. Discuss the relationship between project, program, and portfolio management and their contribution to enterprise success.
5. What are the roles of the project, program, and portfolio managers? What are suggested skills for project managers? What additional skills do program and portfolio managers need?
6. What role does the Project Management Institute play in helping the profession?
7. What functions can you perform with project management software? What are some popular names of low-end, midrange, and high-end project management tools?

EXERCISES

Note: These exercises can be done individually or in teams, in-class, as homework, or in a virtual environment. Learners can either write their results in a paper or prepare a short presentation to show their results.

1. Search the Internet for the terms *project management*, *program management,* and *project portfolio management*. Write down the number of hits that you received for each of these phrases. Find at least three Web sites that provide interesting information on one of the topics, including Project Management Institute's Web site (*www.pmi.org*). Write a one-page paper or prepare a short presentation summarizing key information about these three Web sites. See the companion Web site for some suggested sites.
2. Find an example of a real project with a real project manager. Feel free to use projects in the media (the Olympics, television shows, movies, and so on) or a project from work, if applicable. Write a one-page paper or prepare a short presentation describing the project in terms of its scope, time, and cost goals and each of the project's attributes. Try to include information describing what went right and wrong on the project and the role of the project manager and sponsor. Also describe whether you consider the project to be a success or not and why. Include at least one reference and proper citations.
3. Go to www.gradschools.com and search for graduate schools that offer courses and programs related to project management. Select Business Programs as the Field of Study and Project Management as the Subject. Review schools by location and format. Summarize your findings in a one- to two-page paper or short presentation.
4. Review information from http://project-management-software-review.toptenreviews.com. Read at least four reviews and visit the supplier Web

sites for their products. Write a one-page paper or prepare a short presentation summarizing your findings.

TEAM PROJECTS

1.   Find someone who works as a project manager or is a member of a project team. If possible, find more than one person. Use the interview guidelines below (and on the companion Web site) and then ask the questions in person, via the phone, or via the Internet. Discuss the results with your team, and then prepare a one- to two-page paper or prepare a short presentation to summarize of your findings.

Project Manager Interview Guidelines

Please note that these are guidelines and sample questions only. Use only the questions that seem appropriate, and feel free to add your own.

Note: If the interviewee wants to remain anonymous, that's fine. If not, please include his/her name and place of employment as a project manager in your paper. Let him/her know that you are doing this interview for a class assignment and that the information may be shared with others.

The main purpose of these interviews is for students to gain more insight into what project managers really do, what challenges they face, what lessons they've learned, what concepts/tools you're learning about that they really use, and what suggestions they have for you and other students as future team members and project managers. People often like to tell stories or relate particular situations they were in to get their points across. To this end, here are a few sample questions.

1) How did you get into project management?
2) If you had to rate the job of project manager on a scale of 1-10, with 10 being the highest, how would you rate it?
3) Briefly explain the reason for your rating. What do you enjoy most and what do you like least about being a project manager?
4) Did you have any training or special talents or experiences that qualified you to be a project manager? Are you certified or have you thought about becoming certified as a PMP?
5) What do you feel is the most important thing you do as a project manager? On what task do you spend the most time each day?
6) What are some of the opportunities and risks you have encountered on projects? Please describe any notable successes and failures and what you have learned from them.
7) What are some of the tools, software or otherwise, that you use, and what is your opinion of those tools?
8) What are some steps a project manager can take to improve the effectiveness and efficiency of a team? How does a new project manager gain the respect and

34

loyalty of team members? Can you share any examples of situations you faced related to this topic?

9) What suggestions do you have for working with sponsors and senior managers? Can you share any examples of situations you faced related to this topic?

10) Do you have any suggestions for future project managers, such as any specific preparations they should make, skills they should learn, etc?

2. Go to www.monster.com and search for jobs as a "project manager" or "program manager" in three geographic regions of your choice. Write a one- to two-page paper or prepare a short presentation summarizing what you found.

3. As a team, discuss projects that you are currently working on or would like to work on to benefit yourself, your employers, your family, or the broader community. Come up with at least ten projects, and then determine if they could be grouped into programs. Write a one- to two-page paper or prepare a short presentation summarizing your results.

4. Review the information on project management certification in Appendix C and from the document it mentions (available from www.kathyschwalbe.com). Also review other resources about certification. As a team, discuss your findings and opinions on earning PMP or other certification. Document your findings in a one- to two-page paper or short presentation, citing your references.

COMPANION WEB SITE

Visit the free companion Web site for this text at **www.intropm.com** to access template files, online quizzes, Jeopardy-like games, Microsoft Project files, links to sites mentioned in the text, and other information to help you learn more about this important field. Instructors must contact the author at schwalbe@augsburg.edu to gain access to the instructor site. Anyone can access the student site.

An Introduction to Project Management, Third Edition

KEY TERMS

best practice — An optimal way recognized by industry to achieve a stated goal or objective.

ethics — A set of principles that guide our decision making based on personal values of what is "right" and "wrong".

leader — A person who focuses on long-term goals and big-picture objectives, while inspiring people to reach those goals.

manager — A person who deals with the day-to-day details of meeting specific goals.

portfolio — A collection of projects or programs and other work that are grouped together to facilitate effective management of that work to meet strategic business objectives.

program — A group of projects managed in a coordinated way to obtain benefits and control not available from managing them individually.

program manager — A person who provides leadership and direction for the project managers heading the projects within the program.

project — A temporary endeavor undertaken to create a unique product, service, or result.

project management — The application of knowledge, skills, tools, and techniques to project activities to meet project requirements.

project manager — The person responsible for working with the project sponsor, the project team, and the other people involved in a project to meet project goals.

Project Management Institute (PMI) — International professional society for project managers.

project management knowledge areas — Project integration management, scope, time, cost, quality, human resource, communications, risk, and procurement management.

Project Management Professional (PMP) — Certification provided by PMI that requires documenting project experience, agreeing to follow the PMI code of ethics, and passing a comprehensive exam.

project management tools and techniques — Methods available to assist project managers and their teams; some popular tools in the time management knowledge area include Gantt charts, network diagrams, critical path analysis, and project management software.

project portfolio management — The grouping and managing of projects and programs as a portfolio of investments that contribute to the entire enterprise's success.

project sponsor — The person who provides the direction and funding for a project.

stakeholders — People involved in or affected by project activities.

triple constraint — Balancing scope, time, and cost goals.

END NOTES

[1]Project Management Institute (PMI), *Project Management Salary Survey, Fifth Edition* (2007).

[2]Project Management Institute (PMI), The PMI Project Management Fact Book, Second Edition (2001).

[3]Standish Group, "The CHAOS Report" (*www.standishgroup.com*) (1995).

[4]PriceWaterhouseCoopers, "Boosting Business Performance through Programme and Project Management" (June 2004).

[5]Project Management Institute, Inc., *A Guide to the Project Management Body of Knowledge (PMBOK® Guide), Fourth Edition* (2008), p. 5.

[6]Ibid, p. 6.

[7]Claude Besner and Brian Hobbs, "The Perceived Value and Potential Contribution of Project Management Practices to Project Success," PMI Research Conference Proceedings (July 2006).

[8]Standish Group, "CHAOS Summary 2009" (2009).

[9]Standish Group, "CHAOS 2001: A Recipe for Success" (2001).

[10]Project Management Institute, Inc., *A Guide to the Project Management Body of Knowledge (PMBOK® Guide), Fourth Edition* (2008), p. 9.

[11]Burke, Eric, "Project Portfolio Management," PMI Houston Chapter Meeting (July 10, 2002).

[12]Jennifer Krahn, "Effective Project Leadership: A Combination of Project Manager Skills and Competencies in Context," PMI Research Conference Proceedings (July 2006).

[13]Ultimate Business Library, *Best Practice: Ideas and Insights from the World's Foremost Business Thinkers* (New York: Perseus 2003), p. 1.

[14]Ibid., p. 8.

[15]The Project Management Institute, "PMI Today" (July 2009).

[16]Vanessa Wong, "PMI On Specialization and Globalization," Projects@Work (June 23, 2008).

[17]The Project Management Institute, "PMI Today" (December 2006), p. 12-13.

Chapter 2

Project, Program, and Portfolio Selection

LEARNING OBJECTIVES

After reading this chapter, you will be able to:

- Describe the importance of aligning projects with business strategy, the strategic planning process, and using a SWOT analysis
- Explain the four-stage planning process for project selection and provide examples of applying this model to ensure the strategic alignment of projects
- Summarize the various methods for selecting projects and demonstrate how to calculate net present value, return on investment, payback, and the weighted score for a project
- Discuss the program selection process and distinguish the differences between programs and projects
- Describe the project portfolio selection process and the five levels of project portfolio management

---

OPENING CASE

Marie Scott, the director of the Project Management Office for Global Construction, Inc., was facilitating a meeting with several senior managers throughout the company. The purpose of the meeting was to discuss a process for selecting projects, grouping them into programs, and determining how they fit into the organization's portfolio of projects. She had invited an outside consultant to the meeting to provide an objective view of the theory and practice behind project, program, and portfolio selection.

     She could see that several managers were getting bored with the presentation, while others looked concerned that their projects might be cancelled if the company implemented a new approach for project selection. After the consultant's presentation, Marie had each participant write down his or her questions and concerns and hand them in anonymously for her group to review. She was amazed at the obvious lack of understanding of the need for projects to align with business strategy. How should Marie respond?

ALIGNING PROJECTS WITH BUSINESS STRATEGY

Most organizations face hundreds of problems and opportunities for improvement and consider potential projects to address them. These organizations—both large and small—cannot undertake most of the potential projects identified because of resource limitations and other constraints. Therefore, an organization's overall business strategy should guide the project selection process and prioritization of those projects.

Strategic Planning

Successful leaders look at the big picture or strategic plan of the organization to determine what projects will provide the most value. The same can be said for successful individuals. No one person can do everything, so individuals must pick projects to pursue based on their talents, interests, limitations, and other criteria. **Strategic planning** involves determining long-term objectives by analyzing the strengths and weaknesses of an organization, studying opportunities and threats in the business environment, predicting future trends, and projecting the need for new products and services. Strategic planning provides important information to help organizations identify and then select potential projects.

What Went Wrong?

Unfortunately, when deciding to approve projects, many organizations lack a structured process. Mike Peterson, project management professional (PMP) and director with PricewaterhouseCoopers' Advisory Services, described an organization that decided it needed to implement a new financial system, which is often a very expensive, challenging project. "With little in the way of analysis, they selected a big-name enterprise resource planning package, and hired a boutique firm to assist with the implementation. At no time did they formally define the benefits the new system was meant to usher in; nor did they decide, exactly, which processes were to be redesigned. Their own assumptions were not articulated, timelines were never devised, nor were the key performance indicators needed to track success ever established."[1]

What was the result of this project? It was completed over budget and behind schedule. Instead of helping the company, it prevented it from closing its books for over 12 months. The company undertook a long and costly project, and ultimately failed to improve the organization's effectiveness. The company could have avoided many of the problems it encountered if it had followed a formal, well-defined process to identify and select projects.

SWOT Analysis

Many people are familiar with **SWOT analysis**—analyzing **S**trengths, **W**eaknesses, **O**pportunities, and **T**hreats—which is used to aid in strategic planning. For example, a group of four people who want to start a new business in the film industry could perform a SWOT analysis to help identify potential projects. They might determine the following based on a SWOT analysis:

Strengths:

- As experienced professionals, we have numerous contacts in the film industry.

- Two of us have strong sales and interpersonal skills.

- Two of us have strong technical skills and are familiar with several filmmaking software tools.

- We all have impressive samples of completed projects.

Weaknesses:

- None of us have accounting/financial experience.
- We have no clear marketing strategy for products and services.
- We have little money to invest in new projects.
- We have no company Web site and limited use of technology to run the business.

Opportunities:

- A current client has mentioned a large project she would like us to bid on.
- The film industry continues to grow.
- There are two major conferences this year where we could promote our company.

Threats:

- Other individuals or companies can provide the services we can.
- Customers might prefer working with more established individuals/organizations.
- There is high risk in the film business.

Based on their SWOT analysis, the four entrepreneurs outline potential projects as follows:

- Find an external accountant or firm to help run the business.
- Hire someone to develop a company Web site, focusing on our experience and past projects.
- Develop a marketing plan.
- Develop a strong proposal to get the large project the current client mentioned.
- Plan to promote the company at two major conferences this year.

Some people like to perform a SWOT analysis by using mind mapping. **Mind mapping** is a technique that uses branches radiating out from a core idea to structure thoughts and ideas. The human brain does not work in a linear fashion. People come up with many unrelated ideas. By putting those ideas down in a visual mind map format, you can often generate more ideas than by just creating lists. You can create mind maps by hand, by using sticky notes, using presentation software like PowerPoint, or by using mind mapping software. Mind mapping can be a more structured, focused, and documented approach to brainstorming individually or in small groups.

Figure 2-1 shows a sample mind map for the SWOT analysis presented earlier. This diagram was created using MindManager software by Mindjet. (You can download a free trial of this software from *www.mindjet.com* or use a similar free tool called FreeMind available at *www.freemind.sourceforge.net*.) Notice that this map has four main branches representing strengths, weaknesses, opportunities, and threats. Icons are added to each of those main branches to more visually identify them, such as the thumbs up for strengths and thumbs down for weaknesses. Ideas in each category are added to the appropriate branch. You could also add sub-branches to show ideas under those categories. For example, under the first branch for strengths, you could start adding sub-branches to list the most important contacts you have. This mind map includes branches for project ideas related to different categories, with text markers used to identify the project names. From this visual example, you can see that there are no project ideas identified yet to address strengths or threats, so these areas should be discussed further.

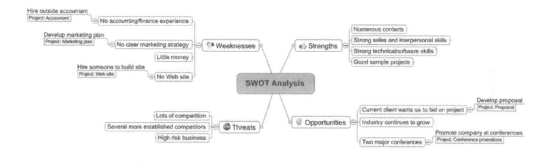

Figure 2-1. Mind map of a SWOT analysis to help identify potential projects (Schwalbe, Information Technology Project Management, Sixth Edition, 2010)

FOUR-STAGE PLANNING PROCESS FOR PROJECT SELECTION

One of the most important factors in project success is selecting the best projects to undertake. In addition to using a SWOT analysis, organizations often follow a detailed planning process for project selection. Figure 2-2 shows a four-stage planning process for selecting projects. Note the hierarchical structure of this model and the results produced from each stage. *It is very important to start at the top of the pyramid to select projects that support the organization's business* strategy. *It is also important to update plans and estimates based on the changing business environment.* The four stages of this process include:

1. *Strategic planning*: The first step of the project selection process is to determine the organization's strategy, goals, and objectives. This information should come from the strategic plan or strategy planning meetings. For example, if a firm's competitive strategy is cost leadership, it should focus on projects that will help it retain its position as a low-cost producer.

2. *Business area analysis*: The second step is to analyze business processes that are central to achieving strategic goals. For example, could the organization make improvements in sales, manufacturing, engineering, information technology (IT), or other business areas to support the strategic plan?

3. *Project planning*: The next step is to start defining potential projects that address the strategies and business areas identified. Managers should discuss the potential projects' scope, time, and cost goals; projected benefits; and constraints as part of this process.

4. *Resource allocation*: The last step in the project planning process is choosing which projects to do and assigning resources for working on them. The amount of resources the organization has available or is willing to acquire will affect decisions on how many projects it can support.

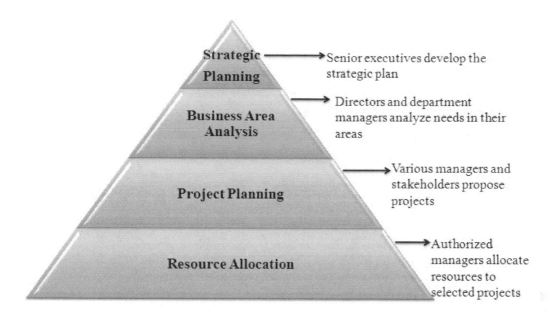

Figure 2-2. Pyramid for the project planning process

METHODS FOR SELECTING PROJECTS

Although people in organizations identify many potential projects as part of their strategic planning process, they also identify projects by working on day-to-day operations. For example, a project manager overseeing an apartment building project might notice that some workers are much more efficient than others are. He or she might suggest a project to provide standardized training on specific skills. A marketing analyst might notice that competitors are using new forms of advertising and suggest a project to respond to this competition. It is important for organizations to encourage workers at all levels as well as customers to submit project ideas because they know firsthand what problems they are encountering and what opportunities might be available.

How do senior managers decide which of the many potential projects their organization should pursue? Some projects directly support competitive strategy and are easy choices, but other project ideas require additional thought and analysis. However, organizations need to narrow down the list of potential projects due to resource and time constraints and focus on projects that will be most beneficial. Most large organizations go through a preliminary project prioritization process annually. For example, early each fall Exxon Corporation's Information Technology (IT) organizations work with all of their internal client organizations worldwide to identify potential IT projects and resource requirements for the following year. This process takes about three weeks, followed by meetings to discuss and prioritize potential projects and agree to cut-off lines based on the availability of funds and other resources. Senior management then reviews the prioritized list of potential projects as part of the corporation's fall company planning and budgeting process.

Selecting projects is not an exact science, but it is a critical part of project, program, and project portfolio management. Many methods exist for selecting from among possible projects. Common techniques are listed here and explained in the following sections:

- Focusing on competitive strategy and broad organizational needs

- Performing net present value analysis or other financial projections

- Using a weighted scoring model

- Implementing a balanced scorecard

- Addressing problems, opportunities, and directives

- Considering project time frame

- Considering project priority

In practice, organizations usually use a combination of these approaches to select projects. Each approach has advantages and disadvantages, and it is up to management to decide the best approach for selecting projects based on their particular organization. In any case, projects should first and foremost address business needs.

Focusing on Competitive Strategy and Broad Organizational Needs

When deciding what projects to undertake, when to undertake them, and to what level, managers must focus on meeting their organizations' many needs. Projects that address competitive strategy are much more likely to be successful because they will be important to the organization's competitive position.

For example, a company might have a competitive strategy of cost leadership, meaning that it attracts customers primarily because its products or services are inexpensive. Wal-Mart (*www.walmart.com*) and Cub Foods (*www.cub.com*) fit into this category; a project to help reduce inventories and, thereby, costs would fit their competitive strategies. Other companies might have a particular focus for their competitive strategies, meaning that they develop products for a particular market niche. Babies"R"Us (*www .babiesrus.com*) and Ron Jon Surf Shop (*www.ronjons.com*) fit into this category; a project to help attract new customers (new parents for Babies"R"Us and new surfers for Ron Jon Surf Shop) would fit their competitive strategies.

In addition to projects that directly tie to competitive strategy, organizations might pursue projects that everyone agrees will meet broad organizational needs. These needs might involve minimizing legal or financial risks, improving the firm's IT infrastructure, improving safety or morale, or providing faster customer service. It is often impossible to estimate the financial value of such projects, but everyone agrees that they do have a high value. As the old proverb says, "It is better to measure gold roughly than to count pennies precisely."

One method for selecting projects based on broad organizational needs is to determine whether they meet three important criteria: need, funding, and will. Do people in the organization agree that the project needs to be done? Does the organization have the capacity to provide adequate funds to perform the project? Is there a strong will to make the project succeed? For example, many visionary chief executive officers (CEOs) can describe a broad need to improve certain aspects of their organizations, such as communications. Although they cannot specifically describe how to improve communications, they might allocate funds to projects that address this need. As projects progress, the organization must reevaluate the need, funding, and will for each project to determine if the projects should be continued, redefined, or terminated.

Performing Financial Projections

Financial considerations are often an important aspect of the project selection process, especially during tough economic times. As authors Dennis Cohen and Robert Graham put it, "Projects are never ends in themselves. Financially they are always a means to an end, cash."[2] Many organizations require an approved business case before pursuing projects, and financial projections are a critical component of the business case. Three primary methods for determining the projected financial value of projects include net present value analysis, return on investment, and payback analysis. Because project managers often deal with business executives, they must understand how to speak their language, which often boils down to understanding these important financial concepts.

Net Present Value Analysis

Net present value (NPV) analysis is a method of calculating the expected net monetary gain or loss from a project by discounting all expected future cash inflows and outflows to the present point in time. (Detailed steps to walk you through the calculation are outlined in the following paragraphs.) An organization should consider only projects with a positive NPV if financial value is a key criterion for project selection. This is because a positive NPV means the return from a project exceeds the **opportunity cost of capital**— the return available by investing the capital elsewhere. For example, is it best to put money into Project A or Project B? Projects with higher NPVs are preferred to projects with lower NPVs if all other factors are equal.

Figure 2-3 illustrates the NPV concept for two different projects. Note that this example starts discounting right away in Year 1 and uses a 10% discount rate for both projects. (The paragraphs that follow explain the discount rate.) You can use the NPV function in Microsoft Excel to calculate the NPV quickly. Detailed steps on performing this calculation manually are provided in Figure 2-4. Note that Figure 2-3 lists the projected benefits first, followed by the costs, and then the calculated cash flow amount. Notice that the sum of the **cash flow**—benefits minus costs, or income minus expenses— is the same for both projects at $5,000. The net present values are different, however, because they account for the time value of money. Money earned today is worth more than money earned in the future. Project 1 had a negative cash flow of $5,000 in the first year, whereas Project 2 had a negative cash flow of only $1,000 in the first year.

Although both projects had the same total cash flows without discounting, these cash flows are not of comparable financial value. NPV analysis, therefore, is a method for making equal comparisons between cash flow for multiyear projects. Although this example shows both projects having the same length, NPV also works for projects of different lengths.

	A	B	C	D	E	F	G
1	Discount rate	10%					
2							
3	**PROJECT 1**	YEAR 1	YEAR 2	YEAR 3	YEAR 4	YEAR 5	**TOTAL**
4	Benefits	$0	$2,000	$3,000	$4,000	$5,000	$14,000
5	Costs	$5,000	$1,000	$1,000	$1,000	$1,000	$9,000
6	Cash flow	($5,000)	$1,000	$2,000	$3,000	$4,000	**$5,000**
7	NPV ──────➤	**$2,316**					
8		Formula =npv(b1,b6:f6)					
9							
10	**PROJECT 2**	YEAR 1	YEAR 2	YEAR 3	YEAR 4	YEAR 5	**TOTAL**
11	Benefits	$1,000	$2,000	$4,000	$4,000	$4,000	$15,000
12	Costs	$2,000	$2,000	$2,000	$2,000	$2,000	$10,000
13	Cash flow	($1,000)	$0	$2,000	$2,000	$2,000	**$5,000**
14	NPV ──────➤	**$3,201**					
15		Formula =npv(b1,b13:f13)					
16							
17							

Note that totals are equal, but NPVs are not because of the time value of money

Figure 2-3. Net present value example (Schwalbe, Information Technology Project Management, Sixth Edition, 2010)

Discount rate	10%					
PROJECT 1	**1**	**2**	**3**	**4**	**5**	**TOTAL**
Costs	$5,000	$1,000	$1,000	$1,000	$1,000	$9,000
Discount factor*	0.91	0.83	0.75	0.68	0.62	
Discounted costs	$4,545	$826	$751	$683	$621	**$7,427**
Benefits	$0	$2,000	$3,000	$4,000	$5,000	$14,000
Discount factor*	0.91	0.83	0.75	0.68	0.62	
Discounted benefits	0	$1,653	$2,254	$2,732	$3,105	**$9,743**

Discounted benefits - discounted costs, or NPV ⟶ **$2,316**

*Note: The discount factors are NOT rounded to two decimal places.

They are calculated using the formula discount factor = 1/(1+discount rate)ˆyear.

You can access this spreadsheet on the companion Web site under Sample Documents.

Figure 2-4. Detailed NPV calculations (Schwalbe, Information Technology Project Management, Sixth Edition, 2010)

There are some items to consider when calculating NPV. Some organizations refer to the investment year for project costs as Year 0 instead of Year 1 and do not discount costs in Year 0. Other organizations start discounting immediately based on their financial procedures; it is simply a matter of preference for the organization. The discount rate can also vary, based on the prime rate and other economic considerations. Financial experts in your organization will be able to tell you what discount rate to use. Some people consider it to be the rate at which you could borrow money for the project. You can enter costs as negative numbers instead of positive numbers, and you can list costs first and then benefits. For example, Figure 2-5 shows the financial calculations a consulting firm provided in a business case for an intranet project. Note that the discount rate is 8%, costs are not discounted right away (note the Year 0), the discount factors are rounded to two decimal places, costs are listed first, and costs are entered as positive numbers. The NPV and other calculations are still the same; only the format is slightly different. Project managers must be sure to check with their organization to find out its guidelines for when discounting starts, what discount rate to use, and what format the organization prefers.

Discount rate		8%					
Assume the project is completed in Year 0				Year			
		0	1	2	3	Total	
Costs		140,000	40,000	40,000	40,000		
Discount factor		1	0.93	0.86	0.79		
Discounted costs		140,000	37,200	34,400	31,600	243,200	
Benefits		0	200,000	200,000	200,000		
Discount factor		1	0.93	0.86	0.79		
Discounted benefits		0	186,000	172,000	158,000	516,000	
Discounted benefits - costs	(140,000)	148,800	137,600	126,400	272,800	←NPV	
Cumulative benefits - costs	(140,000)	8,800	146,400	272,800			
ROI		112%					
		Payback in Year 1					

Figure 2-5. Intranet project NPV example (Schwalbe, Information Technology Project Management, Sixth Edition, 2010)

To determine NPV, follow these steps:

1. Determine the estimated costs and benefits for the life of the project and the products it produces. For example, the intranet project example assumed the project would produce a system in about six months that would be used for three years, so costs are included in Year 0, when the system is developed, and ongoing system costs and projected benefits are included for Years 1, 2, and 3.

2. Determine the discount rate. A **discount rate** is the rate used in discounting future cash flows. It is also called the capitalization rate or opportunity cost of capital. In Figures 2-3 and 2-4, the discount rate is 10% per year, and in Figure 2-5, the discount rate is 8% per year.

3. Calculate and interpret the net present value. There are several ways to calculate NPV. Most spreadsheet software has a built-in function to calculate NPV. For example, Figure 2-3 shows the formula that Excel uses: =npv(discount rate, range of cash flows), where the discount rate is in cell B1 and the range of cash flows for Project 1 are in cells B6 through F6. To use the NPV function, there must be a row in the spreadsheet (or column, depending on how it is organized) for the cash flow each year, which is the benefit amount for that year minus the cost amount. The result of the formula yields an NPV of $2,316 for Project 1

An Introduction to Project Management, Third Edition

and an NPV of $3,201 for Project 2. Because both projects have positive NPVs, they are both good candidates for selection. However, because Project 2 has a higher NPV than Project 1 (38% higher), it would be the better choice between the two. If the two numbers are close, other methods should be used to help decide which project to select.

The mathematical formula for calculating NPV is:

$$\text{NPV} = \sum_{t=0...n} A_t / (1+r)^t$$

where t equals the year of the cash flow, n is the last year of the cash flow, A_t is the amount of cash flow in year t, and r is the discount rate. If you cannot enter the data into spreadsheet software, you can perform the calculations by hand or with a simple calculator. First, determine the annual **discount factor**—a multiplier for each year based on the discount rate and year—and then apply it to the costs and benefits for each year. The formula for the discount factor is $1/(1+r)^t$, where r is the discount rate, such as 8%, and t is the year. For example, the discount factors used in Figure 2-5 are calculated as follows:

Year 0: discount factor = $1/(1+0.08)^0 = 1$

Year 1: discount factor = $1/(1+0.08)^1 = .93$

Year 2: discount factor = $1/(1+0.08)^2 = .86$

Year 3: discount factor = $1/(1+0.08)^3 = .79$

After determining the discount factor for each year, multiply the costs and benefits by the appropriate discount factor. For example, in Figure 2-6, the discounted cost for Year 1 is $40,000 * .93 = $37,200, where the discount factor is rounded to two decimal places. Next, sum all of the discounted costs and benefits each year to get a total. For example, the total discounted costs in Figure 2-5 are $243,200. To calculate the NPV, take the total discounted benefits and subtract the total discounted costs. In this example, the NPV is $516,000 – $243,200 = $272,800.

Return on Investment

Another important financial consideration is return on investment. **Return on investment (ROI)** is the result of subtracting the project costs from the benefits and then dividing by the costs. For example, if you invest $100 today and next year your investment is worth $110, your ROI is ($110 – 100)/100, or 0.10 (10%). Note that the ROI is always a percentage. It can be positive or negative. It is best to consider discounted costs and benefits for multiyear projects when calculating ROI. Figure 2-5 shows an ROI of 112%. You calculate this number as follows:

ROI = (total discounted benefits – total discounted costs)/discounted costs

ROI = (516,000 – 243,200) / 243,200 = 112%

The higher the ROI, the better; an ROI of 112% is outstanding. Many organizations have a required rate of return for projects. The **required rate of return** is the minimum acceptable rate of return on an investment. For example, an organization might have a required rate of return of at least 10% for projects. The organization bases the required rate of return on what it could expect to receive elsewhere for an investment of comparable risk.

You can also determine a project's **internal rate of return (IRR)** by finding what discount rate results in an NPV of zero for the project. You can use the Goal Seek function in Excel (use Excel's Help function for more information on Goal Seek) to determine the IRR quickly. Simply set the cell containing the NPV calculation to zero while changing the cell containing the discount rate. For example, in Figure 2-3, you could set cell B7 to zero while changing cell B1 to find that the IRR for Project 1 is 27%. (Note: The Excel file for Figure 2-3 is provided on the companion Web site under Sample Documents if you want to try this out. Consult additional sources for more information on IRR and other financial concepts.)

Payback Analysis

Payback analysis is another important financial tool to use when selecting projects. **Payback period** is the amount of time it will take to recoup—in the form of net cash inflows—the total dollars invested in a project. In other words, payback analysis determines how much time will lapse before accrued benefits overtake accrued and continuing costs. Payback, if there is one, occurs in the year when the cumulative benefits minus costs reach zero.

For example, assume a project cost $100,000 up front with no additional costs, and its annual benefits were $50,000 per year. Payback period is calculated by dividing the cost of the project by the annual cash inflows ($100,000/$50,000), resulting in 2 years in this simple example. If costs and benefits vary each year, you need to find where the lines for the cumulative costs and benefits cross, or where the cumulative cash inflow is equal to zero. The data used to create the chart in Figure 2-6 is provided above the chart.

Year	Costs	Benefits	Cum Costs	Cum Benefits	Cum Cash Inflows
0	100,000	0	100,000	0	-100,000
1	0	50,000	100,000	50,000	-50,000
2	0	50,000	100,000	100,000	0
3	0	50,000	100,000	150,000	50,000

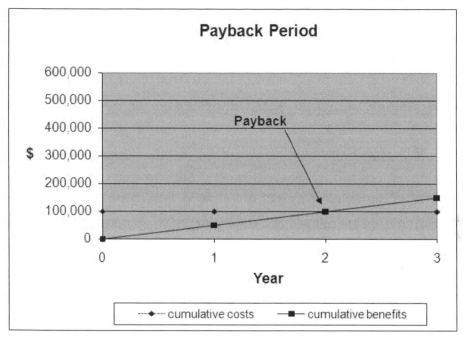

Figure 2-6. Charting the payback period

Template Files Available

A template file charting the payback period is provided on the companion Web site for this text, as well as one for calculating NPV, ROI, and payback for a project (called business case financials). See Appendix C for a list of all template files.

Many organizations have certain recommendations for the length of the payback period of an investment. For example, they might require all IT projects to have a payback period of less than two years or even one year, regardless of the estimated NPV or ROI. Rhonda Hocker, CIO at San Jose–based BEA Systems, Inc. (now owned by Oracle), notes that the general rule at the company is that its IT projects should have a payback period of less than one year. The company also tries to limit project teams to no more than 12 people, who perform the work within four months. Given the economic climate and rapid pace of change in businesses and technology, the company has to focus on delivering positive financial results quickly.[3] However; organizations must also consider long-range goals when making major investments. Many crucial projects, such as drug development or major transportation projects, cannot achieve a payback that quickly or be completed in such a short time period.

To aid in project selection, it is important for project managers to understand the organization's financial expectations for projects. It is also important for management to understand the limitations of financial estimates, because they are just estimates.

Using a Weighted Scoring Model

A **weighted scoring model** is a tool that provides a systematic process for selecting projects based on many criteria. These criteria include such factors as meeting strategic goals or broad organizational needs; addressing specific problems or opportunities; the amount of time it will take to complete the project; the overall priority of the project; and the projected financial performance of the project.

The first step in creating a weighted scoring model is to identify criteria important to the project selection process. It often takes time to develop and reach agreement on these criteria. Holding facilitated brainstorming sessions or using software to exchange ideas can aid in developing these criteria.

For example, suppose your family wants to take a trip. Some possible criteria for selecting which trip to take include the following:

- Total cost of the trip

- Probability of good weather

- Fun activities nearby

- Recommendations

Next, you assign a weight to each criterion. Once again, determining weights requires consultation and final agreement. These weights indicate how much you value each criterion or how important each criterion is. You can assign weights based on percentage, and the sum of all the criteria's weights must total 100%. You then assign numerical scores to each criterion (for example, 0 to 100) for each project (or trip in this example). The scores indicate how much each project (or trip) meets each criterion. At this point, you can use a spreadsheet application to create a matrix of projects, criteria, weights, and scores. Figure 2-7 provides an example of a weighted scoring model to evaluate four different trips. After assigning weights for the criteria and scores for each trip, you calculate a weighted score for each trip by multiplying the weight for each criterion by its score and adding the resulting values.

For example, you calculate the weighted score for Trip 1 in Figure 2-7 as:

$$25\%*60 + 30\%*80 + 15\%*70 + 30\%*50 = 64.5$$

Criteria	Weight	Trip 1	Trip 2	Trip 3	Trip 4
Total cost of the trip	25%	60	80	90	20
Probability of good weather	30%	80	60	90	70
Fun activities nearby	15%	70	30	50	90
Recommendations	30%	50	50	60	90
Weighted Project Scores	**100%**	**64.5**	**57.5**	**75**	**66.5**

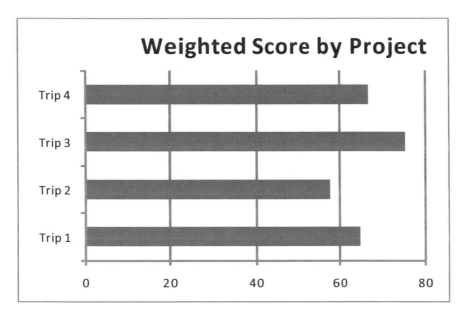

Figure 2-7. Sample weighted scoring model for project selection

Note that in this example, Trip 3 is the obvious choice for selection because it has the highest weighted score. Creating a bar chart to graph the weighted scores for each project allows you to see the results at a glance. If you create the weighted scoring model in a spreadsheet, you can enter the data, create and copy formulas, and perform a "what-if" analysis. For example, suppose you change the weights for the criteria. By having the weighted scoring model in a spreadsheet, you can easily change the weights to update the weighted scores and charts automatically. This capability allows you to investigate various options for different stakeholders quickly. Ideally, the result should be reflective of the group's consensus, and any major disagreements should be documented. A template file for creating a weighted scoring model is provided on the companion Web site for this text.

Many readers of this text are probably familiar with a weighted scoring model because teachers often use them to determine grades. Suppose grades for a class are based on two homework assignments and two exams. To calculate final grades, the teacher would assign a weight to each of these items. Suppose Homework One is worth 10% of the grade, Homework Two is worth 20% of the grade, Test One is worth 20% of the grade, and Test Two is worth 50% of the grade. Students would want to do well on each of these items, but they would focus on performing well on Test Two because it is 50% of the grade.

You can also establish weights by assigning points. For example, a project might receive 100 points if it definitely supports key business objectives, 50 points if it somewhat supports them, and 0 points if it is totally unrelated to key business objectives. With a point model, you can simply add all the points to determine the best projects for selection without having to multiply weights and scores and sum the results.

You can also determine minimum scores or thresholds for specific criteria in a weighted scoring model. For example, suppose an organization decided that it should not consider a project if it does not score at least 50 out of 100 on every criterion. The organization can build this type of threshold into the weighted scoring model to automatically reject projects that do not meet these minimum standards. As you can see, weighted scoring models can aid in project selection decisions.

Implementing a Balanced Scorecard

Dr. Robert Kaplan and Dr. David Norton developed another approach to help select and manage projects that align with business strategy. A **balanced scorecard** is a methodology that converts an organization's value drivers—such as customer service, innovation, operational efficiency, and financial performance—to a series of defined metrics. Organizations record and analyze these metrics to determine how well projects help them achieve strategic goals.

The Balanced Scorecard Institute, which provides training and guidance to organizations using this methodology, quotes Kaplan and Norton's description of the balanced scorecard as follows:

"The balanced scorecard retains traditional financial measures. But financial measures tell the story of past events, an adequate story for industrial age companies for which investments in long-term capabilities and customer relationships were not critical for success. These financial measures are inadequate, however, for guiding and evaluating the journey that information age companies must make to create future value through investment in customers, suppliers, employees, processes, technology, and innovation."[4]

Visit *www.balancedscorecard.org* for more information on using this approach to project selection. This site includes several examples of how organizations use this methodology. For example, the U.S. Defense Finance and Accounting Services (DFAS) organization uses a balanced scorecard to measure performance and track progress in achieving its strategic goals. Their strategy focuses on four perspectives: customer, financial, internal, and growth and learning. Figure 2-8 shows how the balanced scorecard approach ties together the organization's mission, vision, and goals based on these four perspectives. The DFAS continuously monitors this corporate scorecard and revises it based on identified priorities.

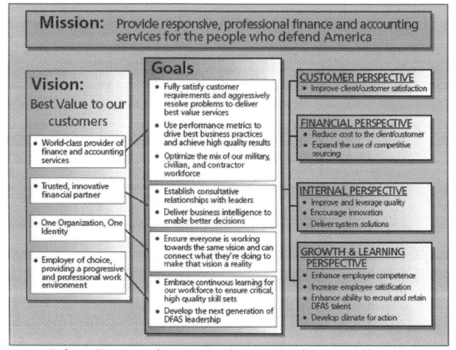

Defense Finance and Accounting Service, "DFAS Strategic Plan," Nov 2001 (http://balancedscorecard.org/files/DFAS-strategic-plan.pdf), p. 13.

Figure 2-8. Balanced scorecard example

Using the Performance Power Grid

David F. Giannetto, author of the 2006 book *The Performance Power Grid: The Proven Method to Create and Sustain Superior Organizational Performance*, argues that the performance power grid approach is much more effective than the balanced scorecard method. He says that the balanced scorecard, developed in the 1980's, has not delivered the desired long-term performance results. The power grid helps managers channel the energy of employees into the proper tasks, processes, and projects every day, which leads to higher productivity and more team focus on the jobs that truly matter. Instead of waiting for monthly data, like many users of the balanced scorecard or similar approaches do, users of the performance power grid approach use real-time data to constantly update important performance metrics. See Gianetto's book or visit www.performancepowergrid.com for more information.

Addressing Problems, Opportunities, and Directives

Another method for selecting projects is based on their response to a problem, an opportunity, or a directive, as described in the following list:

- **Problems** are undesirable situations that prevent an organization from achieving its goals. These problems can be current or anticipated. For example, if a bridge in a major city collapses, that problem must be addressed as soon as possible. If a bridge is known to need repairs to prevent a collapse, a project should be initiated soon to take care of it.

- **Opportunities** are chances to improve the organization. For example, a company might want to revamp its Web site to attract more visitors to the site.

- **Directives** are new requirements imposed by management, government, or some external influence. For example, a college or university may have to meet a requirement to discontinue the use a student's social security number for data privacy.

Organizations select projects for any of these reasons. It is often easier to get approval and funding for projects that address problems or directives because the organization must respond to these categories of projects to avoid hurting the business. For example, several years ago Exxon Corporation realized that it was losing $200,000 each minute its motor fuel store point-of-sale system was down. Getting approval for a $7 million project to re-engineer this critical system was approved and given high priority. Many projects resulting from natural disasters, such as hurricanes and earthquakes, get quick approvals due to their serious nature. Many problems and directives must be resolved quickly, but managers must also consider projects that seek opportunities for improving the organization.

Project Time Frame

Another approach to project selection is based on the time it will take to complete a project or the date by which it must be done. For example, some potential projects must be finished within a specific time period, such as projects that were done to meet Year 2000 issues. If they cannot be finished by this set date, there may be serious consequences. Likewise, if there is a potential project that is only valid if it can be done by a certain time and there is no way your organization can meet the deadline, it should not be considered. Some projects can be completed very quickly—within a few weeks, days, or even minutes. However, even though many projects can be completed quickly, it is still important to prioritize them.

Project Priority

Another method for project selection is the overall priority of the project. Many organizations prioritize projects as being high, medium, or low priority based on the current business environment. For example, if it were crucial to cut operating costs quickly, projects that have the most potential to do so would be given a high priority. The organization should always complete high-priority projects first, even if a lower priority project could be finished in less time. Usually, there are many more potential projects than an organization can undertake at any one time, so it is very important to work on the most important ones first.

As you can see, organizations of all types and sizes can use many approaches to select projects. Many project managers have some say in which projects their organizations select for implementation. Even if they do not, they need to understand the motive and overall business strategy for the projects they are managing. Project managers and team members are often asked to justify their projects, and understanding many of these project selection methods can help them to do so.

PROGRAM SELECTION

After deciding which projects to pursue, organizations need to decide if it is advantageous to manage several projects together as part of a program. There might already be a program that a new project would logically fall under, or the organization might initiate a program and then approve projects for it. Recall that a program is a group of projects managed in a coordinated way to obtain benefits and control not available from managing them individually.

Focusing on Coordination and Benefits

What does it mean to manage a group of projects in a coordinated way? Project managers focus on managing individual projects. Project managers and their teams have to do many things to achieve individual project success. For example, if a project manager is in charge of building a new house for a sponsor, he or she must perform the following tasks, just to name a few:

- Work with local government groups to obtain permits
- Find and manage a land excavation firm to prepare the land
- Work with an architect to understand the house design
- Screen and hire various construction workers
- Find appropriate suppliers for the materials

If a construction firm is in charge of developing several houses in the same geographic area, it makes sense to coordinate these and other tasks for all the housing projects instead of doing them separately.

What benefits and control would be possible by managing projects as part of a program? There are several. For example, potential benefits in the housing program scenario include the following:

- *Saving money*: The construction firm can often save money by using economies of scale. It can purchase materials, obtain services, and hire workers for less money if it is managing the construction of 100 houses instead of just one house.

- *Saving time*: Instead of each project team having to perform similar work, by grouping the projects into a program, one person or group can be responsible for similar work, such as obtaining all the permits for all the houses. This coordination of work usually saves time as well as money.

- *Increasing authority*: A program manager responsible for building 100 houses will have more authority than a project manager responsible for building one house. The program manager can use this authority in multiple situations, such as negotiating better prices with suppliers and obtaining better services in a more timely fashion.

Approaches to Creating Programs

Some new projects naturally fall into existing programs, such as houses being built in a certain geographic area. As another example, many companies use IT, and they usually have a program in place for IT infrastructure projects. Projects might include purchasing new hardware, software, and networking equipment, or determining standards for IT. If a new office opens up in a new location, the project to provide the hardware, software, and networks for that office would logically fall under the infrastructure program.

Other projects might spark the need for developing a new program. For example, Global Construction, Inc., from the opening case might win a large contract to build an office complex in a foreign country. Instead of viewing the contract as either one huge project or part of an existing program, it would be better to manage the work as its own program that comprises several smaller projects. For example, there might be separate project managers for each building. Grouping related projects into programs helps improve coordination through better communications, planning, management, and control. Organizations must decide when it makes sense to group projects together. When too many projects are part of one program, it might be wise to create a new program to improve their management. Remember that the main goal of programs is to obtain benefits and control not available from managing projects separately.

Media Snapshot

Many people enjoy watching the extra features on a DVD that describe the creation of a movie. For example, the extended edition DVD for *Lord of the Rings: The Two Towers* includes detailed descriptions of how the script was created, how huge structures were built, how special effects were made, and how talented professionals overcame numerous obstacles to complete the three movies. Instead of viewing each movie as a separate project, the producer, Peter Jackson, decided to develop all three movies as part of one program.

"By shooting all three films consecutively during one massive production and post-production schedule, New Line Cinema made history. Never before had such a monumental undertaking been contemplated or executed. The commitment of time, resources, and manpower were unheard of as all three films and more than 1,000 effects shots were being produced concurrently with the same director and core cast."[5]

At three years in the making, *The Lord of the Rings* trilogy was the largest production ever to be mounted in the Southern Hemisphere. The production assembled an international cast, employed a crew of 2,500, used over 20,000 days of extras, featured 77 speaking parts, and created 1,200 state-of-the-art computer-generated effects shots. Jackson said that doing detailed planning for all three movies made it much easier than he imagined producing them, and the three movies were completed in less time and for less money by grouping them together. The budget for the three films was reported to be $270 million, and they grossed over $1 billion before the end of 2004.

PROJECT PORTFOLIO SELECTION

Projects and programs have existed for a long time, as has some form of project portfolio management. There is no simple process for deciding how to create project portfolios, but the goal of project portfolio management is clear: to help maximize business value to ensure enterprise success. You can measure business value in several ways, such as in market share, profit margins, growth rates, share prices, and customer or employee satisfaction ratings. Many factors are involved in ensuring enterprise success. Organizations cannot only pursue projects that have the best financial value. They must also consider resource availability (including people, equipment, and cash); risks that could affect success; and other concerns, such as potential mergers, public relations, balancing investments, and other factors that affect enterprise success.

Focusing on Enterprise Success

Project managers strive to make their projects successful and naturally focus on doing whatever they can to meet the goals of their particular projects. Likewise, program managers focus on making their programs successful. Project portfolio managers and other senior managers, however, must focus on how all of an organization's projects fit together to help the entire enterprise achieve success. That might mean canceling or putting several projects on hold, reassigning resources from one project to another, suggesting changes in project leadership, or taking other actions that might negatively affect individual projects or programs to help the organization as a whole. For example, a university might have to close a campus in order to provide quality services at other campuses. Running any large organization is complex, as is project portfolio management.

What Went Right?

Many companies have seen great returns on investment after implementing basic ideas of project portfolio management. For example, Jane Walton, the project portfolio manager for IT projects at Schlumberger, saved the company $3 million in one year by simply organizing the organization's 120 IT projects into one portfolio. Before then, all IT projects and their associated programs were managed separately, and no one looked at them as a whole. Manufacturing companies used project portfolio management in the 1960s, and Walton anticipated the need to justify investments in IT projects just as managers have to justify capital investment projects. She found that 80% of the organization's projects overlapped, and 14 separate projects were trying to accomplish the same thing. By looking at all IT projects and programs together, Schlumberger could make better strategic business decisions. The company canceled several projects and merged others to reduce the newly discovered redundancy.[6]

Leaders are turning to project portfolio management tools to better capture, manage, prioritize, and align investments and resources with the hopes of increasing the amount of business value they can provide. Many vendors promise triple-digit returns on their products. Is that possible? A 2009 study found that a comprehensive project portfolio management tool "is likely to provide an ROI of more than 250%."[7]

Recall that project portfolio management focuses on strategic issues while individual projects often focus on tactical issues. Portfolios should be formed and continuously updated to help the organization as a whole make better strategic decisions. Organizations normally put all projects into one portfolio, but then often break it down into more detailed sub-portfolios, often set up by major departments or other categories. Several companies create a separate portfolio for IT projects. It is often difficult to measure the financial value of many IT projects, yet these projects are often a large investment and have a strong effect on other business areas. For example, if you have to update your financial system to meet new government regulations, such as the 2002 Sarbanes-Oxley Act (also known as SOX), where would it fit in your enterprise project portfolio? (After several major corporate scandals, the Sarbanes-Oxley Act was passed to help restore public confidence in the financial reporting of publicly traded companies in the United States. Companies have spent millions of dollars to be compliant with this act.) You have to do it to stay in business, but you cannot generate a positive return on investment from that particular project.

Best Practice

Many organizations rely on effective new product development (NPD) to increase growth and profitability, yet according to Robert Cooper of McMaster University and the New Product Development Institute in Ontario, Canada, only one in seven product concepts comes to fruition. Why is it that some companies, like Proctor & Gamble, Johnson and Johnson, Hewlett Packard, and Sony are consistently successful in NPD? Because they use a disciplined, systematic approach to NPD projects based on best practices, including focusing NPD on business strategy.

Cooper's study compared companies that were the best at performing NPD with those that were the worst. For example:

- 65.5% of companies performing the best at NPD align projects with business strategy.
- 46% of companies performing the worst at NPD align projects with business strategy.
- 65.5% of best performing NPD companies have their resource breakdown aligned to business strategy, while only 8% of worst performing companies do.

It's easy for a company to say that its projects are aligned with business strategy, but assigning its resources based on that strategy is a measurable action that produces results. Best performing NPD companies are also more customer-focused in identifying new product ideas and put a project manager in charge of their NPD projects:

- 69% of best performing NPD companies identify customer needs and problems based on customer input, while only 15% of worst performing companies do.
- 80% of best performing companies have an identifiable NPD project manager, while only 50% of worst performing companies do.[8]

These best practices apply to all projects:

- Align projects *and* resources with business strategy.
- Focus on customer needs when identifying potential projects.
- Assign project managers to lead the projects.

Sample Approach for Creating a Project Portfolio

Figure 2-9 illustrates one approach for project portfolio management in which there is one large portfolio for the entire organization. Sections of the portfolio are then broken down to improve the management of projects in each particular sector. For example, Global Construction might have the main portfolio categories shown in the left part of Figure 2-9 (marketing, materials, IT, and HR (human resources)) and divide each of those categories further to address their unique concerns. The right part of this figure shows how the IT projects could be categorized in more detail to assist in their management. For example, there are three basic IT project portfolio categories:

1. *Venture*: Projects in this category would help transform the business. For example, Global Construction might have an IT project to provide Webcams and interactive Web-based reporting on construction sites that would be easily accessible by its customers and suppliers. This project could help transform the business by developing more trusting partnerships with customers and suppliers, who could know exactly what is happening with their construction projects.

2. *Growth*: Projects in this category would help the company grow in terms of revenue. For example, Global Construction might have an IT project to provide information on its corporate Web site in a new language, such as Chinese or Japanese. This capability could help the company grow its business in those countries.

3. *Core*: Projects in this category must be accomplished to run the business. For example, an IT project to provide computers for new employees would fall under this category.

Note that the core category of IT projects is labeled as nondiscretionary costs. This means that the company has no choice in whether to fund these projects; it must fund them to stay in business. Projects that fall under the venture or growth category would be discretionary costs because the company can use its own discretion in deciding whether to fund them. Also note the arrow in the center of Figure 2-9. This arrow indicates that the risks, value, and timing of projects normally increase as you go from core to growth to venture projects. However, some core projects can also be high risk, have high value, and require good timing.

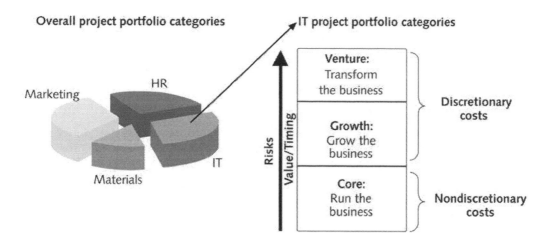

Figure 2-9. Sample project portfolio approach (Schwalbe, Information Technology Project Management, Sixth Edition, 2010)

Five Levels of Project Portfolio Management

As you can imagine, it takes time to understand and apply project portfolio management. You can develop and manage a project portfolio in many ways. Just as projects are unique, so are project portfolios.

An organization can view project portfolio management as having five levels, from simplest to most complex, as follows:

1. Put all of your projects in one list. Many organizations find duplicate or unneeded projects after they identify all the projects on which they are working.

2. Prioritize the projects in your list. It's important to know which projects are most important to an organization so that resources can be applied accordingly.

3. Divide your projects into several categories based on types of investment. Categorizing projects helps you see the big picture, such as how many projects are supporting a growth strategy, how many are helping to increase profit margins, how many relate to marketing, and how many relate to materials. Organizations can create as many categories as they need to help understand and analyze how projects affect business needs and goals.

4. Automate the list. Managers can view project data in many different ways by putting key information into a computerized system. You can enter the project information in spreadsheet software such as Excel. You might have headings for the project name, project manager, project sponsor, business needs addressed, start date, end date, budget, risk, priority, key deliverables, and other items. You can also use more sophisticated tools to help perform project portfolio management, such as enterprise project management software, as described in Chapter 1.

5. Apply modern portfolio theory, including risk-return tools that map project risks. Figure 2-10 provides a sample map to assist in evaluating project risk versus return, or business value. Each bubble represents a project, and the size of the bubble relates to its approved budget (that is, the larger bubbles have larger budgets). Notice that there are not and should not be projects in the lower-right quadrant, which is the location of projects that have low relative value and high risk.

As described in Chapter 1, many project portfolio management software products are available on the market today to help analyze portfolios. Consult references on portfolio theory and project portfolio management software for more details on this topic.

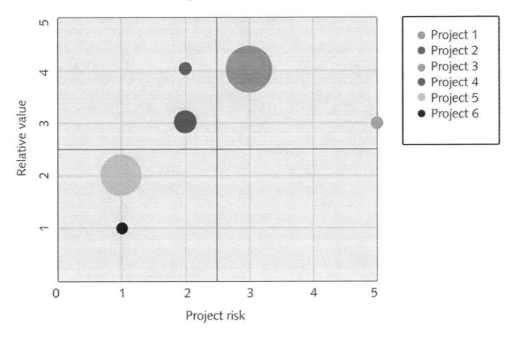

Figure 2-10. Sample project portfolio risk map (Schwalbe, Information Technology Project Management, Sixth Edition, 2010)

Figure 2-11 shows a humorous example of a portfolio management chart listing various fruits, charting them based on their taste and ease of eating. In this example, people would eat a lot more seedless grapes, strawberries, blueberries and peaches and not many grapefruit!

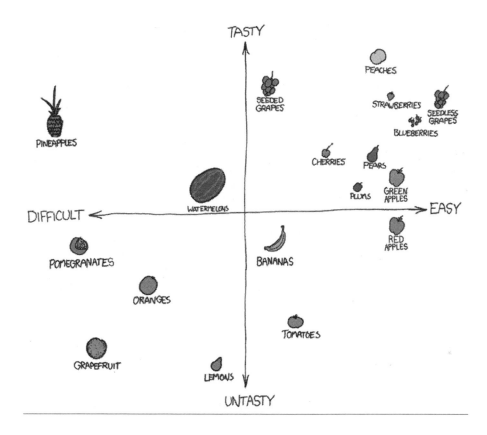

Figure 2-11. Deciding what fruit to eat (www.xkcd.com)

It is important for organizations to develop a fair, consistent, and logical process for selecting projects, programs, and portfolios. Studies show that one of the main reasons people quit their jobs is because they feel they do not make a difference. After employees understand how their work fits into the big picture, they can work more effectively to help themselves and their entire organizations succeed.

CASE WRAP-UP

Marie and her team summarized the inputs from the meeting and discussed them with their CEO, Doug Milis, and other senior managers. They felt people were nervous that the company might not be doing well and that their jobs were in jeopardy. They discussed options for how to proceed and decided that it was important for the CEO to explain the importance of aligning projects with business strategy. Doug and his staff put together a memo and presentation to explain that the company was doing very well, and that they had no intentions of either letting anyone go or cutting major programs. On the contrary, they had far more projects to pursue than they possibly could, and they believed that using project portfolio management would help them select and manage projects better. After everyone heard this information, they were much more open to working with Marie's group to improve their project, program, and portfolio management processes.

CHAPTER SUMMARY

An organization's overall business strategy should guide the project selection process and management of those projects. Many organizations perform a SWOT analysis to help identify potential projects based on their strengths, weaknesses, opportunities, and threats.

The four-stage planning process helps organizations align their projects with their business strategy. The four stages of this model, from highest to lowest, are strategic planning, business area analysis, project planning, and resource allocation.

Several methods are available for selecting projects. Financial methods include calculating and analyzing the net present value, return on investment, and payback period for projects. You can also use a weighted scoring model; implement a balanced scorecard; use a performance power grid; address problems, opportunities, and directives; and consider project time frame and project priority to assist in project selection.

After determining what projects to pursue, it is important to decide if projects should be grouped into programs. The main criteria for program selection are the coordination and benefits available by grouping projects together into a program.

There is no simple process for deciding how to create project portfolios, but the goal of project portfolio management is to help maximize business value to ensure enterprise success. There are five levels of complexity for project portfolio managing, ranging from simply putting all projects in one list to applying modern portfolio theory to analyze risks and returns of a project portfolio.

QUICK QUIZ

1. Which of the following is not part of a SWOT analysis?

    A. strengths

    B. weaknesses

    C. opportunities

    D. tactics

2. A large company continues to be successful by providing new products and services for its market niche of brides. What is its main competitive strategy?

    A. cost leadership

    B. quality

    C. focus

    D. customer service

3. The last step in the four-stage planning process for projects is _____.

    A. resource allocation

    B. project planning

    C. business area analysis

    D. strategic planning

4. It is very important to start at the top of the four-stage planning process pyramid to select projects that support the organization's _____.

    A. vision

    B. business strategy

    C. financial position

    D. culture

5. Which of the following statements is false concerning the financial analysis of projects?

    A. The higher the net present value the better.

    B. A shorter payback period is better than a longer one.

    C. The required rate of return is the discount rate that results in an NPV of zero for the project.

    D. ROI is the result of subtracting the project costs from the benefits and then dividing by the costs.

6. A _____ is a methodology that converts an organization's value drivers—such as customer service, innovation, operational efficiency, and financial performance—into a series of defined metrics.

    A. balanced scorecard

    B. weighted scoring model

    C. net present value analysis

    D. directive

7. Which of the following is not a major benefit of grouping projects into programs?

    A. increasing revenues

    B. increasing authority

    C. saving money

    D. saving time

8. A college approved a project to provide discounts for faculty, students, and staff to use the city's new light-rail system. Under what existing program might this project naturally fit?

    A. academic enrichment program

    B. fund-raising program

    C. entertainment program

    D. transportation program

9. The goal of project portfolio management is to help maximize business value to ensure _____.

   A. profit maximization

   B. enterprise success

   C. risk minimization

   D. competitive advantage

10. Many organizations find duplicate or unneeded projects after they perform which step in project portfolio management?

   A. prioritizing the projects in their list

   B. dividing the projects into several categories based on type of investment

   C. putting all projects in one list

   D. applying modern portfolio theory, including risk-return tools that map project risk

Quick Quiz Answers

1. D; 2. C; 3. A; 4. B; 5. C; 6. A; 7. A; 8. D; 9. B; 10. C

DISCUSSION QUESTIONS

1. Why is it important to align projects to business strategy? What is SWOT analysis? How can you use a mind map to create a SWOT analysis and generate project ideas?

2. What are the stages called in the four-stage planning process for project selection? How does following this process assist in selecting projects that will provide the most benefit to organizations?

3. How do you decide which projects to pursue using net present value analysis? How do return on investment and payback period relate to net present value?

4. What are three main benefits of grouping projects into programs?

5. What are the five levels of project portfolio management?

EXERCISES

Note: These exercises can be done individually or in teams, in class, as homework, or in a virtual environment. Students can either write their results in a paper or prepare a short presentation to show their results.

1.   Perform a financial analysis for a project using the format provided in Figure 2-5. Assume the projected costs and benefits for this project are spread over four years as follows: Estimated costs are $100,000 in Year 1 and $25,000 each year in Years 2, 3, and 4. (*Hint*: Just change the years in the template file from 0, 1, 2, 3, and 4 to 1, 2, 3, and 4. The discount factors will automatically be recalculated.) Estimated benefits are $0 in Year 1 and $80,000 each year in Years 2, 3, and 4. Use an 8% discount rate. Use the business case financials template provided on the companion Web site to calculate and clearly display the NPV, ROI, and year in which payback occurs. In addition, write a paragraph explaining whether you would recommend investing in this project based on your financial analysis.

2.   Create a weighted scoring model to determine which project to select. Assume the criteria are cost, strategic value, risk, and financials, with weights of 15%, 40%, 20%, and 25%, respectively. Enter values for Project 1 as 90, 70, 85, and 50; Project 2 as 75, 80, 90, and 70; and Project 3 as 80 for each criterion. Use the weighted scoring model template provided on the companion Web site to create the model, calculate the weighted score, and graph the results.

3.   Search the Internet to find a real example of how a company or organization uses a structured process to aid in project, program, and/or project portfolio selection. As an alternative, document the process you followed to make a major decision where you had multiple options, such as what college or university to attend, what job to take, where to live, what car to buy, etc. Write a one-page paper or prepare a short presentation summarizing your findings.

4.   Search the Internet for software that helps organizations perform strategic planning, project selection, or project portfolio management. Summarize at least three different tools and discuss whether or not you think these tools are good investments in a one- to two-page paper. Cite your references.

TEAM PROJECTS

1. Find someone who has been involved in the project selection process within an organization. Prepare several interview questions, and then ask him or her the questions in person, via the phone, or via the Internet. Be sure to ask if he or she uses any of the project selection tools discussed in this chapter (for example, ROI, weighted scoring models, balanced scorecards, or other methods). Discuss the results with your team, and then prepare a one- to two-page paper or prepare a short presentation summarizing your findings.

2. Search the Internet to find two good examples of how organizations group projects into programs and two examples of how they create project portfolios. Write a one- to two-page paper or prepare a short presentation summarizing your results, being sure to cite your references.

3. Develop criteria that your class could use to help select what projects to pursue for implementation by your class or another group. For example, criteria might include benefits to the organization, interest level of the sponsor, interest level of the class, and fit with class skills and timing. Determine a weight for each criterion, and then enter the criteria and weights into a weighted scoring model, similar to that shown in Figure 2-7. (You can use the template for a weighted scoring model provided on the companion Web site.) Then review the list of projects you prepared in Chapter 1, Team Project 3, and enter scores for at least five of those projects. Calculate the weighted score for each project. Write a one- to two-page paper or prepare a short presentation summarizing your results.

4. Using your college, university, or an organization your team is familiar with, create a mind map of a SWOT analysis, including at least three branches under each category. Also add sub-branches with at least four potential project ideas. You can create the mind map by hand, or try using software like MindManager (free trial available at *www.mindjet.com*) or FreeMind (available at *www.freemind.sourceforge.net*).

5. As a team, discuss other methods you could use to select class projects. Be sure to review the other methods described in this chapter (besides a weighted scoring model). Document your analysis of each approach as it applies to this situation in a two- to three-page paper or 10-minute presentation.

COMPANION WEB SITE

Visit the free companion Web site for this text at **www.intropm.com** to access template files, online quizzes, Jeopardy-like games, Microsoft Project files, links to sites mentioned in the text, and other information to help you learn more about this important field. Instructors must contact the author at schwalbe@augsburg.edu to gain access to the instructor site. Anyone can access the student site.

KEY TERMS

balanced scorecard — A methodology that converts an organization's value drivers to a series of defined metrics.

cash flow — Benefits minus costs, or income minus expenses.

directives — The new requirements imposed by management, government, or some external influence.

discount factor — A multiplier for each year based on the discount rate and year.

discount rate — The rate used in discounting future cash flows.

internal rate of return (IRR) — The discount rate that results in an NPV of zero for a project.

mind mapping — A technique that uses branches radiating out from a core idea to structure thoughts and ideas.

net present value (NPV) analysis — A method of calculating the expected net monetary gain or loss from a project by discounting all expected future cash inflows and outflows to the present point in time.

opportunities — Chances to improve the organization.

opportunity cost of capital — The return available by investing the capital elsewhere.

payback period — The amount of time it will take to recoup, in the form of net cash inflows, the total dollars invested in a project.

problems — Undesirable situations that prevent the organization from achieving its goals.

required rate of return — The minimum acceptable rate of return on an investment.

return on investment (ROI) — (Benefits minus costs) divided by costs.

strategic planning — The process of determining long-term objectives by analyzing the strengths and weaknesses of an organization, studying opportunities and threats in the business environment, predicting future trends, and projecting the need for new products and services.

SWOT analysis — Analyzing **S**trengths, **W**eaknesses, **O**pportunities, and **T**hreats.

weighted scoring model — A technique that provides a systematic process for basing project selection on numerous criteria.

END NOTES

[1]Mike Peterson, "Why Are We Doing This Project?" Projects@Work, (*www.projectsatwork.com*) (February 22, 2005).

[2]Dennis J. Cohen and Robert J. Graham, *The Project Manager's MBA.* San Francisco: Jossey-Bass (2001), p. 31.

[3]Marc L. Songini, "Tight Budgets Put More Pressure on IT," *Computer World* (December 2, 2002).

[4]The Balanced Scorecard Institute, "What Is a Balanced Scorecard?" (*www.balancedscorecard.org*) (accessed June 2009).

[5]The Compleat Sean Bean Web Site, "Lord of the Rings" (February 23, 2004).

[6]Scott Berinato, "Do the Math," *CIO Magazine* (October 1, 2001).

[7]Craig Symons, "The ROI of Project Portfolio Management Tools," Forrester Research (May 8, 2009).

[8]Robert G. Cooper, "Winning at New Products: Pathways to Profitable Intervention," PMI Research Conference Proceedings (July 2006).

Chapter 3
Initiating Projects

LEARNING OBJECTIVES

After reading this chapter, you will be able to:

- Describe the five project management process groups, map them to the project management knowledge areas, discuss other project management methodologies and why organizations often develop their own, and understand the importance of top management commitment and organizational standards in project management
- Discuss the initiating process used by Global Construction, Inc., including pre-initiating tasks, breaking large projects down into smaller projects, and initiating tasks
- Prepare a business case to justify the need for a project
- Identify project stakeholders and perform a stakeholder analysis
- Create a project charter to formally initiate a project
- Describe the importance of holding a good project kick-off meeting

OPENING CASE

Marie Scott worked with other managers at Global Construction, Inc. to decide what projects their firm should undertake to meet business needs. Construction is a low-margin, very competitive industry, and productivity improvements are crucial to improving shareholder returns. After participating in several strategic planning and project selection workshops, one of the opportunities the company decided to pursue was just-in-time training. Several managers pointed out that Global Construction was spending more than the industry average on training its employees, especially in its sales, purchasing, engineering, and information technology departments, yet productivity for those workers had not improved much in recent years. They also knew that they needed to transfer knowledge from many of their retiring workers to their younger workers. Global Construction, Inc. still offered most courses during work hours using an instructor-led format, and the course topics had not changed in years.

Several managers knew that their competitors had successfully implemented just-in-time training programs so that their workers could get the type of training they needed when they needed it. For example, much of the training was provided over the Internet, so employees could access it anytime, anywhere. Employees were also able to ask questions of instructors as well as experts within the company at any time via the Internet to help them perform specific job duties. In addition, experts documented important knowledge and let other workers share their suggestions. Management believed that Global Construction could reduce training costs and improve productivity by successfully implementing a project to provide just-in-time training on key topics and promote a more collaborative working environment.

Mike Sundby, the vice president of human resources, was the project's champion. After successfully completing a Phase I Just-In-Time Training study to decide how they should proceed with the overall project, Mike and his directors selected Kristin Maur to lead Phase II of the project. Kristin suggested partnering with an outside firm to help with some of the project's technical aspects. Mike asked Kristin to start forming her project team and to prepare important initiating documents, including a detailed business case, a stakeholder register and management strategy, and a project charter for the project. He was also looking forward to participating in the official kick-off meeting.

PROJECT MANAGEMENT PROCESS GROUPS

Recall from Chapter 1 that project management consists of nine project management knowledge areas: project integration, scope, time, cost, quality, human resource, communications, risk, and procurement management. Another important concept to understand is that projects involve five project management process groups: initiating, planning, executing, monitoring and controlling, and closing. Applying these process groups in a consistent, structured fashion increases the chance of project success. This chapter briefly describes each project management process group and then describes the initiating process in detail through a case study based on Global Construction's Just-In-

Time Training project. Subsequent chapters describe the other process groups and apply them to the same project.

Project management process groups progress from initiating activities to planning activities, executing activities, monitoring and controlling activities, and closing activities. A **process** is a series of actions directed toward a particular result. All projects use the five process groups as outlined in the following list:

- **Initiating processes** include actions to begin projects and project phases. To initiate a project such as the Just-In-Time Training project, someone must develop a project charter and hold a kick-off meeting to officially start the project. This chapter will describe these and other initiating tasks in detail.

- **Planning processes** include devising and maintaining a workable scheme to ensure that the project meets its scope, time, and cost goals as well as organizational needs. There are often many different plans to address various project needs as they relate to each knowledge area. For example, as part of project scope management for the Just-In-Time Training project, the project team will develop a scope statement to plan the work that needs to be done to develop and provide the products and services produced as part of the project. As part of project time management, the project team will create a detailed schedule that lets everyone know when specific work will start and end. As part of procurement management, the project team will plan for work that will be done by external organizations to support the project. Chapters 4 and 5 describe the planning tasks in detail.

- **Executing processes** include coordinating people and other resources to carry out the project plans and produce the deliverables of the project or phase. A **deliverable** is a product or service produced or provided as part of a project. For example, a project to construct a new office building would include deliverables such as blueprints, cost estimates, progress reports, the building structure, windows, plumbing, and flooring. The Just-In-Time Training project would include deliverables such as a training needs survey, training materials, and classes. Chapter 6 describes executing tasks in detail.

- **Monitoring and controlling processes** measure progress toward achieving project goals, monitor deviation from plans, and take corrective action to match progress with plans and customer expectations. For example, the main objective of the Just-In-Time Training project is to provide training to help employees be more productive. If the first training course does not improve productivity or meet other customer expectations, the project team should take corrective action to deliver more suitable training courses. As another example, if the project team continues to miss deadlines in the schedule for the Just-In-Time Training project, the project manager should lead the team in taking corrective action, such as developing a more realistic schedule or securing additional resources to help meet deadlines. Chapter 7 describes monitoring and controlling tasks in detail.

An Introduction to Project Management, Third Edition

- **Closing processes** include formalizing acceptance of the project or phase and bringing it to an orderly end. Administrative tasks are often involved in this process group, such as archiving project files, closing out contracts, documenting lessons learned, and receiving formal acceptance of the deliverables. It is also important to plan for a smooth transition of the results of the project to the responsible operational group. For example, after the Just-In-Time Training project is completed, the training department will need to schedule and provide courses developed as part of the project. The planning for this transition should be done as part of the closing process group. Chapter 8 describes closing tasks in detail.

The process groups are not isolated events. For example, project managers must perform monitoring and controlling processes throughout the project's life span. The level of activity and length of each process group varies for every project. Normally, executing tasks require the most resources and time, followed by planning tasks. Initiating and closing tasks are usually the shortest (at the beginning and end of a project or phase, respectively), and they require the least amount of resources and time. However, every project is unique, so there can be exceptions.

Many people ask for guidelines on how much time to spend in each process group. In his 2006 book, *Alpha Project Managers: What the Top 2% Know That Everyone Else Does Not*, Andy Crowe collected data from 860 project managers in various companies and industries in the United States. He found that the best or "alpha" project managers spent more time on every process group than their counterparts except for execution, as follows:

- Initiating: 2% vs. 1%

- Planning: 21% vs. 11%

- Executing: 69% vs. 82%

- Controlling: 5% vs. 4%

- Closing: 3% vs. 2%[1]

This breakdown suggests that the most time should be spent on executing, followed by planning. Note the importance of spending a fair amount of time on planning, which should lead to less time spent on execution.

Note that process groups apply to entire projects as well as to project phases. A **phase** is a distinct stage in project development, and most projects have distinct phases. For example, the Just-In-Time Training project includes phases called study or feasibility, course design and development, course administration, and course evaluation. In this case, the study or feasibility phase was done as a separate project. The other phases were done in a second, larger project. To ensure that they continue to meet current organizational needs, projects should pass successfully through each phase before continuing.

Mapping the Process Groups to the Knowledge Areas

You can map the process group into the nine project management knowledge areas. For example, project integration management includes the following processes:

- Develop project charter (during the initiating process group).

- Develop project management plan (during the planning process group).

- Direct and manage project execution (during the executing process group).

- Monitor and control project work and perform integrated change control (during the monitoring and controlling process group).

- Close the project or phase (during the closing process group).

Based on the *PMBOK® Guide, Fourth Edition*, there are 42 total processes in project management. Figure 3-1 provides a big-picture view of the relationships among these processes, the time in which they are typically completed, and the knowledge areas into which they fit.

Knowledge area	Project management process groups				
	Initiating	Planning	Executing	Monitoring and Controlling	Closing
Project integration management	Develop project charter	Develop project management plan	Direct and manage project execution	Monitor and control project work; perform integrated change control	Close project or phase
Project scope management		Collect requirements; define scope; create WBS		Verify scope; control scope	
Project time management		Define activities; sequence activities; estimate activity resources; estimate activity durations; develop schedule		Control schedule	
Project cost management		Estimate costs; determine budget		Control costs	
Project quality management		Plan quality	Perform quality assurance	Perform quality control	
Project human resource management		Develop human resource plan	Acquire project team; develop project team; manage project team		
Project communications management	Identify stakeholders	Plan communications	Distribute information; manage stakeholders expectations	Report performance	
Project risk management		Plan risk management; identify risks; perform qualitative risk analysis; perform quantitative risk analysis; plan risk reponses		Monitor and control risk	
Project procurement management		Plan procurements	Conduct procurements	Administer procurements	Close procurements

PMBOK® Guide, Fourth Edition, p. 43

Figure 3-1. Project management process groups and knowledge areas mapping

This chapter describes in detail the processes followed and the outputs produced while initiating the Just-In-Time Training project. The *PMBOK® Guide, Fourth Edition*, suggests that the main outputs of initiating include a stakeholder register, stakeholder management strategy, and a project charter. In addition to these three outputs, this chapter also includes a kick-off meeting as an initiating output as well as some outputs produced during a pre-initiating process.

You can access templates to help create many of the documents created in project management on the companion Web site for this text, as summarized in Appendix C. A **template** is a file with a preset format that serves as a starting point for creating various documents so that the format and structure do not have to be re-created. A template can also ensure that critical information is not left out or overlooked. The remaining chapters of this text follow a similar format to describe the processes and outputs used for the Just-In-Time Training project for planning, executing, monitoring and controlling, and closing. To help you visualize outputs for each process group, Figure 3-2, shown later in the chapter, summarizes the outputs for the initiating process group. Similar figures or tables are provided in the following chapters as well.

Several organizations use PMI's information as a foundation for developing their own project management methodologies, as described in the next section. Notice in Figure 3-1 that the majority of project management processes occur as part of the planning process group. Because each project is unique, project teams are always trying to do something that has not been done before. To succeed at unique and new activities, project teams must do a fair amount of planning. Recall, however, that the most time and money is normally spent on executing because that is where the project's products and/or services (for example, the buildings for a construction project, the training courses for a training project, and so on) are produced. It is good practice for organizations to determine how project management will work best in their own organizations.

Developing a Project Management Methodology

Some organizations spend a great deal of time and money on training efforts for general project management skills, but after the training, a project manager might still not know how to tailor their project management skills to the organization's particular needs. Because of this problem, some organizations develop their own internal project management methodologies. The *PMBOK® Guide* is a **standard** that describes best practices for *what* should be done to manage a project. A **methodology** describes *how* things should be done.

Besides using the *PMBOK® Guide* as a basis for a project management methodology, many organizations use others, such as the following:

- ***PRojects IN Controlled Environments (PRINCE2)***: Originally developed for information technology projects, PRINCE2 was released in 1996 as a generic project management methodology by the U.K. Office of Government Commerce (OCG). It is the defacto standard in the U.K. and is used in over 50 countries. (See *www.prince2.com* for more information.) PRINCE2 defines 45 separate sub-processes and organizes these into eight process groups as follows:

1. Starting Up a Project

2. Planning

3. Initiating a Project

4. Directing a Project

5. Controlling a Stage

6. Managing Product Delivery

7. Managing Stage Boundaries

8. Closing a Project

- *Agile methodologies*: Many software development projects use agile methodologies, meaning they use an iterative workflow and incremental delivery of software in short iterations. Several popular agile methodologies include extreme programming, scrum, feature driven development, and lean software development. See Web sites like *www.agilealliance.org* for more information.

- *Rational Unified Process (RUP) framework*: RUP is an iterative software development process that focuses on team productivity and delivers software best practices to all team members. According to RUP expert Bill Cottrell, "RUP embodies industry-standard management and technical methods and techniques to provide a software engineering process particularly suited to creating and maintaining component-based software system solutions."[2] Cottrell explains how you can tailor RUP to include the PMBOK process groups, since several customers asked for that capability. There are several other project management methodologies specifically for software development projects such as Joint Application Development (JAD), Rapid Application Development (RAD), and Extreme Programming. (See Web sites like *www.ibm.com/software/awdtools/rup* for more information.)

- *Six Sigma*: Many organizations have projects underway that use Six Sigma methodologies. The work of many project quality experts contributed to the development of today's Six Sigma principles. In their book, The Six Sigma Way, authors Peter Pande, Robert Neuman, and Roland Cavanagh define Six Sigma as "a comprehensive and flexible system for achieving, sustaining and maximizing business success. Six Sigma is uniquely driven by close understanding of customer needs, disciplined use of facts, data, and statistical analysis, and diligent attention to managing, improving, and reinventing business processes."[3] Six Sigma's target for perfection is the achievement of no more than 3.4 defects, errors, or mistakes per million opportunities. The two main methodologies used on Six Sigma projects: DMAIC (Define, Measure, Analyze, Improve, and Control) is used to improve an existing business process, and DMADV (Define, Measure, Analyze, Design, and Verify) is used to create new product or process designs to achieve

An Introduction to Project Management, Third Edition

predictable, defect-free performance. (See Web sites like *www.isixsigma.com* for more information.)

Many organizations tailor a standard or methodology to meet their unique needs. For example, if organizations use the *PMBOK® Guide* as the basis for their project management methodology, they still have to do a fair amount of work to adapt it to their work environment.

For example, the *PMBOK® Guide, Fourth Edition* lists *what* information a project charter, as described later in this chapter, should address:

- Project purpose or justification

- Measureable project objectives and related success criteria

- High-level requirements

- High-level project description

- High-level risks

- Summary milestone schedule

- Summary budget

- Project approval requirements

- Assigned project manager, responsibility, and authority level

- Name and authority of the sponsor or other person(s) authorizing the project charter

However, the *PMBOK® Guide* does not provide information on *how* the previously listed project charter requirements should be created, when, or by whom. Also, many organizations prefer that project charters be fairly short documents. They might create separate documents with project justification information or approval requirements, if those are lengthy documents. Successful organizations have found that they need to develop and follow a customized, formal project management process that describes not only what needs to be done, but also how it should be done in their organizations. They also must involve key stakeholders and ensure that projects are aligned with organizational needs.

What Went Right?

William Ibbs and Justin Reginato completed a five-year study to help quantify the value of project management. Among their findings are the following points:

- Organizations with more mature project management practices have better project performance, which result in projects being completed on time and within budget much more often than most projects.
- Project management maturity is strongly correlated with more predictable project schedule and cost performance.
- Organizations that follow good project management methodologies have lower direct costs of project management (6–7 percent) than those that do not (11–20 percent).[4]

Several experts have warned against cutting back on project and portfolio management during tough economic times. "Portfolio management can help focus on the projects that are most profitable, while project management can help you execute those projects more efficiently. For example, According to David Muntz, CIO at Baylor Health Care System, "Making informed decisions about which projects to work on is critical at a time when Baylor Health is being especially fiscally prudent."[5]

Part of creating and following a project management methodology includes the creation and use of templates. Companies that excel in project management know that it does not make sense to reinvent the wheel by having every project manager decide how to create standard documents, such as project charters and business cases. They also know that top management commitment and organizational standards are crucial for project success.

The Importance of Top Management Commitment

Without top management commitment, many projects will fail. Some projects have a senior manager called a **champion** who acts as a key proponent for a project. Projects are part of the larger organizational environment, and many factors that might affect a project are out of the project manager's control. Top management commitment is crucial for the following reasons:

- Project managers need adequate resources. The best way to hurt a project is to withhold the required money, human resources, and/or visibility for the project. If project managers have top management commitment, they will also have adequate resources and be able to focus on completing their specific projects.

- Project managers often require approval for unique project needs in a timely manner. For example, a project team might have unexpected problems and need additional resources halfway through the project, or the project manager might need to offer special pay and benefits to attract and retain key project personnel. With top management commitment, project managers can meet these specific needs in a timely manner.

- Project managers must have cooperation from people in other parts of the organization. Because most projects cut across functional areas, top management must help project managers deal with the political issues that often arise in these types of situations. If certain functional managers are not responding to project managers' requests for necessary information, top management must step in to encourage the functional managers to cooperate.

- Project managers often need someone to mentor and coach them on leadership issues. Many project managers come from technical positions and are inexperienced as managers. Senior managers should take the time to pass on advice on how to be good leaders. They should encourage new project managers to take classes to develop leadership skills and allocate the time and funds for them to do so.

The Need for Organizational Standards

Another problem in most organizations is not having standards or guidelines to follow that could help in performing project management functions. These standards or guidelines might be as simple as providing standard forms or templates for common project documents, examples of good project documentation, or guidelines on how the project manager should perform certain tasks, such as holding a kick-off meeting or providing status information. Providing status information might seem like common sense to senior managers, but many new project managers have never given a project status report and are not used to communicating with a wide variety of project stakeholders. Top management must support the development of these standards and guidelines and encourage or even enforce their use.

Some organizations invest heavily in project management by creating a project management office or center of excellence. A **project management office (PMO)** is an organizational entity created to assist project managers in achieving project goals. Some organizations develop career paths for project managers. Some require that all project managers have some type of project management certification and that all employees have some type of project management training. The implementation of all of these standards demonstrates an organization's commitment to project management and helps ensure project success.

Many people learn best by example. The following section describes an example of how Global Construction applied initiating processes to the Just-In-Time Training project. It uses some of the ideas from the *PMBOK® Guide* and additional ideas to meet the unique needs of this project and organization. Several templates illustrate how project teams prepare various project management documents. You can download these templates from the companion Web site for this text.

PRE-INITIATING AND INITIATING PROCESS FOR GLOBAL CONSTRUCTION'S JUST-IN-TIME TRAINING PROJECT

Figure 3-2 illustrates the process that Global Construction will follow for starting the Just-In-Time Training project. Notice that several tasks are completed *before* the project initiation starts. First, the project is approved through a formal project selection process and is given the go-ahead. Second, senior managers perform several activities as part of pre-initiating, as described in the following section. Finally, initiating begins as the project manager works with the team and other stakeholders to identify and understand project stakeholders, create the project charter, and hold a kick-off meeting.

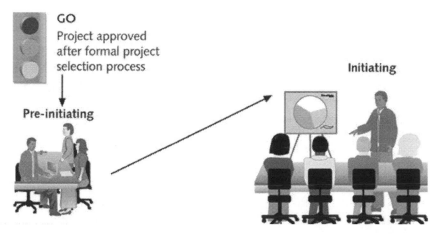

Senior management work together to:

- **Determine scope, time, and cost constraints**

- **Identify the project sponsor**

- **Select the project manager**

- **Develop a business case for the project**

- **Review processes/expectations**

- **Determine if the project should be divided into two or more smaller projects**

Project managers lead efforts to:

- **Identify and understand project stakeholders**

- **Create the project charter**

- **Hold a kick-off meeting**

Figure 3-2. Initiating process summary

PRE-INITIATING TASKS AND OUTPUTS

It is good practice to lay the groundwork for a project before it officially starts. After a project is approved, senior managers should meet to accomplish the following tasks:

- Determine the scope, time, and cost constraints for the project

- Identify the project sponsor

- Select the project manager

- Develop a business case for the project, if required

- Meet with the project manager to review the process and expectations for managing the project

- Determine if the project should be divided into two or more smaller projects

The first three tasks seem obvious. Of course you need to determine project constraints and decide who will sponsor and manage the project. Many projects require a formal business case before investing a significant amount of money in a project, as described later in this section. But why is it necessary to perform these last two tasks? Many organizations have organizational processes and procedures in place for managing projects. It is very important for project managers to understand them as well as the expectations for the project. For example, will there be formal management reviews for the project, and if so, how often will they be held? Are there any regulations, standards, or guidelines related to the project? Is there historical information or are there reports on lessons learned from past projects that might apply to the project? Senior managers should also share their wisdom with project managers to get the project off to a good start. For example, they might recommend key people who would be good team members for the project or offer suggestions based on past experiences.

Many people know from experience that it is easier to successfully complete a small project than a large one. It often makes sense to break large projects down into two or more smaller projects. For Global Construction's Just-In-Time Training project, senior management decided to use this approach. They knew that when scope, time, and cost goals for a large project were unclear, it would help to have a Phase I project to clarify the situation. For a large training project, there is often a study project done first before investing in a larger project.

Lucy Camarena, training director, would sponsor the study project, called the Just-In-Time Training Phase I project. Mike Sundby, the vice president of human resources, would act as the project champion. Lucy assigned one of her senior staff members, Ron Ryan, to manage the project. The scope, time, and cost goals and a summary of the approach and assumptions are provided in Figure 3-3.

Scope Goals

- Investigate and document the training taken in the last two years by all internal employees.

- Determine what courses were taken, the cost of all training, the process for approving/assigning training, and the evaluation of the training by participants, if available.

- Survey employees to get their input on what training they believe they'll need in the next two years, how they'd like to take the training (i.e., instructor-led in-house, instructor-led through a local college, university, or training company, Web-based, CD/ROM, etc.). Also hold focus groups to determine training needs.

- Recommend how to provide the most valuable training for Global Construction employees in the next two years.

- Determine the scope, time, and cost goals for the development and implementation of the Just-In-Time Training Phase II project.

Time Goals: Three months

Cost Goals: **$50,000**

Approach/Assumptions:

- All of the costs would be for internal labor.

- All managers and employees would receive information about this study project.

- A response rate of 30% would be acceptable for the survey.

- The project team would do extensive research to back up their recommendations.

- The team would also provide detailed monthly reports and presentations to a steering committee.

- The final deliverables would include a one-hour final presentation and a comprehensive project report documenting all of the information and recommendations.

Figure 3-3. Summary information for Just-In-Time Training Phase I project

Senior managers were satisfied with the results of the Phase I project, but they realized that they did not want someone from the HR department to lead the Phase II project. Instead, they wanted a manager from one of their key operating divisions—such as sales, engineering, or purchasing—to lead the project. It was important to have buy-in for this new training program from the operating groups, and a strong project manager from one of those areas would likely have more respect and influence than one from HR. Someone from operations would also know firsthand what type of training people in operations would need. HR posted the position internally, and a selection committee decided that Kristin Maur, a former purchasing specialist and now a sales manager, was the best person to lead the Just-In-Time Training Phase II project.

As mentioned earlier, senior managers at Global Construction knew that it was good practice to have experienced managers from operations lead projects that were critical to the operational areas. They also knew that they needed support from several senior managers in the operating divisions as well as other areas, such as IT. So they asked key managers from several divisions to be on a project steering committee to oversee the project. As its name implies, a project steering committee steers a project in the right direction by overseeing it and providing guidance to the project manager. The people on the steering committee are important stakeholders on the project.

A key document often produced during the pre-initiation phase of project is a business case. As the name implies, a **business case** is a document that provides financial justification for investing in a project. Some organizations list different project management requirements based on the dollar value of a project. For example, a project estimated to cost less than $50,000 might not require a business case. A project estimated to cost more than $1 million might need an extensive business case signed off by the Chief Financial Officer.

Successful organizations initiate projects to meet business needs, and a common business need is to spend money wisely. As described in the opening case, Global Construction believed they could reduce training costs and improve productivity by successfully implementing a project to provide just-in-time training on key topics. The Phase I project provided a wealth of information to help write a business case for the Phase II project. Kristin and Lucy reviewed this information carefully and worked together to create the business case. They also had one of the company's financial managers review the information for accuracy.

Contents of a Business Case

Like most project documents, the contents of a business case will vary to meet individual project needs. Typical information included in a business case includes the following:

- Introduction/Background

- Business Objective

- Current Situation and Problem/Opportunity Statement

- Critical Assumptions and Constraints

- Analysis of Options and Recommendations

- Preliminary Project Requirements

- Budget Estimate and Financial Analysis

- Schedule Estimate

- Potential Risks

- Exhibits

Because this project is relatively small and is for an internal sponsor, the business case is not as long as many other business cases. The following section shows the initial business case for the Just-In-Time Training project.

Sample Business Case

Kristin reviewed all of the information created from the Phase I project and drafted a business case. She reviewed it with her sponsor, Lucy (the training director) and had Peter from finance review the financial section. Peter told Kristin to be very conservative by not including any benefit projections that were based on productivity improvements. She still estimated that the project would have a 27 percent discounted return on investment and payback in the second year after implementation (which is denoted as year 3 in Exhibit A in the Sample business case) after implementing the new training program. The resulting business case, including a detailed financial analysis, is provided in Figure 3-4.

Business Case

1.0 Introduction/ Background
Global Construction employs 10,000 full-time employees in ten different counties and fifteen states in the United States. They spend an average of $1,000 per employee for training (not including tuition reimbursement), which is higher than the industry average. However, the productivity of workers, especially in the sales, purchasing, engineering, and information technology departments has not improved much in recent years. In the fast-paced, ever-changing construction market, training employees about new products, new technologies, and soft skills across a globally dispersed company with different populations is a challenge. By redesigning training, Global Construction can reduce training costs and improve productivity.

2.0 Business Objective
Global Construction's strategic goals include continuing growth and profitability. They must have a highly skilled workforce to continue to compete in a global environment. Current training programs, however, are expensive and outdated. Theycan reduce costs by providing more targeted and timely training to their employees and by taking advantage of new technologies and business partnerships. Global Construction can also increase profits by improving productivity, especially by improving supplier management and negotiation skills.

3.0 Current Situation and Problem/Opportunity Statement

Global Construction has not updated its training approach or course offerings in the past five years. Most training is provided on-site during business hours and uses a traditional instructor-led approach with little or no technology involved. Department managers often request slots for various courses, but then they send whoever is available to the course since the department has already paid for it. Therefore, there is often a mismatch between skills needed by employees and the skills taught in a course. The current training is expensive and ineffective. Many employees would like training in key subjects that are currently not provided and that would use more modern approaches and technologies. If the training is directly related to their jobs or interests, employees are willing to take it on their own time, if needed. Survey results indicated that employees are most in need of training in supplier management, negotiating skills, project management, Six Sigma (a quality management methodology) and software applications (i.e., spreadsheet and Web development tools).

4.0 Critical Assumptions and Constraints

This project requires strong participation and cooperation from a wide variety of people. A project steering committee will be formed to provide close oversight and guidance. Some of the requested training will be outsourced, as will development of unique courses. The project will include investigating and taking advantage of new training technologies, such as multimedia and Web-based courses that workers could take on their own time. Employees will also be able to contact instructors and internal experts via the Internet for guidance in performing current work tasks as part of this project.

5.0 Analysis of Options and Recommendation

There are three options for addressing this opportunity:

1. Do nothing. The business is doing well, Global Construction can continue to conduct training as they have done in the past.
2. Instead of providing any internal training, give each employee up to $1,000 to spend on outside training as approved by his/her supervisor. Require employees to stay with the company for one year after using training funds or return the money.
3. Design and implement a new training program as part of this project.

Based on the financial analysis and discussions with key stakeholders, option 3 is the best option.

6.0 Preliminary Project Requirements

The main requirements of this project include the following:

1. Based on survey results, the only current training that does not need to change is the Six Sigma training. No changes will be made in that area. The tuition reimbursement program will continue as is.
2. Training for improving supplier management and negotiating skills, especially international negotiations, have the highest priority since they are most important to the business today and in the next few years. Internal staff will work with outside firms to develop a customized approach to this training that takes advantage of internal experts and new technologies.
3. Demand is also high for training in project management and software applications. The project team will analyze several approaches for this training, including in-house courses, courses offered by local colleges/universities, and computer-based/online courses. They will develop and implement the best combination of approaches for these courses.
4. The project will include updating the corporate Intranet site to explain the new training program, to allow employees to sign up for and evaluate courses, and to track training demand and expenses.
5. The project team will develop an approach for measuring the effect of training on productivity on an annual basis.

7.0 Budget Estimate and Financial Analysis

A preliminary estimate of costs for the entire project is $1,000,000. Half of the cost is for internal labor, $250,000 is for outsourced labor, and $250,000 is for outsourced training programs. These are preliminary estimates that will be revised, as more details become known. Projected benefits are estimated very conservatively. Since the average amount spent on training last year was $1,000/employee, only a 10% or $100/employee reduction was assumed, and no benefits are included for improved productivity. Exhibit A summarizes the projected costs and benefits and shows the estimated net present value (NPV), return on investment (ROI), and the year in which payback occurs. It also lists assumptions made in performing this preliminary financial analysis. All of the financial estimates are very encouraging. The estimated payback is in the second year after implementing the new training program. The NPV is $505,795, and the discounted ROI based on a three-year implementation is 27 percent.

8.0 Schedule Estimate

The sponsor would like to see the entire project completed within one year. Courses will be provided as soon as they are available. The impact of training on productivity will be assessed one year after training is completed and annually thereafter.

9.0 Potential Risks

There are several risks involved with this project. The foremost risk is a lack of interest in the new training program. Employee inputs are crucial for developing the improving training and realizing its potential benefits on improving productivity. There are some technical risks in developing courses using advanced technologies. There are also risks related to outsourcing much of the labor and actual course materials/instruction. The main business risk is investing the time and money into this project and not realizing the projected benefits.

10.0 Exhibits Exhibit A: Financial Analysis

Discount rate	8%				
Assume the project is completed in Year 1					
			Year		
	1	2	3	4	Tota
Costs	1,000,000	400,000	400,000	400,000	
Discount factor	0.93	0.86	0.79	0.74	
Discounted costs	**925,926**	**342,936**	**317,533**	**294,012**	**1,880,406**
Benefits	-	1,000,000	1,000,000	1,000,000	
Discount factor (rounded to two decimal places)	0.93	0.86	0.79	0.74	
Discounted benefits	**-**	**860,000**	**790,000**	**740,000**	**2,390,000**
Discounted benefits - costs	(925,926)	517,064	472,467	445,988	**509,594**
Cumulative benefits - costs	(925,926)	(408,861)	63,606	509,594	
ROI ⟶	27%				
		Payback in Year 3			
Assumptions					
Costs for the project are based on the following:					
Internal labor costs: $500,000					
Outsourced labor costs: $250,000					
Outsourced training programs: $250,000					
After implementation, maintenance costs are estimated at 40% of total development cost					
Benefits are estimated based on the following:					
$100/employee/year X 10,000 employees					
No benefits are included for increased productivity					

Figure 3-4. Sample business case

Now that important pre-initiating tasks were completed, Kristin Maur was ready to tackle important tasks to initiate the Just-In-Time Training project.

INITIATING TASKS AND OUTPUTS

The main tasks normally involved in project initiation are as follows:

- Identifying and understanding project stakeholders
- Creating the project charter
- Holding a kick-off meeting

Key outputs of initiating, as described in the *PMBOK® Guide, Fourth Edition*, include a stakeholder register, stakeholder management strategy, and project charter as shown in Figure 3-5. Even though it is not part of the PMBOK® Guide, Kristin's company also requires a formal kick-off meeting as part of the initiating process. The following sections of this chapter describe each of these outputs in detail for the larger Just-In-Time Training Phase II project, hereafter referred to as the Just-In-Time Training project.

Knowledge area	Initiating process	Outputs
Project integration management	Develop project charter	Project charter
Project communications management	Identify stakeholders	Stakeholder register Stakeholder management strategy

Figure 3-5. Initiating processes and outputs

Identifying and Understanding Project Stakeholders

Recall from Chapter 1 that project stakeholders are the people involved in or affected by project activities. Stakeholders can be internal to the organization or external.

- Internal project stakeholders generally include the project sponsor, project team, support staff, and internal customers for the project. Other internal stakeholders include top management, other functional managers, and other project managers. Because organizations have limited resources, projects affect top management, other functional managers, and other project managers by using some of the organization's limited resources.

- External project stakeholders include the project's customers (if they are external to the organization), competitors, suppliers, and other external groups that are potentially involved in or affected by the project, such as government officials and concerned citizens.

How does a project manager identify key project stakeholders and find out more about them? The best way is by asking around. There might be formal organizational charts or biographies that can provide some information, but the main goal is to help project managers manage relationships with key stakeholders. Talking to other people who have worked with those stakeholders usually provides the best information. For example, in this case, Kristin Maur knew who some of the key stakeholders were but did not know any of them well. It did not take her long, however, to get the information she needed.

Because the purpose of project management is to meet project requirements and satisfy stakeholders, it is critical that project managers take adequate time to identify, understand, and manage relationships with all project stakeholders. Two tools to help accomplish these tasks include a stakeholder register and a stakeholder management strategy

Sample Stakeholder Register and Stakeholder Management Strategy

A **stakeholder register** is a document that includes details related to the identified project stakeholders. Figure 3-6 provides an example of a part of the stakeholder register for Kristin's project. Notice that it includes only basic stakeholder information, such as name, position, if they are internal or external to the organization, role on the project, and contact information. Since this document would be available to other people in their organization, Kristin was careful not to include information that might be sensitive, such as how strongly the stakeholder supported the project or how much influence they had. She would keep these and other issues in mind discretely and use them in developing the stakeholder management strategy.

Name	Position	Internal/ External	Project Role	Contact Information
Mike Sundby	VP of HR	Internal	Project champion	msundy@globalconstruction.com
Lucy Camerena	Training Director	Internal	Project sponsor	lcamerena@globalconstruction.com
Ron Ryan	Senior HR staff member	Internal	Led the Phase I project	rryan@globalconstruction.com

Figure 3-6. Sample stakeholder register

A **stakeholder management strategy** is an approach to help increase the support of stakeholders throughout the project. It is helpful to start preparing a stakeholder management strategy during initiation and adding information to it during the planning process.

The type of information included in a stakeholder management strategy includes the following:

- Names of key stakeholders
- Their level of interest in the project
- Their influence on the project
- Potential management strategies for each stakeholder

Because a stakeholder management strategy often includes sensitive information, it should *not* be part of the official project documents, which are normally available for all stakeholders to review. In many cases, only project managers and a few other team members should be involved in preparing the stakeholder management strategy. In most cases, the strategy is not even written down, and if it is, its distribution is strictly limited.

Figure 3-7 provides an example of a stakeholder management strategy that Kristin Maur could use to help her manage the Just-In-Time Training project. It is important for project managers to take the time to develop this strategy to help them meet stakeholder needs and expectations. In addition, as new stakeholders are added to the project and more information is provided, the strategy should be updated. Early in this project, for example, all of the stakeholders are internal to the company; later on, however, there will be external stakeholders as well.

Name	Level of Interest	Level of Influence	Potential Management Strategies
Mike Sundby	High	High	Mike is very outgoing and visionary. Great traits for a project champion. He is concerned about financials and has an MBA. Keep him informed and ask for his advice as needed.
Lucy Camerena	High	High	Lucy has a Ph.D. in education and knows training at this company. She is very professional and easy to work with, but she can stretch out conversations. Make sure she reviews important work before showing it to other managers.
Ron Ryan	Medium	Medium	Ron led the Phase I project and is upset that he was not asked to lead this Phase II project. He's been with the company over 20 years and can be a good resource, but he could also sabotage the project. Ask Lucy to talk to him to avoid problems. Perhaps give him a small consulting role on the project.

Figure 3-7. Sample stakeholder management strategy

Figure 3-8 provides a humorous example of analyzing a stakeholder's needs. A couple is dressed up to go to the prom, but another opportunity presents itself. Each person must know the other pretty well before suggesting the alternate idea!

Figure 3-8. Analyzing "formal" stakeholder needs (www.xkcd.com)

Creating a Project Charter

After top management determines which projects to pursue, it is important to let the rest of the organization know about these projects. Management needs to create and distribute documentation to authorize project initiation. This documentation can take many different forms, but one common form is a project charter. A **project charter** is a document that formally recognizes the existence of a project and provides a summary of the project's objectives and management. It authorizes the project manager to use organizational resources to complete the project. Ideally, the project manager will play a major role in developing the project charter.

Instead of project charters, some organizations initiate projects using a simple letter of agreement, whereas others use much longer documents or formal contracts. When Global Construction initiates a building project for an outside organization, it still creates a separate charter and attaches it to the contract, which is usually a much longer, more complex document. (You will see an example of a contract for outsourced work for this project in Chapter 5.) *A crucial part of the project charter is the sign-off section, where key project stakeholders sign the document to acknowledge their agreement on the need for the project.*

Contents of a Project Charter

Contents of a project charter will also vary to meet individual project needs. Typical information included in a project charter includes the following:

- The project's title and date of authorization

- The project manager's name and contact information

- A summary schedule or timeline, including the planned start and finish dates; if a summary milestone schedule is available, it should also be included or referenced

- A summary of the project's estimated cost and budget allocation

- A brief description of the project objectives, including the business need or other justification for authorizing the project

- Project success criteria, including project approval requirements and who signs off on the project

- A summary of the planned approach for managing the project, which should describe stakeholder needs and expectations, important assumptions, and constraints, and refer to related documents, such as a communications management plan, as available

- A roles and responsibilities matrix

- A sign-off section for signatures of key project stakeholders

- A comments section in which stakeholders can provide important comments related to the project

Project charters are normally short documents. Some are only one-page long, whereas others might be several pages long. Some charters include signatures of team members, while others do not. The following section shows the project charter for the Just-In-Time Training project.

Sample Project Charter

Kristin drafted a project charter and had the project team members review it before showing it to Lucy. Lucy made a few minor changes, which Kristin incorporated, and then all the key stakeholders who would be working on the project signed the project charter. Figure 3-9 shows the final project charter. Note that Lucy stated her concern about totally changing most training programs and terminating several contracts with local trainers. Also note that Tim Nelson, director of supplier management, wanted to be heavily involved in deciding how to provide the supplier management training. Kristin knew that she would have to consider these concerns when managing the project.

Project Title: Just-In-Time Training Project	
Project Start Date: July 1	**Projected Finish Date:** June 30 (one year later)

Budget Information: The firm has allocated $1,000,000 for this project. Approximately half of these costs will be for internal labor, while the other half will be for outsourced labor and training programs.

Project Manager: Kristin Maur, (610) 752-4896, kmaur@globalconstruction.com

Project Objectives: Develop a new training program that provides just-in-time training to employees on key topics, including supplier management, negotiating skills, project management, and software applications (spreadsheets and Web development). Reduce the training cost per employee by 10%, or $100/employee/year. Develop an approach for measuring productivity improvements from this approach to training on an annual basis.

Success Criteria: This project will be successful if it reduces training cost per employee by 10% or $100/employee/year. It should also be completed on time, be run professionally, and meet all of the requirements. The project sponsor will determine if the project is a success or not.

Approach:

- Terminate all internal training courses except the Six Sigma training once new courses are developed
- Communicate to all employees the plans to improve internal training and let them know that tuition reimbursement will continue as is.
- Work closely with internal managers and employees to determine the best approaches for providing training in supplier management, negotiating skills, project management, and software applications.
- Research existing training and work with outside experts to develop several alternatives for providing each training topic.
- Develop and implement new training.
- Take advantage of new training approaches and technologies and encourage employees to take some training during non-work hours.
- Encourage experts within the company to mentor other workers on current job duties.
- Determine a way to measure the effectiveness of the training and its impact on productivity on an annual basis.

Roles and Responsibilities:			
Name and Signature	*Role*	*Position*	*Contact Information*
Mike Sundby *Mike Sundby*	Project Champion	VP of HR	msundby@ globalconstruction.com
Lucy Camerena *Lucy Camerena*	Project Sponsor	Training Director	lcamerena@ globalconstruction.com
Kristin Maur *Kristin Maur*	Project Manager	Project Manager	kmaur@ globalconstruction.com
Julia Portman *Julia Portman*	Steering Committee Member	VP of IT	jportman@ globalconstruction.com
Tim Nelson *Tim Nelson*	Steering Committee Member	Supplier Management Director	tnelson@ globalconstruction.com
Mohamed Abdul *Mohamed Abdul*	Team Member	Senior programmer/ analyst	mabdul@ globalconstruction.com
Kim Johnson *Kim Johnson*	Team Member	Curriculum designer	kjohnson@ globalconstruction.com
Etc.			

Comments: (Handwritten or typed comments from above stakeholders, if applicable)
"I am concerned about people's reactions to cancelling most internal training and totally changing most training classes. I also hate to terminate some contracts with local training firms we've used for several years. We should try to get some of them involved in this project." Lucy
"I want to review all of the information related to providing the supplier management training. We need to make something available quickly." Tim

Figure 3-9. Sample project charter

Because many projects fail because of unclear requirements and expectations, starting with a project charter makes sense. If project managers are having difficulty obtaining support from project stakeholders, for example, they can refer to what everyone agreed to in the project charter. After the charter is completed, it is good practice to hold an official kick-off meeting for the project.

An Introduction to Project Management, Third Edition

Media Snapshot

Many people enjoy watching television shows like Trading Spaces, where participants have two days and $1,000 to update a room in their neighbor's house. Since the time and cost are set, it is the scope that has the most flexibility. Examples of some of the work completed include new flooring, light fixtures, paint, new shelves, or artwork to brighten up a dull room.

Designers on these shows often have to change initial scope goals due to budget or time constraints. For example, designers often go back to local stores to exchange items, such as lights, artwork, or fabric, for less expensive items to meet budget constraints. Or they might describe a new piece of furniture they'd like the carpenter to build, but the carpenter changes the design or materials to meet time constraints. Occasionally designers can buy more expensive items or have more elaborate furniture built because they underestimated costs and schedules.

Another important issue related to project scope management is meeting customer expectations. Who wouldn't be happy with a professionally designed room at no cost to them? Although most homeowners on Trading Spaces are very happy with work done on the show, some are obviously disappointed. Unlike most projects where the project team works closely with the customer, homeowners have little say in what gets done and cannot inspect the work along the way. They walk into their newly decorated room with their eyes closed. Modernizing a room can mean something totally different to a homeowner and the interior designer. For example, one woman was obviously shocked when she saw her bright orange kitchen with black appliances. Another couple couldn't believe there was moss on their bedroom walls. What happens when the homeowners don't like the work that's been done? Part of agreeing to be on the show includes signing a release statement acknowledging that you will accept whatever work has been done. Too bad you can't get sponsors for most projects to sign a similar release statement. It would make project scope management much easier!

Holding a Project Kick-Off Meeting

Experienced project managers know that it is crucial to get projects off to a great start. Holding a good kick-off meeting is an excellent way to do this. A **kick-off meeting** is a meeting held at the beginning of a project so that stakeholders can meet each other, review the goals of the project, and discuss future plans. The kick-off meeting is often held after the business case and project charter are completed, but it could be held sooner, as needed.

Project kick-off meetings are often used to get support for a project and clarify roles and responsibilities. If there is a project champion, as there is for this project, he or she should speak first at the kick-off meeting and introduce the project sponsor and project manager. If anyone seems opposed to the project or unwilling to support it, the project champion—an experienced senior manager—should be able to handle the situation.

As discussed earlier in the chapter, there is normally a fair amount of work done before an official kick-off meeting for a project. At a minimum, the project manager and sponsor should have met several times, and other key stakeholders should have been involved in developing the project charter. The project manager should make sure the right people are invited to the kick-off meeting and send out an agenda in advance. For a small project, a kick-off meeting might be an informal meeting of the project team held in a social environment. The main idea is to get the project off to a good start. Ideally the kick-off meeting should be held face-to-face so stakeholders can physically meet each other and be able to pick up on each others' body language.

Sample Kick-Off Meeting Agenda

All project meetings with major stakeholders should include an agenda. Figure 3-10 provides the agenda that Kristin provided for the Just-In-Time Training project kick-off meeting. Notice the main topics in an agenda:

- Meeting objective

- Agenda (lists in order the topics to be discussed)

- A section for documenting action items, who they are assigned to, and when each person will complete the action

- A section to document the date and time of the next meeting

---

Just-In-Time Training Project
Kick-off Meeting
July 16

Meeting Objective: Get the project off to an effective start by introducing key stakeholders, reviewing project goals, and discussing future plans

Agenda:

- Introductions of attendees
- Review of the project background
- Review of project-related documents (i.e., business case, project charter)
- Discussion of project organizational structure
- Discussion of project scope, time, and cost goals
- Discussion of other important topics
- List of action items from meeting

Action Item	Assigned To	Due Date

Date and time of next meeting:

Figure 3-10. Sample kick-off meeting agenda

It is good practice to focus on results of meetings, and having sections for documenting action items and deciding on the next meeting date and time on the agenda helps to do so. It is also good practice to document meeting minutes, focusing on key decisions and action items, and to send them to all meeting participants and other appropriate stakeholders within a day or two of a meeting. Meeting minutes are valuable to people who could not attend a meeting since it summarizes key discussions and results of the meeting. If there is a project Web site or other place for storing project information, the meeting minutes should be stored there.

CASE WRAP-UP

Kristin was pleased with work completed in initiating the Just-In-Time Training project, as were the project sponsor and other key stakeholders. Kristin met weekly with the project steering committee to review project progress. She found the committee to be very helpful, especially when dealing with several challenges they encountered. For example, it was difficult finding a large enough conference room for the kick-off meeting and setting up the Webcast to allow other stakeholders to participate in the meeting. She was also a bit nervous before running the meeting, but Lucy and Mike, the project sponsor and champion, helped her relax and stepped in when people questioned the need for the project. There were also indications that several key departments would not be represented at the kick-off meeting, but Mike made sure that they were. Kristin could see how important senior management support was on this project, in particular for obtaining buy-in from all parts of the organization.

CHAPTER SUMMARY

The five project management process groups are initiating, planning, executing, monitoring and controlling, and closing. These processes occur at varying levels of intensity throughout each phase of a project, and specific outcomes are produced as a result of each process.

Mapping the main activities of each project management process group into the nine project management knowledge areas provides a big picture of what activities are involved in project management. Some organizations develop their own project management methodologies, often using the standards found in the *PMBOK® Guide* as a foundation. It is important to tailor project management methodologies to meet the organization's particular needs.

Global Construction's Just-In-Time Training project demonstrates the process of initiating a project. After a project is approved, senior managers often meet to perform several pre-initiating tasks, as follows:

- Determining the scope, time, and cost constraints for the project

- Identifying the project sponsor

- Selecting the project manager

- Developing a business case for the project, if required

- Meeting with the project manager to review the process and expectations for managing the project

- Determining if the project should be divided into two or more smaller projects

The main tasks normally involved in project initiation are the following:

- Identifying and understanding project stakeholders

- Creating the project charter

- Holding a kick-off meeting

Descriptions of how each of these tasks was accomplished and samples of related outputs are described in the chapter.

An Introduction to Project Management, Third Edition

QUICK QUIZ

1.   In which of the five project management process groups is the most time and money usually spent?

    A. initiating

    B. planning

    C. executing

    D. monitoring and controlling

    E. closing

2.   In which of the five project management process groups are activities performed that relate to each knowledge area?

    A. initiating

    B. planning

    C. executing

    D. monitoring and controlling

    E. closing

3.   The best or "alpha" project managers spend more time on every process group than other project managers except for which one?

    A. initiating

    B. planning

    C. executing

    D. monitoring and controlling

4.   What document provides justification for investing in a project?

    A. project charter

    B. business case

    C. net present value analysis

    D. stakeholder register

5. What document formally recognizes the existence of a project and provides direction on the project's objectives and management?

    A. project charter

    B. business case

    C. stakeholder register

    D. stakeholder management strategy

6. What is a crucial part of the project charter—a section in which key project stakeholders acknowledge their agreement on the need for the project?

    A. project objectives

    B. approach

    C. roles and responsibilities

    D. sign-off

7. Which project document should not be made available to all key project stakeholders due to its sensitive nature?

    A. project charter

    B. business case

    C. stakeholder register

    D. stakeholder management strategy

8. All project meetings with major stakeholders should include.

    A. an agenda

    B. food

    C. name tags

    D. all of the above

9. Preparing a stakeholder register and management strategy are part of which knowledge area?

    A. project integration management

    B. project human resource management

    C. project communications management

    D. project risk management

10.   Which of the following is not an output of initiating in the *PMBOK® Guide, Fourth Edition*?

A. project charter

B. stakeholder register

C. stakeholder management strategy

D. kick-off meeting

Quick Quiz Answers

1. C; 2. B; 3. C; 4. B; 5. A; 6. D; 7. D; 8. A; 9. C; 10. D

DISCUSSION QUESTIONS

1.   Briefly describe what happens in each of the five project management process groups (initiating, planning, executing, monitoring and controlling, and closing). On which process should team members spend the most time? Why? Why is it helpful to follow a project management methodology?

2.   What pre-initiating tasks were performed for the Just-In-Time Training project? Does it make sense to do these tasks? What are the main initiating tasks?

3.   Describe the purpose of a business case and its main contents.

4.   What is the main purpose of developing a stakeholder management strategy? When should it be done, and who should see the results?

5.   Why should projects have a project charter? What is the main information included in a project charter?

6.   Discuss the process for holding a project kick-off meeting. Who should attend? What key topics should be on the agenda?

EXERCISES

1. Find an example of a large project that took more than a year to complete, such as a major construction project. You can ask people at your college, university, or work about a recent project, such as a major fund raising campaign, information systems installation, or building project. You can also find information about projects online such as the Big Dig in Boston (*www.masspike.com/bigdig*), the Patronas Twin Towers in Malaysia, and many other building projects (*www.greatbuildings.com*). Why was the project initiated? Describe some of the pre-initiating and initiating tasks completed for the project. Write a one-page paper or prepare a short presentation summarizing your findings.

2. Review the business case for the Just-In-Time Training project. Do you think there is solid business justification for doing this project? Why or why not? What parts of the business case do you think could be stronger? How? Rewrite a section that you believe can be improved. Write a one-page paper or prepare a short presentation summarizing your findings.

3. Search the Internet for "project charter." Find at least three good references that describe project charters. Write a one-page paper or prepare a short presentation summarizing your findings.

4. Review the project charter for the Just-In-Time Training project. How does this document help clarify what work will be done on the project? Is the success criteria clear for this project? What questions do you have about the scope of the project? Write a one-page paper or prepare a short presentation summarizing your ideas.

TEAM PROJECTS

1. Your organization has decided to initiate a project to raise money for an important charity. Assume that there are 1,000 people in your organization. Use the pre-initiating tasks described in this chapter to develop a strategy for how to proceed. Be creative in describing your organization; the charity; the scope, time, and cost constraints for the project; and so on. Document your ideas in a one- to two-page paper or a short presentation.

2. You are part of a team in charge of a project to help people in your company (500 people) lose weight. This project is part of a competition, and the top "losers" will be featured in a popular television show. Assume that you have six months to complete the project and a budget of $10,000. Develop a project charter for this project using the sample provided in this chapter. Be creative in developing detailed information to include in the charter.

3. Using the information you developed in Team Project 1 or 2, role-play the kick-off meeting for this project. Follow the sample agenda provided in this chapter.

An Introduction to Project Management, Third Edition

4. Perform the initiating tasks for one of the case studies provided in Appendix C. If you are working on a real team project, perform the applicable pre-initiating and initiating tasks for that project. Be sure to work closely with your project sponsor to get the project off to a good start.

5. As a team, research two different project management methodologies (other than using the *PMBOK® Guide*), such as PRINCE2, RUP, Six Sigma, etc. Summarize your findings in a two- to three-page paper or a short presentation. Try to include examples of projects managed using each methodology.

COMPANION WEB SITE

Visit the free companion Web site for this text at **www.intropm.com** to access template files, online quizzes, Jeopardy-like games, Microsoft Project files, links to sites mentioned in the text, and other information to help you learn more about this important field. Instructors must contact the author at schwalbe@augsburg.edu to gain access to the instructor site. Anyone can access the student site.

KEY TERMS

agile methodologies — Popular software development methodologies that use an iterative workflow and incremental delivery of software in short iterations.

business case — A document that provides justification for investing in a project.

champion — A senior manager who acts as a key proponent for a project.

closing processes — The actions that involve formalizing acceptance of the project or phase and bringing it to an orderly end.

deliverable — A product or service produced or provided as part of a project.

executing processes — The actions that involve coordinating people and other resources to carry out the project plans and produce the deliverables of the project.

initiating processes — The actions to begin projects and project phases.

kick-off meeting — A meeting held at the beginning of a project so that stakeholders can meet each other, review the goals of the project, and discuss future plans.

methodology — A plan that describes how things should be done to manage a project.

monitoring and controlling processes — The actions taken to measure progress toward achieving project goals, monitor deviation from plans, and take corrective action.

phase — A distinct stage in project development.

planning processes — The actions that involve devising and maintaining a workable scheme to ensure that the project meets its scope, time, and cost goals as well as organizational needs.

process — A series of actions directed toward a particular result.

project charter — A document that formally recognizes the existence of a project and provides a summary of the project's objectives and management.

project management office (PMO) — An organizational entity created to assist project managers in achieving project goals.

project management process groups — The progression from initiating activities to planning activities, executing activities, monitoring and controlling activities, and closing activities.

PRojects IN Controlled Environments (PRINCE2) — A project management methodology with eight process groups developed in the U.K.

Rational Unified Process (RUP) framework — A project management methodology that uses an iterative software development process that focuses on team productivity and delivers software best practices to all team members.

Six Sigma — A comprehensive and flexible system for achieving, sustaining, and maximizing business success; uniquely driven by close understanding of customer needs, disciplined use of facts, data, and statistical analysis, and diligent attention to managing, improving, and reinventing business processes.

stakeholder register — A document that includes details related to the identified project stakeholders

stakeholder management strategy — An approach to help increase the support of stakeholders throughout the project.

standard — A document that describes best practices for what should be done to manage a project.

template — A file with a preset format that serves as a starting point for creating various documents so that the format and structure do not have to be re-created.

END NOTES

[1]Andy Crowe, *Alpha Project Managers: What the Top 2% Know That Everyone Else Does Not*, Velociteach Press (2006).

[2]Bill Cottrell, "Standards, compliance, and Rational Unified Process, Part I: Integrating RUP and the PMBOK," *IBM Developerworks* (May 10, 2004).

[3]Peter S. Pande, Robert P. Neuman, and Roland R. Cavanagh, *The Six Sigma Way*. New York: McGraw-Hill (2000), p. xi.

[4]William Ibbs and Justin Reginato, *Quantifying the Value of Project Management*, Project Management Institute (2002).

[5]Meridith Levinson, "Why Project and Portfolio Management Matter More At Recession Time," CIO.com (November 10, 2008).

Chapter 4
Planning Projects, Part 1
(Project Integration, Scope, Time, and Cost Management)

LEARNING OBJECTIVES

After reading this chapter, you will be able to:

- Describe the importance of creating plans to guide project execution, and list several planning tasks and outputs for project integration, scope, time, and cost management
- Discuss project integration management planning tasks, and explain the purpose and contents of a team contract and a project management plan
- Explain the project scope management planning tasks, and create requirements documents, a requirements management plan, a requirements traceability matrix, a project scope statement, a work breakdown structure (WBS), and a WBS dictionary
- Describe the project time management planning tasks, and prepare an activity list and attributes, milestone list, project schedule network diagram, activity resource requirements, activity duration estimates, and project schedule
- Discuss the project cost management planning tasks, and create a cost estimate, cost performance baseline, and project funding requirements

---

OPENING CASE

Kristin Maur continued to work with her project team and other key stakeholders on the Just-In-Time Training project. She knew that it was crucial to do a good job in planning all aspects of the project, and she strongly believed that execution would be much smoother if they had good plans to follow. She also knew that it was important to involve the people who would be doing the work in actually planning the work, and that planning was an iterative process. Involving key people in the planning process and keeping the plans up to date had been her main challenges on past projects, so Kristin focused proactively on those areas.

Kristin and her team were fortunate to have many templates to use in developing several planning documents. They could also review examples of planning documents from past and current projects available on Global Construction's intranet site and use project management software to enter key planning data. Kristin also found that the project steering committee that had been set up during project initiation gave her very helpful advice. Several experienced members warned her to be thorough in planning but not to become bogged down in too much detail.

INTRODUCTION

Many people have heard the following sayings:

- If you fail to plan, you plan to fail.

- If you don't know where you're going, any road will take you there.

- What gets measured gets managed.

All of these sayings emphasize the fact that planning is crucial to achieving goals. Successful project managers know how important it is to develop, refine, and follow plans to meet project goals, and they know how easy it is to become sidetracked if they do not have good plans to follow. They also know that people are more likely to perform well if they know what they are supposed to do and when.

PROJECT PLANNING SHOULD GUIDE PROJECT EXECUTION

Planning is often the most difficult and unappreciated process in project management. Often, people do not want to take the time to plan well, but theory and practice show that good planning is crucial to good execution. *The main purpose of project planning is to guide project execution.* To guide execution, plans must be realistic and useful, so a fair amount of effort must go into the project planning process.

What Went Wrong?

Based on their experiences, many people have a dim view of plans. Top managers often require a plan, but then no one tracks whether the plan was followed. For example, one project manager said he would meet with each project team leader within two months to review their project plans, and he even created a detailed schedule for these reviews. He canceled the first meeting due to another business commitment; he rescheduled the next meeting for unexplained personal reasons. Two months later, the project manager had still not met with over half of the project team leaders. Why should project team members feel obligated to follow their own plans when the project manager obviously does not follow his?

Recall from Chapter 3 that project planning involves devising and maintaining a workable scheme to ensure that the project meets its scope, time, and cost goals as well as organizational needs. Also, recall that planning includes tasks related to each of the nine project management knowledge areas. This chapter describes the types of planning performed in four of the knowledge areas—project integration, scope, time, and cost management—and summarizes the planning done for Global Construction's Just-In-Time Training project. Chapter 5 focuses on planning in the other five knowledge areas—quality, human resource, communications, risk, and procurement management.

SUMMARY OF PLANNING TASKS AND OUTPUTS

The *PMBOK® Guide, Fourth Edition* lists over 50 documents that project teams can produce as part of project planning. Other experts suggest even more potential planning documents. Every project is unique, so project managers and their teams must determine which planning outputs are needed for their projects and how they should be created.

Figure 4-1 summarizes the project planning outputs for integration, scope, time, and cost management listed in the *PMBOK® Guide, Fourth Edition*. This chapter provides samples of some of these outputs, as well as a few additional ones, such as a team contract. All of these planning documents, as well as other project-related information, will be available to all team members on a project Web site. Global Construction has used project Web sites for several years, and everyone agrees that they significantly facilitate communications.

Knowledge area	Planning process	Outputs
Project integration management	Develop project management plan	Project management plan
Project scope management	Collect requirements	Requirements documents
		Requirements management plan
		Requirements traceability matrix
	Define scope	Project scope statement
		Project document updates
	Create WBS	WBS
		WBS dictionary
		Scope baseline
		Project document updates
Project time management	Define activities	Activity list
		Activity attributes
		Milestone list
	Sequence activities	Project schedule network diagrams
		Project document updates
	Estimate activity resources	Activity resource requirements
		Resource breakdown structures
		Project document updates
	Estimate activity durations	Activity duration estimates
		Project document updates
	Develop schedule	Project schedule
		Schedule baseline
		Schedule data
		Project document updates
Project cost management	Estimate costs	Activity cost estimates
		Basis of estimates
		Project document updates
	Determine budget	Cost performance baseline
		Project funding requirements
		Project document updates

Figure 4-1. Planning processes and outputs for project integration, scope, time, and cost management

      The following sections describe planning tasks and outputs in the first four knowledge areas and then provide examples of applying them to the Just-In-Time Training project at Global Construction. You can consider many of these planning tasks as following a chronological order, especially for the scope, time, and cost tasks. You need to plan the project scope and determine what activities need to be done before you can develop a detailed project schedule. Likewise, you need a detailed project schedule before you can develop a cost performance baseline. Of course, human resource planning and assignment to the project team must also be accomplished as part of project human resource management, as described in the next chapter. As noted earlier, there are many interdependencies between various knowledge areas and process groups.

PROJECT INTEGRATION MANAGEMENT PLANNING TASKS

Project integration management involves coordinating all the project management knowledge areas throughout a project's life span. The main planning tasks performed as part of project integration management include creating a team contract and developing the project management plan.

Team Contracts

Global Construction believes in using **team contracts** to help promote teamwork and clarify team communications. After core project team members have been selected, they meet to prepare a team contract. The process normally includes reviewing a template and then working in small groups of three to four people to prepare inputs for the team contract. Creating smaller groups makes it easier for everyone to contribute ideas. Each group then shares their ideas on what the contract should contain, and then they work together to form one project team contract. Ideally, the contract should be finished in a one- to two-hour meeting. The project manager should attend the meeting and act as a coach or facilitator, observing the different personalities of team members and seeing how well they work together. It is crucial to emphasize the importance of the project team throughout the project's life cycle. The team contract should provide the groundwork for how the project team will function.

Sample Team Contract

Figure 4-2 shows the team contract created for the Just-In-Time Training project. Notice that the main topics covered include the following: code of conduct, participation, communication, problem solving, and meeting guidelines.

Everyone involved in creating the team contract should sign it. As new project team members are added, the project manager should review ground rules with them and have them read and sign the contract as well.

Team Contract

Project Name: Just-In-Time Training Project

Project Team Members Names and Sign-off:

<u>Name</u>	<u>Date</u>
Kristin Maur	*July 9*
Other team members	

Code of Conduct: As a project team, we will:
- Work proactively, anticipating potential problems and preventing their occurrence.
- Keep other team members informed of information related to the project.
- Focus on what is best for the entire project team.

Participation: We will:
- Be honest and open during all project activities.
- Provide the opportunity for equal participation.
- Be open to new approaches and consider new ideas.
- Let the project manager know well in advance if a team member has to miss a meeting or may have trouble meeting a deadline for a given task.

Communication: We will:
- Keep discussions on track and have one discussion at a time.
- Use the telephone, e-mail, a project Web site, instant messaging, and other technology to assist in communicating.
- Have the project manager or designated person facilitate all meetings and arrange for phone and videoconferences, as needed.
- Work together to create the project schedule and related information and enter actuals, issues, risks, and other information into our enterprise project management system by 4 p.m. every Friday.

Problem Solving: We will:
- Only use constructive criticism and focus on solving problems, not blaming people.
- Strive to build on each other's ideas.
- Bring in outside experts when necessary.

Meeting Guidelines: We will:
- Plan to have a face-to-face meeting of the entire project team every Tuesday morning.
- Arrange for telephone or videoconferencing for participants as needed.
- Hold other meetings as needed.
- Develop and follow an agenda for all meetings.
- Record meeting minutes and send them out via e-mail within 24 hours of all project meetings, focusing on decisions made and action items and issues from each meeting.

Figure 4-2. Sample team contract

Project Management Plans

To coordinate and integrate information across all project management knowledge areas and across the organization, there must be a good project management plan. A **project management plan**, which is a deliverable for the project integration management knowledge area, is a document used to coordinate all project planning documents and to help guide a project's execution and control. Plans created in the other knowledge areas are subsidiary parts of the overall project management plan. Project management plans facilitate communication among stakeholders and provide a baseline for progress measurement and project control, as discussed in detail in Chapter 7. A **baseline** is a starting point, a measurement, or an observation that is documented so that it can be used for future comparison. The project management plan briefly describes the overall scope, time, and cost performance baselines for the project. Specific plans in each of those knowledge areas provide more detailed baseline information. For example, the project management plan might provide a high-level budget baseline for the entire project, whereas the cost performance baseline prepared as part of the project cost management knowledge area (explained later in this chapter) provides detailed cost projections by WBS by month.

Project management plans should be dynamic, flexible, and receptive to change when the environment or project changes. These plans should greatly assist the project manager in leading the project team and assessing project status. Just as projects are unique, so are project plans. For a small project involving a few people over a couple of months, a project charter, team contract, scope statement, and Gantt chart might be the only project planning documents needed; there would not be a need for a separate project management plan. A large project involving 100 people over three years would benefit from having a detailed project management plan and separate plans for each knowledge area. It is important to tailor all planning documentation to fit the needs of specific projects. Because all project plans should help guide the completion of the particular project, they should be only as detailed as needed for each project.

There are, however, common elements to most project management plans, as follows:

- Introduction/overview of the project

- Project organization

- Management and technical processes

- Work to be performed

- Schedule information

- Budget information

- References to other project planning documents

Sample Project Management Plan

Figure 4-3 provides partial information from the initial project management plan for Global Construction's Just-In-Time Training project. Of course, the actual document would be longer because this is a one-year, $1 million project involving many different stakeholders, including outside suppliers. The document would also be updated as needed. It is important to mark the date and version number on the document to avoid confusion. Also note that project organization varies on projects, so it is helpful to provide a high-level project organizational chart in the project management plan. On some projects, the project sponsor and project champion are the same person, but not always. Projects that cross functional boundaries, as the Just-In-Time Training project does, often benefit from having a high-level project champion, such as a vice president, from a key functional area.

Project Management Plan Version 1.0
September 17

Project Name: Just-In-Time Training Project
Introduction/Overview of the Project
Global Construction employs 10,000 full-time employees in ten different counties and fifteen states in the U.S. The company spends, on average, $1,000 per employee for training (not including tuition reimbursement), which is higher than the industry average. By redesigning training, Global Construction can reduce training costs and improve productivity. The main goal of this project is to develop a new training program that provides just-in-time training to employees on key topics, including supplier management, negotiating skills, project management, and software applications.

Project Organization

The basic organization of the project is provided in Figure 1. The project sponsor, Lucy Camerena, will have the final say on major decisions, with consultation from the project steering committee and project champion, Mike Sundby. The project sponsor should have time to thoroughly review important project information and provide timely feedback to the project manager. The project manager in this case reports to the project sponsor, and the team leaders, and supplier project managers report to the project manager.

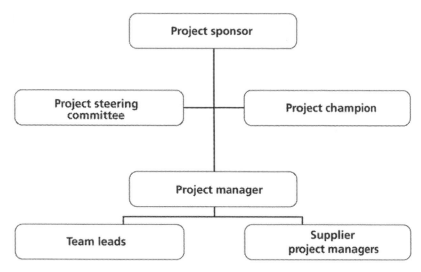

FIGURE 1   Project organizational chart

Figure 1. Project Organizational Chart

Management and Technical Processes

Management Processes:

1. Management Review Process: The project steering committee will meet at least monthly to provide inputs and review progress on this project.

2. Progress Measurement Process: The project steering committee will review project progress during project review meetings, and they can also review information as needed by viewing reports on the enterprise project management software. Post project progress will also be measured to see if the project met its goals. These goals include reducing the training cost per employee by $100/person/year and receiving positive results from survey participants on the effectiveness of the training.

3. Change Approval Process: See Attachment 1 based on corporate standards.

4. Supplier Management Process: See Attachment 2 based on corporate standards.

An Introduction to Project Management, Third Edition

Technical Processes:

1. Enterprise Project Management Software: All tasks, costs, resources, issues, and risks will be tracked for this project using our enterprise project management software. Data must be entered on a weekly basis, at a minimum, to provide timely information.

2. Supplier Evaluation: The project team will coordinate with the purchasing department to follow our standard procedures for selecting and working with suppliers. See Attachment 2 for corporate standards.

3. Productivity Improvement: The project team will work with the finance department and quality assurance department to develop and implement a system to measure improvements in employee productivity that result from this new training program. The finance department will report on this information annually beginning one year after the first new training course is offered.

Work to be Performed

Summary: Research, develop or purchase, and implement a new just-in-time training program covering the topics of supplier management, negotiating skills, project management, and software applications and determine a way to measure the effectiveness of the training and its impact on productivity on an annual basis. See the scope statement, WBS, and other scope documents for further detail.

Schedule Information

The entire project will be completed in one year with a projected completion date of June 30. See the project schedule and other time management documents for further detail.

Budget Information

The total budget for this project is $1,000,000. Approximately half of these costs will be for internal labor, while the other half will be for outsourced labor and training programs. See the cost estimate and cost performance baseline for further detail.

References to Other Project Planning Documents

All current project plans created for this project are provided in Appendix A. Initial documents and revisions are available on the project Web site.

Figure 4-3. Sample project management plan

PROJECT SCOPE MANAGEMENT PLANNING TASKS

Project scope management involves defining and controlling what work is or is not included in a project. The main planning tasks performed as part of project scope management include collecting requirements, defining scope, and creating the WBS. The main documents produced are requirements documents, a requirements management plan, a requirements traceability matrix, a scope statement, a WBS, and a WBS dictionary.

Collecting Requirements

The *PMBOK® Guide, Fourth Edition*, defines a **requirement** as "a condition or capability that must be met or possessed by a system, product, service, result, or component to satisfy a contract, standard, specification, or other formal document." It is important to document requirements in enough detail so that they can be measured during project execution. After all, meeting scope goals is often based on meeting documented requirements.

The main outputs of collecting requirements include:

- requirements documents, which can range from a single-page checklist to a room full of notebooks with text, diagrams, images, etc.

- a **requirements management plan**, which describes how project requirements will be analyzed, documented and managed, and

- a **requirements traceability matrix (RTM)**, which is a table that lists requirements, various attributes of each requirement, and the status of the requirements to ensure that all of them are addressed

There are several ways to collect requirements. Interviewing stakeholders one-on-one is often very effective, although it can be very expensive and time-consuming. Holding focus groups, facilitated workshops, and using group creativity and decision-making techniques to collect requirements are normally faster and less expensive than one-on-one interviews. Questionnaires and surveys can be very efficient ways to collect requirements as long as key stakeholders provide honest and thorough information. Observation can also be a good technique for collecting requirements, especially for projects that involve improving work processes and procedures. Prototyping is a commonly used technique for collecting requirements for software development projects.

The project's size, complexity, importance, and other factors will affect how much effort is spent on collecting requirements. For example, a team working on a project to upgrade the entire corporate accounting system for a multibillion dollar company with more than 50 geographic locations should spend a fair amount of time collecting requirements. A project to upgrade the hardware and software for a small accounting firm with only five employees, on the other hand, would need a much smaller effort. In any case, it is important for a project team to decide how they will collect and manage requirements. It is crucial to gather inputs from key stakeholders and align the scope, a key aspect of the entire project, with business strategy, as described in Chapter 2.

Sample Requirements Management Plan

There were many requirements involved in the Just-In-Time Training project. Some requirements, such as the type of training to be provided, are described in the project charter. However, Kristin knew from past experience that it was important to do a good job collecting and managing requirements. She worked with her team to develop a requirements management plan. Important contents of this plan include information related to:

-

- Planning, tracking, and reporting requirements

- Performing configuration management activities, such as initiating, analyzing, authorizing, tracking, and reporting changes to requirements

- Prioritizing requirements

- Using product metrics

- Tracing requirements

Figure 4-4 shows a sample requirement management plan.

Requirements Management Plan Version 1.0
September 30

Project Name: Just-In-Time Training Project

Planning, tracking, and reporting requirements:

Information from the Phase I project, the business case, and the project charter will provide valuable information in determining requirements for this project, as will many existing corporate standards and processes. A survey will also be used to gather requirements. All requirements will be documented where appropriate. For example, requirements related to course prerequisites will be documented in course descriptions. Requirements related to facilities, class size, etc. will be documented in the scope statement. Requirements will be tracked by the person in charge of each related deliverable and reported as part of our normal reporting processes (i.e. weekly status reports, monthly review meetings, etc.)

Performing configuration management activities:

Requirements can be introduced by several means, such as existing written requirements, suggestions provided from our survey, or direct suggestions from stakeholders. Appropriate project stakeholders will analyze, authorize, track, and report changes to requirements. The project manager must be informed in advance of potential changes to requirements and be involved in the decision process to approve those changes. Any change that will impact the project's cost or schedule significantly must be approved by the project steering committee.

Prioritizing requirements:

All requirements will be designated as 1, 2 or 3, for mandatory, desirable, or nice-to-have, respectively. Emphasis will be placed on meeting all mandatory requirements, followed by desirable and then nice-to-have requirements.

Using product metrics:

Several product metrics will be used to help in managing requirements. For example, each training class will be compared to similar classes to evaluate its content, length, and quality with similar classes. Course evaluations will be used as the main metric in evaluating the course and instructor.

Tracing requirements:

All mandatory requirements will be included in the requirements traceability matrix. Desirable and nice-to-have requirements will be documented in a separate matrix and be addressed only as time and resources allow. The matrix will be created using the company's template file for this document.

Figure 4-4. Sample requirements management plan

Sample Requirements Traceability Matrix

Figure 4-5 provides an example of a few requirements traceability matrix (RTM) entries for the Just-In-Time Training project. Remember that the main purpose of an RTM is to maintain the linkage from the source of each requirement through its decomposition to implementation and verification. For example, the first entry is related to survey questions. The project team knew they had to develop a survey for the project to help assess training needs, and the project steering committee decided in a meeting that they should review and approve the survey questions before the survey went out. They wanted to make sure that there were objective and open-ended questions in the survey, as documented in their project steering committee meeting minutes. The second entry concerns the course evaluations for the new courses that will be developed. The company has documented standards that must be followed for course evaluations.

Require-ment no.	Name	Category	Source	Status
R26	Survey questions	Survey	Project steering committee minutes	Complete. The survey questions were reviewed and approved by the steering committee.
R31	Course evaluations	Assessment	Corporate training standards	In process. The course evaluations have not been created yet.

Figure 4-5. Sample requirements traceability matrix

Defining Scope

Good scope definition is crucial to project success because it helps improve the accuracy of time, cost, and resource estimates; defines a baseline for performance measurement and project control; and aids in communicating clear work responsibilities. Work that is not included in the scope statement should not be done. The main techniques used in defining scope include expert judgment, product analysis, alternatives identification, and facilitated workshops. The main outputs of scope definition are the scope statement and project document updates.

The project charter, requirements documentation, and **organizational process assets** (i.e. policies and procedures related to project management, past project files, and lessons-learned reports from previous, similar projects) are all inputs for creating the initial scope statement. The scope statement should be updated as more information becomes available. Although contents vary, scope statements should include, at a minimum, a product scope description, product user acceptance criteria, and detailed information on all project deliverables. It is also helpful to document project boundaries, constraints, and assumptions. The scope statement should also reference supporting documents, such as product specifications and corporate policies, which often affect how products or services are produced.

Sample Scope Statement

Kristin worked closely with her team to develop the first version of the scope statement, reviewing available information and meeting several times with key stakeholders to develop a thorough document. Part of the scope statement is shown in Figure 4-6. Kristin knew that this document would change as they finalized more details of the project scope. Note that some details have been added and changes have been made since the project charter was completed. For example, class size has been added, more information on the needs assessment and survey has been provided, and the success criteria were changed slightly.

Scope Statement, Version 1.0
August 1

Project Title: Just-In-Time Training Project
Project Justification: (Not included in this sample)
Product Characteristics and Requirements:
This project will produce three levels of courses, executive, introductory, and advanced, in the following subject areas: supplier management, negotiating skills, project management, and software applications (spreadsheets and Web development). Details on each course are provided below:

1. Supplier management training: The Supplier Management Director estimates the need to train at least 200 employees each year in supplier management. There should be three levels of courses: an executive course, an introductory course, and an advanced course. Course materials should be developed as a joint effort with internal experts, outside training experts, if needed, and key suppliers. This training must be tailored to our business needs. A partnership might be developed to maximize the effectiveness of the training and minimize development costs. Different delivery methods should be explored, including instructor-led, CD/ROM, and Web-based training. About half of employees would prefer an instructor-led approach, and about half would prefer a self-paced course they could take at their convenience.

2. Negotiating skills training: Employees from the Supplier Management and other departments would benefit from this training. There should be several courses offered, including a basic course, a course tailored to negotiating contracts, and a course tailored to international negotiations. Different delivery methods should be explored, including instructor-led, CD/ROM, and Web-based.

Etc.

Product User Acceptance Criteria
The courses produced as part of this project will be considered successful if they are all available within one year and the average course evaluations for each course are at least 3.0 on a 5.0 scale.
Deliverables
Project Management-Related Deliverables
Team contract, project charter, project management plan, requirements management plan, scope statement, WBS, etc.

Product-Related Deliverables:
1. Supplier management training:
      1.1. Needs assessment: A survey will be conducted to determine the learning objectives for the executive, introductory, and advanced courses
      1.2 Research of existing training: A study will be done to identify current training courses and materials available
      1.3. Partnerships: Partnership agreements will be explored to get outside training organizations and suppliers to work on developing and providing training
      1.4. Course development: Appropriate materials will be developed for each course. Materials could take various formats, including written, video, CD/ROM, or Web-based. Materials should include interactivity to keep learners engaged.
      1.5. Pilot course: A pilot course will be provided for the introductory supplier management course. Feedback from the pilot course will be incorporated into following courses.
2. Negotiating skills training:
      2.1. Needs assessment: A survey will be conducted to determine the learning objectives for the basic negotiations, contract negotiations, and international negotiations courses.
      2.2 Research of existing training: A study will be done to identify current training courses and materials available.
      Etc.

Figure 4-6. Sample scope statement

As more information becomes available and decisions are made related to project scope—such as specific products that will be purchased or changes that have been approved—the project team should update the project scope statement. Different iterations of the scope statement should be named Version 1.0, Version 2.0, and so on. These updates might also require changes to the project management plan. For example, if the team decides to purchase products or services for the project from a supplier with whom it has never worked, the project management plan should include information on working with that new supplier.

An up-to-date project scope statement is an important document for developing and confirming a common understanding of the project scope. It describes in detail the work to be accomplished on the project and is an important tool for ensuring customer satisfaction and preventing **scope creep**, which is the tendency for project scope to continually increase.

Creating the Work Breakdown Structure

A **work breakdown structure (WBS)** is a deliverable-oriented grouping of the work involved in a project that defines the total scope of the project. In other words, the WBS is a document that breaks all the work required for the project into discrete tasks, and groups those tasks into a logical hierarchy. Because most projects involve many people and many different deliverables, it is important to organize and divide the work into logical parts based on how the work will be performed. The WBS is a foundation document in project management because it provides the basis for planning and managing project schedules, costs, resources, and changes. Because the WBS defines the total scope of the project, some project management experts believe that work should not be done on a project if it is not included in the WBS. Therefore, it is crucial to develop a good WBS.

A WBS is often depicted in a graphical format, similar to an organizational chart. The name of the entire project is the top box, called level 1, and the main groupings for the work are listed in the second tier of boxes, called level 2. This level numbering is based on PMI's *Practice Standard for Work Breakdown Structure, Second Edition (2006)*. Each of those boxes can be broken down into subsequent tiers of boxes to show the hierarchy of the work. Project teams often organize the WBS around project products, project phases, or other logical groupings. People often like to create a WBS in a graphical format first to help them visualize the whole project and all of its main parts. You can also show a WBS in tabular form as an indented list of tasks showing the groupings of the work. Note that the term "task" is used to describe each level of work in the WBS. For example, in Figure 4-7, the following items can be referred to as tasks: the level 2 item called Concept, the level 3 item below that called Define requirements, and the level 4 item below that called Define user requirements. Tasks that are decomposed into smaller tasks are called summary tasks.

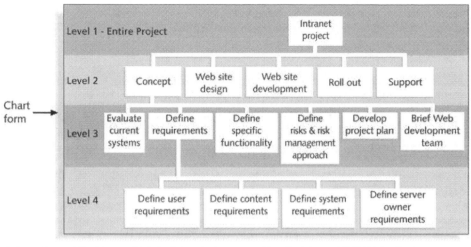

Chart form →

Tabular form with Microsoft Project Numbering

1.0 Concept
    1.1 Evaluate current systems
    1.2 Define requirements
        1.2.1 Define user requirements
        1.2.2 Define content requirements
        1.2.3 Define system requirements
        1.2.4 Define server owner requirements
    1.3 Define specific functionality
    1.4 Define risks and risk management
        approach
    1.5 Develop project plan
    1.6 Brief Web development team
2.0 Web site design
3.0 Web site development
4.0 Roll out
5.0 Support

Tabular form with PMI Numbering

1.1 Concept
    1.1.1 Evaluate current systems
    1.1.2 Define requirements
        1.1.2.1 Define user requirements
        1.1.2.2 Define content requirements
        1.1.2.3 Define system requirements
        1.1.2.4 Define server owner requirements
    1.1.3 Define specific functionality
    1.1.4 Define risks and risk management
        approach
    1.1.5 Develop project plan
    1.1.6 Brief Web development team
1.2 Web site design
1.3 Web site development
1.4 Roll out
1.5 Support

Figure 4-7. WBS in chart and tabular form (Schwalbe, Information Technology Project Management, Sixth Edition, 2010)

Figure 4-7 shows a sample WBS in both chart and tabular form. Notice that both of these formats show the same information. Many documents, such as contracts, use the tabular format. Project management software also uses this format. The WBS becomes the contents of the Task Name column in Microsoft Project, and the hierarchy or level of tasks is shown by indenting and numbering tasks within the software. The numbering shown in the tabular form on the left in Figure 4-7 coincides with numbering done in Microsoft Project and other sources. The numbering shown in the tabular form on the right in Figure 4-7 is based on PMI's *Practice Standard for Work Breakdown Structures, Second Edition*. Be sure to check with your organization to see what numbering scheme they prefer to use for work breakdown structures.

In Figure 4-7, the lowest level of the WBS is level 4. A **work package** is a task at the lowest level of the WBS. In this figure, tasks 1.2.1, 1.2.2, 1.2.3, and 1.2.4 based on numbering on the left are work packages. The other tasks would probably be broken down further. However, some tasks can remain at a level 3 in the WBS. Some might be broken down to level 5 or 6, depending on the complexity of the work. A work package also represents the level of work that the project manager monitors and controls. You can think of work packages in terms of accountability and reporting. If a project has a relatively short time frame and requires weekly progress reports, a work package might represent work completed in one week or less. On the other hand, if a project has a very long time frame and requires quarterly progress reports, a work package might represent work completed in one month or more. A work package might also be the procurement of a specific product or products, such as an item or items purchased from an outside source.

The sample WBS shown here seems somewhat easy to construct and understand. *Nevertheless, it is very difficult to create a good WBS.* To create a good WBS, you must understand both the project and its scope, and incorporate the needs and knowledge of the stakeholders. The project manager and the project team must decide as a group how to organize the work and how many levels to include in the WBS. Many project managers have found that it is better to focus on getting the top levels done well to avoid being distracted by too much detail.

Many people confuse tasks on a WBS with specifications. Tasks on a WBS represent work that needs to be done to complete the project. For example, if you are creating a WBS to redesign a kitchen, you might have level 2 categories called design, purchasing, flooring, walls, cabinets, and appliances. Under flooring, you might have work packages to remove the old flooring, install the new flooring, and install the trim. You would not have items like "12′ by 14′ of light oak" or "flooring must be durable" on a WBS.

Another concern when creating a WBS is how to organize it so that it provides the basis for the project schedule. You should focus on what work needs to be done, not when it will be done. In other words, the tasks do not have to be developed as a sequential list of steps. If you do want some time-based flow for the work, you can create a WBS using the project management process groups of initiating, planning, executing, monitoring and controlling, and closing as level 2 in the WBS. By doing this, not only does the project team follow good project management practice, but the WBS tasks can be mapped more easily against time.

Approaches to Developing Work Breakdown Structures

Because it is so important to create a good WBS, this section describes several approaches you can use to develop them. These approaches include:

- Using guidelines

- The analogy approach

- The top-down approach

- The bottom-up approach

- The mind-mapping approach

Using Guidelines

If guidelines for developing a WBS exist, it is very important to follow them. Some organizations—for example, the U.S. Department of Defense (DOD)—prescribe the form and content for WBSs for particular projects. Many DOD projects require contractors to prepare their proposals based on the DOD-provided WBS. For example, a large contract for purchasing hardware and software might prescribe a WBS with level 2 WBS items that included hardware, off-the-shelf software, software development, training, project management, and the like. The hardware item could include several level 3 items, such as servers, laptops, printers, and network hardware. Many government projects include project management as a level 2 item to make sure that work is not forgotten.

The Analogy Approach

Another approach for constructing a WBS is the analogy approach, where you use a similar project's WBS as a starting point. For example, many organizations have sample WBSs from past projects. Many software products, like Microsoft Project 2010, include several templates for WBSs for various types of projects that can be used as a starting point for creating a new WBS. (See Appendix A for information on using templates.) While starting with a WBS from a similar project can save a lot of time, it is important that project managers and their teams address their unique project needs and how work will be done when creating their WBSs.

The Top-down Approach

Most project managers consider the top-down approach of WBS construction to be conventional. To use the top-down approach, start with the largest items of the project and break them into their subordinate items. This process involves refining the work into greater and greater levels of detail. For example, Figure 4-7 shows how work was broken down to level 4 for part of the intranet project. After breaking down or decomposing the top-level items, resources should then be assigned at the work-package level. The top-down approach is best suited to project managers and teams who have vast technical insight and a big-picture perspective.

The Bottom-up Approach

In the bottom-up approach, team members first identify as many specific tasks related to the project as possible. They then aggregate the specific tasks and organize them into summary activities, or higher levels in the WBS. For example, a group of people might be responsible for creating a WBS to create a brand new product. They could begin by listing detailed tasks they think they would need to do in order to create the product and then group the tasks into categories. Then, they would group these categories into higher-level categories. Some people have found that writing all possible tasks down on sticky notes and then placing them on a wall helps them see all the work required for the project and develop logical groupings for performing the work. The bottom-up approach can be very time consuming, but it can also be a very effective way to create a WBS. Project teams often use the bottom-up approach for projects that represent entirely new products or approaches to doing a job, or to help create buy-in and synergy with a project team.

Mind Mapping

Some project managers like to use mind mapping to help develop WBSs. As described in Chapter 2, mind mapping is a technique that uses branches radiating out from a core idea to structure thoughts and ideas. This more visual, less structured approach to defining and then grouping tasks can unlock creativity among individuals and increase participation and morale among teams. You can create mind maps by hand, by using sticky notes, using presentation software like PowerPoint, or by using mind mapping software.

Figure 4-8 shows a diagram that uses mind mapping to create a WBS for an information technology upgrade project. This figure was created using MindManager software by Mindjet (www.mindjet.com). The circle in the center represents the entire project. Each of the four main branches radiating out from the center represents the main tasks or level 2 items for the WBS. Different people at the meeting creating this mind map might have different roles in the project, which could help in deciding the tasks and WBS structure. For example, the project manager would want to focus on all of the project management tasks, and he or she might also know that they will be tracked in a separate budget category. People who are familiar with acquiring or installing hardware and software might focus on that work. Branching off from the main task called "Update inventory" are two subtasks, "Perform physical inventory" and "Update database." Branching off from the "Perform physical inventory" subtask are three further subdivisions, labeled Building A, Building B, and Building C. The team would continue to add branches and items until they have exhausted ideas on what work needs to be performed.

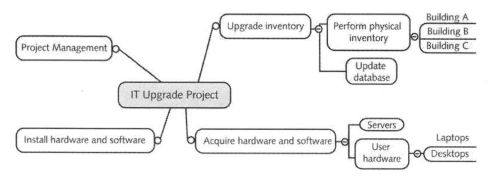

Figure 4-8. Sample mind-mapping technique for creating a WBS (Schwalbe, **Information Technology Project Management, Sixth Edition, 2010**)

After discovering WBS items and structure using the mind-mapping technique, you could then translate the information into chart or tabular form, as described earlier. A feature of MindManager software is that you can export your map into Microsoft Project. The WBS is entered in the Task List column, with the structure automatically created based on the mind map. Figure 4-9 shows the resulting Microsoft Project file for the information technology upgrade project.

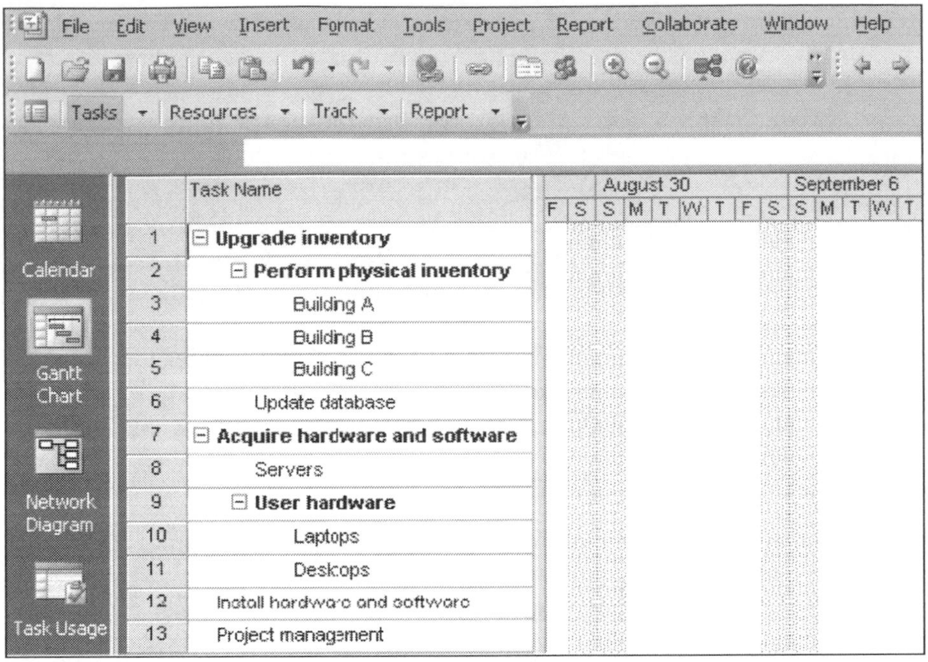

Figure 4-9. Microsoft Project file with WBS generated from a mind map (Schwalbe, Information Technology Project Management, Sixth Edition, 2010)

Mind mapping can be used for developing WBSs using the top-down or bottom-up approach or a combination of the two. For example, you could conduct mind mapping for an entire project by listing the whole project in the center of a document, adding the main categories on branches radiating out from the center, and then adding branches for appropriate subcategories. You could also develop a separate mind-mapping diagram for each major deliverable and then merge them to create one large diagram for the entire project. You can also add items anywhere on a mind-mapping document without following a strict top-down or bottom-up approach. After the mind-mapping documents are complete, you can convert them into a chart or tabular WBS form.

Sample WBS

The Just-In-Time Training project team decided to use the project management process groups for the level 2 tasks in its WBS, following a top-down approach. They also reviewed WBSs of similar projects as they created theirs. (Remember that the process groups include initiating, planning, executing, monitoring and controlling, and closing.) The level 3 tasks under "Executing" (where the products and services of the project are produced) included course design and development, course administration, course evaluation, and stakeholder communications. The project team knew that they had to have strong communications to make the project a success, so they created a separate WBS level 3 category for communications under "Executing." They focused on the product deliverables they had to produce in breaking down the course design and development task by having level 4 categories based on the types of courses: supplier management, negotiating skills, project management, and software applications.

Figure 4-10 shows part of the initial WBS Kristin and her team created. You will see this same information later in this chapter as the task names in the Gantt chart. Some tasks have been broken down into more detail while others have not. Many tasks might be broken into more levels for the actual WBS used in the project. Recall that the scope statement should list and describe all the work required for the project. To define the scope of the project accurately, it is very important to ensure consistency between the project charter, scope statement, WBS, Gantt chart, and related documents. It is also very important to involve the entire project team and other stakeholders in creating and reviewing the WBS. *People who will do the work should help to plan the work* by creating the WBS. It is important to let workers be creative and know that they have a say in how their work is done. Having group meetings to develop a WBS helps everyone understand *what* work must be done for the entire project and *how* it should be done, given the people involved. It also helps to identify where coordination between different work packages will be required.

Work Breakdown Structure (WBS) for the
Just-In-Time Training Project
August 1

1. Initiating
    1.1. Prepare stakeholder analysis
    1.2. Prepare business case
    1.3. Create project charter
    1.4. Hold project kickoff meeting
    1.5. Develop preliminary scope statement
2. Planning
    2.1. Project integration management
        2.1.1. Create team contract
        2.1.2. Develop project management plan
    2.2. Project scope management
        2.2.1. Develop scope statement
        2.2.2. Create WBS and WBS dictionary
    2.3. Project time management
    2.4. Project cost management
    2.5. Project quality management
    2.6. Project human resource management
    2.7. Project communications management
    2.8. Project risk management
    2.9. Project procurement management

3. Executing
   3.1. Course design and development
      3.1.1. Supplier management training
         3.1.1.1. Needs assessment
            3.1.1.1.1. Develop survey
            3.1.1.1.2. Administer survey
            3.1.1.1.3. Analyze survey results
         3.1.1.2. Research of existing training
         3.1.1.3. Partnerships
            3.1.1.3.1. Research potential partners for providing training
            3.1.1.3.2. Meet with potential partners
            3.1.1.3.3. Develop partnership agreements
         3.1.1.4. Course development
            3.1.1.4.1. Develop executive course
            3.1.1.4.2. Develop introductory course
            3.1.1.4.3. Develop advanced course
         3.1.1.5. Pilot course
            3.1.1.5.1. Plan pilot course
            3.1.1.5.2. Hold pilot course
            3.1.1.5.3. Prepare report on pilot course
            3.1.1.5.4. Review results of pilot course
      3.1.2. Negotiating skills training
      3.1.3. Project management training
      3.1.4. Software applications training
   3.2. Course administration
   3.3. Course evaluation
   3.4. Stakeholder communications
      3.4.1. Communications regarding project and changes to training
         3.4.1.1. Prepare emails, posters, memos, and other information
         3.4.1.2. Plan and hold meetings
         3.4.1.3. Prepare information for the corporate intranet
      3.4.2. Communications regarding productivity improvements
4. Monitoring and controlling
5. Closing

Figure 4-10. Sample WBS

Creating the WBS Dictionary

Many of the tasks listed on a WBS can be rather vague. What exactly does WBS item 3.1.1.1.2, "Administer survey" mean, for example? The person responsible for this task for the Just-In-Time Training project might think that it does not need to be broken down any further, which could be fine. However, the task should be described in more detail so that everyone has the same understanding of what it involves. What if someone else has to perform the task? What would you tell him or her to do? What will it cost to complete the task? How many resources are required? How long will it take to complete? Information that is more detailed is needed to answer these and other questions. Of course you must use common sense in deciding how much documentation is needed. For a simple task, verbal instructions might be sufficient.

A **WBS dictionary** is a document that describes WBS tasks in detail. The format of the WBS dictionary can vary based on project needs. It might be appropriate to have just a short paragraph describing each work package. For a more complex project, an entire page or more might be needed for the work-package descriptions. Some projects might require that each WBS dictionary item describe the responsible person or organization, resource requirements, estimated costs, and other information. Other projects might not require a WBS entry for every single WBS task.

Sample WBS Dictionary Entry

The project manager should work with his or her team and sponsor to determine the level of detail needed in the WBS dictionary. Project teams often review WBS dictionary entries from similar tasks to get a better idea of how to create these entries. They should also decide where this information will be entered and how it will be updated. For the Just-In-Time Training project, Kristin and her team will enter all of the WBS dictionary information into their enterprise project management system. Figure 4-11 provides an example of one of the entries.

WBS Dictionary Entry
August 1

Project Title: Just-In-Time Training Project
WBS Item Number:3.1.1.1.2
WBS Item Name: Administer survey

Description: The purpose of the survey for the supplier management training is to determine the learning objectives for the executive, introductory, and advanced supplier management courses (see WBS item 3.1.1.1.1 for additional information on the survey itself). The survey will be administered online using the standard corporate survey software. After the project steering committee approves the survey, the IT department will send it to all employees of grade level 52 or higher in the purchasing, accounting, engineering, information technology, sales, marketing, manufacturing, and human resource departments. The project champion, Mike Sundby, VP of Human Resources, will write an introductory paragraph for the survey. Department heads will mention the importance of responding to this survey in their department meetings and will send an e-mail to all affected employees to encourage their inputs. If the response rate is less than 30% one week after the survey is sent out, additional work may be required.

Figure 4-11. Sample WBS dictionary entry

The approved project scope statement and its associated WBS and WBS dictionary form the **scope baseline**. Performance in meeting project scope goals is based on the scope baseline.

PROJECT TIME MANAGEMENT PLANNING TASKS

Project time management involves the processes required to ensure timely completion of a project. The main planning tasks performed as part of project time management are defining activities, sequencing activities, estimating activity resource, estimating activity durations, and developing the project schedule. The main documents produced are an activity list and attributes, a milestone list, a network diagram, the activity resource requirements, the activity duration estimates, and a project schedule. Samples of these documents are provided later in this section.

Defining Activities

Project schedules grow out of the basic documents that initiate a project. The project charter often mentions planned project start and end dates, which serve as the starting points for a more detailed schedule. The project manager starts with the project charter and then develops a project scope statement and WBS, as discussed in the previous section. Using this information with the scope statement, WBS, WBS dictionary, project management plan, and other related information, the project team begins to develop a schedule by first clearly defining all the activities it needs to perform.

Creating the Activity List and Attributes

The **activity list** is a tabulation of activities to be included on a project schedule. The list should include the activity name, an activity identifier or number, and a brief description of the activity. The **activity attributes** provide schedule-related information about each activity, such as predecessors, successors, logical relationships, leads and lags, resource requirements, constraints, imposed dates, and assumptions related to the activity. The activity list and activity attributes should be in agreement with the WBS and WBS dictionary. Recall that a work package is the lowest level task in a WBS. Activities in the activity list are based on the detailed work required to complete each work package.

The goal of the activity definition process is to ensure that project team members have a complete understanding of all the work they must do as part of the project scope so that they can start scheduling the work. For example, one of the work packages in the WBS for the Just-In-Time Training project is "Prepare report on pilot course." The project team would have to understand what that means before it can make schedule-related decisions. How long should the report be? Does it require a survey or extensive research to produce it? What skill level does the report writer need to have? Further defining the task will help the project team determine how long it will take to do and who should do it.

The WBS is often expanded during the activity definition process as the project team members further define the activities required for performing the work. For example, the task "Prepare report on pilot course" might be broken down into several subtasks describing the steps involved in producing the report, such as developing a survey, administering the survey, analyzing the survey results, conducting interviews, writing a draft report, editing the report, and finally producing the report.

To avoid too much detail, some people prefer *not* to include these additional schedule-related activities in the WBS. They keep the lowest level of the WBS at the previously defined work package and describe detailed activities separately in the activity list and schedule. With most project management software, however, it is easy to include *all* the activity data in one place and then view information at whatever level of detail is desired. In this example, the activity list refers to the lowest level of work described for the project.

The project team should review the activity list and activity attributes with project stakeholders. If they do not, they could produce an unrealistic schedule and deliver unacceptable results. For example, if a project team simply estimated that it would take one day for the "Prepare report on pilot course" task and had an intern or trainee write a two-page report to complete that task, the result could be a furious sponsor who expected extensive research, surveys, and a 50-page report. Clearly defining the work and having a realistic schedule for all activities is crucial to project success.

Sample Activity List and Attributes

Kristin and her team developed an activity to assist in developing the project schedule. Figure 4-12 provides a sample entry in the activity list. Notice the detailed information provided, such as the predecessors, successors, resource requirements, and assumptions. As you can see from this sample, Kristin and her team would have to work closely with other stakeholders to define this information.

Activity List and Attributes
August 1

Project Name: Just-In-Time Training Project
WBS Item Number:3.1.1.1.2
WBS Item Name: Administer survey
Predecessors: 3.1.1.1.1 Develop survey
Successors: 3.1.1.1.3 Analyze survey results
Logical Relationships: finish-to-start
Leads and Lags: None
Resource Requirements: IT personnel, corporate survey software, corporate Intranet
Constraints: None
Imposed dates: None
Assumptions: The survey for the supplier management training will be administered online using the standard corporate survey software. It should include questions measured on a Likert scale. For example, a question might be as follows: I learned a lot from this course. Respondents would enter 1 for Strongly Agree, 2 for Agree, 3 for Undecided, 4 for Disagree, or 5 for Strongly Disagree. There also should be several open-ended questions, such as "What did you like most about the pilot course? What did you like least about the pilot course?" After the project steering committee approves the survey, the IT department will send it to all employees of grade level 52 or higher in the purchasing, accounting, engineering, information technology, sales, marketing, manufacturing, and human resource departments. The project champion, Mike Sundby, VP of Human Resources, will write an introductory paragraph for the survey. Department heads will mention the importance of responding to this survey in their department meetings and will send an e-mail to all affected employees to encourage their inputs. If the response rate is less than 30% one week after the survey is sent out, additional work may be required, such as a reminder e-mail to follow-up with people who have not responded to the survey.

Figure 4-12. Sample activity list and attributes

Creating a Milestone List

To ensure that all major activities are accounted for, project teams often create a milestone list. A **milestone** is a significant event on a project. It often takes several activities and a lot of work to complete a milestone, but the milestone itself is like a marker to help in identifying necessary activities. There is usually no cost or duration associated with a milestone. Milestones are also useful tools for setting schedule goals and monitoring progress, and project sponsors and senior managers often focus on major milestones when reviewing projects. For example, milestones for many projects include sign-off of key documents; completion of specific products; and completion of important process-related work, such as awarding a contract to a supplier. Milestone names are generally written in past tense, such as "Contract awarded."

Sample Milestone List

Kristin and her team reviewed the draft WBS and activity list to develop an initial milestone list. They reviewed the list with their sponsor and other key stakeholders. Project teams often estimate completion dates for milestones early in the scheduling process and adjust them after going through additional time management planning steps such as activity sequencing, activity resource estimating, duration estimating, and schedule development. Figure 4-13 shows part of the milestone list for the Just-In-Time Training project. This section focuses on the milestones related to the needs assessment for supplier management training (WBS item 3.1.1.1). Kristin knew her team had to complete this survey early in the project and that the results would affect many of the other tasks required for the project. Her team might need to see all the milestones provided in Figure 4-13, but the steering committee might only need to see the last milestone, "Survey results reported to steering committee." The steering committee might focus on other milestones, including the project kick-off meeting, results of the pilot course, dates for each training class provided as part of the project, results of the course evaluations, and projected end date for the project. Using project management software, such as Project 2010, makes it easy to filter information and create reports so that different people can focus on their own tasks and milestones. See Appendix A for more details on using Project 2010.

Milestone List
August 1

Project Name: Just-In-Time Training Project

Milestone	Initial Estimated Completion Date*
Draft survey completed	8/3
Survey comments submitted	8/8
Survey sent out by IT	8/10
Percentage of survey respondents reviewed	8/17
Survey report completed	8/22
Survey results reported to steering committee	8/24

*Note: Dates are in U.S. format. 8/3 means August 8.

Figure 4-13. Sample milestone list

Best Practice

Many people use the SMART criteria to help define milestones. The SMART criteria are guidelines suggesting that milestones should be:

- Specific
- Measureable
- Assignable
- Realistic
- Time-framed

    For example, completing the draft survey, as listed in Figure 4-13 is specific, measurable, and assignable if everyone knows what should be in the draft survey, how and to whom it should be distributed, and who is responsible for creating the survey. Completing the draft survey is realistic and able to be time-framed if it is an achievable event and scheduled for completion at an appropriate time.

    You can also use milestones to help reduce schedule risk by following these best practices:

- Define milestones early in the project and include them in the Gantt chart to provide a visual guide.
- Keep milestones small and frequent.
- The set of milestones must be all-encompassing.
- Each milestone must be binary, meaning it is either complete or incomplete.
- Carefully monitor the milestones on the critical path (described later in this chapter).[3]

Sequencing Activities

After defining project activities, the next step in project time management is activity sequencing. Activity sequencing involves reviewing the activity list and attributes, project scope statement, and milestone list to determine the relationships or dependencies between activities. It also involves evaluating the reasons for dependencies and the different types of dependencies.

A **dependency** or **relationship** relates to the sequencing of project activities or tasks. For example, does a certain activity have to be finished before another one can start? Can the project team do several activities in parallel? Can some overlap? Determining these relationships or dependencies between activities has a significant impact on developing and managing a project schedule.

There are three basic reasons for creating dependencies among project activities:

- **Mandatory dependencies** are inherent in the nature of the work being performed on a project. They are sometimes referred to as hard logic because their relationships are unavoidable. For example, you cannot hold training classes until the training materials are ready, and the training materials cannot be created until the objectives of the course are determined.

- **Discretionary dependencies** are defined by the project team. For example, a project team might follow good practice and not start detailed design work until key stakeholders sign off on all of the analysis work. Discretionary dependencies are sometimes referred to as soft logic and should be used with care because they might limit later scheduling options.

- **External dependencies** involve relationships between project and non-project activities. The installation of new software might depend on delivery of new hardware from an external supplier. Even though the delivery of the new hardware might not be in the scope of the project, it should have an external dependency added to it because late delivery will affect the project schedule.

As with activity definition, it is important that project stakeholders work together to define the activity dependencies that exist on their project. If you do not define the sequence of activities and estimate their durations, you cannot use some of the most powerful schedule tools available to project managers: network diagrams and critical path analysis. The main output of activity sequencing is a network diagram.

Network Diagrams

Network diagrams are the preferred technique for showing activity sequencing. A **network diagram** is a schematic display of the logical relationships among, or sequencing of, project activities. Some people refer to network diagrams as PERT charts. PERT is described later in this section. Figure 4-14 shows a sample network diagram for Project X, which uses the arrow diagramming method (ADM), or activity-on-arrow (AOA) approach. (Note: This approach is shown first because the diagrams are easier to understand and create. Its main limitation is that it can only show finish-to-start dependencies, as described later in this section.)

Note the main elements on this network diagram. The letters A through I represent activities with dependencies that are required to complete the project. These activities come from the WBS and activity definition process described earlier. The arrows represent the activity sequencing, or relationships between tasks. For example, Activity A must be done before Activity D, Activity D must be done before Activity F, and Activity F must be done before Activity H.

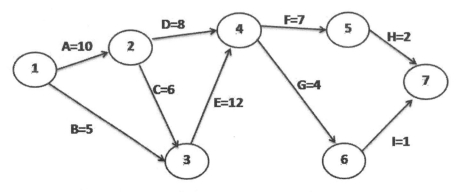

Note: Assume all durations are in days;
A=10 means Activity A has a duration of 10 days.

Figure 4-14. Activity-on-arrow (AOA) network diagram for Project X

The format of this network diagram uses the **activity-on-arrow (AOA)** approach, or the **arrow diagramming method (ADM)**—a network diagramming technique in which activities are represented by arrows and connected at points called nodes to illustrate the sequence of activities. A **node** is simply the starting and ending point of an activity. The first node signifies the start of a project, and the last node represents the end of a project.

Keep in mind that the network diagram represents activities that must be done to complete the project. It is not a race to get from the first node to the last node. *Every* activity on the network diagram must be completed for the project to finish. It is also important to note that not every single item on the WBS needs to be on the network diagram; only activities with dependencies need to be shown on the network diagram. However, some people like to have start and end milestones and to list every activity. It is a matter of preference. For projects with hundreds of activities, it might be simpler to include only activities with dependencies on a network diagram.

Assuming you have a list of the project activities and their start and finish nodes, follow these steps to create an AOA network diagram:

1. Find all of the activities that start at Node 1. Draw their finish nodes, and draw arrows between Node 1 and each of those finish nodes. Put the activity letter or name on the associated arrow. If you have a duration estimate, write that next to the activity letter or name, as shown in Figure 4-14. For example, A = 10 means that the duration of Activity A is ten days, weeks, or other standard unit of time. Also be sure to put arrowheads on all arrows to signify the direction of the relationships.

2. Continue drawing the network diagram, working from left to right. Look for bursts and merges. A **burst** occurs when two or more activities follow a single node. A **merge** occurs when two or more nodes precede a single node.

An Introduction to Project Management, Third Edition

For example, in Figure 4-14, Node 1 is a burst because it goes into Nodes 2 and 3. Node 4 is a merge preceded by Nodes 2 and 3.

3. Continue drawing the AOA network diagram until all activities are included on the diagram.

4. As a rule of thumb, all arrowheads should face toward the right, and no arrows should cross on an AOA network diagram. You might need to redraw the diagram to make it look presentable.

Even though AOA network diagrams are generally easy to understand and create, a different method is more commonly used: the precedence diagramming method. The **precedence diagramming method (PDM)** is a network diagramming technique in which boxes represent activities. It is particularly useful for visualizing different types of time dependencies. AOA diagrams can only show the most common type of dependency, finish-to-start.

Figure 4-15 illustrates the types of dependencies that can occur among project activities, based on a Help screen from Project 2007. This screen shows that task A is the predecessor or "from" task and B is the successor or "to" task. After you determine the reason for a dependency between activities (mandatory, discretionary, or external), you must determine the type of dependency. Note that the terms "activity" and "task" are used interchangeably, as are "relationship" and "dependency." The four types of dependencies, or relationships, between activities include the following:

- *Finish-to-start:* A relationship in which the successor or "to" activity (Activity B) cannot start until the predecessor "from" activity" (Activity A) is finished. For example, you cannot provide training until after the training materials are available. Finish-to-start is the most common type of relationship, or dependency, and AOA network diagrams use only finish-to-start dependencies.

- *Start-to-start:* A relationship in which the successor activity cannot start until the predecessor activity starts. For example, as soon as you start a project review meeting, you can start documenting attendees, serving refreshments, taking minutes, and so on.

- *Finish-to-finish:* A relationship in which the successor activity cannot finish before the predecessor activity finishes. For example, quality control efforts cannot finish before production finishes, although the two activities can be performed at the same time.

- *Start-to-finish:* A relationship in which the successor activity cannot finish before the predecessor activity starts. This type of relationship is rarely used, but it is appropriate in some cases. For example, an organization might strive to stock raw materials just in time for the manufacturing process to begin. A delay in the start of the manufacturing process should delay completion of stocking the raw materials. Another example is when an employee cannot leave his/her current job until a replacement is found. Project 2007's Help screen provides the following example: The roof trusses for your construction project are built offsite. Two of the tasks in your project are "Truss delivery" and "Assemble roof." The "Assemble roof" task cannot be completed until the "Truss delivery" task begins.

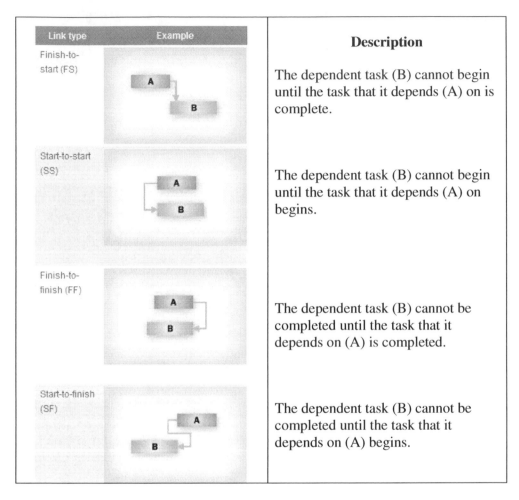

Link type	Example	Description
Finish-to-start (FS)		The dependent task (B) cannot begin until the task that it depends (A) on is complete.
Start-to-start (SS)		The dependent task (B) cannot begin until the task that it depends (A) on begins.
Finish-to-finish (FF)		The dependent task (B) cannot be completed until the task that it depends on (A) is completed.
Start-to-finish (SF)		The dependent task (B) cannot be completed until the task that it depends on (A) begins.

Figure 4-15. Task dependency types

Figure 4-16 illustrates Project X (shown originally in Figure 4-14) using the precedence diagramming method. Notice that the activities are placed inside boxes, which represent the nodes on this diagram. Arrows show the relationships between activities. For example, Activity D has a relationship of dependency with Activity A. This figure was created using Microsoft Project, which automatically places additional information inside each node. Each task box includes the start and finish date, labeled "Start" and "Finish"; the task ID number, labeled "ID"; the task's duration, labeled "Dur"; and the names of resources, if any, assigned to the task, labeled "Res." The border of the boxes for tasks on the critical path (discussed later in this section) appears automatically in red in the Microsoft Project network diagram view. In Figure 4-16, the boxes for critical tasks (A, C, E, F, and H) are shown in black. See Appendix A for detailed information on using Project 2010.

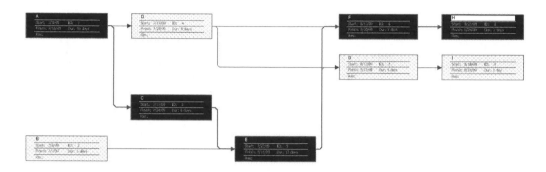

Figure 4-16. Precedence diagramming method network diagram for Project X

Although the AOA diagram might seem easier to understand, the precedence diagramming method is used more often than AOA network diagrams. Its main advantage is that it allows you to show different types of dependencies among tasks, whereas AOA network diagrams use only finish-to-start dependencies.

Kristin and her team reviewed all the project activities and determined which ones had dependencies. They also determined which tasks could be overlapped (or have "lead" time) and which needed some "lag" time, or a gap in time. See Appendix A for more information on lead and lag time. For example, they wanted to wait 30 days after holding the first supplier management course before holding the second one, which meant they needed to create a dependency with 30 days of lag time between the two courses. If the first class was held earlier or later than planned, the date for the second course would automatically adjust to follow it 30 days later. They entered the information into Microsoft Project to begin building a detailed Gantt chart for the project, as described later in this section. The Microsoft Project file would be integrated with their enterprise project management system to have all information in one place.

Estimating Activity Resources

Before you can estimate the duration for each activity, you must have a good idea of the quantity and type of resources (people, equipment, and materials) that will be assigned to each activity. It is important that the people who help determine what resources are necessary include people who have experience and expertise in similar projects and with the organization performing the project.

Important questions to answer in activity resource estimating include the following:

- How difficult will it be to do specific activities on this project?

- Is there anything unique in the project's scope statement that will affect resources?

- What is the organization's history in doing similar activities? Has the organization done similar tasks before? What level of personnel did the work?

- Does the organization have appropriate people, equipment, and materials available for performing the work? Are there any organizational policies that might affect the availability of resources?

- Does the organization need to acquire more resources to accomplish the work? Would it make sense to outsource some of the work? Will outsourcing increase or decrease the amount of resources needed and when they will be available?

It is important to thoroughly brainstorm and evaluate alternatives related to resources, especially on projects that involve people from multiple disciplines and companies. Because most projects involve many human resources and the majority of costs are for salaries and benefits, it is often effective to solicit ideas from different people and to address resource-related issues early in a project. The resource estimates should also be updated as more detailed information becomes available.

Sample Activity Resource Requirements

A key output of the resource estimating process is documentation of activity resource requirements. This list can take various formats. For the Just-In-Time Training project, Kristin met with her team, her sponsor, and the project steering committee, as needed, to discuss resource requirements for the project. They also discussed which training might be best to outsource, which would be best to perform with internal resources, and which should use both internal and external resources. They entered important resource information for each task in their enterprise project management software.

Figure 4-17 provides an example of one of the resource requirement entries for the activity described earlier in the WBS dictionary entry called "Administer survey."

Activity Resource Requirements
August 1

Project Name: Just-In-Time Training Project
WBS Item Number:3.1.1.1.2
WBS Item Name: Administer survey
Description: Internal members of our IT department will perform this task. The individuals must be knowledgeable in using our online survey software so they can enter the actual survey into this software. They must also know how to run a query to find the e-mail addresses of employees of grade level 52 or higher in the purchasing, accounting, engineering, information technology, sales, marketing, manufacturing, and human resource departments.

Figure 4-17. Sample activity resource requirements information

Estimating Activity Duration

After working with key stakeholders to define activities, determine their dependencies, and estimate their resources, the next process in project time management is to estimate the duration of activities. It is important to note that **duration** includes the actual amount of time spent working on an activity *plus* elapsed time. For example, even though it might take one workweek or five workdays to do the actual work, the duration estimate might be two weeks to allow extra time needed to obtain outside information or to allow for resource availability. Do not confuse duration with **effort**, which is the number of workdays or work hours required to complete a task. A duration estimate of one day could be based on eight hours of work or 80 hours of work. Duration relates to the time estimate, not the effort estimate. Of course, the two are related, so project team members must document their assumptions when creating duration estimates and update the estimates as the project progresses.

The outputs of activity duration estimating include updates to the activity attributes, if needed, and duration estimates for each activity. Duration estimates are provided as a discrete number, such as four weeks; as a range, such as three to five weeks; or as a three-point estimate. A **three-point estimate** is an estimate that includes an optimistic, most likely, and pessimistic estimate, such as three weeks, four weeks, and five weeks, respectively. The optimistic estimate is based on a best-case scenario, whereas the pessimistic estimate is based on a worst-case scenario. The most likely estimate, as it sounds, is an estimate based on a most likely or expected scenario.

A three-point estimate is required for performing PERT estimates. **Program Evaluation and Review Technique (PERT)** is a network analysis technique used to estimate project duration when there is a high degree of uncertainty about the individual activity duration estimates. By using the PERT weighted average for each activity duration estimate, the total project duration estimate accounts for the risk or uncertainty in the individual activity estimates. To use PERT, you calculate a weighted average for the duration estimate of each project activity using the following formula:

PERT weighted
    average = optimistic time + 4 x most likely time + pessimistic time
                                       6

Sample Activity Duration Estimates

Many project teams use one discrete estimate—the most likely estimate—to estimate activity durations. For example, Kristin's team could enter these discrete estimates into their enterprise project management system. If Kristin's project team used PERT to determine the schedule for the Just-In-Time Training project, they would have to collect numbers for the optimistic, most likely, and pessimistic duration estimates for each project activity. For example, suppose the person assigned to administer the survey for the supplier management training estimated that it would take two workdays to do this activity. Without using PERT, the duration estimate for that activity would be two workdays. Suppose an optimistic time estimate for this activity is one workday, and a pessimistic time estimate is nine workdays. Applying the PERT formula, you get the following:

PERT weighted average = 1 workdays + 4 x 2 workdays + 9 workdays
                                       6
                          = 3 workdays

Instead of using the most likely duration estimate of two workdays, the project team would use three workdays. The main advantage of PERT is that it attempts to address the risk associated with duration estimates. Because many projects exceed schedule estimates, PERT might help in developing schedules that are more realistic.

PERT also has disadvantages: It involves more work because it requires several duration estimates, and there are better probabilistic (based on probability) methods for assessing schedule risk, such as Monte Carlo simulations. To perform a Monte Carlo simulation, in addition to the three-point estimate, you also collect probabilistic information for each activity duration estimate. For example, Kristin would ask the person assigned to administer the survey for the supplier management training for an optimistic, pessimistic, and most likely estimate and the probability of completing that activity between the optimistic and most likely time estimates. For this project, however, Kristin and her team decided to enter realistic discrete estimates for each activity instead of using PERT or a Monte Carlo simulation. She stressed that people who would do the work should provide the estimate, and they should have 50 percent confidence in meeting each estimate. If some tasks took longer, some took less time, and some were exactly on target, they should still meet their overall schedule.

Developing the Project Schedule

Schedule development uses the results of all the preceding project time management processes to determine the start and end dates of project activities and of the entire project. There are often several iterations of all the project time management processes before a project schedule is finalized. The ultimate goal of schedule development is to create a realistic project schedule that provides a basis for monitoring project progress for the time dimension of the project. Project managers must lead their teams in creating realistic schedules and then following them during project execution.

What Went Right?

The International Project Management Association (IPMA) provides annual awards for Project Excellence (PE). In 2008, Foster Wheeler won the award for designing and building the Lomellina 2 waste-to-energy plant, which annually processes 180,000 tons of refuse-derived fuel and generates 25 megawatts of electricity. They used experience from the first project and worked closely with their customer to develop and follow an aggressive schedule for the plant. CEO Marco Moresco said, "We are indeed extremely pleased to be the 2008 winner of this prestigious international award. The Lomellina 2 project is one of many successful Foster Wheeler projects that demonstrate the extent to which world-class project management tools and procedures are deeply embedded in our organization worldwide. The Lomellina 2 team delivered a high quality facility in a very challenging schedule of 26 months from kick-off to commercial operation and we are proud that the Lomellina 2 team has achieved international recognition for their achievements."[4]

The main output of the schedule development process is the project schedule, which is often displayed in the form of a Gantt chart.

Gantt charts provide a standard format for displaying project schedule information by listing project activities and their corresponding start and finish dates in a calendar format. Figure 4-18 shows a simple Gantt chart for Project X, described earlier, created with Microsoft Project. Recall that this example only uses finish-to-start dependencies and no lead or lag time. See Appendix A for examples and instructions for using other types of dependencies.

Recall that the activities on the Gantt chart should coincide with the activities on the WBS, the activity list, and the milestone list. Before showing a Gantt chart for the Just-In-Time Training project, it is important to explain a fundamental concept that assists project teams in developing and meeting project schedules: critical path analysis.

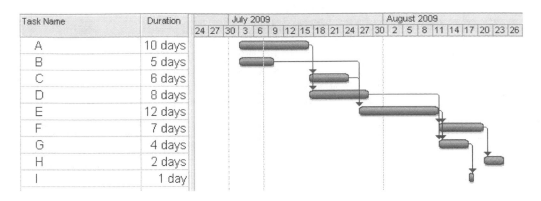

Task Name	Duration
A	10 days
B	5 days
C	6 days
D	8 days
E	12 days
F	7 days
G	4 days
H	2 days
I	1 day

Figure 4-18. Gantt chart for Project X

Critical Path Analysis

Many projects fail to meet schedule expectations. **Critical path method (CPM)**—also called **critical path analysis**—is a network diagramming technique used to predict total project duration. This important tool will help you combat project schedule overruns. A **critical path** for a project is the series of activities that determine the *earliest* time by which the project can be completed. It is the *longest* path through the network diagram and has the least amount of slack or float. **Slack** or **float** is the amount of time an activity may be delayed without delaying a succeeding activity or the project finish date. There are normally several tasks done in parallel on projects, and most projects have multiple paths through a network diagram. The longest path or the path containing the critical tasks is what is driving the completion date for the project. Remember that you are not finished with the project until you have finished *all* the tasks.

Calculating the Critical Path

To find the critical path for a project, you must first develop a good network diagram as described earlier, which requires a good activity list based on the WBS. To create a network diagram, you must determine the dependencies of activities and also estimate their durations. Calculating the critical path involves adding the durations for all activities on each path through the network diagram. The longest path is the critical path.

Figure 4-19 shows the AOA network diagram for Project X again. Note that you can use either the AOA or the precedence diagramming method to determine the critical path on projects. Figure 4-19 shows all the paths—a total of six—through the network diagram. Note that each path starts at the first node (1) and ends at the last node (7) on the AOA network diagram. This figure also shows the length or total duration of each path through the network diagram. These lengths are computed by adding the durations of each activity on the path. Because path A-C-E-F-H at 37 days has the longest duration, it is the critical path for the project.

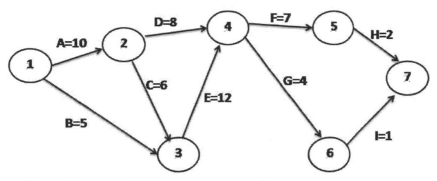

Note: Assume all durations are in days.

Path 1: A-D-F-H   Length = 10+8+7+2 =27
Path 2: A-D-G-I   Length = 10+8+4+1=23
Path 3: A-C-E-F-H   Length = 10+6+12+7+2=37
Path 4: A-C-E-G-I   Length = 10+6+12+4+1 = 33
Path 5: B-E-F-H   Length = 5+12+7+2=26
Path 6: B-E-G-I   Length = 5+12+4+1=22

Figure 4-19. Critical path calculation for Project X

On a humorous note, Figure 4-20 shows what looks like a network diagram from a cartoon illustrating how viruses travel.

Figure 4-20. Another use of a network diagram (www.xkcd.com)

What does the critical path really mean? *The critical path shows the shortest time in which a project can be completed.* If one or more of the activities on the critical path takes longer than planned, the whole project schedule will slip *unless* the project manager takes corrective action.

Project teams can be creative in managing the critical path. For example, Joan Knutson, a well-known author and speaker in the project management field, often describes how a gorilla helped Apple computer complete a project on time. Team members worked in an area with cubicles, and whoever was in charge of a task currently on the critical path had a big, stuffed gorilla on top of his or her cubicle. Everyone knew that that person was under the most time pressure, so they tried not to distract him or her. When a critical task was completed, the person in charge of the next critical task received the gorilla.

Growing Grass Can Be on the Critical Path

People are often confused about what the critical path is for a project or what it really means. Some people think the critical path includes the most critical activities. However, the critical path focuses on the time dimension of a project. The fact that its name includes the word "critical" does *not* mean that it includes all critical activities in terms of scope, quality, resources, or other areas. For example, Frank Addeman, executive project director at Walt Disney Imagineering, explained in a keynote address at the May 2000 PMI-ISSIG Professional Development Seminar that growing grass was on the critical path for building Disney's Animal Kingdom theme park. This 500-acre park required special grass for its animal inhabitants, and some of the grass took years to grow. The project manager did not assign his top people to watching grass grow! He did use this information, however, to delay the start of other more expensive activities to make effective use of resources. Another misconception is that the critical path is the shortest path through the network diagram. In areas such as transportation modeling, multiple network diagrams are drawn in which identifying the shortest path is the goal. For a project, however, each task or activity must be done in order to complete the project. It is not a matter of choosing the shortest path.

Other aspects of critical path analysis may cause confusion. Can there be more than one critical path on a project? Does the critical path ever change? In the Project X example, suppose that Activity G has a duration estimate of eight days instead of four days. This new duration estimate would make the length of Path 4 equal to 37days. Now the project has two paths (paths 3 and 4) of the longest duration, so there are two critical paths. Therefore, there *can* be more than one critical path on a project. Project managers should closely monitor performance of activities on the critical path to avoid late project completion. If there is more than one critical path, project managers must keep their eyes on all of them.

The critical path on a project can change as the project progresses. For example, suppose Activity B from Figure 4-19 has problems and ends up taking 17 days instead of 5 to finish. Assuming no other task durations change, path 5, B-E-F-H, becomes the new critical path with a duration of 38. Therefore, the critical path can change on a project.

Using Critical Path Analysis to Make Schedule Trade-Offs

It is important to know what the critical path is throughout the life of a project so that the project manager can make trade-offs. If the project manager knows that one of the tasks on the critical path is behind schedule, he needs to decide what to do about it. Should the schedule be renegotiated with stakeholders? Should more resources be allocated to other items on the critical path to make up for that time? Is it okay if the project finishes behind schedule? By keeping track of the critical path, the project manager and his team take a proactive role in managing the project schedule.

It is common for stakeholders to want to shorten a project schedule estimate. Your team may have done its best to develop a project schedule by defining activities, determining sequencing, and estimating resources and durations for each activity. The results of this work may have shown that your team needs 10 months to complete the project. Your sponsor might ask if the project can be done in eight or nine months. Rarely do people ask you to take longer than you suggested. By knowing the critical path, the project manager and his team can use several duration compression techniques to shorten the project schedule. One technique is to reduce the duration of activities on the critical path. The project manager can shorten the duration of critical path activities by allocating more resources to those activities or by changing their scope.

Crashing is a technique for making cost and schedule trade-offs to obtain the greatest amount of schedule compression for the least incremental cost. For example, suppose one of the items on the critical path for the Just-In-Time Training project was to design and develop an advanced course for supplier management. If this task is yet to be done and was originally estimated to take four weeks based on key people working 25 percent of their time on this task, Kristin could suggest that people work 50 percent of their time to finish the task faster. This change might cost some additional money if people had to work paid overtime, but it could shorten the project end date by two weeks. By focusing on tasks on the critical path that could be finished more quickly for either no extra cost or a small cost, the project schedule could be shortened. The main advantage of crashing is shortening the time it takes to finish a project. The main disadvantage of crashing is that it often increases total project costs. If used too often, however, crashing can affect staff negatively by lowering morale or causing burnout.

Another technique for shortening a project schedule is fast tracking. **Fast tracking** involves doing activities in parallel that you would normally do in sequence. For example, Kristin's project team may have planned not to start any of the work on the negotiating skills training until they finished most of the work on the supplier management training. Instead, they could consider performing several of these tasks in parallel to shorten the schedule. As with crashing, the main advantage of fast tracking is that it can shorten the time it takes to finish a project. The main disadvantage of fast tracking is that it can end up lengthening the project schedule, because starting some tasks too soon often increases project risk and results in rework.

Importance of Updating Critical Path Data

In addition to finding the critical path at the beginning of a project, it is important to update the schedule with actual data. After the project team completes activities, the project manager should document the actual duration of each of those activities. He or she should also document revised estimates for activities in progress or yet to be started. These revisions often cause a project's critical path to change, resulting in a new estimated completion date for the project. Again, proactive project managers and their teams stay on top of changes so that they can make informed decisions and keep stakeholders informed of, and involved in, major project decisions.

Critical Chain Scheduling

Another more advanced scheduling technique that addresses the challenge of meeting or beating project finish dates is an application of the Theory of Constraints called critical chain scheduling. The **Theory of Constraints (TOC)** is a management philosophy developed by Eliyahu M. Goldratt and discussed in his books *The Goal* and *Critical Chain*.[5] The Theory of Constraints is based on the fact that, like a chain with its weakest link, any complex system at any point in time often has only one aspect or constraint that limits its ability to achieve more of its goal. For the system to attain any significant improvements, that constraint must be identified, and the whole system must be managed with it in mind. **Critical chain scheduling** is a method of scheduling that considers limited resources when creating a project schedule and includes buffers to protect the project completion date.

An important concept in critical chain scheduling is the availability of scarce resources. Some projects cannot be done unless a particular resource is available to work on one or several tasks. For example, if a television station wants to produce a show centered on a particular celebrity, it must first check the availability of that celebrity. As another example, if a particular piece of equipment is needed full time to complete each of two tasks that were originally planned to occur simultaneously, critical chain scheduling acknowledges that you must either delay one of those tasks until the equipment is available or find another piece of equipment in order to meet the schedule. Other important concepts related to critical chain scheduling include multitasking and time buffers.

Multitasking occurs when a resource works on more than one task at a time. This situation occurs frequently on projects. People are assigned to multiple tasks within the same project or different tasks on multiple projects. For example, suppose someone is working on three different tasks, Task 1, Task 2, and Task 3, for three different projects, and each task takes 10 days to complete. If the person did not multitask, and instead completed each task sequentially, starting with Task 1, then Task 1 would be completed after day 10, Task 2 would be completed after day 20, and Task 3 would be completed after day 30, as shown in Figure 4-21. However, because many people in this situation try to please all three people who need their tasks completed, they often work on the first task for some time, then the second, then the third, then go back to finish the first task, then the second, and then the third, as shown in Figure 4-22. In this example, the tasks were all half-done one at a time, then completed one at a time. Task 1 is now completed at the end of day 20 instead of day 10, Task 2 is completed at the end of day 25 instead of day 20, and Task 3 is still completed on day 30. This example illustrates how multitasking can delay task completions. Multitasking also often involves wasted setup time, which increases total duration.

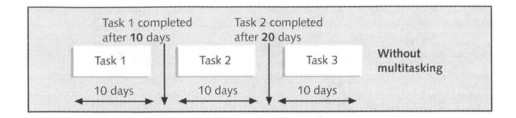

Figure 4-21. Three tasks without multitasking (Schwalbe, Information Technology Project Management, Sixth Edition, 2010)

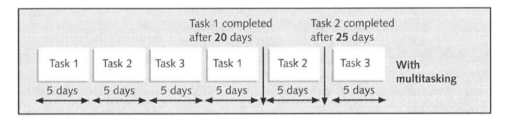

Figure 4-22. Three tasks with multitasking (Schwalbe, Information Technology Project Management, Sixth Edition, 2010)

Critical chain scheduling assumes that resources do not multitask or at least minimize multitasking. Someone should not be assigned to two tasks simultaneously on the same project when critical chain scheduling is in effect. Likewise, critical chain theory suggests that projects be prioritized so people working on more than one project at a time know which tasks take priority. Preventing multitasking avoids resource conflicts and wasted setup time caused by shifting between multiple tasks over time. In fact, a 2006 cover story for Time Magazine discussed the negative effects of multi-tasking, especially with the advent of new technologies. "Decades of research (not to mention common sense) indicate that the quality of one's output and depth of thought deteriorate as one attends to ever more tasks. Some are concerned about the disappearance of mental downtime to relax and reflect."[6]

An essential concept to improving project finish dates with critical chain scheduling is to change the way people make task estimates. Many people add a safety or **buffer**, which is additional time to complete a task, to an estimate to account for various factors. These factors include the negative effects of multitasking, distractions and interruptions, fear that estimates will be reduced, Murphy's Law, etc. **Murphy's Law** states that if something can go wrong, it will. Critical chain scheduling removes buffers from individual tasks and instead creates a **project buffer**, which is additional time added before the project's due date. Critical chain scheduling also protects tasks on the critical chain from being delayed by using **feeding buffers**, which are additional time added before tasks on the critical chain that are preceded by non-critical-path tasks.

Figure 4-23 provides an example of a network diagram constructed using critical chain scheduling. Note that the critical chain accounts for a limited resource, X, and the schedule includes use of feeding buffers and a project buffer in the network diagram. The tasks marked with an X are part of the critical chain, which can be interpreted as being the critical path using this technique. The task estimates in critical chain scheduling should be shorter than traditional estimates because they do not include their own buffers. Not having task buffers should mean less occurrence of **Parkinson's Law**, which states that work expands to fill the time allowed. In other words, if you included a buffer in a task estimate and you did not need it, you would still use it. The feeding and project buffers protect the date that really needs to be met—the project completion date.

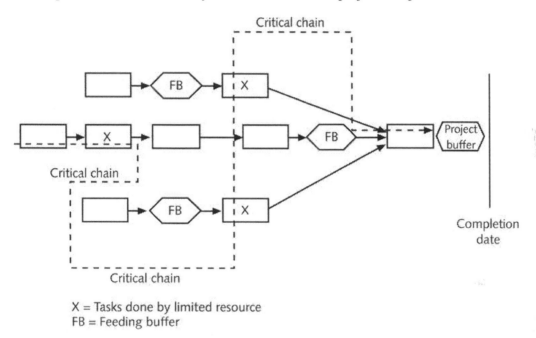

X = Tasks done by limited resource
FB = Feeding buffer

Figure 4-23. Example of critical chain scheduling[7]

As you can see, critical chain scheduling is a fairly complicated yet powerful tool that involves critical path analysis, resource constraints, and changes in how task estimates are made in terms of buffers. Several organizations have reported successes with this approach. Some consider critical chain scheduling one of the most important new concepts in the field of project management.

Sample Project Schedule

Kristin worked with her team to define project activities, determine activity sequencing, describe activity resources, estimate activity durations, and make schedule trade-offs to perform all of the work required for the project within one year, as desired by the project sponsor.

Figure 4-24 provides part of the resulting Gantt chart the team will use to guide their project schedule. To fit the information on one page, the executing tasks have been collapsed, which means that you cannot see the tasks under that category but you can expand them on the computer screen. Notice that the items in the Task Name column come from the WBS, and duration estimates are entered in the "Duration" column. Also notice the flow between the initiating, planning, executing, monitoring and controlling, and closing tasks. Dependencies between activities are shown by the entries in the "Predecessors" column and the arrows connecting symbols on the Gantt chart. You can download and review the entire Microsoft Project file from the companion Web site for this text and learn how to use Project 2010 by reading the section of Appendix A.

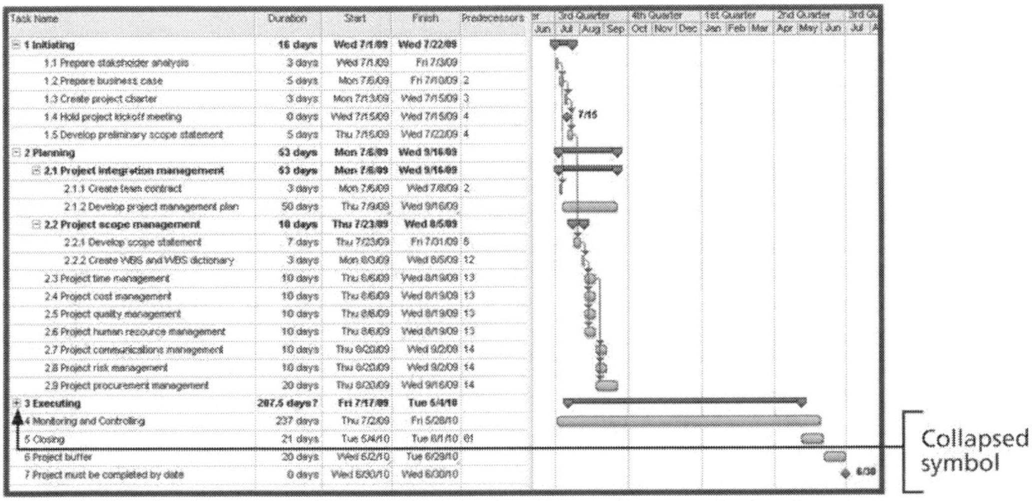

Figure 4-24. Sample project schedule

Figure 4-25 shows another view of the Gantt chart for the Just-In-Time Training project, showing all of the summary tasks (represented by thick black lines) and milestones (represented by black diamonds). Note that the milestones include the schedule items that the project manager and the project steering committee would be most interested in monitoring and controlling to make sure the project stays on schedule. You will learn more about monitoring and controlling projects in Chapter 7.

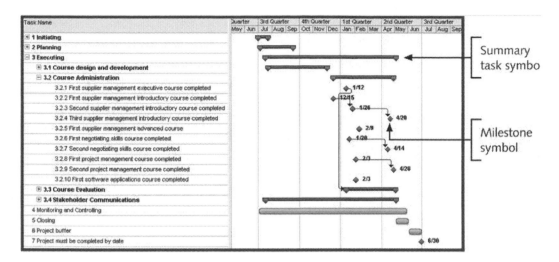

Figure 4-25. Sample Gantt chart showing summary tasks and milestones

By using project management software like Project 2010, you can easily see different levels of detail in the schedule information. Also note that Kristin decided to include a project buffer to account for unexpected factors. This buffer (shown as the second to last item in the Task Name column in Figure 4-24) will help ensure that the project is completed on time. Kristin has learned from past projects that no matter how well you try to schedule everything, it can still be a challenge to finish on time without a mad rush at the end. For this reason, she decided to include a 20-day project buffer, which the project steering committee thought was an excellent idea.

PROJECT COST MANAGEMENT PLANNING TASKS

Project cost management includes the processes required to ensure that a project team completes a project within an approved budget. The main planning tasks performed as part of project cost management are estimating costs and determining the budget. Estimating costs involves developing an approximation or estimate of the costs of the resources needed to complete a project. Cost budgeting involves allocating the overall cost estimate to individual tasks over time to establish a baseline for measuring performance. The main documents produced include a cost estimate and a cost performance baseline.

Estimating Costs

Project teams normally prepare cost estimates at various stages of a project, and these estimates should be fine-tuned as time progresses. Before management approves a project, someone must develop a rough estimate of what it will cost to complete the project. After the project manager and team are assigned to a project, they normally prepare a more detailed cost estimate. If this estimate is substantially different from the initial budgeted amount, the project manager should negotiate with the project sponsor to increase or decrease the budget, or to make changes to the scope or time goals to meet cost constraints. As more detailed information becomes available, the project team should update the cost estimates and continue negotiating with the sponsor to meet project goals.

In addition to creating cost estimates, it is also important to provide supporting details for the estimates. The supporting details include the ground rules and assumptions used in creating the estimate, the description of the project (including references to the scope statement, WBS, and WBS dictionary) that was used as a basis for the estimate, and details on the cost estimation tools and techniques used to create the estimate. These supporting details should make it easier to prepare an updated estimate or similar estimate as needed.

A large percentage of total project costs are often labor costs. Many organizations estimate the number of people or hours they need for major parts of a project over the life cycle of the project. They also determine the labor rate to apply based on the category of labor. It is important to work with people in the organization's finance and accounting departments to determine these labor rates and apply the appropriate amounts for benefits and overhead so that total labor costs are included in the estimate.

Cost Estimation Tools and Techniques

As you can imagine, developing a good cost estimate is difficult. Fortunately, several tools and techniques are available to assist in creating them. Three commonly used techniques for creating estimates include the following:

- **Analogous estimates**, also called **top-down estimates**, use the actual cost of a previous, similar project as the basis for estimating the cost of the current project. This technique requires a good deal of expert judgment and is generally less costly than others are, but it can also be less accurate. Analogous estimates are most reliable when the previous projects are similar in fact, not just in appearance.

- **Bottom-up estimates** involve estimating individual activities and summing them to get a project total. The size of the individual activities and the experience of the estimators drive the accuracy of the estimates. If a detailed WBS is available for a project, the project manager could have each person responsible for a work package develop his own cost estimate for that particular work package. The project manager would then add all of the cost estimates to create cost estimates for each higher-level WBS item and finally for the entire project. This approach can increase the accuracy of the cost estimate, but it can also be time intensive and, therefore, expensive to develop.

- **Parametric modeling** uses project characteristics (parameters) in a mathematical model to estimate project costs. A parametric model might provide an estimate of $5 per square foot for flooring, for example, based on the type of flooring, total square feet required, and location of the job. Parametric models are most reliable when the historical information used to create the model is accurate, the parameters are readily quantifiable, and the model is flexible in terms of the size of the project.

Sometimes it makes sense to use more than one approach for creating a cost estimate, and sometimes more than one approach is used on different parts of a project. For example, a project team might develop an analogous estimate and a parametric model for an entire project or a key part of the project, such as software development, and compare the results. If the estimates were far apart, the team would need to collect more information to develop a better estimate.

Sample Cost Estimate

Every cost estimate is unique, just as every project is unique. This section includes a step-by-step approach for developing the major parts of the cost estimate for the Just-In-Time Training project. Of course, this example is much shorter and simpler than a real cost estimate would be, but it illustrates an easy-to-follow process and uses several of the tools and techniques described earlier.

It is important to first clarify and document the ground rules and assumptions for the estimate. For the Just-In-Time Training project cost estimate, these include the following:

- This project was preceded by a project that provided valuable information, such as the training taken in the last two years by all internal employees, the cost of all training, the process for approving/assigning training, the evaluation of the training by participants, what training employees would need in the next two years, how they would like to take the training (that is, instructor-led in-house; instructor-led through a local college, university, or training company; or online).

- There is a WBS for the project, as described earlier. The level 2 and some of the level 3 categories are shown as follows:

    1. Initiating

    2. Planning

    3. Executing

        3.1 Course design and development

        3.2 Course administration

        3.3 Course evaluation

        3.4 Stakeholder communications

    4. Monitoring and controlling

    5. Closing

- Costs must be estimated by WBS and by month. The project manager will report progress on the project using earned value analysis, which requires this type of estimate.

An Introduction to Project Management, Third Edition

- Costs will be provided in U.S. dollars. Because the project length is one year, discounted cash flows are not needed.

- There will be a project manager who spends three-quarters of her time on the project, and three core team members assigned to the project half-time. Two of the team members will be from the training department and one will be from the supplier management department. Additional internal resources from various departments will support the project as needed and charge their time to the project.

- The project steering committee members' time is not directly charged to the project. Internal labor costs include a 40 percent overhead charge as well as a 30 percent benefits charge. For example, if the direct labor rate is $30/hour, the burdened rate, or the rate including benefits and overhead, is $30*1.3*1.4=$55 (rounded to the nearest whole-dollar amount).

- The project cost estimate does not include any hardware, software, or facilities that will be used to develop and administer the courses.

- The project team should purchase training materials and related products and services from qualified suppliers to take advantage of their expertise and to reduce internal costs. Estimates are based on analogous projects and will be updated as contracts are awarded.

- Labor costs for employees to cover their salaries while they attend training classes are not included in this estimate.

- Because several risks are related to this project, the estimate includes 10 percent of the total estimate as reserves.

- A computer model of the project estimate will be developed to facilitate the changing of inputs, such as labor rates or the number of labor hours for various activities.

Fortunately, the project team can easily access cost estimates and actual information from similar projects. A great deal of information is available from the Phase I project, and the team can talk to supplier personnel from the past project to help them develop the estimate.

Because the estimate must be provided by WBS monthly, Kristin and her team reviewed the draft of the project schedule and made further assumptions. They decided first to estimate the cost of each WBS task and then determine when the work would be performed, even though costs might be incurred at times other than when the work was actually performed. Their budget expert had approved this approach for the estimate. Further assumptions and information for estimating the costs for each WBS category are as follows:

1. *Initiating*: The team used the actual labor costs charged to the project for project initiation activities.

2. *Planning*: The team used actual labor costs to date and added the projected hours and costs per hour to develop this part of the estimate.

3. *Executing*:

    3.1 *Course design and development:* The team used labor hour and rate estimates for internal and external staff, plus estimates for purchasing existing course materials for each course (that is, supplier management, negotiating skills, project management, and software applications). Some of the purchased costs were based on the number of students using the materials each year. The majority of project costs should be applied to this category.

    3.2 *Course administration:* Estimates were made based on the number of courses and number of people expected to take each course using various delivery methods (that is, instructor-led, CD-ROM, Web-based).

    3.3 *Course evaluation:* The team estimated labor hours and rates.

    3.4 *Stakeholder communications:* The team estimated labor hours and rates.

4. *Monitoring and controlling:* The team estimated labor hours and rates.

5. *Closing:* The team estimated labor hours and rates.

6. *Reserves:* As directed, reserved costs were estimated at 10 percent of the total estimate.

The project team developed a cost model using the preceding information. Figure 4-26 shows a spreadsheet that summarizes the costs by WBS based on that information. There are columns for entering the number of labor hours and the costs per hour. Several tasks are estimated using this approach. There are also some short comments within the estimate, such as reserves being 10 percent of the total estimate. With this computerized model, you can easily change input variables, such as number of hours or cost per hour, to revise the estimate.

WBS Categories	Internal Labor	S/hour	Internal $ Total	External Labor	S/hour	External $ Total	Total Labor	Non-labor $	Total Cost
1. Initiating	200	$ 65	$ 13,000			$ -	$ 13,000		$ 13,000
2. Planning	600	$ 60	$ 36,000			$ -	$ 36,000		$ 36,000
3. Executing			$ -			$ -	$ -		$ -
3.1 Course design and development			$ -			$ -	$ -		$ -
3.1.1 Supplier management training	600	$ 60	$ 36,000	600	$ 150	$90,000	$ 126,000	$ 100,000	$ 226,000
3.1.2 Negotiating skills training	300	$ 55	$ 16,500	300	$ 150	$45,000	$ 61,500	$ 50,000	$ 111,500
3.1.3 Project management training	400	$ 60	$ 24,000	400	$ 150	$60,000	$ 84,000	$ 50,000	$ 134,000
3.1.4 Software applications training	400	$ 60	$ 24,000	400	$ 150	$60,000	$ 84,000	$ 50,000	$ 134,000
3.2 Course administration	400	$ 55	$ 22,000	300	$ 250	$75,000	$ 97,000	$ 80,000	$ 177,000
3.3. Course evaluation	300	$ 55	$ 16,500			$ -	$ 16,500		$ 16,500
3.4 Stakeholder communications	300	$ 55	$ 16,500			$ -	$ 16,500		$ 16,500
4. Monitoring and Controlling	500	$ 55	$ 27,500			$ -	$ 27,500		$ 27,500
5. Closing	200	$ 55	$ 11,000			$ -	$ 11,000		$ 11,000
Subtotal									$ 903,000
Reserves			$ -			$ -	$ -		90,300.0
Total	4,200		243,000	2,000		330,000	573,000	330,000	$ 993,300

Assumptions

Internal labor rates include benefits and overhead. Average hourly rates are based on skill levels and departments of stakeholders.

External labor rates are based on historical averages; may change as contracts are awarded.

Non-labor costs include purchasing licenses for using training materials, books, CD/ROMs, travel expenses, etc.

Non-labor costs may change as contracts are awarded.

Reserves are calculated by taking 10% of the total estimate.

Figure 4-26. Sample cost estimate

It is very important to have several people review the project cost estimate, including the ground rules and assumptions. It is also helpful to analyze the total dollar value as well as the percentage of the total amount for each major WBS category. For example, a senior executive could quickly look at the Just-In-Time Training project cost estimate and decide whether the costs are reasonable and whether the assumptions are well documented. In this case, Global Construction had budgeted $1 million for the project, so the estimate was right in line with that amount. The WBS level 2 and 3 tasks also seem to be at appropriate percentages of the total cost based on similar past projects. In some cases, a project team might also be asked to provide a range estimate for each task instead of one discrete amount.

After the total cost estimate is approved, Kristin's team can then allocate costs for each month based on the project schedule and when costs will be incurred. Many organizations also require that the estimated costs be allocated into certain budget categories, such as compensation or travel.

Cost Budgeting

Project cost budgeting involves allocating the project cost estimate to tasks over time. These tasks are based on the work breakdown structure for the project. The WBS, therefore, is a required input to the cost budgeting process. Likewise, the project scope statement, WBS dictionary, activity cost estimates and supporting detail, project schedule, and other plans provide useful information for cost budgeting.

The main goal of the cost budgeting process is to produce a cost performance baseline (or simply cost baseline). A **cost performance baseline** is a time-phased budget that project managers use to measure and monitor cost performance. Estimating costs for each major project activity over time provides project managers and top management with a foundation for project cost control using earned value management, as described in Chapter 7. See the *Brief Guide to Microsoft Project 2010* in Appendix A for information on using Project 2010 for cost control.

Sample Cost Performance Baseline

The Just-In-Time Training project team used the cost estimate from Figure 4-26 along with the project schedule and other information to allocate costs for each month. Figure 4-27 provides an example of a cost performance baseline for this project. Again, it is important for the team to document the assumptions they made when developing the cost performance baseline and have several experts review it. The cost performance baseline should also be updated as more information becomes available.

						Month							
	1	2	3	4	5	6	7	8	9	10	11	12	Total Cost
WBS Categories													
1. Initiating	13,000												$ 13,000
2. Planning	6,000	16,000	8,000	1,000	1,000	1,000	1,000	1,000	1,000				$ 36,000
3. Executing			-			-	/						$ -
3.1 Course design and development			-			-	-						$ -
3.1.1 Supplier management training			5,000	73,667	73,667	73,667							$226,000
3.1.2 Negotiating skills training			5,000	35,500	35,500	35,500							$111,500
3.1.3 Project management training			5,000	43,000	43,000	43,000							$134,000
3.1.4 Software applications training			5,000	43,000	43,000	43,000							$134,000
3.2 Course administration						17,000	53,333	53,333	53,333				$177,000
3.3.Course evaluation							3,000	3,000	3,000	7,500			$ 16,500
3.4 Stakeholder communications		1,500	1,500	1,500	1,500	1,500	1,500	1,500	1,500	1,500	1,500	1,500	$ 16,500
4. Monitoring and Controlling	1,000	2,000	2,000	2,000	3,000	3,500	3,000	3,000	2,000	3,000	2,000	1,000	$ 27,500
5. Closing											8,000	3,000	$ 11,000
Subtotal													$903,000
Reserves*			-			-	-					90,300	$ 90,300
Total	20,000	19,500	31,500	199,667	200,667	218,167	61,833	61,833	60,833	12,000	11,500	95,800	993,300

*Reserves are all entered in month 12

Figure 4-27. Sample cost performance baseline

CASE WRAP-UP

Kristin learned a lot by leading her team during the planning phase of the Just-In-Time Training project. She did her best to get key stakeholders involved, including those who had little experience in planning. She could see that some people jumped to the planning details right away while others wanted to do as little planning as possible. She continued to consult members of the project steering committee for their advice, especially in helping everyone see how crucial it was to understand and document the scope, time, and cost of the project to provide a good baseline for measuring progress.

CHAPTER SUMMARY

Successful project managers know how important it is to develop, refine, and follow plans to meet project goals. It is important to remember that the main purpose of project plans is to guide project execution. Planning is done in all nine project management knowledge areas. This chapter summarizes the planning tasks and outputs for integration, scope, time, and cost management.

Planning tasks for integration management include developing a team contract and a project management plan. Samples of these documents are provided for the Just-In-Time Training project.

Planning tasks for scope management include creating a requirements management plan, a requirements traceability matrix, a scope statement, a WBS, and a WBS dictionary. Samples of these documents are provided for the Just-In-Time Training project.

Planning tasks for time management include developing a project schedule by creating an activity list and attributes, a milestone list, network diagrams, activity resource requirements, and activity duration estimates. Samples of these documents are provided for the Just-In-Time Training project. It is also important to understand critical path analysis to make schedule trade-off decisions. Critical chain scheduling can also help in scheduling when there are scarce resources involved in a project.

Planning tasks for cost management include developing a project cost estimate and a cost performance baseline. Samples of these documents are provided for the Just-In-Time Training project.

QUICK QUIZ

1. What can project teams create to help promote teamwork and clarify team communications?

   A. a project Web site

   B. a team-building plan

   C. a team roster

   D. a team contract

2. The main purpose of project planning is to:

   A. obtain funding for the project

   B. guide project execution

   C. clarify roles and responsibilities

   D. keep senior managers informed

3. Project teams develop a _____ to coordinate all other project plans.

   A. strategic plan

   B. project management plan

   C. master plan

   D. project Web site

4. A _____ is a deliverable-oriented grouping of the work involved in a project that defines the total scope of the project.

   A. contract

   B. Gantt chart

   C. WBS

   D. network diagram

5.   A _____ is a task at the lowest level of the WBS that represents the level of work that the project manager uses to monitor and control the project.

A. WBS dictionary

B. budget item

C. line item

D. work package

6.   What is the first step in planning a project schedule?

A. developing a budget

B. developing an activity list

C. assigning resources to the project

D. determining activity sequencing

7.   What is the most common type of dependency between activities?

A. finish-to-start

B. start-to-finish

C. start-to-start

D. finish-to-finish

8.   The _____ method is a network diagramming technique used to predict total project duration.

A. PERT

B. Gantt chart

C. critical path

D. crashing

9.   What cost estimating technique uses project characteristics in a mathematical model to estimate project costs?

A. parametric modeling

B. fast-track estimating

C. analogous estimating

D. critical chain

10.   A _____ is a time-phased budget that project managers use to measure and monitor cost performance.

   A. cost performance baseline

   B. cost estimate

   C. life-cycle budget

   D. cash flow analysis

Quick Quiz Answers

1. D; 2. B; 3. B; 4. C; 5. D; 6. B; 7. A; 8. C; 9. A; 10. A

DISCUSSION QUESTIONS

1.   Why does having good plans help project teams during project execution? Why is it difficult to develop good plans?

2.   What are the main planning tasks performed as part of project integration management? What are the main documents created, and what are some of their main contents?

3.   What are the main planning tasks performed as part of project scope management? What are some approaches for creating a WBS? Why is it important to develop a good WBS? What do you think about the scope planning documents prepared by the Just-In-Time Training project team? Do they seem too broad or too detailed in certain areas?

4.   What are the main planning tasks performed as part of project time management? What is the critical path for a project, and why is it important to know which tasks are on the critical path? When should you consider critical chain scheduling?

5.   What are the main planning tasks performed as part of project cost management? What is the difference between a cost estimate and a cost performance baseline? Why is it important to have clear ground rules and assumptions for a cost estimate?

EXERCISES

1. Find an example of a large project that took more than a year to complete, such as a major construction project. You can ask people at your college, university, or work about a recent project, such as a major fund raising campaign, information systems installation, or building project. You can also find information about projects online such as the Big Dig in Boston (www.masspike.com/bigdig), the Patronas Twin Towers in Malaysia, and many other building projects (www.greatbuildings.com). Describe some of the tasks done in planning the integration, scope, time, and cost aspects of the project. Write a one-page paper or prepare a short presentation summarizing your findings.

2. Review the sample scope statement in Figure 4-6. Assume you are responsible for planning and then managing the course development for the introductory supplier management course. What additional information would you want to know to develop a good schedule and cost estimate, and why? Write a one-page paper or prepare a short presentation summarizing your response.

3. Create a WBS for building a new house by using the mind mapping approach. Assume that the WBS Level 2 categories include managing the project, finding property, securing a loan, designing the entire home, building the entire home, and providing landscaping and external items, including a hot tub and swimming pool. Break at least two Level 2 items down to Level 4. Try to use MindManager software from www.mindjet.com, if possible. You can also create the mind map by hand or using similar mind-mapping software.

4. Consider Figure 4-28. All duration estimates are in days, and the network proceeds from Node 1 to Node 9. (*Note*: Instructors should see the Instructor's Manual for similar exercises.)

Activity	Initial node	Final node	Duration estimate
A	1	2	2
B	2	3	2
C	2	4	3
D	2	5	4
E	3	6	2
F	4	6	3
G	5	7	6
H	6	8	2
I	6	7	5
J	7	8	1
K	8	9	2

Figure 4-28. Network diagram data for a small project

a. Draw an AOA network diagram representing the project. Put the node numbers in circles and draw arrows from node to node, labeling each arrow with the activity letter and estimated duration.

b. Identify all the paths on the network diagram and note how long they are, using Figure 4-19 as a guide for how to represent each path.

c. What is the critical path for this project, and how long is it?

d. What is the shortest possible time it will take to complete this project?

e. Enter the information into Project 2010. See the *Brief Guide to Microsoft Project 2010* in Appendix A for detailed instructions on using this software. View the network diagram and task schedule table to see the critical path and float or slack for each activity. Print the Gantt chart and network diagram views and the task schedule table. Write a short paper that interprets this information for someone unfamiliar with project time management.

5. Create a cost estimate/model for redecorating a room using spreadsheet software. Assume you have one month and $5,000 to spend. Develop a WBS for the project and create a cost model based on your WBS. Document the assumptions you made in preparing the estimate and provide explanations for key numbers.

TEAM PROJECTS

1.	Your organization initiated a project to raise money for an important charity. Assume that there are 1,000 people in your organization. Also assume that you have six months to raise as much money as possible, with a goal of $100,000. Develop a scope statement, WBS, and Gantt chart for the project. Be creative in deciding how you will raise the money and the major work packages required to complete the project. Assume that the only costs are volunteer labor, so you do not need to prepare a cost estimate.

2.	You are part of a team in charge of a project to help people in your company (500 people) lose weight. This project is part of a competition, and the top "losers" will be featured in a popular television show. Assume that you have six months to complete the project and a budget of $10,000. Develop a scope statement, WBS, Gantt chart, and cost estimate for the project.

3.	Using the information you developed in Project 1 or 2 role-play a meeting to review one of these planning documents with key stakeholders. Determine who will play what role (project manager, team member from a certain department, senior managers, and so on). Be creative in displaying different personalities (a senior manager who questions the importance of the project to the organization, a team member who is very shy or obnoxious).

4.	Perform the planning tasks (only for the knowledge areas covered in this chapter) for one of the case studies provided in Appendix C. Remember to be thorough in your planning so that your execution goes smoothly.

5.	As a team, find at least six examples of Gantt charts for various types of projects. Discuss the similarities and differences between how the WBSs are structured, how durations and dependencies are entered, etc. Also discuss the quality of these examples. Document your results in a two- to three-page paper or a 15–20 minute presentation. Include screen shots of the files and citations for where and when you found them in an appendix.

COMPANION WEB SITE

Visit the free companion Web site for this text at **www.intropm.com** to access template files, online quizzes, Jeopardy-like games, Microsoft Project files, links to sites mentioned in the text, and other information to help you learn more about this important field. Instructors must contact the author at schwalbe@augsburg.edu to gain access to the instructor site. Anyone can access the student site.

KEY TERMS

activity attributes — Information that provides schedule-related information about each activity, such as predecessors, successors, logical relationships, leads and lags, resource requirements, constraints, imposed dates, and assumptions related to the activity.

activity list — A tabulation of activities to be included on a project schedule.

activity-on-arrow (AOA) approach, or the **arrow diagramming method (ADM)** — A network diagramming technique in which activities are represented by arrows and connected at points called nodes to illustrate the sequence of activities.

analogous estimates, or **top-down estimates** — The estimates that use the actual cost of a previous, similar project as the basis for estimating the cost of the current project.

baseline — A starting point, a measurement, or an observation that is documented so that it can be used for future comparison; also defined as the original project plans plus approved changes.

bottom-up estimates — Cost estimates created by estimating individual activities and summing them to get a project total.

buffer — Additional time to complete a task, added to an estimate to account for various factors.

burst — An occurrence when two or more activities follow a single node on a network diagram.

cost performance baseline — A time-phased budget that project managers use to measure and monitor cost performance.

crashing — A technique for making cost and schedule trade-offs to obtain the greatest amount of schedule compression for the least incremental cost.

critical chain scheduling — A method of scheduling that takes limited resources into account when creating a project schedule and includes buffers to protect the project completion date.

critical path — The series of activities that determine the *earliest* time by which the project can be completed; it is the *longest* path through the network diagram and has the least amount of slack or float.

critical path method (CPM), or **critical path analysis** — A network diagramming technique used to predict total project duration.

dependency, or **relationship** — The sequencing of project activities or tasks.

discretionary dependencies — The dependencies that are defined by the project team.

duration — The actual amount of time spent working on an activity *plus* elapsed time.

effort — The number of workdays or work hours required to complete a task.

external dependencies — The dependencies that involve relationships between project and non-project activities.

fast tracking — A schedule compression technique where you do activities in parallel that you would normally do in sequence.

feeding buffers — Additional time added before tasks on the critical path that are preceded by non-critical-path tasks.

Gantt charts — A standard format for displaying project schedule information by listing project activities and their corresponding start and finish dates in a calendar format.

mandatory dependencies — The dependencies that are inherent in the nature of the work being performed on a project.

merge — A situation when two or more nodes precede a single node on a network diagram.

milestone — A significant event on a project.

multitasking — When a resource works on more than one task at a time.

Murphy's Law — If something can go wrong, it will.

network diagram — A schematic display of the logical relationships among, or sequencing of, project activities.

node — The starting and ending point of an activity on an activity-on-arrow network diagram.

organizational process assets — Policies and procedures related to project management, past project files, and lessons-learned reports from previous, similar projects.

parametric modeling — A technique that uses project characteristics (parameters) in a mathematical model to estimate project costs.

Parkinson's Law — Work expands to fill the time allowed.

precedence diagramming method (PDM) — A network diagramming technique in which boxes represent activities.

Program Evaluation and Review Technique (PERT) — A network analysis technique used to estimate project duration when there is a high degree of uncertainty about the individual activity duration estimates.

project buffer — The additional time added before a project's due date to account for unexpected factors.

project management plan — A document, which is a deliverable for the project integration management knowledge area, used to coordinate all project planning documents and to help guide a project's execution and control.

requirement — A condition or capability that must be met or possessed by a system, product, service, result, or component to satisfy a contract, standard, specification, or other formal document.

requirements management plan — A plan that describes how project requirements will be analyzed, documented and managed.

requirements traceability matrix (RTM) — A table that lists requirements, various attributes of each requirement, and the status of the requirements to ensure that all of them are addressed.

scope baseline — The approved project scope statement and its associated WBS and WBS dictionary.

scope creep — The tendency for project scope to continually increase.

slack or **float** — The amount of time an activity may be delayed without delaying a succeeding activity or the project finish date.

team contract — A document created to help promote teamwork and clarify team communications.

Theory of Constraints (TOC) — A management philosophy that states that any complex system at any point in time often has only one aspect or constraint that is limiting its ability to achieve more of its goal.

three-point estimate — An estimate that includes an optimistic, most likely, and pessimistic estimate.

work breakdown structure (WBS) — A deliverable-oriented grouping of the work involved in a project that defines the total scope of the project.

work breakdown structure (WBS) dictionary — A document that describes detailed information about WBS tasks.

work package — A task at the lowest level of the WBS.

END NOTES

[1]Ross Foti, "The Best Winter Olympics, Period," *PM Network* (January 2004) p. 23.

[2]Ibid, p. 23.

[3]Luc K. Richard, "Reducing Schedule Risk, Parts 1 and 2," (*www.Gantthead.com*) (November 10, 2003 and January 31, 2005).

[4]OilVoice, "Foster Wheeler Wins Project Excellence Award at IPMA 22nd World Congress in Rome" (December 9, 2008).

[5]Goldratt, Eliyahu, *Critical Chain and The Goal.* Great Barrington, MA: The North River Press (1997 and 2004).

[6]Claudia Wallis, "The Multitasking Generation," *Time Magazine* (March 19, 2006).

[7]Goldratt, Eliyahu, *Critical Chain.* p. 218.

Chapter 5

Planning Projects, Part 2
(Project Quality, Human Resource, Communications, Risk, and Procurement Management)

LEARNING OBJECTIVES

After reading this chapter, you will be able to:

- List several planning tasks and outputs for project quality, human resource, communications, risk, and procurement management
- Discuss the project quality management planning tasks, and explain the purpose and contents of a quality management plan, project dashboard, quality metrics, and quality checklists
- Explain the project human resource management planning tasks, and create a human resource plan
- Describe the project communications management planning tasks, and describe the importance of using a project communications management plan and project Web site
- Discuss the project risk management planning tasks, and explain how a risk management plan, a probability/impact matrix, a risk register, and risk-related contractual agreements are used in risk management planning
- Discuss the project procurement management planning tasks, and explain a make-or-buy analysis, procurement management plans, requests for proposal/quote, contract statements of work, and supplier evaluation matrices

OPENING CASE

Kristin and her team continued to plan various aspects of the Just-In-Time Training project. About half of her project's budget was allocated for external labor and outsourced training programs, but Kristin and her team were still unsure about what sources to use for most of the training. Kristin had worked with many construction suppliers before, but she had never had to select or negotiate contracts with educational consultants or training companies. She knew that developing and providing quality training courses was very important to this project; however, she also knew that successfully planning the human resource, communications, risk, and procurement management dimensions were also important—especially because the project involved so many different stakeholders. Because some of the plans in these areas might affect the initial scope, time, and cost plans, Kristin knew that she had to focus on project integration management to pull all these plans together and effectively lead the team in preparing and then executing these plans.

Fortunately, Global Construction had well-defined processes for planning all aspects of projects, and the project steering committee provided helpful advice, especially in the areas in which Kristin had little experience. She also relied heavily on her team members and other stakeholders to help create all the initial plans for the project. Because they knew that many of the plans would require updates, they built in as much flexibility as possible.

INTRODUCTION

Everyone knows that it is important to effectively plan the scope, time, and cost dimensions of a project and to develop the overall project management plan as part of integration management. However, some project managers neglect planning in the other knowledge areas—quality, human resource, communications, risk, and procurement management. It is important to skillfully plan *all* of these areas because they are all crucial to project success. This chapter summarizes key information on planning in these knowledge areas and specific actions that Kristin and her team took. The next chapter shows how these plans provide the basis for executing tasks.

SUMMARY OF PLANNING TASKS AND OUTPUTS

Figure 5-1 shows the project planning outputs for quality, human resource, communications, risk, and procurement management based on the *PMBOK® Guide, Fourth Edition*. As mentioned in Chapter 4, these planning documents, as well as other project-related information, will be available to all team members for the Just-In-Time Training Project. This chapter provides samples of some of these outputs, as well as a few additional ones, such as a project dashboard and Web site.

Knowledge area	Planning process	Outputs
Project quality management	Plan quality	Quality management plan
		Quality metrics
		Quality checklists
		Process improvement plan
		Project document updates
Project human resource management	Develop human resource plan	Human resource plan
Project communications management	Plan communications	Communications management plan
		Project document updates
Project risk management	Plan risk management	Risk management plan
	Identify risks	Risk register
	Perform qualitative risk analysis	Risk register updates
	Perform quantitative risk analysis	Risk register updates
	Plan risk responses	Risk register updates
		Project management plan updates
		Risk related contract decisions
		Project document updates
Project procurement management	Plan procurements	Procurement management plan
		Procurement statement of work
		Make-or-buy decisions
		Procurement documents
		Source selection criteria
		Change requests

Figure 5-1. Planning processes and outputs for project quality, human resource, communications, risk, and procurement management

The following sections describe planning tasks in the quality, human resource, communications, risk, and procurement management knowledge areas, and then provide examples of applying them to the Just-In-Time Training project at Global Construction. Templates for creating several of these planning documents are available on the companion Web site for this text.

PROJECT QUALITY MANAGEMENT PLANNING TASKS

Project quality management ensures that the project will satisfy the stated or implied needs for which it was undertaken. Key outputs produced as part of project quality management include a quality management plan, quality metrics, and quality checklists. Before describing these outputs, it is important to understand what quality is and why it is an important part of project management.

The International Organization for Standardization (ISO) defines **quality** as "the degree to which a set of inherent characteristics fulfill requirements" (ISO9000:2000). Other experts define quality based on conformance to requirements and fitness for use. **Conformance to requirements** means that the project's processes and products meet written specifications. For example, Kristin's project team might write specifications stating that a course must cover certain topics and be written in English, Chinese, and Japanese. As part of quality management, Kristin's team would verify that the training vendors meet those written requirements. **Fitness for use**, on the other hand, means that a product can be used as it was intended. For example, a training vendor might develop a course in English and then translate it into Chinese and Japanese, but the translations might be faulty, causing confusion to learners. These translated courses, then, would not be fit for use, even though they might have met the written specifications.

Recall that project management involves meeting or exceeding stakeholder needs and expectations. To understand what quality means to the stakeholders, the project team must develop good relationships with them—especially the main customer for the project. *After all, the customer ultimately decides that the quality level is acceptable.* Many projects fail because the project team focuses only on meeting the written requirements for the main products being produced and ignores other stakeholder needs and expectations for the project.

Quality, therefore, must be considered on an equal level of importance with project scope, time, and cost. If a project's stakeholders are not satisfied with the quality of the project management or the resulting products or services, the project team will need to adjust scope, time, and cost to satisfy stakeholder needs and expectations. Meeting only written requirements for scope, time, and cost is not sufficient.

Quality Planning and the Quality Management Plan

Quality planning includes identifying which quality standards are relevant to the project and how best to satisfy those standards. It also involves designing quality into the products and services of the project as well as the processes involved in managing the project. It is important to describe important factors that directly contribute to meeting customer requirements. The scope baseline, stakeholder register, cost performance baseline, schedule baseline, risk register, enterprise environmental factors, and organizational process assets (i.e. policies related to quality and related standards and regulations) are all important inputs to the quality planning process.

The quality management plan describes how the project management team will implement quality policies. Like other project plans, its format and contents vary based on the particular project and organizational needs. It can be a long, formal document or short and informal.

Sample Quality Management Plan

Kristin and her team worked together to create a quality management plan for the Just-In-Time Training project (see Figure 5-2). The primary purpose of the plan was to ensure that all the products and services produced as part of the project are of known quality and sufficient quantity to meet customer expectations.

Quality Management Plan

August 20

Project Name: Just-In-Time Training Project

Introduction

The main goal of this project is to develop a new training program that provides just-in-time training to employees on key topics, including supplier management, negotiating skills, project management, and software applications.

Quality Standards

The standards that apply to this project are summarized as follows:

1. Survey standards: See Attachment 1 for corporate standards for developing and administering surveys to employees. Quantitative and qualitative information will be collected. Quantitative data will use a 5-point Likert scale as much as possible. A corporate expert on surveys will review the survey before it is administered.

2. Supplier selection standards: See Attachment 2 for corporate standards regarding supplier selection. Past performance and developing partnerships will be key issues for this project.

3. Training standards: See Attachment 3 for corporate standards regarding training. The training provided as part of this project will be available in several formats, including instructor-led, CD/ROM, and web-based. Employees will have access to CD/ROM and web-based training at any time to meet individual and business needs on a just-in-time manner.
Etc.

Metrics

Metrics measure quality performance. Several metrics apply to this project, and more may be developed as the project progresses. The project team will use a few key metrics as follows:

1. Survey response rate: For the survey to be successful, a response rate of at least 30% must be achieved.

2. Course evaluations: All course participants must complete a course evaluation in order for their training to be tracked in our corporate professional development system. In addition to evaluations on more detailed topics, there will be an overall course rating. The average course rating should be at 3.0 or better on a 5.0 scale.

Etc.

Problem Reporting and Corrective Action Processes

Project plans will include clear roles and responsibilities for all stakeholders. The person responsible for an individual task should report problems to appropriate managers (see the project organizational chart) and work with them to determine and implement corrective actions. Major problems should be brought to the attention of the project manager, who should elevate problems that might affect project success, including meeting scope, time, cost, and quality goals, to the project steering committee and then the project sponsor. It is crucial to address problems as early as possible and develop several alternative solutions.

Supplier Quality and Control

The project manager will closely monitor work performed by suppliers, with assistance from our supplier management department. All contracts must clearly state quality standards, metrics, etc. Etc.

Figure 5-2. Sample quality management plan

Quality Metrics

A **metric** is a standard of measurement. Metrics allow organizations to measure their performance in certain areas and to compare them over time or with other organizations. Examples of common metrics used by organizations include failure rates of products produced, availability of goods and services, and customer satisfaction ratings.

Individual projects also have metrics. Before deciding on the metrics to use for a particular project, it is important to clarify the project goals, business case for the project, and success criteria. Knowing this information, you can then decide what data will give you the information you need, and how to collect it.

For example, the Just-In-Time Training project's success criteria, as documented in the project charter, included metrics based on:

- *Time*: Completing the project within one year

- *Customer satisfaction*: Achieving an average course evaluation of at least 3.0 on a 5.0 scale

- *Cost reduction*: Recouping the cost of the project in reduced training costs within two years after project completion

Global Construction's senior management, therefore, should collect and analyze data to ensure these metrics, as well as other metrics related to the project, are being met, such as how well they are meeting general scope, time, and cost goals. Many organizations use charts to keep track of metrics, such as a **project dashboard**—a graphical screen summarizing key project metrics.

BEST PRACTICE

Dragan Milosevic, author of the Project Management Toolbox, has done several studies to investigate what companies that excel in project delivery capability do differently from others. After analyzing data from hundreds of companies, he found four key practices these best-performing companies follow:

1. They build an integrated project management toolbox. In other words, they use several standard and advanced project management tools. They tailor these tools to their organizations and provide employees with lots of templates.
2. They grow competent project leaders, emphasizing business and soft skills. These organizations identify good project leaders and provide training, mentoring, and a career path for them.
3. They develop streamlined, consistent project delivery processes. Project management methodologies are well defined and followed.
4. And probably the hardest of all, they install a sound but comprehensive set of project performance metrics. It is difficult defining, measuring, and tracking metrics across an organization, but in order to improve project delivery capability, these metrics are crucial.[1]

Sample Project Dashboard and Quality Metrics Description

Figure 5-3 provides a sample project dashboard that could be used on the Just-In-Time Training Project. Most dashboards use red, yellow, and green to indicate the status of each metric, where green indicates the metric is on target, yellow means it is slightly off target/caution, and red indicates the metric is off target/problem area. (This example uses different shades of gray.) It also describes how the metric is measured and explains the reason for the status rating. You will learn more about earned value charts, a tool for measuring overall scope, time, and cost goals, in Chapter 7.

Just-In-Time Training Project Dashboard
As of January 20

Metric Name	Description	Status	How measured	Explanation
Scope	Meeting project scope goals	◉	Earned value chart	On target
Time	Completing the project within one year	◉	Earned value chart	On target
Cost	Staying within budget – under $1 million	○	Earned value chart	A little over budget
Survey response	Must be at least 30%	◉	Surveys received/sent	Got 33% response
Customer satisfaction	Average course rating of at least 3.0/5.0	○	Course evaluations	Goal part of success criteria
	–Number of course evaluations received	38	Feed from online system	All course participants must complete
	–Average course rating	2.7	Feed from online system	CD/ROM course had low ratings
Cost reduction	Recoup investment within two years	N/A	Cost/employee for training	Can't measure until project is completed
Courses developed	Meeting milestones for development	◉	Milestone dates	Course development on target
Number of people trained	Meeting goals of people trained	○	Filling scheduled classes	Last minute cancellations

◉ = on target
○ = slightly off target/caution
● = off target/problem area

Figure 5-3. Sample project dashboard

As mentioned in the sample quality management plan, two important metrics related to the Just-In-Time Training project include the survey response rate and course evaluation ratings. Figure 5-4 provides more information on these metrics.

Quality Metrics
August 20

Project Name: Just-In-Time Training Project

The following quality metrics apply to this project:

1. Survey response rate: In order for the survey to be successful, a response rate of at least 30% must be achieved. Most surveys will be administered online using the standard corporate survey software, which can track the response rate automatically. If the response rate is less than 30% one week after the survey is sent out, the project manager will alert the project steering committee to determine corrective action.

2. Course evaluations: All course participants must complete a course evaluation so that their training can be tracked in our corporate professional development system. In addition to evaluations on more detailed topics, there will be an overall course rating. The average course rating should be at least 3.0, with 5 being the highest score. Surveys should include questions measured on a Likert scale. For example, a question might be as follows: "My overall evaluation of this course is ……" Respondents would select 1 for Poor, 2 for Fair, 3 for Average, 4 for Good, or 5 for Excellent.

Etc.

Figure 5-4. Sample quality metrics description

Quality Checklists

A **checklist** is a list of items to be noted or consulted. Checklists help project teams verify that a set of required topics or steps has been covered or performed. A single project can have many different checklists. For example, there can be checklists related to interviewing project team members, selecting suppliers, reviewing important documents, ensuring a room is ready for training, and so on.

Sample Quality Checklist

Kristin and her team developed several checklists for their project and used others that were already available on the corporate intranet. Figure 5-5 is a sample checklist that the company uses for ensuring that training rooms are in proper order.

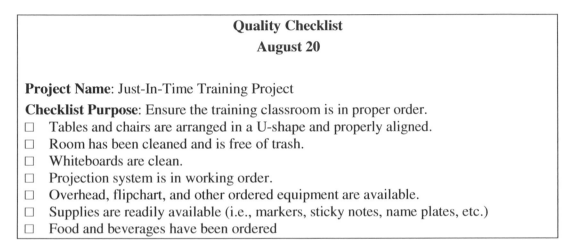

Quality Checklist
August 20

Project Name: Just-In-Time Training Project

Checklist Purpose: Ensure the training classroom is in proper order.
☐   Tables and chairs are arranged in a U-shape and properly aligned.
☐   Room has been cleaned and is free of trash.
☐   Whiteboards are clean.
☐   Projection system is in working order.
☐   Overhead, flipchart, and other ordered equipment are available.
☐   Supplies are readily available (i.e., markers, sticky notes, name plates, etc.)
☐   Food and beverages have been ordered

Figure 5-5. Sample quality checklist

PROJECT HUMAN RESOURCE MANAGEMENT PLANNING TASKS

Many corporate executives have said, "People are our most important asset." People determine the success and failure of organizations and projects. Project human resource management is concerned with making effective use of the people involved with a project. The main output produced as part of project human resource management planning is creating a human resource plan which includes a project organizational chart, a responsibility assignment matrix, a resource histogram, and a staffing management plan. Chapter 6, which covers project execution, includes much more information on project human resource management, as Kristin encounters some problems related to this topic. Planning human resources effectively will help her face these challenges.

Project Organizational Charts

After identifying the important skills and types of people needed to staff a project, the project manager should work with top management and project team members to create an organizational chart for the project. Similar to a company's organizational chart, a

project organizational chart is a graphical representation of how authority and responsibility is distributed within the project. The size and complexity of the project determines how simple or complex the organizational chart is.

Sample Project Organizational Chart

Figure 5-6 shows a project organizational chart that Kristin put together. After supplier project managers and other personnel were assigned, Kristin would fill in more of the chart. Notice that Kristin has a direct reporting line to the project sponsor, and the project team leaders and supplier project managers would report to her. Also note that the project steering committee and project sponsor have a strong role on the project. Sometimes, dotted lines are used to represent indirect reporting relationships.

Just-In Time Training Project Organizational Chart
August 20

Figure 5-6. Sample project organizational chart

Responsibility Assignment Matrices

A **responsibility assignment matrix (RAM)** is a matrix that maps the work of the project as described in the work breakdown structure (WBS) to the people responsible for performing the work. A RAM allocates work to responsible and performing organizations, teams, or individuals, depending on the desired level of detail. For smaller projects, it is best to assign WBS activities to individuals. For larger projects, it is more effective to assign the work to organizational units or teams. In addition to using a RAM to assign detailed work activities, you can use a RAM to define general roles and responsibilities on projects. This type of RAM can include the stakeholders in the project. The project team should decide what to use as categories in the RAM and include a key to explain those categories. For example, a RAM can show whether stakeholders are accountable for (A) or just participants (P) in part of a project, and whether they are required to provide input (I), review (R), or sign off (S) on parts of a project. This simple tool enables the project manager to efficiently communicate the roles of project team members and expectations of important project stakeholders.

Sample Responsibility Assignment Matrix

Some organizations, including Global Construction, use **RACI charts**—a type of responsibility assignment matrix that shows **R**esponsibility (who does the task), **A**ccountability (who signs off on the task or has authority for it), **C**onsultation (who has information necessary to complete the task), and **I**nformed (who needs to be notified of task status/results) roles for project stakeholders. Figure 5-7 shows a RACI chart that Kristin developed for the supplier management training part of the project. Jamie and Mohamed were early members of the project team, and Supplier A represents the supplier who would be selected to provide the supplier management training courses.

Notice that the RACI chart lists tasks vertically and individuals or groups horizontally, and that each intersecting cell contains at least one of the letters R, A, C, or I. For the first task, needs assessment, Kristin is accountable for getting it done, Jamie is responsible for doing the work, Mohamed is providing information in a consultative role, and Supplier A will be informed about it. Each task may have multiple R, C, or I entries, but there can only be one A entry to clarify which particular individual or group has accountability for each task (only one A in a matrix row). One person can also have multiple roles for each task, such as being responsible and accountable. (Note that some people switch the meaning of the R and A. It is important to clarify people's roles on projects.)

Just-In-Time Training Project RACI Chart
August 20

Tasks	Kristin	Jamie	Mohamed	Supplier A
Needs assessment	A	R	C	I
Research of existing training	I	R, A	C	I
Partnerships	R, A	I	I	C
Course development	A	C	C	R
Course administration	I	A	R	I
Course evaluation	I	A	R	I
Stakeholder communications	R, A	C	C	C

R: Responsible   A: Accountable   C: Consulted   I: Informed

Figure 5-7. Sample RACI chart

Resource Histograms

A **resource histogram** is a column chart that shows the number of resources required for or assigned to a project over time. In planning project staffing needs, senior managers often create a resource histogram in which columns represent the number of people (or person hours, if preferred) needed in each skill category, such as managers, IT specialists, and HR specialists. By stacking the columns, you can see the total number of people needed each month. After resources are assigned to a project, you can view a resource histogram for each person to see how his or her time has been allocated. You can create resource histograms using spreadsheets or project management software.

Sample Resource Histogram

Kristin worked with other managers to estimate how many internal resources they would need for the Just-In-Time Training project over time. They decided that in addition to herself (the project manager, or PM), they would require people from human resources (HR), supplier management (SM), information technology (IT), the project management office (PMO), and the contracting department. After contracts were written, Kristin could request a similar resource histogram from each supplier to review overall staffing for the project. Figure 5-8 is the resulting resource histogram for internal resources, showing the total number of people, or head count, by month. For example, it shows the need for a project manager (PM) .75 time for all 12 months, 1 HR person (or several HR people part-time, adding up to 1 total person) for all 12 months, etc. If needed, Kristin could also develop a similar chart showing the estimated number of hours per month. She could also use resource histograms to see where people might be overallocated, as described in Chapter 7.

Type of Resource	Meaning	Month											
		1	2	3	4	5	6	7	8	9	10	11	12
PM	Project Manager	0.75	0.75	0.75	0.75	0.75	0.75	0.75	0.75	0.75	0.75	0.75	0.75
HR	Human Resources	1	1	1	1	1	1	1	1	1	1	1	1
SM	Supplier Management	0.5	0.5	0.5	0.5	0.5	0.5	0.5	0.5	0.5	0.5	0.5	0.5
IT	Information Technology	0.25	0.5	0.5	0.5	0.25	0.25	0.25	0.25	0.25	0.25	0.25	0.25
Contracting	Contracting	0	0	0.25	0.25	0.25	0.25	0.25	0.25	0.25	0.25	0.25	0.25
PMO	Project Management Office	0	0.5	0.5	0.5	0.5	0	0	0	0	0	0	0
Miscellaneous	Miscellaneous	0.25	0.25	0.25	0.25	0.25	0.5	0.5	0.5	0.5	0.25	0.25	0.25

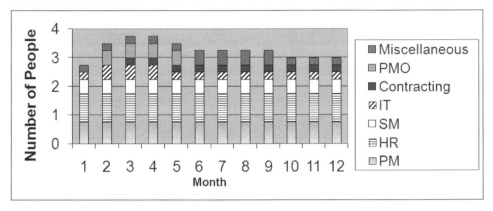

Figure 5-8. Sample resource histogram

Staffing Management Plans

A **staffing management plan** describes when and how people will be added to and removed from a project. The level of detail can vary based on the type of project. The staffing management plan describes the number of and types of people needed to work on the project. It also describes how these resources will be acquired, trained, rewarded, and reassigned after their work on the project is completed. All these issues are important to meeting the needs of the project, the employees, and the organization.

Sample Staffing Management Plan

Figure 5-9 provides part of a staffing management plan that Kristin created for the Just-In-Time Training project.

Staffing Management Plan
August 20

Project Name: Just-In-Time Training Project

Introduction

The main goal of this project is to develop a new training program that provides Just-In-Time training to employees on key topics, including supplier management, negotiating skills, project management, and software applications.

Staffing Requirements

This project will require the following internal staff:

- Project manager (PM) (Kristin was assigned 3/4 time)

- Project team members from the HR department (two people assigned half-time) to help with all the project training

- Project team member from the supplier management (SM) department (assigned half-time) to assist with the supplier management training

- Information technology (IT) department staff to help with technical support and the software applications training

- Project management (PMO) staff to help with the project management training

- Contracting department staff to assist in administering the project contracts. See the resource histogram in Attachment A for projected staffing needs over time.

Staff Assignments

The project manager will work through functional managers to assign individuals to the project. The project manager will interview potential candidates to determine suitability. If particular expertise is required for part of the project, the functional managers will plan to make experts available. Employees will be paid overtime if needed.

Training, Rewards, and Reassignment

Ideally, people assigned to this project will have appropriate experience or be willing to learn quickly on-the-job. The project manager will do his or her best to provide a challenging and enjoyable work environment. Assignment to the project will not affect an individual's salary, but the project manager will write a performance evaluation and recommend appropriate rewards. If an individual is not performing as expected, the project manager will work with him or her and the appropriate functional manager to determine whether corrections can be made or if reassignment is necessary.

Attachment A: Resource histogram

Figure 5-9. Sample staffing management plan

PROJECT COMMUNICATIONS MANAGEMENT PLANNING TASKS

Many experts agree that the greatest threat to the success of any project is a failure to communicate. It is often said that project managers spend 90% of time communicating. Yet many project managers fail to take the time to plan for it. Even though having a communications management plan does not guarantee that all project communications will flow smoothly, it certainly helps.

What Went Wrong?

An amusing example of miscommunication comes from a director of communications at a large firm:

I was asked to prepare a memo reviewing our company's training programs and materials. In the body of the memo in one of the sentences, I mentioned the "*pedagogical approach*" used by one of the training manuals. The day after I routed the memo to the executive committee, I was called into the HR director's office, and told that the executive vice president wanted me out of the building by lunch. When I asked why, I was told that she wouldn't stand for perverts (pedophiles?) working in her company. Finally, he showed me her copy of the memo, with her demand that I be fired—and the word "*pedagogical*"—circled in red. The HR manager was fairly reasonable, and once he looked the word up in his dictionary and made a copy of the definition to send back to her, he told me not to worry. He would take care of it. Two days later, a memo to the entire staff came out directing us that no words that could not be found in the local Sunday newspaper could be used in company memos. A month later, I resigned. In accordance with company policy, I created my resignation memo by pasting words together from the Sunday paper.[2]

Figure 5-10 provides another humorous example of miscommunication based on selfishness and bad timing. (It's a take-off from the story about the woman who cuts her long hair to buy her husband a chain for his watch while he sells his watch to buy a comb for her hair.)

Figure 5-10. Poor communications (www.xkcd.com)

Project communications management involves generating, collecting, disseminating, and storing project information. Key outputs produced for the Just-In-Time Training project include a communications management plan and a project Web site.

Communications Management Plan

Because project communication is so important, every project should include a **communications management plan**—a document that guides project communications. The communications management plan will vary with the needs of the project, but some type of written plan should always be prepared. The communications management plan should address the following items:

- Stakeholder communications requirements

- Information to be communicated, including format, content, and level of detail

- Identification of who will receive the information and who will produce it

- Suggested methods or guidelines for conveying the information

- Description of the frequency of communication

- Escalation procedures for resolving issues

An Introduction to Project Management, Third Edition

- Revision procedures for updating the communications management plan

- A glossary of common terminology used on the project

Sample Communications Management Plan

Kristin and her team drafted a communications management plan (for the Just-In-Time Training project as shown in Figure 5-11. The project steering committee reviewed it and provided suggestions on how to keep communication lines open. They advised Kristin to stress the importance of communications with *all* project stakeholders. They also mentioned the fact that people communicate in different ways and recommended that her team not be afraid of over-communicating by providing the same information in multiple formats. The steering committee noted that it is not enough to provide formal documents; Kristin and her team should use face-to-face communications, e-mails, phone calls, and other communications media to ensure optimal communications. Recall that the WBS for this project included an item called stakeholder communications to ensure good project communications.

Communication Management Plan Version 1.0
August 28

Project Name: Just-In-Time Training Project

1.   Stakeholder Communications Requirements

Because this project involves many people from all over the company as well as outside suppliers, the project team will use surveys, interviews, checklists, and other tools and techniques to determine the communications requirements for various stakeholders. Employees will have specific communications needs in that several training programs are being totally changed, and they will likely be uncomfortable with those changes. Suppliers will have communications needs to ensure that they are developing courses that will meet our organization's needs. Internal experts providing content will have communications needs related to providing useful information and products.

2.   Communications Summary

The following table summarizes various stakeholders, communications required, the delivery method or format of the communications, who will produce the communications, and when it will be distributed or the frequency of distribution. All communications produced will be archived and available on the project web site. As more communications items are defined, they will be added to this list. The project team will use various templates and checklists to enhance communications. The team will also be careful to use the appropriate medium (that is, face-to-face meeting, phone, e-mail, hard copy, web site, and so on) and follow corporate guidelines for effective communications. Note the comments/guidelines as well.

Stakeholders	Communications Name	Delivery Method/Format	Producer	Due Date/ Frequency
Project steering committee	Weekly status report	Hard copy and short meeting	Kristin Maur	Wed. mornings at 9 AM

Sponsor and champion	Monthly status report	Hard copy and short meeting	Kristin Maur	First Thursday of month at 10 AM
Affected employees	Project announcement	Memo, e-mail, intranet site, and announcement at department meetings	Lucy Camerena and Mike Sundby	July 1
Project team	Weekly status report	Short meeting	All team members	Tues. afternoons at 2:00.

3. Guidelines

- Make sure people understand your communications. Use common sense techniques to check comprehension, such as having them explain what you mean in their own words. Don't overuse/misuse e-mail or other technologies. Short meetings or phone calls can be very effective.
- Use templates as much as possible for written project communications. The project web site includes a link to all project-related templates.
- Use the titles and dates of documents in e-mail headings and have recipients acknowledge receipt.
- Prepare and post meeting minutes within 24 hours of a meeting.
- Use checklists where appropriate, such as reviewing product requirements and conducting interviews.
- Use corporate facilitators for important meetings, such as kickoff meetings and supplier negotiations.

4. Escalation Procedures for Resolving Issues

Issues should be resolved at the lowest level possible. When they cannot be resolved, affected parties should alert their immediate supervisors of the issues. If it is critical to the project or extremely time-sensitive, the issue should be brought directly to the project manager. If the project manager cannot resolve an issue, he or she should bring it to the project steering committee or appropriate senior management, as required.

5. Revision Procedures for this Document

Revisions to this plan will be approved by the project manager. The revision number and date will be clearly marked at the top of the document.

6. Glossary of Common Terminology

actual cost — the total direct and indirect costs incurred in accomplishing work on an activity during a given period.

baseline — the original project plan plus approved changes.

Etc.

Figure 5-11. Sample communications management plan

Project Web Sites

In the past few years, more and more project teams have started posting all or part of their project information to project Web sites. Project Web sites provide a centralized way of delivering project documents and other communications. Note that some organizations use a different type of repository to store information, such as a SharePoint site. Some teams also create **blogs**—easy-to-use journals on the Web that allow users to write entries, create links, and upload pictures, while allowing readers to post comments to particular journal entries. Project teams can develop project Web sites using Web-authoring tools, such as SharePoint Designer or Macromedia Dreamweaver; enterprise project management software, if available; or a combination of the two approaches. Part of the Web site might be open to outside users, whereas other parts might be accessible only by certain stakeholders. It is important to decide if and how to use a project Web site to help meet project communications requirements.

Sample Project Web Site

Kristin and her team entered detailed project information into the company's enterprise project management software. From within that system, Kristin could control who could and could not see various types of information. In addition, she worked with her team and the IT department to create a simple project Web site using a project Web site template of Microsoft FrontPage. This site would be available on the corporate intranet. Kristin's team felt it was important to let all employees access basic information about the project. Figure 5-12 shows the home page of the Web site for the Just-In-Time Training project. It includes summary information, such as project objectives, new information, and key milestones. It also includes links to information on team members, the project schedule, the project archive, a search feature, a discussions feature, and contact information.

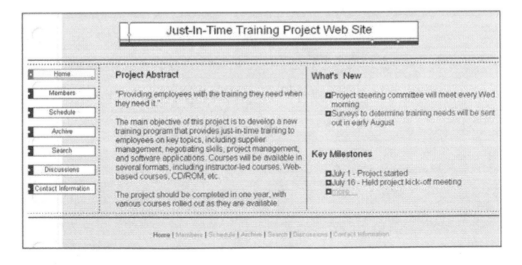

Figure 5-12. Sample project Web site

PROJECT RISK MANAGEMENT PLANNING TASKS

Although it is a frequently overlooked aspect of project management, good risk management can often result in significant improvements in the chance of a project succeeding. What is risk as it relates to a project? PMI defines a project **risk** as an uncertainty that can have a *negative or positive* effect on meeting project objectives. Note that some people only view risks as negative and call positive risks opportunities. Key outputs of project risk management planning include a risk management plan, a probability/impact matrix, a risk register, and risk-related contractual agreements.

Risk Management Plans

A risk management plan documents the procedures for managing risk *throughout the life of a project*. Project teams should hold several planning meetings early in the project's life cycle to help develop the risk management plan. The project team should review project documents as well as corporate risk management policies, risk categories, lessons learned from past projects, and templates for creating a risk management plan. It is also important to review the risk tolerances of various stakeholders. For example, if the project sponsor is risk-averse, the project might require a different approach to risk management than if the project sponsor were a risk seeker.

A risk management plan outlines how risk management will be performed on a particular project. Like other specific knowledge area plans, it becomes a subset of the project management plan. The general topics that a risk management plan should address include the methodology for risk management, roles and responsibilities, budget and schedule estimates for risk-related activities, risk categories, probability and impact matrices, and risk documentation. The level of detail included in the risk management plan will vary with the needs of the project.

In addition to a risk management plan, many projects also include contingency plans, fallback plans, and contingency reserves.

- **Contingency plans** are predefined actions that the project team will take if an identified risk event occurs. For example, if the project team knows that the new version of a product they need might not be available in time, they might have a contingency plan to use the existing, older version of the product.

- **Fallback plans** are developed for risks that have a high impact on meeting project objectives, and are put into effect if attempts to reduce the risk are not effective. For example, a new college graduate might have a main plan and several contingency plans on where to live after graduation, but if none of those plans work out, a fallback plan might be to live at home for a while. Sometimes the terms *contingency plan* and *fallback plan* are used interchangeably, and some people view fallback plans as contingency plans of last resort.

- **Contingency reserves** or **contingency allowances** are funds held by the project sponsor that can be used to mitigate cost or schedule overruns if unknown risks occur. For example, if a project appears to be off course because the staff is not experienced with a new technology and the team had not identified that as a risk, the project sponsor might provide additional funds from contingency reserves to hire an outside consultant to train and advise the project staff in using the new technology. All of these contingency plans, fallback plans, and contingency reserves show the importance of taking a proactive approach to managing project risks.

Sample Risk Management Plan

Kristin knew that it was important to plan efficiently for the risk management of the Just-In-Time Training project. There were several uncertainties, both negative and positive, associated with this project. Kristin asked Ron Ryan, the project manager of the Phase I project, to assist her in drafting the first version of the risk management plan. She also received input from the project steering committee, and as her team and suppliers were identified, they would work together to update the plan as needed. Figure 5-13 shows the initial risk management plan.

Risk Management Plan
September 3

Project Name: Just-In-Time Training Project
1. Methodology
The project team will review data available from the Phase I project and past training programs within Global Construction to assist in risk management planning. They will also review information related to external projects similar to this one. The team will use several tools and techniques, including brainstorming, surveys, and risk-related checklists to assist in risk management.
2. Roles and Responsibilities
The project manager will be responsible for leading the team and other stakeholders in performing risk-related activities. As detailed tasks and deliverables are determined, the project manager will delegate those tasks as appropriate.
3. Budget and Schedule
As specific risk-related tasks and deliverables are determined, budget and schedule information will be provided.
4. Risk Categories
General categories and subcategories for risk on this project include business risks (suppliers and cash flow), technical risks (course content, hardware, software, and network), organizational risks (executive support, user/employee support, supplier support, and team support), and project management risks (estimates, communication, and resources).
5. Risk Probability and Impact
Risk probability and impact will initially be estimated as high, medium, or low based on expert advice. If more advanced scoring is needed, the project team will determine an appropriate approach.
6. Risk Documentation
All risk-related information will be summarized in a risk register. Detailed documentation will be available in a secure area on the project web site.

Figure 5-13. Sample risk management plan

Probability/Impact Matrices

It is important to evaluate risks to determine which ones need the most attention. **Risk events** refer to specific, uncertain events that may occur to the detriment or enhancement of the project. For example, negative risk events might include the performance failure of a product produced as part of a project, delays in completing work as scheduled, increases in estimated costs, supply shortages, litigation against the company, and labor strikes. Examples of positive risk events include completing work sooner than planned or at an unexpectedly reduced cost, collaborating with suppliers to produce better products, and obtaining good publicity from the project.

There are two important dimensions of risk events: *probability* of the risk event occurring and the *impact* or consequence if the risk does occur. People often describe a risk event probability or impact as being high, medium, or low. For example, a meteorologist might predict that there is a high probability of severe rain showers on a certain day. If that happens to be your wedding day and you are planning a large outdoor wedding, the impact or consequences of severe showers would also be high.

A project manager can chart the probability and impact of risk events on a probability/impact matrix or chart. One side (axis) of a probability/impact matrix or chart lists the relative *probability* of a risk event occurring, and the other side (axis) of the chart shows the relative *impact* of the risk event occurring. To use this approach, project stakeholders identify and list the risk events related to their projects. They then label each risk event as being high, medium, or low in terms of its probability of occurrence and level of impact. The project manager then summarizes the results in a probability/impact matrix. Project teams should initially focus on risk events that fall in the high sections of the probability/impact matrix and develop strategies for minimizing negative risk events and maximizing positive ones.

Sample Probability/Impact Matrix

Kristin Maur worked with several project stakeholders early in the project to begin identifying several negative and positive risk events related to the Just-In-Time Training project. She held a brainstorming session in which over 100 risk events were identified. To differentiate between the two, she asked participants to identify negative risk events and then positive ones. After people identified a risk event and wrote it down on a sticky note, Kristin asked them to mark each one as having a high, medium, or low probability of occurrence and impact. Kristin had posted on the whiteboard large probability/impact matrices—one for negative risk events and another for positive risk events. Everyone put their sticky notes in the appropriate sections of the appropriate matrix. They then examined the results to combine and reword risk events to improve collaboration and avoid duplicates.

Figure 5-14 shows part of the resulting probability/impact matrix. For example, risks 1 and 4 are listed as high in both categories of probability and impact. Risk 6 is high in the probability category but low in the impact category. Risk 9 is high in the probability category and medium in the impact category. Risk 12 is low in the probability category but high in the impact category. The team then discussed in detail how they planned to respond to risks in the medium and high categories, Risks 1, 4, and 9, bolded in Figure 5-14, and documented the results in the risk register, as described in the following section.

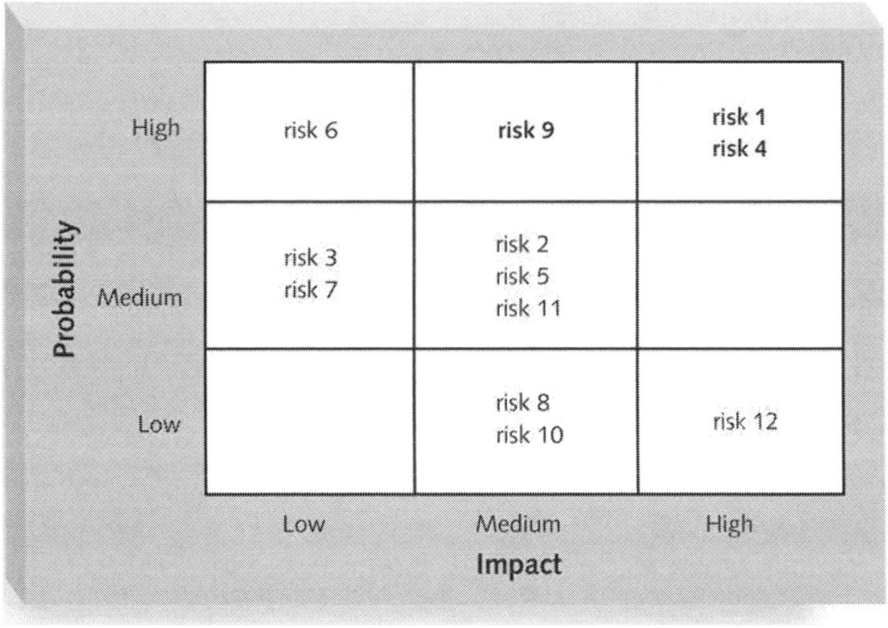

Figure 5-14. Sample probability/impact matrix (Schwalbe, Information Technology Project Management, Sixth Edition, 2010)

Risk Registers

A **risk register** is a document that contains results of various risk management processes, often displayed in a table or spreadsheet format. It is a tool for documenting potential risk events and related information. The risk register often includes the following main headings:

- *An identification number for each risk event:* The project team might want to sort or quickly search for specific risk events, so they need to identify each risk with some type of unique descriptor, such as an identification number.

- *A rank for each risk event:* The rank can be indicated as high, medium, or low, or it can be a number, with 1 being the highest-ranked risk. The project team would have to determine these rankings.

- *The name of the risk event:* For example, defective product, poor survey results, reduced consulting costs, or good publicity.

- *A description of the risk event:* Because the name of a risk event is often abbreviated, it helps to provide a detailed description in the risk register. For example, reduced consulting costs might be expanded in the description to say that the organization might be able to negotiate lower-than-average costs for a particular consultant because the consultant enjoys working for the company in that particular location.

- *The category under which the risk event falls:* For example, a defective product might fall under the broader category of technology.

- *The root cause of the risk event:* It is important to find the **root cause** of a problem—the real or underlying reason a problem occurs. By finding the root cause, you can deal with it directly rather than dealing with the symptoms of the problem. You can help identify the root cause of problems by creating a cause-and-effect or fishbone diagram (see Chapters 6 and 7), or continually asking why until you find a root cause. For example, the root cause of a defective product, like a defective computer, might be a defective hard drive. Instead of purchasing a brand-new computer or wasting time on other potential causes of the defect, knowing that you need to replace the hard drive provides valuable information that you can act on to fix the problem.

- *Triggers for each risk event:* **Triggers** are indicators or symptoms of actual risk events. For example, a clicking noise or increasing number of bad sectors would be triggers of a bad hard drive. Documenting potential risk triggers also helps the project team identify more potential risk events.

- *Potential responses to each risk event:* There can be one or more potential responses to each risk event.

- *The risk owner, or person who will own or take responsibility for the risk event:* One person should be responsible for monitoring each risk event.

- *The probability of the risk event occurring:* The chance of the risk event becoming a reality is rated as high, medium, or low.

- *The impact to the project if the risk event occurs:* The impact to project success if the risk event actually occurs can be rated as high, medium, or low.

- *The status of the risk event:* Did the risk event occur? Was the response strategy completed? Is the risk event no longer relevant to the project? For example, a clause may have been written into a contract to address the risk event of a defective product so that the supplier would have to replace the item at no additional cost.

Sample Risk Register

Kristin began developing a risk register after she and the other stakeholders had prepared the probability/impact matrix. Figure 5-15 shows the format of the risk register and one of the entries. Note that the risk event identification (ID) number is shown in the first column, followed by the rank of the risk event. The risk events are sorted by rank order. As information is added, deleted, or changed, the risk register will be updated on the project Web site.

No.	Rank	Risk	De-scrip-tion	Cate-gory	Root Cause	Trig-gers	Potential Respon-ses	Risk Owner	Proba-bility	Impact	Status
R15	1										
R21	2										
R7	3										

Risk Register
September 3

Project Name: Just-In-Time Training Project

To understand the risk register more fully, imagine that the following data is entered for the first risk in the register.

- No.: R15
- Rank: 1
- Risk: Poor survey response
- Description: Many people dislike surveys and avoid filling them out, or if they do, they don't offer good or honest feedback
- Category: Organizational/user support risk
- Root cause: People don't want to take the time and think their inputs aren't important
- Triggers: Low survey response rate the first few days, incomplete surveys.
- Risk Responses: Make sure senior management emphasizes the importance of this project and the survey for designing good courses. Have the functional managers personally mention the survey to their people and stress its importance. Offer a reward to the department with the most responses. Ensure that the survey instructions say it will take ten minutes or less to complete. Extend the deadline for survey responses.
- Risk owner: Mike Sundby, Project champion
- Probability: Medium
- Impact: High
- Status: PM will set up the meeting within the week with the project steering committee to decide which response strategies to implement.

Figure 5-15. Sample risk register

Risk-Related Contract Decisions

Many projects, including the Just-In-Time Training project, involve outside suppliers. Work done by outside suppliers or sellers should be well documented in **contracts**, which are mutually binding agreements that obligate the seller to provide the specified products or services, and obligate the buyer to pay for them. Project managers should include clauses in contracts to help manage project risks. For example, sellers can agree to be responsible for certain negative risks and incur the costs themselves if they occur. Or there can be incentive or penalty clauses in contracts based on seller performance to encourage positive risks and discourage negative risks. Project teams can also use certain types of contracts, such as fixed-price contracts, to reduce their risk of incurring higher costs than expected. Competition for supplying goods and services can also help reduce negative risks and enhance positive risks on projects.

Sample Risk-Related Contract Decisions

Kristin's team had not yet prepared any contractual documents for the Just-In-Time Training project, but they did have access to several other contracts that Global Construction had used in the past. Kristin had come from the supplier management area of the company, so she had personal experience working with suppliers and contracts. She also knew several people who could advise her on writing risk-related contractual agreements. Figure 5-16 provides a list of a few risk-related contract decisions or agreements that Kristin's team would consider for this project. Kristin received these guidelines from the project team's representative from the contracting department. These agreements can take the form of contracts or clauses within contracts that can help prevent negative risk events and promote positive ones related to the project. Kristin also knew that the company's legal professionals would have to review all contracts because they were legally binding.

Guidelines for Risk-Related Contract Decisions/Agreements

The following guidelines are provided for your consideration as you make decisions develop contracts/agreements between Global Construction (the buyer) and its suppliers (the sellers). Be sure to work with a member of the contracting department to write your specific contracts. All contracts must be reviewed and signed by the legal department, as well.

- Contract termination clauses: These clauses list circumstances under which the buyer and/or seller can terminate a contract and how final payment will be settled. All the contracts must include a termination clause.
- Incentive clauses: These clauses provide incentives for the seller to provide goods or services at certain times, of certain quality, and so on. Incentive clauses can include extra payments or profit sharing, if appropriate.
- Penalty clauses: These clauses specify penalties that will be applied when the seller does not provide goods or services as specified in the contract. For example, if a product is delivered late, the seller might be required to pay a certain dollar amount for each day the product is late.
- Fixed price contracts: To minimize the negative risk of paying more than planned for specific goods or services, Global Construction issues fixed priced contracts, which specify that the seller agrees to a fixed price and bears the risk if it costs more to provide the goods or services than originally assumed.
- Competitive contracts: In many situations Global Construction can use competition to help reduce risks. In addition to reviewing bids from several sellers, a good strategy may be to award two small contracts and then award the following larger contract to the seller that does the best job on the first job.

Figure 5-16. Sample guidelines for risk-related contractual agreements

The example in the following What Went Right? passage shows another contractual approach for managing positive risk on a large project. By having suppliers visibly compete against each other, the buyers reduced their risks and benefited from competition.

What Went Right?

The Petronis Twin Towers in Malaysia are famous landmarks in Kuala Lumpur. They were the tallest buildings constructed at the time, and the first large construction project to use GPS (Global Positioning System). Over 7000 people were working on the site during the peak of construction. The project management team decided to use competition to help keep the project on time and on budget. The Japanese firm Hazama Corporation led the construction of Tower 1, and the Korean firm Samsung Engineering Co. led the construction of Tower 2. Because the towers were constructed simultaneously, everyone could see the progress of the two competitors as the 88-story towers rose into the sky. "Construction of the towers was fast paced, thanks in part to the decision to grant two contracts, one for each tower, to two separate contractors. This naturally created a competitive environment, to the benefit of the building."[3]

As you can see, risk management planning addresses procurement-related topics, such as preparing risk-related contractual agreements. The following section addresses planning tasks directly related to project procurement management.

PROJECT PROCUREMENT MANAGEMENT PLANNING TASKS

Project procurement management includes acquiring or procuring goods and services for a project from outside the organization. As the business world continues to become more competitive and global, more and more projects include procurement. Many project managers realize the advantages of buying goods and services required for their projects, especially as sellers with better goods and services continue to become increasingly available. They also realize that they can find qualified sellers throughout the world. Remember that project managers strive to do what is best for the project and the organization, and that often means acquiring goods and services from the outside. Good procurement management often provides a win-win situation for both buyers and sellers.

Key outputs produced by planning procurements include make-or-buy analysis, procurement management plans, procurement statements of work, procurement documents, source selection criteria, and change requests.

Make-or-Buy Analysis

With a make-or-buy decision, an organization decides if it would benefit more by making a product or performing a service itself, or by buying the product or service from a supplier. If there is no need to buy products or services from outside the organization, the organization can avoid the costs involved in managing procurement management processes. **Make-or-buy analysis** involves estimating the internal costs of providing a product or service, and comparing that estimate to the cost of outsourcing.

Many organizations also use a lease-or-buy analysis to decide if they should purchase or lease items for a particular project. For example, suppose you need a piece of equipment for a project that has a purchase price of $12,000. Assume it also has a daily operational cost of $400. Suppose you can lease the same piece of equipment for $800 per day, including the operational costs. You can set up an equation that shows the amount of time it will take for the purchase cost to equal the lease cost. In this way, you can determine when it makes sense financially to buy rather than lease the equipment. In the equation that follows, d = the number of days you need the piece of equipment.

$$\$12,000 + \$400d = \$800d$$

Subtracting $400d from both sides, you get:

$$\$12,000 = \$400d$$

Dividing both sides by $400, you get:

$$d = 30,$$

which means that the purchase cost equals the lease cost in 30 days. Therefore, if you need the equipment for less than 30 days, it would be more economical to lease it. If you need the equipment for more than 30 days, you should purchase it. Note that this simple example assumes there is no disposal value for the purchased item and does not include any tax considerations.

Figure 5-17 graphically shows the costs each day to lease or buy the equipment in the preceding example. Notice that the lines cross at Day 30, showing that the costs are the same to lease or buy the equipment that day. Before Day 30, the lease line is lower than the buy line, meaning it is less expensive to lease the item if it is needed for less than 30 days. After Day 30, the buy line is lower, meaning it is less expensive to buy the item after Day 30.

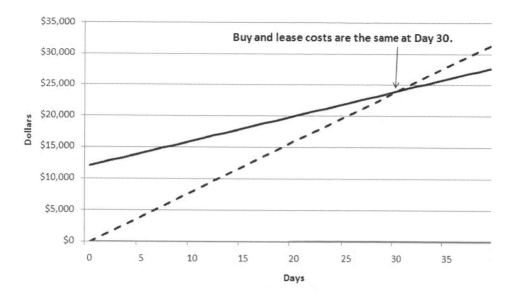

Figure 5-17. Comparing the cost of leasing versus buying

Sample Make-or-Buy Analysis

Kristin and her team needed to make several make-or-buy decisions for the Just-In-Time Training project. They knew that they wanted to outsource most of the development and delivery for much of the new training, but because internal expertise existed, it might make sense to do some of the work in-house.

For example, based on information collected in the Phase I project, it was suggested that Global Construction could probably identify internal people to conduct some of the face-to-face training or provide online advice for several courses. Internal resources would be much less expensive than external contractors. In particular, one of the requirements for the Just-In-Time Training project was to provide instructor-led basic project management training and facilitation for online materials. To train 100 employees, there would be five, two-day instructor-led classes with 20 participants in each class in the first year. There would also be 500 hours of online facilitation.

One specific suggestion was to have current employees conduct the basic project management training—the "make" option—instead of having an outside firm provide the training—the "buy" option. There were a couple of project management professionals (PMPs) in the training department with experience in teaching face-to-face and online courses. They had taken college courses in basic project management and knew of excellent books with online materials. They also knew of several companies that conducted their own in-house courses for basic project management training and then brought in an outside expert, often a qualified college professor, who would conduct advanced courses. They found that college professors or other independent consultants provided high-quality training for much less than most training firms.

Figure 5-18 summarizes the make-or-buy analysis for the basic project management training. In this case, Kristin's team recommended doing the training in-house; for much of the other training, however, they did not have internal experts or training materials available.

Make-Or-Buy Analysis
September 1

Project Name: Just-In-Time Training Project

Background: Global Construction wants to train 100 employees and will consider having the employees sent to an outside course (Buy option) or provide the education using internal employees (Make option). Assuming 20 participants/class and 2 days average course length, 10 total days of training will be needed. Assume 500 of online facilitation will be needed as well (5 hours per participant).

Decision Being Analyzed: Project management training

Option 1: (Make): Use in-house instructors for the instructor-led basic project management training and facilitation for online materials (includes purchasing course materials)

Estimated cost per hour for in-house trainer (excludes participant time): $60

Estimated training hours: 80 (10 total days of training X 8 hours per day)

Subtotal: $4,800 (80 hours X $60 per hour)

Materials cost: $7500 ($75/participant/course, 100 participants total)

Estimated cost per hour for online facilitation (excludes employee time): $60

Estimated hours: 500

Subtotal: $30,000 (500 hours X $60 per hour)

   Total: $42,300 ($4,800 + $7,500 + $30,000)

Option 2: (Buy): Outsource instructor-led basic project management training and facilitation for online materials (includes course materials)

Estimated cost for class per participant = (Estimated Cost X Number of Days) = $500 X 2 days = $1,000

Cost of instructor-led classes ($1,000 X 100 participants)

Subtotal: $100,000

Estimated cost per hour for online facilitation (excludes student time): $100

Estimated hours: 500

Subtotal: $50,000 (500 hours X $100 per hour)

   Total $150,000 ($100,000 + $50,000)

Cost Difference: $150,000 - $42,300 = $107,700

Recommendation: Because we have qualified internal staff and can purchase suitable materials, we recommend Option 1, in which we conduct the basic project management training in-house.

Figure 5-18. Sample make-or-buy analysis

Procurement Management Plans

A procurement management plan is a document that describes how the procurement processes will be managed, from developing documentation for making outside purchases or acquisitions to contract closure. Like other project plans, the contents of procurement management plans vary with project needs. Topics that can be included in a procurement management plan are as follows:

- Guidelines on types of contracts to be used in different situations

- Standard procurement documents or templates to be used, if applicable

- Guidelines for creating contract work breakdown structures, statements of work, and other procurement documents

- Roles and responsibilities of the project team and related departments, such as the purchasing or legal department

- Guidelines on using independent estimates for evaluating sellers' cost proposals

- Suggestions on managing multiple providers

- Processes for coordinating procurement decisions, such as make-or-buy decisions, with other project areas

- Constraints and assumptions related to purchases and acquisitions

- Lead times for purchases and acquisitions

- Risk-mitigation strategies for purchases and acquisitions, such as insurance contracts and bonds

- Guidelines for identifying prequalified sellers and organizational lists of preferred sellers

- Procurement metrics to assist in evaluating sellers and managing contracts

Types of Contracts

Contract type is a key consideration in a procurement management plan. Different types of contracts can be used in different situations. Three broad categories of contracts are fixed price, or lump sum; cost reimbursable; and time and material. A single contract can actually include all three of these categories, if it makes sense for that particular procurement. For example, you could have a contract with a seller that includes purchasing specific products for a fixed price or lump sum, some services that are provided on a cost-reimbursable basis, and other services that are provided on a time-and-material basis. It is important to understand and decide which approaches to use to meet particular project needs.

- **Fixed-price contracts** or **lump-sum contracts** involve a fixed total price for a well-defined product or service. The buyer incurs little risk or uncertainty in this situation because the price is predetermined. Sellers often pad their estimates somewhat to reduce their risk, while keeping in mind that their price must still be competitive. For example, using a two-week, fixed-price contract, Global Construction could hire a consultant to develop a survey to determine requirements for its new supplier management training courses under the Just-In-Time Training project. Fixed-price contracts generally have well-defined deliverables and deadlines, and may include incentives for meeting or exceeding selected project objectives. For example, the contract could include an incentive fee that would be paid for early delivery of the survey. A firm-fixed price (FFP) contract has the least amount of risk for the buyer, followed by a fixed-price incentive (FPI) contract.

- **Cost-reimbursable contracts** involve payment to the seller for direct and indirect actual costs. For example, the salaries for people working directly on a project and materials purchased for a specific project are direct costs, whereas the cost of providing a work space for those workers, office furniture, electricity, a cafeteria, and so on, are indirect costs. Indirect costs are often calculated as a percentage of direct costs. Cost-reimbursable contracts often include fees such as a profit percentage, and they can also include incentives for meeting or exceeding selected project objectives. For example, many contracts to build homes are cost-reimbursable contracts. The buyer might expect the home to cost a certain amount, but the total cost could vary if any of the costs of individual goods or services increase or decrease. The buyer reimburses the contractor for costs incurred, and pays a fee or profit percentage as well. Buyers absorb more of the risk with cost-reimbursable contracts than they do with fixed-price contracts. For example, if the cost of wood doubles, the buyer would have to absorb the additional cost. See the Media Snapshot for a great example of using incentives to build a bridge more quickly.

- **Time-and-material contracts** are a hybrid of both fixed-price and cost-reimbursable contracts. For example, an independent consultant might have a contract with a company based on a fee of $100 per hour for his or her services plus a fixed price of $10,000 for providing specific materials for the project. The materials fee might also be based on approved receipts for purchasing items, with a ceiling of $10,000. The consultant would send an invoice to the company each week or month, listing the materials fee, the number of hours worked, and a description of the work produced. This type of contract is often used for services that are needed when the work cannot be clearly specified and total costs cannot be estimated in a contract. Many consultants prefer time-and-material contracts.

Unit pricing can also be used in various types of contracts to require the buyer to pay the supplier a predetermined amount per unit of service. The total value of the contract is a function of the quantities needed to complete the work. For example, many companies use unit price contracts for purchasing computer hardware. If the company purchases only one unit, the cost is $1,000. If it purchases 10 units, the cost is $10,000 if there were no volume discounts involved, but this type of pricing often does involve volume discounts. For example, if the company purchases between 5 and 50 units, the contracted cost is $900 per unit. If it purchases over 50 units, the cost reduces to $800 per unit. This flexible pricing strategy is often advantageous to both the buyer and the seller.

Media Snapshot

Contract type and incentives can be extremely effective. On August 1, 2007, tragedy struck Minneapolis, Minnesota when a bridge on I-35W crossing the Mississippi River suddenly collapsed, killing 13 motorists, injuring 150 other people, and leaving a mass of concrete and steel in the river and on its banks. The Minnesota Department of Transportation (MnDOT) acted quickly to find a contractor to rebuild the bridge. They also provided a strong incentive to finish the bridge as quickly as possible, ensuring quality and safety along the way.

Peter Sanderson, project manager for the joint venture of Flatiron-Manson, hired to build the bridge, led his team in completing the project three months ahead of schedule, and the new bridge opened on September 18, 2008. The contractors earned $25 million in incentive fees on top of their $234 million contract for completing the bridge ahead of schedule. The financial incentive motivated the project team to coordinate their work using around the clock shifts and to develop innovative ways to pour concrete in the dead of winter.

Why did MnDOT offer such a large incentive fee for finish the project early? "I-35W in Minneapolis is a major transportation artery for the Twin Cities and entire state. Each day this bridge has been closed, it has cost road users more than $400,000," MnDOT Commissioner Tom Sorel remarked. "Area residents, business owners, motorists, workers and others have been affected by this corridor's closure. The opening of this bridge reconnects our community." [4]

Sample Procurement Management Plan

Figure 5-19 displays a section of a procurement management plan for the Just-In-Time Training project.

Procurement Management Plan
September 17

Project Name: Just-In-Time Training Project
Guidelines on Types of Contracts: To reduce Global Construction's risk, contracts for the Just-In-Time Training project should be fixed price as often as possible. When goods or services cannot be well defined, cost-reimbursable or time and material contracts may be used. The representative from the contracting department assigned to this project will work with the project manager to determine the appropriate contract type for each contract developed.

Standard procurement documents or templates: Global Construction's intranet site includes many sample documents and templates for project procurement. The project team will review these documents and templates and use them as often as possible.

Guidelines for creating procurement documents: Global Construction's intranet site provides guidelines for creating many procurement documents. The Just-In-Time Training project team should review their current work breakdown structure and scope statement to provide the basis for contract work breakdown structures and statements of work.

Roles and responsibilities: The project manager is the main contact for all procurement matters directly related to the Just-In-Time Training project. The representative from the contracting department assigned to this project will coordinate with other staff in the contracting and legal departments, as needed.
Etc.

Figure 5-19. Sample procurement management plan

Procurements Documents: Requests for Proposal or Quote

When organizations decide to procure goods or services, they often create documents to describe what they plan to procure and how potential sellers should respond. Two common examples of procurement documents include a Request for Proposal (RFP) and a Request for Quote (RFQ).

- A **Request for Proposal (RFP)** is a document used to solicit proposals from prospective suppliers. A **proposal** is a document in which sellers describe what they will do to meet the requirements of a buyer. It can be expensive and time-consuming to prepare a good RFP or proposal for a large contract, such as building a new bridge or designing a complex information system. For smaller contracts, it would take less time and money. For example, there are several different ways to meet many of Global Construction's training needs. Kristin and her team can write and issue an RFP that outlines training needs so that suppliers can respond with their unique proposals describing how they would meet those needs.

- A **Request for Quote (RFQ)** is a document used to solicit quotes or bids from prospective suppliers. A **bid** (also called a quote) is a document prepared by sellers providing pricing for standard items that have been clearly defined by the buyer. For example, if Kristin's team decided to use a specific book for training courses, they could ask for bids from different sellers for those books. Creating and responding to RFQs is usually a much quicker process than the process of responding to RFPs. Selections are often made based on the lowest bid.

RFPs and RFQs can be issued in several ways. The organization might contact one or several preferred sellers directly and send the RFP or RFQ only to them. To reach more sellers, the organization might post the information on its Web site, or advertise on other sites or in newspapers. Project managers must carefully consider which approaches are most appropriate in various situations.

Topics addressed in an RFP usually include the following:

- Purpose of the RFP
- Background information, describing the organization issuing the RFP and the project itself
- Basic requirements for the products and/or services being proposed
- Hardware and software environment (for technology-related proposals)
- RFP process, describing how sellers should prepare and submit their proposals
- Statement of work and schedule information
- Appendices providing more detailed information, as appropriate

A simple RFP might be three- to five-pages long, whereas an RFP for a larger, more complicated procurement might be hundreds of pages long.

Sample Requests for Proposal

Kristin knew that the project would require several RFPs and RFQs, but it was still very early in the project. Kristin asked the project steering committee for advice because she knew how important it was to develop good procurement documents. They suggested that Kristin's team work with the contracting department to issue an RFP for expert advice to help make major procurement decisions related to the project. The RFP would be for a fixed-price contract to hire an expert to help develop a list of qualified sellers for developing the courses for the Just-In-Time Training project. Figure 5-20 shows the RFP. Lucy, the project sponsor and training director for Global Construction, suggested that they send the RFP to several preferred vendors. They estimated that the work required to develop this qualified-sellers list should take no more than a couple weeks and cost no more than $5,000.

Request for Proposal
August 1

Project Name: Just-In-Time Training Project
RFP Name: Qualified Sellers List for Just-In-Time Training Project
Purpose of RFP
Global Construction wants to improve training in supplier management, negotiating skills, project management, and software for its employees. In the fast-paced, ever-changing construction market, effectively training employees across a globally dispersed company with different populations is a challenge. By redesigning our current training, Global Construction can reduce training costs and improve productivity. In addition to traditional instructor-led courses provided on-site, we also want to allow our employees to learn about specific topics on a just-in-time basis by having quick access to materials and expert advice. The purpose of this RFP is to hire experts to help us find qualified sellers to develop and deliver these new training courses.

Background Information
Global Construction employs 10,000 full-time employees in ten different counties and fifteen states in the U.S. We want to increase the productivity of our employees, especially in the sales, purchasing, engineering, and information technology departments. The Just-In-Time Training Project, a one-year project, began on July 2. A key part of this project is working with outside firms to develop and provide just-in-time training in supplier management, negotiating skills, project management, and software applications. See Appendix A for detailed information on the project and specific training needs.

Basic Requirements
The basic requirements for this work include the following:
1. Develop a list of qualified sellers to develop and provide the training as described in Appendix A.
2. Provide a summary description and detailed evaluation of each seller. Provide company brochures, web sites, annual reports, and other appropriate information.
3. Work with Global Construction to develop an evaluation system to evaluate each seller.
4. Provide an objective evaluation of each seller using this evaluation system.
5. Develop a list of the top five sellers for each course.
6. Provide recommendations for developing partnerships/relationships with each of the top five sellers.
7. Complete the above work no later than September 9.

RFP Process
Prospective sellers will send written proposals to Global Construction no later than August 10. To prepare your proposal, use the outline in Appendix B, and examine Appendix C for our evaluation criteria. We expect to award the contract no later than August 20.

An Introduction to Project Management, Third Edition

Statement of Work and Schedule Information See Appendix D for a statement of work. The work must be completed no later than September 9. **Appendices** Appendix A: Just-In-Time Training Project Documents Appendix B: Proposal Outline Appendix C: Evaluation Criteria Appendix D: Statement of Work

Figure 5-20. Sample RFP

Contract Statements of Work

Another important procurement document is a **contract statement of work (SOW)**, a document that describes the goods or services to be purchased. As shown in Figure 5-20, the SOW should be included with the RFP to clarify the work that needs to be performed. The contract SOW is a type of scope statement that describes the work in sufficient detail to allow prospective suppliers to both determine if they are capable of providing the goods and services required and to determine an appropriate price for the work. A contract SOW should be clear, concise, and as complete as possible. It should describe all services required and include performance information, such as the location and timing of the work. It is important to use appropriate words in a contract SOW—for example, *must* instead of *may*. *Must* implies that something has to be done; *may* implies that there is a choice involved. The contract SOW should specify the products and services required for the project, use industry terms, and refer to industry standards.

Sample Contract Statement of Work

Figure 5-21 shows the contract statement of work for the qualified-sellers list described in the RFP.

Contract Statement of Work **August 1** **Project Name**: Just-in-Time Training Project **Contract Name**: Qualified Sellers List **Scope of Work:** 1. Develop a list of qualified sellers to develop and provide the training as described in Appendix A. 2. Provide a summary description and detailed evaluation of each seller. Provide company brochures, web sites, annual reports, and other appropriate information. 3. Work with Global Construction to develop an evaluation system to evaluate each seller. 4. Provide an objective evaluation of each seller using this evaluation system. 5. Develop a list of the top five sellers for each course.

6. Provide recommendations for developing partnerships/relationships with each of the top five sellers.

7. Complete the above work no later than September 9.

Location of Work:

The seller can perform the work at any location. The seller must physically meet with representatives from Global Construction in our corporate office at least twice during the term of the contract.

Period of Performance:

Work is expected to start on or around August 20and end no later than September 9. The seller will prepare a detailed schedule for all work required, including dates for deliverables and meetings. After meeting with representatives from Global Construction to review and update the schedule, the seller will agree to the schedule for this work.

Deliverables Schedule:

The seller will prepare a detailed schedule for all of the work required, including dates for all deliverables and meetings. After meeting with representatives from Global Construction to review and update the schedule, the seller will agree to the schedule for this work.

Applicable Standards:

The seller will use standard software to produce the required documentation for this project. Draft and final documents will be sent via e-mail.

6. Acceptance Criteria:

The seller will work closely with the project manager, Kristin Maur, to clarify expectations and avoid problems in providing acceptable work. Kristin will provide written acceptance/non-acceptance of all deliverables.

7. Special Requirements:

The seller's staff assigned to work on this contract must verify appropriate education and experience. The seller will work with Global Construction to make all travel arrangements and minimize travel costs.

Figure 5-21. Sample contract statement of work

Source Selection Criteria and the Supplier Evaluation Matrix

It is highly recommended that buyers use formal supplier evaluation procedures to help select sellers. In addition to reviewing their proposals or quotes, buyers should also review sellers' past performance, talk to recent customers, interview their management team, and request sample products or demos, if applicable. After doing a thorough evaluation, many organizations summarize criteria and evaluations using a **supplier evaluation matrix**—a type of weighted scoring model. Recall from Chapter 2 that a weighted scoring model provides a systematic process for selection based on numerous criteria. For example, suppliers are often evaluated on criteria related to cost, quality, technology, past performance, and management. The weights for all of the criteria must add up to 100%.

Sample Supplier Evaluation Matrix

Kristin knew her team would have to evaluate suppliers for various goods and services as part of the Just-In-Time Training project. Kristin and her team reviewed Global Construction's previously used supplier evaluation matrices, and then prepared a simple matrix to evaluate the suppliers for the qualified-sellers list, as shown in Figure 5-22. This figure was created using the weighted scoring model template from the companion Web site, and it shows results based on three suppliers. In this example, Supplier 2 has the highest weighted score, so that supplier would be selected.

Just-In-Time Training Project Supplier Evaluation Matrix
September 9

Criteria	Weight	Supplier 1	Supplier 2	Supplier 3
Past performance	30%	70	90	70
Cost	25%	80	75	70
Educational background	25%	70	75	70
Management Approach	20%	85	80	70
Weighted Scores		**75.5**	**80.5**	**70**

Figure 5-22. Sample supplier evaluation matrix

CASE WRAP-UP

Kristin was pleased with the progress on planning tasks for the Just-In-Time Training project. Several members of her project team and the project steering committee had complimented Kristin on her ability to get key stakeholders involved. They also liked the way she admitted her own areas of weakness and sought out expert advice. Kristin was grateful for the steering committee's suggestion to hire an outside firm early in the project to help find qualified suppliers for the training courses. Everyone felt confident that the project team had a handle on risk management. Kristin felt ready to tackle the challenges she would face in leading her team during project execution.

CHAPTER SUMMARY

Successful project managers know how important it is to develop, refine, and follow plans to meet project goals. This chapter summarizes the planning tasks and outputs for quality, human resource, communications, risk, and procurement management.

Planning outputs related to quality management include a quality management plan, a project dashboard, quality metrics descriptions, and a quality checklist. Sample outputs are provided for the Just-In-Time Training project.

Planning outputs related to human resource management include creating a human resource plan, which includes a project organizational chart, responsibility assignment matrix, resource histogram, and staffing management plan. Sample outputs are provided for the Just-In-Time Training project.

Planning outputs related to communications management include developing a communications management plan and project Web site. Sample outputs are provided for the Just-In-Time Training project.

Planning outputs related to risk management include developing a risk management plan, a probability/impact matrix, a risk register, and risk-related contract decisions. Sample updates are provided for the Just-In-Time Training project.

Planning outputs related to procurement management include performing a make-or-buy analysis and preparing a procurement management plan, requests for proposal/quote, a contract statement of work, and source selection criteria (such as a supplier evaluation matrix). Sample outputs are provided for the Just-In-Time Training project.

QUICK QUIZ

1. _____ is defined as the degree to which a set of inherent characteristics fulfill requirements.

   A. Fitness for use

   B. Conformance to requirements

   C. Metrics

   D. Quality

2. _____ allow organizations to measure their performance in certain areas—such as failure rates, availability, and reliability—and compare them over time or with other organizations.

   A. Ratings

   B. Metrics

   C. Quality-control charts

   D. Checklists

3. A RACI chart is a type of _____.

   A. project organizational chart

   B. resource histogram

   C. responsibility assignment matrix

   D. project dashboard

4. A _____ describes when and how people will be added to and taken off of a project.

   A. project organizational chart

   B. resource histogram

   C. responsibility assignment matrix

   D. staffing management plan

5. Topics such as who will receive project information and who will produce it, suggested methods or guidelines for conveying the information, frequency of communication, and escalation procedures for resolving issues should be described in a _____.

    A. communications management plan

    B. staffing management plan

    C. team contract

    D. scope statement

6. Suppose you are a member of Kristin's team and you are having difficulties communicating with one of the supplier management experts who is providing important content for a class you are developing. What strategy might you use to help improve communications?

    A. put all communications in writing

    B. put all communications on your project Web site

    C. use several different methods to communicate with this person

    D. ask Kristin to find a better person to provide the technical content

7. What two dimensions should you use when evaluating project risks?

    A. probability and impact

    B. cost and schedule

    C. negative and positive

    D. source and responsibility

8. A _____ is a document that contains results of various risk management processes, often displayed in a table or spreadsheet format.

    A. risk event

    B. trigger

    C. risk register

    D. risk management plan

9. You can purchase an item you need for a project for $10,000 and it has daily operating costs of $500, or you can lease the item for $700 per day. On which day will the purchase cost be the same as the lease cost?

   A. day 5

   B. day 10

   C. day 50

   D. day 100

10. You want to have the least risk possible in setting up a contract to purchase goods and services from an outside firm. As the buyer, what type of contract should you use?

   A. fixed price

   B. unit price

   C. cost reimbursable

   D. time and materials

Quick Quiz Answers

1. D; 2. B; 3. C; 4. D; 5. A; 6. C; 7. A; 8. C; 9. C; 10. A

DISCUSSION QUESTIONS

1. What is the main purpose of a project quality management plan? What are two metrics besides those provided in this chapter that Kristin and her team could use on the Just-In-Time Training project? Besides ensuring that classrooms are ready for training, where else might they use a checklist on the project?

2. What is the main purpose of a staffing management plan? What tool should you use to graphically show total staffing needs for a project? What tool should you use to clarify roles and responsibilities for tasks?

3. Why is it so difficult to ensure good communication on projects? What strategies can any project team use to improve communications?

4. Why is risk management often neglected on projects? Why is it important to take the time to identify and rank risks throughout the project's life?

5. What is the difference between an RFP and an RFQ? Give an example of the appropriate use of each.

EXERCISES

1. Find an example of a large project that took more than a year to complete. You can ask people at your college, university, or work about a recent project, such as a major fund raising campaign, information systems installation, or building project. You can also find information about projects online such as the Big Dig in Boston (*www.masspike.com/bigdig*), the Patronas Twin Towers in Malaysia, and many other building projects (*www.greatbuildings.com.*) Describe some of the tasks performed in planning the quality, human resource, communications, risk, and procurement aspects of the project. Write a one-page paper or prepare a short presentation summarizing your findings.

2. Search the Internet for "project dashboard." Find at least three different charts or examples that can be used on a project dashboard. Document your findings in a two-page paper or short presentation, including screen shots of the charts you find and your assessment of their value.

3. Your company is planning to launch an important project starting January 1, which will last one year. You estimate that you will need one half-time project manager; two full-time business analysts for the first six months; two full-time marketing analysts for the whole year; four full-time business interns for the months of June, July, and August; and one full-time salesperson for the last three months. Use spreadsheet software such as Microsoft Excel to create a stacked-column chart showing a resource histogram for this project, similar to the one shown in Figure 5-8. Be sure to include a legend to label the types of resources needed, and use appropriate titles and axis labels. You can use the resource histogram template on the companion Web site to make this exercise easier.

4. List three negative risk events and three positive risk events for the Just-In-Time Training project. Briefly describe each risk, and then rate each one as high, medium, or low in terms of probability and impact. Plot the results on a probability/impact matrix. Also, prepare an entry for one of the risks for the risk register.

5. Assume the source selection criteria for evaluating proposals for a project is as follows:

    - Management approach 15%

    - Technical approach 15%

    - Past performance 20%

    - Price 20%

    - Interview results and samples 30%

Use Figure 5-22 as a guide and the weighted scoring model template from the companion Web site to calculate the total weighted scores for three proposals. Enter scores for Proposal 1 as 80, 90, 70, 90, and 80, respectively. Enter scores for Proposal 2 as 90, 50, 95, 80, and 95. Enter scores for Proposal 3 as 60, 90, 90, 80, and 65. Add a paragraph summarizing the results and your recommendation on the spreadsheet. Print your results on one page.

TEAM PROJECTS

1.   Your organization initiated a project to raise money for an important charity. Assume that there are 1,000 people in your organization. Also, assume that you have six months to raise as much money as possible, with a goal of $100,000. Create a checklist to use in soliciting sponsors for the fundraiser, a responsibility assignment matrix for various stakeholders, a project Web site (just the home page), a probability/impact matrix with six potential negative risks, and a request for quote for obtaining items your team will need. Be creative in your responses. Remember that this project is entirely run by volunteers.

2.   You are part of a team in charge of a project to help people in your company (500 people) lose weight. This project is part of a competition, and the top "losers" will be featured in a popular television show. Assume that you have six months to complete the project and a budget of $10,000. Develop metrics for the project, a project organizational chart, a communications management plan, and a risk register with at least three entries for the project.

3.   Using the information you developed in Team Project 1 or 2, role-play a meeting to review one of these planning documents with key stakeholders. Determine who will play what role (project manager, team member from a certain department, senior managers, and so on). Be creative in displaying different personalities (a senior manager who questions the importance of the project to the organization, a team member who is very shy or obnoxious).

4.   Develop a project dashboard for your team project, using Figure 5-3 as an example. Be sure to include at least eight different metrics. Document your results in a one-page paper or short presentation, showing the actual dashboard you created.

5.   Perform the planning tasks (only for the knowledge areas covered in this chapter) for one of the case studies provided in Appendix C. Remember to be thorough in your planning so that your execution goes smoothly. Be sure to have your sponsor and other stakeholders provide inputs on your plans.

COMPANION WEB SITE

Visit the free companion Web site for this text at **www.intropm.com** to access template files, online quizzes, Jeopardy-like games, Microsoft Project files, links to sites mentioned in the text, and other information to help you learn more about this important field. Instructors must contact the author at schwalbe@augsburg.edu to gain access to the instructor site. Anyone can access the student site.

KEY TERMS

bid — A document prepared by sellers providing pricing for standard items that have been clearly defined by the buyer.

blogs — Easy-to-use journals on the Web that allow users to write entries, create links, and upload pictures, while allowing readers to post comments to particular journal entries.

checklist — A list of items to be noted or consulted.

communications management plan — A document that guides project communications.

conformance to requirements — The process of ensuring that the project's processes and products meet written specifications.

contingency plans — The predefined actions that the project team will take if an identified risk event occurs.

contingency reserves or **contingency allowances** — The funds held by the project sponsor that can be used to mitigate cost or schedule overruns if unknown risks occur.

contracts — The mutually binding agreements that obligate the seller to provide the specified products or services, and obligate the buyer to pay for them.

contract statement of work (SOW) — A document that describes the goods or services to be purchased.

cost-reimbursable contract — A contract that involves payment to the seller for direct and indirect actual costs.

fallback plans — The plans that are developed for risks that have a high impact on meeting project objectives, and are put into effect if attempts to reduce the risk are not effective.

fitness for use — The ability of a product to be used as it was intended.

fixed-price or **lump-sum contract** — A type of contract that involves a fixed price for a well-defined product or service.

make-or-buy analysis — The process of estimating the internal costs of providing a product or service and comparing that estimate to the cost of outsourcing.

metric — A standard of measurement.

project dashboard — A graphic screen summarizing key project metrics.

project organizational chart — A graphical representation of how authority and responsibility is distributed within the project.

proposal — A document in which sellers describe what they will do to meet the requirements of a buyer.

quality — The degree to which a set of inherent characteristics fulfill requirements.

RACI charts — A type of responsibility assignment matrix that shows **R**esponsibility, **A**ccountability, **C**onsultation, and **I**nformed roles for project stakeholders.

Request for Proposal (RFP) — A document used to solicit proposals from prospective suppliers.

Request for Quote (RFQ) — A document used to solicit quotes or bids from prospective suppliers.

resource histogram — A column chart that shows the number of resources required for or assigned to a project over time.

responsibility assignment matrix (RAM) — A matrix that maps the work of the project as described in the WBS to the people responsible for performing the work.

risk — An uncertainty that can have a negative or positive effect on meeting project objectives.

risk events — The specific, uncertain events that may occur to the detriment or enhancement of the project.

risk register — A document that contains results of various risk management processes, often displayed in a table or spreadsheet format.

root cause — The real or underlying reason a problem occurs.

staffing management plan — A plan that describes when and how people will be added to and taken off of a project.

time-and-material contract — A type of contract that is a hybrid of both a fixed-price and cost-reimbursable contract.

triggers — The indicators or symptoms of actual risk events.

228

END NOTES

[1] Dragan Milosevic, Portland State University, "Delivering Projects: What the Winners Do," PMI Conference Proceedings (November 2001).

[2] Jokes Unlimited, "Quotes from Companies," (http://www.jokesunlimited.com/jokes/quotes_from_companies.html) (Accessed June 2009).

[3] Cesar Pelli and Michael J. Crosbie, "Building Petronas Towers," *Architecture Week* (February 19, 2003).

[4] Rohland, Dick, "I-35W Bridge Completion Brings Closure to Minneapolis," ConstructionEquipmentGuide.com (October 4, 2008).

Chapter 6
Executing Projects

LEARNING OBJECTIVES

After reading this chapter, you will be able to:

- List several tasks and outputs of project execution
- Discuss what is involved in directing and managing project execution as part of project integration management, including the importance of producing promised deliverables, implementing solutions to problems, evaluating work performance information, and requesting changes to a project
- Explain the importance of recommending corrective actions and updating project – related information as part of quality assurance
- Describe the executing tasks performed as part of human resource management, summarize important concepts related to managing people, and explain what is involved in leveling resources, assigning staff, reviewing resource calendars, and assessing team performance
- Discuss important communications concepts, and describe the executing tasks performed as part of communications management
- Explain the executing tasks performed as part of procurement management, and describe what is involved in selecting sellers and preparing contract awards

---

OPENING CASE

Kristin reviewed initial project plans with the steering committee for the Just-In-Time Training project. Committee members felt that everything was going well so far and that it was time to commit more resources to the project. At later steering committee meetings, Kristin brought up several challenges she was facing in executing the project plans. For example, Jamie, the supplier management expert assigned to her team half-time, was not working out. In addition, there were several conflicts between various stakeholders on how to perform certain tasks, and several people complained about a lack of communication about the project. The IT people supporting the project were overallocated, yet some of their tasks were on the critical path for the project. The prototype for the supplier management introductory course was not as well received as the team had hoped, and Kristin was afraid that the seller might demand more money to make major changes to the course. Kristin would need to use her experience—especially her soft (interpersonal) skills—as well as advice from the project steering committee to deal with these and other challenges.

INTRODUCTION

Whereas project planning is considered to be the most unappreciated project management process group, project execution is the most noticed. Of course, good plans are important, but it is even more important to execute them well. In fact, the June 21, 1999, issue of *Fortune* summarized research showing that without a doubt, the main reason chief executive officers (CEOs) failed was poor execution. Failed CEOs simply did not get things done, were indecisive, and did not deliver on commitments. The same is true for project managers and all leaders. Stakeholders expect to see results from their projects through effective execution.

What Went Wrong?

"The results are not acceptable," stated President Bush four days after Hurricane Katrina caused major damage to New Orleans and surrounding areas. After Federal Emergency Management Agency (FEMA) officials returned in January 2005 from a tour of the tsunami devastation in Asia, New Orleans was the number one disaster they discussed. Officials had drawn up dozens of plans and conducted preparedness drills for years, but despite all the warnings, Hurricane Katrina overwhelmed government agencies, and many people suffered from slow response to their needs for emergency aid. The mayor of New Orleans, C. Ray Nagin, blasted the government for its lack of an immediate response. "I've talked directly with the president, I've talked to the head of the Homeland Security, I've talked to everybody under the sun, I've been out there."[1] People were disappointed with the poor execution of disaster relief efforts during the first few days, and officials took corrective actions to address the challenges caused by the hurricane.

Recall that, in general, the majority of a project's time and budget is spent on project execution. Many of the tasks and outputs created in the other process groups are fairly similar from project to project, but no two projects are ever executed in the exact same way. Why? Because projects involve uncertainty. No one can ever predict the challenges that project teams will face in trying to meet project goals. This chapter summarizes the main tasks involved in executing projects and discusses some challenges that Kristin faced in managing the execution of the Just-In-Time Training project.

SUMMARY OF EXECUTING TASKS AND OUTPUTS

Figure 6-1 summarizes processes and outputs of project execution by knowledge area, based on the *PMBOK® Guide, Fourth Edition*. Notice that not every knowledge area is included, and change requests, project management plan updates, and project document updates are outputs of several of these knowledge areas. Although there are many planning tasks related to scope, time, cost, and risk management, these knowledge areas do not have tasks directly related to project execution. Changes to the triple constraint and risk management are addressed in the next chapter on project monitoring and control. This chapter focuses on tasks and outputs that project teams perform to execute projects, and provides specific examples for Global Construction's Just-In-Time Training project.

Knowledge area	Executing process	Outputs
Project integration management	Direct and manage project execution	Deliverables
		Work performance data
		Change requests
		Project management plan updates
		Project document updates
Project quality management	Perform quality assurance	Organizational process asset updates
		Change requests
		Project management plan updates
		Project document updates
Project human resource management	Acquire project team	Project staff assignments
		Resource calendars
		Project management plan updates
		Team performance assessment
	Develop project team	Enterprise environmental factors updates
		Change request
		Project management plan updates
	Manage project team	Enterprise environmental factors updates
		Organizational process assets updates
Project communications management	Distribute information	Organizational process assets updates
	Manage stakeholder expectations	Organizational process assets updates
		Change requests
		Project management plan updates
		Project document updates
Project procurement management	Conduct procurements	Selected sellers
		Procurement award
		Resource calendars
		Change requests
		Project management plan updates
		Project documents updates

Figure 6-1. Executing processes and outputs

EXECUTING TASKS FOR PROJECT INTEGRATION MANAGEMENT

As part of project integration management, the project manager must perform the task of directing and managing stakeholders to complete the project. Project managers can follow several important practices to help accomplish this challenging job:

- *Coordinate planning and execution:* As mentioned earlier, the main purpose of project planning is to guide execution. If the project manager and team did a good job planning, the plans will be easier to execute. As things change, team members need to update the plans to keep everyone working on the same page.

- *Develop and use soft skills:* Several studies of project managers suggest that soft skills (for example, strong leadership, effective team building, strong communication, motivation, negotiation, conflict management, and problem solving) are crucial to the success of project managers, especially during project execution. Project managers must lead by example in demonstrating the importance of creating good project plans and then following them in project execution. Project managers often create plans for things they need to do themselves, such as meeting with key stakeholders, reviewing important information, and so on. If project managers follow through on their own plans, their team members are more likely to do the same.

- *Provide a supportive organizational culture:* Good project execution requires a supportive organizational culture. For example, organizational procedures can help or hinder project execution. If an organization has useful guidelines and templates for project management that everyone in the organization follows, it will be easier for project managers and their teams to plan and do their work. If the organization uses the project plans as the basis for performing and monitoring progress during execution, the culture will promote the relationship between good planning and execution. Even if the organizational culture is not supportive, project managers can create a supportive culture within their own project and work on improving the culture in other parts of the organization.

- *Break the rules when needed:* Even with a supportive organizational culture, project managers might sometimes find it necessary to break the rules to produce project results in a timely manner. When project managers break the rules, politics will play a role in the results. For example, if a particular project requires use of nonstandard software, the project manager must use his or her political skills to convince concerned stakeholders of the need to break the rules.

- *Capitalize on product, business, and application area knowledge:* The application area of the project directly affects project execution because the products of the project are produced during project execution. For example, if a project involves constructing a new building, the project manager and other stakeholders would need to use their expertise in architecture, engineering, and construction to produce the product successfully. Project managers should use their expertise to guide their team and make important decisions.

- *Use project execution tools and techniques:* For example, following a project management methodology and using a project management information system can help project execution go more smoothly. The project management methodology should include guidelines on how to communicate project status, handle conflicts, work with suppliers and other stakeholders, and perform other important tasks.

As listed in Figure 6-1, the main outputs produced during execution as part of project integration management are deliverables, work performance data, change requests, project management plan updates, and project document updates. Updating the project management plan and other project documents is self explanatory. These other outputs will be described in more detail, along with a discussion of how to solve problems that often occur during execution.

Deliverables

Most project sponsors would say that the most important output of any project is its deliverables. Recall that deliverables are products or services produced or provided as part of a project. They include product and process-related items. For the Just-In-Time Training project at Global Construction, key product-related deliverables include the training materials and courses (instructor-led, Web-based, and CD-ROM). Process-related deliverables related to developing and delivering those training materials and courses include researching existing training and meeting with potential partners.

Sample Deliverables

Because the Just-In-Time Training project is fictitious, it is impossible to show the actual training materials, courses, and other deliverables produced during execution. Because you are probably reading this book as part of a course and have taken other courses in both an instructor-led or online fashion, you have some feel for what training materials and courses are like. Recall that several of the training courses for this project must be available on a just-in-time basis (that is, they must be available whenever the employee wants to learn), so deliverables must be created to provide effective Web-based and/or CD-ROM instruction. Note the word *effective*. The main objective of this training is to provide employees with the knowledge and skills they need to do their jobs when they need it. Just because training is available around the clock does not mean that it is effective. The section on quality later in this chapter describes the importance of ensuring quality during project execution.

Work Performance Data

One of Kristin's main jobs during project execution was collecting, assessing, and communicating work performance data. Kristin used the "management by wandering around" (MBWA) approach, meaning she informally observed and talked to her project team members, suppliers, and other stakeholders as much as possible. She wanted to know firsthand how project activities were progressing, and she wanted to offer suggestions as often as possible. Of course, she also used more formal communications, such as status reports, the project dashboard (which summarized key project metrics, as described in Chapter 5), survey results, and course evaluations, to address work performance on the project.

Sample Work Performance Data

A common way to summarize work performance data is by using a milestone report. Recall that a milestone is a significant event on a project, such as completing a major deliverable or awarding a major contract. Figure 6-2 provides part of a milestone report for the Just-In-Time Training project. Notice that in addition to listing the milestones, the report lists the planned date for completion (in month/day format), the status, the person responsible for the milestone, and issues/comments. Project 2010 also includes a standard milestone report, as described in Appendix A. You can also create customized reports in Project 2010 to tailor the content and format of reports.

Just-In-Time Training Project Milestone Report
September 1

Milestone	Date	Status	Responsible	Issues/Comments
Researched existing training	8/13	Complete	Jamie (replaced by Abner)	Many basic courses available, but not much advanced/tailored training. (Note: Replaced Jamie with better candidate for project after Jamie completed this task)
Supplier management training survey results reported to steering committee	8/24	Completed	Kristin	Great feedback. Many people stressed the need to have instructor-led training and mentors for soft skills development
Meetings with potential partners	9/21	In progress	Kristin/Contracting	May need more time for meetings
Partnership agreements completed	9/28	Not started yet	Kristin/Contracting	May need more time to set up agreements

An Introduction to Project Management, Third Edition

Developed executive course	11/9	Not started yet	TBD Supplier	
Developed introductory course	11/9	Not started yet	TBD Supplier	
Developed advanced course	11/23	Not started yet	TBD Supplier	
Held pilot course	11/23	Not started yet	TBD Supplier	
Pilot course results reported to steering committee	11/30	Not started yet	Kristin	

Figure 6-2. Sample milestone report for reporting work performance data

Change Requests

Often, a number of requests for changes emerge during project execution. Recall that a process for handling changes should be defined during project planning as part of the project management plan. Chapter 7, which covers monitoring and controlling projects, provides detailed information on handling changes. It is important during project execution to formally and informally request appropriate changes. Project managers, team members, suppliers, and other stakeholders can make change requests, so it is important to have a good process in place for handling them.

Sample Change Request

Successful project teams use well-defined processes and standard forms for requesting project changes. Some changes are requested using other established change processes. For example, when Kristin requested that Jamie be replaced with Abner as the project team member from the supplier management department, she used Global Construction's personnel transfer process. Jamie's department head and the human resources department handled necessary paperwork for the reassignment. For other change requests—especially those that may impact achieving scope, time, or cost goals of the project—a formal change request form should be submitted through the appropriate channels. Figure 6-3 provides a sample of a completed change request form for the Just-In-Time Training project. It is important to have a good justification for the requested change and address the benefits of incurring any additional costs. In this case, if the additional $550 is not provided, the entire project will be delayed.

Just-In-Time Training Project Change Request

Project Name: Just-In-Time Training Project

Date Request Submitted: September 22

Title of Change Request: Increase time to develop partnerships for supplier management training

Change Order Number: A200-17

Submitted by: Kristin Maur

Change Category: __Scope   __Schedule   <u>X</u> Cost __Technology __Other

Description of change requested:

In order to avoid a schedule slip and have appropriate internal resources available, we are requesting the approval of paid overtime for creating and distributing the survey for the supplier management course.

Events that made this change necessary or desirable:

The IT person assigned to our project has several other important projects on-hand. If these tasks are delayed, the entire project will be delayed.

Justification for the change/why it is needed/desired to continue/complete the project:

We must send out and analyze the survey in a timely manner since we need the information to develop the first supplier management course and select an appropriate supplier.

Impact of the proposed change on:

Scope: None   **Schedule:** None   **Cost:** $550

Staffing: One IT person will work 10 hours of paid overtime basis over a period of several weeks.

Risk: Low. This person suggested the paid overtime and has successfully worked overtime in the past.

Other: None

Suggested implementation if the change request is approved: Include the overtime pay in the normal paycheck.

Required approvals:

Name/Title	Date	Approve/Reject
Evan George/Affected Employee		
Stella Jacobs/Employee's Supervisor		
Julia Portman, VP of IT		

Figure 6-3. Sample change request

Implemented Solutions to Problems

Of course, all project teams face numerous problems. Some surface early during project initiation or planning, but some do not occur until project execution, when many things are happening at once. Many problems can be avoided by doing a good job of initiating, planning, or monitoring and controlling the project, but other problems cannot be avoided. Some common problems encountered during project execution include the following:

1. The project sponsor and/or other senior managers are not very supportive of the project.

2. Project stakeholders, such as people who would use the products and services the project is attempting to create, are not sufficiently involved in project decision-making.

3. The project manager is inexperienced in managing people, working in a particular organization, or understanding the application area of the project.

4. The project objectives/scope are unclear.

5. Estimates for time and cost goals are unreliable or unrealistic.

6. Business needs/technology changes have impacted the project.

7. People working on the project are incompetent or unmotivated.

8. There are poor conflict-management procedures.

9. Communications are poor.

10. Suppliers are not delivering as promised.

The first five problems should have been addressed during project initiation or planning (and were addressed in previous chapters), but they can also cause difficulties during execution. Addressing business and technology changes are discussed in the next chapter on monitoring and controlling. The last four problems are discussed in this chapter and presented in the context of the Just-In-Time Training project.

Sample Implemented Solutions to Problems

Kristin Maur had been working hard to direct and manage project execution, but she encountered several problems. The following sections discuss the problems of incompetent or unmotivated people working on the project and poor conflict-management procedures. Later sections discuss strategies for improving communications and supplier delivery.

Issues with Competence and Motivation

Jamie, the project team member assigned to work half-time from the supplier management department, was not contributing much to the project. Jamie's main role was to provide expertise in developing the supplier management courses. She was well qualified for this assignment, having over 10 years' experience with Global Construction managing major accounts with suppliers. (Recall that supplier management was the most important training topic for the project.) Kristin knew that Jamie was very good at negotiating with and managing suppliers, but Jamie felt that she was assigned to the project primarily because she was available, having recently finished another large project. Although Jamie was assigned to work on this project from its start, she was on vacation for most of the first month and seemed uninterested in the project when she was around. Kristin tried her best to motivate her, but she could see that Jamie was simply not the right person for the project. (See a later section in this chapter on motivation.) Kristin talked to Jamie directly, and she admitted that she would much rather deal directly with suppliers than work on this training project. Just two months into the project, Kristin used her experience and contacts within the company to find a suitable replacement. She worked through the project steering committee and other managers to quickly approve the personnel change.

Poor Conflict Management

Most large projects are high-stake endeavors that are highly visible within organizations. They require tremendous effort from team members, are expensive, require significant resources, and can have an extensive impact on the way work is done in an organization. When the stakes are high, conflict is never far away, and even small projects with low budgets have conflicts—it is a natural part of work and life in general. Project managers should lead their teams in developing norms for dealing with various types of conflicts that might arise. For example, team members should know that disrespectful behavior toward any project stakeholder is inappropriate, and that team members are expected to try to work out small conflicts themselves before elevating them to higher levels. The team contract, created during project planning, should address team conduct and conflict management.

Blake and Mouton (1964) delineated five basic modes for handling conflicts. Each strategy can be considered as being high, medium, or low on two dimensions: importance of the task or goal, and importance of the relationship between the people having the conflict.

1. *Confrontation*: When using the **confrontation mode**, project managers directly face a conflict using a problem-solving approach that allows affected parties to work through their disagreements. This approach is also called the problem-solving mode. It is best used when *both the task and the relationship are of high importance.* For example, Kristin confronted Jamie when she was not working well on the project. They discussed the problem and decided it was best for both parties for Jamie to leave the project team. They also discussed who could take her place. This mode reflects a win/win approach.

2. *Compromise*: With the **compromise mode**, project managers use a give-and-take approach to resolve conflicts, bargaining and searching for solutions that

will bring some degree of satisfaction to all the parties in a dispute. This give-and-take approach works best when both the task and the relationship are of medium importance. For example, suppose one of Kristin's stakeholders wanted to add a new topic to one of the courses for no extra cost, and the supplier wanted payment for it, as agreed to in their contract. They could compromise and add the new topic at a discounted cost. This mode reflects a lose/lose approach, since both parties are giving up something.

3. *Smoothing*: When using the **smoothing mode**, the project manager de-emphasizes or avoids areas of differences and emphasizes areas of agreement. This method is best used when the *relationship is of high importance and the task is of low importance.* For example, two members of the project steering committee might totally disagree on whether they should provide incentive bonuses to suppliers for achieving outstanding ratings on courses. Kristin could use the smoothing mode to ensure that the relationship between the steering committee members remains harmonious by discussing with these team members the areas in which they agree and by downplaying the topic of bonuses during meetings.

4. *Forcing*: The **forcing mode** can be viewed as the win-lose approach to conflict resolution. People exert their viewpoints even though they contradict the viewpoints of others. This approach is appropriate when *the task is of high importance and the relationship is of low importance.* For example, if you are competing against another firm for a contract, it may be appropriate to use the forcing mode.

5. *Withdrawal*: When using the **withdrawal mode**, project managers retreat or withdraw from an actual or potential disagreement. This approach is the least desirable conflict-handling mode. It may be appropriate when *both the task and the relationship are of low importance.*

More recent studies recognize a sixth conflict-handling mode:

6. *Collaborating*: Using the **collaborating mode**, decision makers incorporate different viewpoints and insights to develop consensus and commitment.

Effective project managers often use confrontation or collaborating for conflict resolution instead of the other modes. The term *confrontation* may be misleading. This mode focuses on a win-win problem-solving approach, in which all parties work together to find the best way to solve the conflict.

Project managers must also realize that not all conflict is bad. In fact, conflict can often be good. Conflict often produces important results, such as new ideas, better alternatives, and motivation to work harder and more collaboratively. Project team members might become stagnant or develop **groupthink**—conformance to the values or ethical standards of a group—if there are no conflicting viewpoints on various aspects of a project. Research suggests that task-related conflict, which is derived from differences over team objectives and how to achieve them, often improves team performance.

Emotional conflict, however, which stems from personality clashes and misunderstandings, often depresses team performance. Project managers should create an environment that encourages and maintains the positive and productive aspects of conflict.

EXECUTING TASKS FOR PROJECT QUALITY MANAGEMENT

It is one thing to develop a plan for ensuring quality on a project; it is another to ensure delivery of quality products and services. The main quality management task required during execution is quality assurance. **Quality assurance** includes all the activities related to satisfying the relevant quality standards for a project. For example, it was important for the Just-In-Time Training project that the course materials included content that would meet participants' needs. Kristin made sure that the people developing those materials reviewed results of the needs assessment, were experts in the field, and reviewed the content with Global Construction, Inc. managers in those areas (supplier management, negotiating skills, project management, and software applications). Another goal of quality assurance is continual quality improvement. Many companies understand the importance of quality assurance and have entire departments dedicated to this discipline. These companies have detailed processes in place to make sure that their products and services conform to various quality requirements. They also know they must produce products and services at competitive prices. To be successful in today's competitive business environment, successful companies develop their own best practices and evaluate other organizations' best practices to continuously improve the way they do business. See Chapter 9 for more information on and examples of best practices in project management.

Top management and project managers can impact the quality of projects most significantly by implementing quality assurance. Key outputs of quality assurance include change requests, project management plan updates, and project document updates. Another output is updates to organizational process assets. Recall that organizational process assets include formal and informal plans, policies, procedures, guidelines, information systems, financial systems, management systems, lessons learned, and historical information that can be used to influence a project's success.

Quality Assurance Techniques

It is important for organizations to use common techniques to identify areas in which they would benefit from taking actions to improve quality. Several quality improvement techniques include benchmarking, quality audits, and cause-and-effect diagrams.

- **Benchmarking** generates ideas for quality improvements by comparing specific project practices or product characteristics to those of other projects or products within or outside of the organization itself. For example, one reason that Global Construction initiated the Just-In-Time Training project was because it discovered that its cost of training per employee was higher than that of similar firms. The amount of money that organizations spend on training is a benchmark. As another example, many organizations have overall course ratings using a Likert scale, with 1 being the lowest rating and 5 being the highest. A benchmark for a good rating might be an average rating of 3.0 or higher. If training participants rated the prototype supplier management course lower than 3.0 on average, then Kristin's team would need to take corrective actions to improve the quality of the course.

- A **quality audit** is a structured review of specific quality management activities that helps identify lessons learned, which could improve performance on current or future projects. In-house auditors or third parties with expertise in specific areas can perform quality audits, which can be either scheduled or random. Recall that several of the main goals of the Just-In-Time Training project were to reduce training costs at Global Construction, provide training when it was needed, and improve employee productivity. By establishing measurement techniques for monitoring these goals and performing an audit to see how well they are being met, Kristin's team can see how well they are doing in meeting specific goals. For example, they could send out a monthly survey asking employees if they are getting training when they need it and if it is helping improve their productivity. A quality audit could be done periodically to review the survey results. If there is a sudden decrease in ratings, Kristin's team would need to take corrective actions.

- **Cause-and-effect diagrams**—also called fishbone diagrams (because their structure resembles a fishbone) or Ishikawa diagrams (named after their creator)—can assist in ensuring and improving quality by finding the root causes of quality problems. Recall from Chapter 5 that a root cause is the real or underlying reason a problem occurs. Kristin and her team created several of these diagrams to find the root causes of quality problems, as described in the next section.

Sample Quality Assurance Technique: Cause and Effect Diagram

After training participants rated the prototype supplier management course less than 3.0 on average, Kristin's team knew they had to recommend corrective actions. They first decided to analyze what the root cause of the problem really was. The prototype course was available in three formats: instructor-led, Web-based, and CD-ROM. The Web-based and CD-ROM courses were virtually identical, except participants in the Web-based course could also access interactive discussion boards and chat rooms as they accessed the course via the Internet. The evaluations for the instructor-led course were actually above average; however, the Web-based and CD-ROM courses were rated below average.

The student evaluation forms provided some open-ended feedback, so Kristin and her team decided to use that information plus other possible causes of the low ratings to prepare a cause-and-effect diagram, as shown in Figure 6-4. The main effect is the low course ratings, and potential causes are grouped into several main categories: content, interactivity, speed, and graphics/fonts. Potential subcategories are listed in each area, such as "too simple" and "not enough examples" under content. Kristin and her team contacted the participants in the prototype courses to get more specific information to help identify the root cause(s) of the low ratings. When they discovered that the majority of respondents rated the CD-ROM course poorly because it lacked interactivity, they discussed the option of supplementing the course with the Web-based interactivity features, such as the discussion board and chat room. Respondents were generally enthusiastic about the Web-based course, except for those who accessed it with a slow Internet connection. A simple solution would be to have them use the CD-ROM for most of the course and use the Internet for the discussion board and chat room. Because the other potential causes were not the main reasons for the low ratings, they were not addressed.

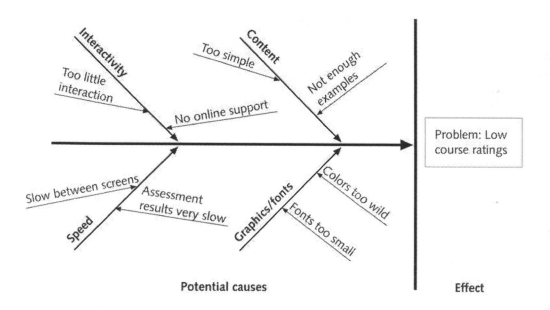

Figure 6-4. Sample cause-and-effect diagram

Kristin and her team recommended that the discussion board and chat room features of the Web-based course be integrated into the CD-ROM course. The supplier who developed both courses said it would be a very simple change and would not affect time or cost estimates.

EXECUTING TASKS FOR PROJECT HUMAN RESOURCE MANAGEMENT

Effective project human resource management is crucial to project execution. The main tasks project managers perform include acquiring, developing, and managing the project team. Key outputs include project staff assignments, resource calendars, team performance assessment, change requests, and updates to the project management plan and organizational process assets.

Resource calendars are simply calendars for each resource showing work assignment dates. Before discussing project staff assignments and team performance assessment, it is important to understand basic concepts related to dealing with people in a work setting. Key concepts include motivation, influence, and effectiveness.

Motivation

Psychologists, managers, coworkers, teachers, parents, and most people in general still struggle to understand what motivates people, or why they do what they do. **Intrinsic motivation** causes people to participate in an activity for their own enjoyment. For example, some people love to read, write, or play an instrument because it makes them feel good. **Extrinsic motivation** causes people to do something for a reward or to avoid a penalty. For example, some young children would prefer *not* to play an instrument, but do so to receive a reward or avoid a punishment. Why do some people require no external motivation whatsoever to produce high-quality work while others require significant external motivation to perform routine tasks? Why can't you get someone who is extremely productive at work to do simple tasks at home? Mankind will continue to try to answer these overarching questions, but a basic understanding of motivational theory will help anyone who has to work or live with other people.

Maslow's Hierarchy of Needs

Abraham Maslow, a highly respected psychologist who rejected the dehumanizing negativism of psychology in the 1950s, is best known for developing a hierarchy of needs. In the 1950s, proponents of Sigmund Freud's psychoanalytic theory were promoting the idea that human beings were not the masters of their destiny and that their actions were governed by unconscious processes dominated by primitive sexual urges. During the same period, behavioral psychologists saw human beings as controlled by the environment. Maslow argued that both schools of thought failed to recognize unique qualities of human behavior: love, self-esteem, belonging, self-expression, and creativity. He argued that these unique qualities enable people to make independent choices, which give them full control over their destiny.

Figure 6-5 shows the basic pyramid structure of **Maslow's hierarchy of needs**, which states that people's behaviors are guided or motivated by a sequence of needs. At the bottom of the hierarchy are physiological needs, such as air, water, and food. After physiological needs are satisfied, safety needs—such as shelter from bad weather, lack of physical or mental abuse, and a low-crime environment—guide behavior. After safety needs are satisfied, social needs—such as having friends, belonging to groups, and having a sense of community—come to the forefront, and so on up the hierarchy. Examples of esteem needs include personal achievement, recognition, and respect, whereas self-actualization needs include a sense of fulfillment and belief that one is working to his or her potential. The order of these needs in the pyramid is significant. Maslow suggests that each level of the hierarchy is a prerequisite for the level above. For example, it is not possible for people to consider self-actualization if they have not addressed basic needs concerning security and safety. People in an emergency situation, such as a flood or hurricane, cannot be concerned with personal growth but will be motivated solely by the requirements of personal survival. After a particular need is satisfied, however, it no longer serves as a potent motivator of behavior.

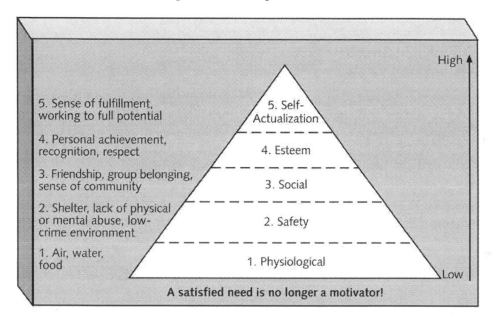

Figure 6-5. Maslow's hierarchy of needs (Schwalbe, Information Technology Project Management, Sixth Edition, 2010)

The bottom four needs in Maslow's hierarchy—physiological, safety, social, and esteem needs—are referred to as deficiency needs, and the highest level, self-actualization, is considered a growth need. Only after meeting deficiency needs can individuals act on growth needs. Self-actualized people are problem-focused, have an appreciation for life, are concerned about personal growth, and can have peak experiences.

Most people working on corporate projects probably have their basic physiological and safety needs met. If someone has a sudden medical emergency or is laid off from work, however, physiological and safety needs move to the forefront. To motivate project team members, the project manager needs to understand each person's motivation, especially with regard to social, esteem, and self-actualization needs. For example, team members new to a company and city might be motivated by social needs. To address social needs, a project manager could organize gatherings and social events for new workers. If a project manager knew a team member was interested in pursuing an advanced degree, he or she could offer suggestions on graduate programs, provide information on tuition reimbursement policies, and allow the team member some scheduling flexibility to balance work and school.

Maslow's hierarchy conveys a message of hope and growth. People can work to control their own destinies and naturally strive to achieve higher and higher needs. Some cultures disagree with Maslow's philosophy and have other beliefs on motivation. Recent brain research also suggests that there are physiological reasons for certain behaviors. In any case, successful project managers know that to provide appropriate motivation and maximize team performance, they must both meet project goals and understand team members' personal goals and needs.

Herzberg's Motivation-Hygiene Theory

Frederick Herzberg, a psychologist and professor, is best known for distinguishing between motivational factors and hygiene factors when considering motivation in work settings. He called factors that cause job satisfaction motivators, and factors that cause dissatisfaction hygiene factors. A hygiene factor is a basic necessity, such as air-conditioning during hot weather. Air-conditioning does not in itself provide team satisfaction, but without it you would have disgruntled staff on hot workdays.

Head of Case Western University's psychology department, Herzberg wrote the book *Work and the Nature of Man* in 1966 and the famous *Harvard Business Review* article "One More Time: How Do You Motivate Employees?" in 1968. Herzberg analyzed the factors that affected productivity among a sample of 1,685 employees. Popular beliefs at that time were that work output was most improved through larger salaries, more supervision, or a more attractive work environment. According to Herzberg, these hygiene factors would cause dissatisfaction if not present but would not motivate workers to do more if present. Herzberg found that people were motivated to work mainly by feelings of personal achievement and recognition. Motivators, Herzberg concluded, included achievement, recognition, the work itself, responsibility, advancement, and growth.

In his books and articles, Herzberg explained why attempts to use positive factors such as reducing time spent at work, implementing upward-spiraling wages, offering fringe benefits, providing human relations and sensitivity training, and so on did not instill motivation. He argued that people want to actualize themselves; they need stimuli for their growth and advancement needs in accordance with Maslow's hierarchy of needs. Factors such as achievement, recognition, responsibility, advancement, and growth produce job satisfaction and are work motivators.

McClelland's Acquired-Needs Theory

David McClelland proposed that an individual's specific needs are acquired or learned over time and shaped by life experiences. The main categories of acquired needs include achievement, affiliation, and power. Normally, one or two of these needs is dominant in individuals.

- *Achievement*: People with a high need for achievement (nAch) seek to excel and tend to avoid both low-risk and high-risk situations to improve their chances of achieving something worthwhile. Achievers need regular feedback and often prefer to work alone or with other high achievers. Managers should give high achievers challenging projects with achievable goals. Achievers should receive frequent performance feedback, and although money is not an important motivator to them, it is an effective form of feedback.

- *Affiliation*: People with a high need for affiliation (nAff) desire harmonious relationships with other people and need to feel accepted by others. They tend to conform to the norms of their work group and prefer work that involves significant personal interaction. Managers should try to create a cooperative work environment to meet the needs of people with a high need for affiliation.

- *Power*: People with a need for power (nPow) desire either personal power or institutional power. People who need personal power want to direct others and can be seen as bossy. People who need institutional, or social, power want to organize others to further the goals of the organization. Management should provide those seeking institutional power with the opportunity to manage others, emphasizing the importance of meeting organizational goals.

The Thematic Apperception Test (TAT) is a tool to measure the individual needs of different people using McClelland's categories. The TAT presents subjects with a series of ambiguous pictures and asks them to develop a spontaneous story for each picture, assuming they will project their own needs into the story.

McGregor's Theory X and Theory Y

Douglas McGregor was one of the great popularizers of a human relations approach to management, and he is best known for developing Theory X and Theory Y. In his research, documented in his 1960 book *The Human Side of Enterprise,* McGregor found that although many managers spouted the right ideas, they actually followed a set of assumptions about worker motivation that he called Theory X (sometimes referred to as classical systems theory). People who believe in Theory X assume that workers dislike and avoid work if possible, so managers must use coercion, threats, and various control schemes to get workers to make adequate efforts to meet objectives. Theory X managers assume that the average worker wants to be directed and prefers to avoid responsibility, has little ambition, and wants security above all else. When research seemed to demonstrate that these assumptions were not valid, McGregor suggested a different series of assumptions about human behavior that he called Theory Y (sometimes referred to as human relations theory). Managers who believe in Theory Y assume that individuals do not inherently dislike work but consider it as natural as play or rest. The most significant rewards are the satisfaction of esteem and self-actualization needs, as described by Maslow. McGregor urged managers to motivate people based on these more valid Theory Y notions.

Thamhain and Wilemon's Influence Bases

Many people working on a project do not report directly to project managers, and project managers often do not have control over project staff that report to them. For example, people are free to change jobs. If they are given work assignments they do not like, many workers will simply quit or transfer to other departments or projects. H. J. Thamhain and D. L. Wilemon investigated the approaches project managers use to deal with workers and how those approaches relate to project success. They identified nine influence bases available to project managers:

1. *Authority:* The legitimate hierarchical right to issue orders

2. *Assignment:* The project manager's perceived ability to influence a worker's assignment to future projects

3. *Budget:* The project manager's perceived ability to authorize the use of discretionary funds

4. *Promotion:* The ability to improve a worker's position

5. *Money:* The ability to increase a worker's pay and benefits

6. *Penalty:* The project manager's perceived ability to dispense or cause punishment

7. *Work challenge:* The ability to assign work that capitalizes on a worker's enjoyment of doing a particular task, which taps an intrinsic motivational factor

8. *Expertise:* The project manager's perceived specialized knowledge that others deem important

9. *Friendship:* The ability to establish friendly personal relationships between the project manager and others

Top management grants authority to the project manager, but not necessarily the power to control personnel assignments, budgets, promotions, and penalties. Team members, however, may misperceive their project manager's sphere of influence and expect him to have the power, for example, to grant promotions and transfers. If project managers' power is limited, they can still influence workers by providing challenging work, and they can increase the power of their influence by using expertise and friendship.

Thamhain and Wilemon found that projects were more likely to fail when project managers relied too heavily on using *authority, money, or penalty* to influence people. When project managers used *work challenge and expertise* to influence people, projects were more likely to succeed. The effectiveness of work challenge in influencing people is consistent with Maslow's and Herzberg's research on motivation. The importance of expertise as a means of influencing people makes sense on projects that involve special knowledge. For example, people working on a project to build a spaceship would expect the project manager to have appropriate education and experience in that area. They would also be impressed if he or she had actually worked on other space projects or traveled into space.

Covey's Effectiveness Research

Stephen Covey, author of *The 7 Habits of Highly Effective People* and several other books, expanded on the work done by Maslow, Herzberg, and others to develop an approach for helping people and teams become more effective. Covey's first three habits of effective people—be proactive, begin with the end in mind, and put first things first—help people achieve a private victory by becoming independent. After achieving independence, people can then strive for interdependence by developing the next three habits—think win/win; seek first to understand, then to be understood; and synergize. (**Synergy** is the concept that the whole is equal to more than the sum of its parts.) Finally, everyone can work on Covey's seventh habit—sharpen the saw—to develop and renew their physical, spiritual, mental, and social/emotional selves.

Project managers can apply Covey's seven habits to improve effectiveness on projects, as follows:

1. *Be proactive:* Covey, like Maslow, believes that people have the ability to be proactive and choose their responses to different situations. Project managers must be proactive, anticipate, and plan for problems and inevitable changes on projects. They can also encourage team members to be proactive in their work.

2. *Begin with the end in mind:* Covey suggests that people focus on their values, what they really want to accomplish, and how they really want to be remembered in their lives. He suggests writing a mission statement to help achieve this habit. Many organizations and projects have mission statements that help them focus on their main purpose.

3. *Put first things first:* Covey developed a time-management system and matrix to help people prioritize their time. He suggests that most people need to spend more time doing things that are important but not urgent. Important but not urgent activities include planning, reading, and exercising. Project managers should focus on important and not urgent activities, such as developing various project plans, building relationships with major project stakeholders, and mentoring project team members. They also need to avoid focusing only on important and urgent activities—that is, putting out fires.

An Introduction to Project Management, Third Edition

4. *Think win/win:* Covey presents several paradigms of interdependence, with "think win/win" being the best choice in most situations. When you use a win/win paradigm, parties in potential conflict work together to develop new solutions that make them all winners. Project managers should strive to use a win/win approach in making decisions, but sometimes, especially in competitive situations, they must use a win/lose paradigm.

5. *Seek first to understand, then to be understood:* **Empathic listening** is listening with the intent to understand by putting yourself in the shoes of the other person. You forget your personal interests and focus on truly understanding the other person and feeling what he or she is feeling. To really understand other people, you must learn to focus on others first. When you practice empathic listening, you can begin two-way communication. Making empathic listening a habit enables project managers to fully understand their stakeholders' needs and expectations.

6. *Synergize:* In projects, a project team can synergize by creating collaborative products that are much better than a collection of individual efforts. For example, engineers helped the crew of the *Apollo 13* return to Earth safely by working together to develop a solution to their potentially deadly technical problems. One person came up with an idea, which prompted another person to have an idea, and so on. The team devised a solution that no one person could have discovered. Covey also emphasizes the importance of valuing differences in others to achieve synergy. Synergy is essential to many complex projects; in fact, several major breakthroughs in technology, such as manned flight, drug development, and various computer technologies, occurred because of synergy.

7. *Sharpen the saw:* When you practice sharpening the saw, you take time to renew yourself physically, spiritually, mentally, and socially. The practice of self-renewal helps people avoid burnout. Project managers must make sure that they themselves and their project team have time to retrain, reenergize, and occasionally even relax to avoid burnout.

Several experts suggest that empathic listening is a powerful skill for project managers and their teams to possess. Understanding what motivates key stakeholders and customers can mean the difference between project success and project failure. After project managers and team members begin to practice empathic listening, they can communicate and work together to tackle problems more effectively.

Before you can practice empathic listening, you first have to get people to talk to you. In many cases, you must work on developing a rapport with other people before they will really open up to you. **Rapport** is a relationship of harmony, conformity, accord, or affinity. Without rapport, people cannot begin to communicate, or the strong person might dominate the weaker one. For example, if you meet someone for the first time and find that you cannot communicate, you need to focus on developing rapport.

One technique for establishing rapport is using a process called mirroring. **Mirroring** is the matching of certain behaviors of the other person. Although establishing rapport involves a number of complex human interactions, the simple technique of mirroring can sometimes help. You can mirror someone's voice tone and/or tempo, breathing, movements, or body postures. For example, when Kristin was negotiating with suppliers, she found that some of them were very abrupt, while she was fairly laid back. Kristin would use mirroring by matching the supplier's posture or voice tone to develop rapport and a strong negotiating position. In fact, mirroring was one of the skills emphasized in the negotiations course the Just-In-Time Training project team was developing.

What Went Right?

A young business consultant who worked in the IT department of a major aerospace firm met with a senior project manager and his core team. The project involved providing updated electronic kits for a major aircraft program. The company was losing money on the project because the upgrade kits were not being delivered on time. Most buyers had written severe late-penalty fees into their contracts, and other customers were threatening to take their business elsewhere. The project manager blamed it all on the IT department for not letting his staff access the information system directly to track the status of kit development and delivery. The tracking system was old and difficult to use.

The business consultant was warned that this project manager was very difficult to work with. When the project manager entered the meeting room with three of his staff, all older men, he threw his books on the table and started yelling at the young consultant and her even younger assistant. Instead of backing down, the consultant mirrored the project manager's behavior and started yelling right back at him. He stood back, paused, and said, "You're the first person who's had the guts to stand up to me. I like that!" After that brief introduction, rapport was established, and everyone began communicating and working together as a team to solve the problem at hand.

You should, of course, take this message with a grain of salt. Few circumstances merit or benefit from yelling matches, but once in a while they cut through the tangle of human complexities. (The story is completely true; the author of this book, who very rarely yells at anyone, was the business consultant and had just completed a weeklong course on communications skills.)

You can see from the material covered in this chapter so far that many important topics related to motivation, influence, and effectiveness are relevant to project management. Projects are done by and for people, so it is important for project managers and team members to understand and practice key concepts related to these topics. Kristin must keep these topics in mind and use her knowledge and skills to successfully execute the project.

Acquiring the Project Team and Making Project Staff Assignments

There's a saying that the project manager who is the smartest person on the team has done a poor job of recruiting. After developing a staffing management plan during project planning, project managers must work with other managers in their organizations to assign personnel to their project or to acquire additional human resources needed to staff their project. Project managers with strong influencing and negotiating skills are often good at getting internal people to work on their project. However, the organization must ensure that people assigned to the project best fit the project's requirements, and that these people are motivated to remain on the project.

Several organizations, publications, and Web sites address the need for good staff acquisition and retention. William C. Taylor, cofounder of *Fast Company* magazine and a renowned speaker, also believes that people today are more demanding and have higher expectations of their jobs than just earning a paycheck. His company's research has found that the top three reasons people leave their jobs (by choice) are because:

1. They feel they do not make a difference.

2. They do not get proper recognition.

3. They are not learning anything new or growing as a person.

Best Practice

Best practices can also be applied to include the best places for people to work. For example, Fortune Magazine lists the "100 Best Companies to Work For" in the United States every year, with Google taking the honors in 2007 and 2008. Working Mothers Magazine lists the best companies in the U.S. for women based on benefits for working families. The Timesonline (www.timesonline.co.uk) provides the Sunday Times list of the 100 Best Companies to Work For, a key benchmark against which UK companies can judge their performance as employers. The Great Place to Work Institute, which produces Fortune's "100 Best Companies to Work For," uses the same selection methodology for more than 20 international lists, including "Best Companies to Work For" lists in all 15 countries of the European Union, Brazil, Korea, and a number of other countries throughout Latin America and Asia. Companies make these lists based on feedback from their best critics: their own employees. Quotes from employees often show why certain companies made the lists:

- "It is a friendly, courteous, caring hospital. We generally care about our co-workers and our patients. I can always get the help and support that I need to function in this hospital. This goes from the top all the way down to the cleaning people."

- "This is the best place I have ever worked. There's an open door policy. Every one is allowed to voice their opinion."

- "I get information about everything—profits, losses, problems. Relationships with people are easier here. It's more direct and open."[2]

Figure 6-6 shows a cartoon describing how many people feel about Google.

Figure 6-6. Best place to work if you can get hired (www.xkcd.com)

Resource Loading and Leveling

Once people are assigned to projects, there are two techniques available to project managers that help them use project staff most effectively: resource loading and resource leveling. **Resource loading** refers to the amount of individual resources an existing schedule requires during specific time periods. Resource loading helps project managers develop a general understanding of the demands a project will make on the organization's resources, as well as on individual people's schedules. Project managers often use resource histograms, as described in Chapter 5, to depict period-by-period variations in resource loading. A histogram can be very helpful in determining staffing needs or in identifying staffing problems.

A resource histogram can also show when work is being overallocated to a certain person or group. **Overallocation** means more resources than are available are assigned to perform work at a given time. For example, Figure 6-7 provides a sample resource histogram created in Microsoft Project. The data was actually from one of the template files Microsoft used to provide with the software. This histogram illustrates how much one individual, Joe Franklin, is assigned to work on the project each week. The percentage numbers on the vertical axis represent the percentage of Joe's available time that is allocated for him to work on the project. The top horizontal axis represents time in weeks. Note that Joe Franklin is overallocated most of the time. For example, for most of March and April and part of May, Joe's work allocation is 300 percent of his available time. If Joe is normally available eight hours per day, this means he would have to work 24 hours a day to meet this staffing projection! Many people don't use the resource assignment features of project management software properly. See Appendix A for detailed information on using Project 2010.

An Introduction to Project Management, Third Edition

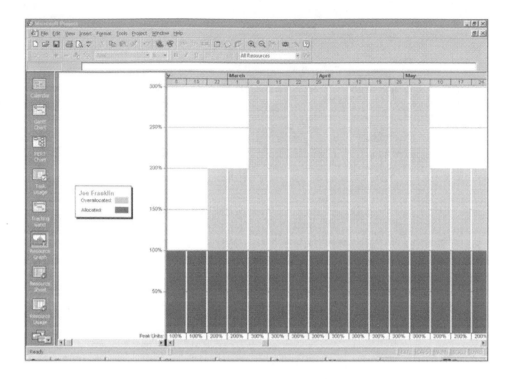

Figure 6-7. Sample resource histogram showing an overallocated individual

Resource leveling is a technique for resolving resource conflicts by delaying tasks. It is a form of network analysis in which resource management concerns drive scheduling decisions (start and finish dates). The main purpose of resource leveling is to create a smoother distribution of resource usage. Project managers examine the network diagram for areas of slack or float, and to identify resource conflicts. For example, you can sometimes remove overallocations by delaying noncritical tasks, which does not result in an overall schedule delay. Other times you will need to delay the project completion date to reduce or remove overallocations. See Appendix A for information on using Project 2010 to level resources using both of these approaches. Overallocation is one type of resource conflict. If a certain resource is overallocated, the project manager can change the schedule to remove resource overallocation. If a certain resource is underallocated, the project manager can change the schedule to try to improve the use of the resource. Resource leveling, therefore, aims to minimize period-by-period variations in resource loading by shifting tasks within their slack allowances.

Figure 6-8 illustrates a simple example of resource leveling. The network diagram at the top of this figure shows that Activities A, B, and C can all start at the same time. Activity A has a duration of two days and will take two people to complete; Activity B has a duration of five days and will take four people to complete; and Activity C has a duration of three days and will take two people to complete. The histogram on the lower-left of this figure shows the resource usage if all activities start on day one. The histogram on the lower right of Figure 6-8 shows the resource usage if Activity C is delayed two days, its total slack allowance. Notice that the lower-right histogram is flat or leveled; that is, its pieces (activities) are arranged to take up the least space (lowering the highest number of workers needed). You may recognize this strategy from the computer game Tetris, in which you earn points for keeping the falling shapes as level as possible. The player with the most points (most level shape allocation) wins.

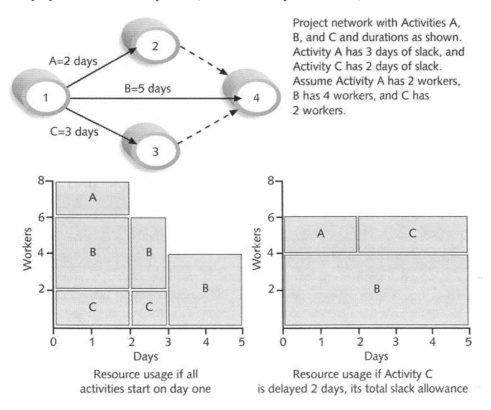

Figure 6-8. Resource leveling example (Schwalbe, Information Technology Project Management, Sixth Edition, 2010)

Resource leveling has several benefits:

- When resources are used on a more constant basis, they require less management. For example, it is much easier to manage a part-time project member who is scheduled to work 20 hours per week on a project for the next three months than it is to manage the same person who is scheduled to work 10 hours one week, 40 the next, 5 the next, and so on.

- Resource leveling may enable project managers to use a just-in-time inventory type of policy for using subcontractors or other expensive resources. For example, a project manager might want to level resources related to work that must be done by particular subcontractors such as testing consultants. This leveling might allow the project to use four outside consultants full-time to do testing for four months instead of

An Introduction to Project Management, Third Edition

spreading the work out over more time or needing to use more than four people. The latter approach is usually more expensive.

- Resource leveling results in fewer problems for project personnel and accounting departments. Increasing and decreasing labor levels and particular human resources often produce additional work and confusion. For example, if a person with expertise in a particular area is only assigned to a project two days a week and another person they need to work with is not assigned to the project those same days, they cannot work well together. The Accounting department might complain when subcontractors charge a higher rate for billing less than 20 hours a week on a project. The accountants will remind project managers to strive for getting the lowest rates possible.

- Resource leveling often improves morale. People like to have some stability in their jobs. It is very stressful for people not to know from week to week or even day to day what projects they will be working on and with whom they will be working.

Sample Project Staff Assignments

Kristin worked with managers in the human resource department and other managers to staff the internal project team members for the Just-In-Time Training project. She also made staffing changes, such as replacing Jamie, the supplier management expert assigned to the team. Although Jamie had great qualifications, she was not a good fit for the project. Jamie needed a break after coming off of a big project, and she did not feel that she would personally enjoy working on the Just-In-Time Training project. Kristin updated the project staff by replacing Jamie with Abner. Kristin was also involved with other staffing updates as people joined and left the project team.

To keep everyone up to date on current project staffing assignments, Kristin provided a current team roster on the project Web site, including team member names, roles, and contact information. As suppliers were added to the project, she included supplier staff information as well. Figure 6-9 provides a sample of part of the team roster for the Just-In-Time Training project.

Team Roster
September 1

Project Name: Just-In-Time Training Project

Name	Role on Project	Position	Email	Phone	Location
Mike Sundby	Project Champion	VP of HR	mike_sundby@ globalconstruction.com		
Lucy Camerena	Project Sponsor	Training Director	lucy_camerena@ globalconstruction.com		
Kristin Maur	Project Manager	Project Manager	kristin_maur@ globalconstruction.com		
Mohamed Abdul	Team Member	Senior programmer/ analyst	mohamed_abdul@ globalconstruction.com		
Kim Johnson	Team Member	Curriculum designer	kim_johnson@ global construction.com		
Abner Tomas	Team Member	Supply management expert	abner_tomas@ globalconstruction.com		

Figure 6-9. Sample team roster

Developing the Project Team and Assessing Team Performance

Even if a project manager has successfully recruited enough skilled people to work on a project, he or she must ensure that people can work together as a team to achieve project goals. Many failed projects have been staffed by highly talented individuals; however, it takes teamwork to complete projects successfully. The main goal of team development is to help people work together more effectively to improve project performance.

Dr. Bruce Tuckman published his four-stage model of team development in 1965 and modified it to include an additional stage in the 1970s. The **Tuckman model** describes five stages of team development:

1. *Forming* involves the introduction of team members, either at the initiation of the team or as new members are introduced. This stage is necessary, but little work is actually achieved.

2. *Storming* occurs as team members have different opinions as to how the team should operate. People test each other, and there is often conflict within the team.

An Introduction to Project Management, Third Edition

3. *Norming* is achieved when team members have developed a common working method, and cooperation and collaboration replace the conflict and mistrust of the previous phase.

4. *Performing* occurs when the emphasis shifts to reaching the team goals rather than working on team process. Relationships are settled, and team members are likely to build loyalty toward each other. At this stage, the team is able to manage tasks that are more complex and cope with greater change. Note that not all teams are able to progress through the team development stages to reach the performance level.

5. *Adjourning* involves the breakup of the team after they successfully reach their goals and complete the work. Teams might also adjourn due to poor performance or project cancellation.

There is an extensive body of literature on team development. This section highlights a few important tools and techniques for team development, including training, team-building activities, and reward and recognition systems. Keep in mind that having teams focus on completing specific tasks is often the most effective way to help teams be productive.

Training

Project managers often recommend that people take specific training courses to improve individual and team development. For example, Kristin recommended that Mohamed, the IT member of her project team, take training courses in designing e-learning courses so that he could contribute even more to this project. Early in the project, Kristin also organized a special team-building session for her internal project team. In addition to traditional, instructor-led training, many organizations provide e-learning opportunities for their employees so that they can learn specific skills at any time and any place, similar to several of the courses being developed for the Just-In-Time Training project. It is important to make sure that the timing and delivery methods for the training are appropriate for specific situations and individuals.

Team-Building Activities

Many organizations provide in-house team-building training activities, and many also use specialized services provided by external companies that specialize in this area. Two common approaches to team-building activities include using physical challenges and psychological preference indicator tools.

Sometimes, organizations have teams of people go through certain physically challenging activities to help them develop as a team. Military basic training or boot camps provide one example. Men and women who want to join the military must first make it through basic training, which often involves several strenuous physical activities such as rappelling off towers, running and marching in full military gear, going through obstacle courses, passing marksmanship training, and mastering survival training. Many non-military organizations use a similar approach by sending teams of people to special locations, where they work as a team to navigate white-water rapids, climb mountains or rocks, participate in ropes courses, and so on.

More often, organizations have teams participate in mental team-building activities in which they learn about themselves, about each other, and how to work as a group most effectively. It is important for people to understand and value each other's differences to work effectively as a team. Two common tools used in mental team building include the Myers-Briggs Type Indicator and the Wilson Learning Social Styles Profile. Effective teams include a variety of personalities. The main purpose of these tools is to help people understand each other and learn to adjust their personal communication styles to work well as a team.

The **Myers-Briggs Type Indicator (MBTI)** is a popular tool for determining personality preferences. During World War II, Isabel B. Myers and Katherine C. Briggs developed the first version of the MBTI based on psychologist Carl Jung's theory of psychological type. The four dimensions of psychological type in the MBTI are as follows:

1. *Extrovert/Introvert (E/I):* This first dimension determines if you are generally extroverted or introverted. The dimension also signifies whether people draw their energy from other people (extroverts) or from inside themselves (introverts). About 75 percent of people in the general population are extroverts.

2. *Sensation/Intuition (S/N):* This second dimension relates to the manner in which you gather information. Sensation (or Sensing) type people take in facts, details, and reality and describe themselves as practical. Intuitive type people are imaginative, ingenious, and attentive to hunches or intuition. They describe themselves as innovative and conceptual. About 75 percent of people in the general population have a preference for sensation.

3. *Thinking/Feeling (T/F):* This third dimension represents thinking judgment and feeling judgment. Thinking judgment is objective and logical, and feeling judgment is subjective and personal. The general population is generally split evenly between these two preferences.

4. *Judgment/Perception (J/P):* This fourth dimension concerns people's attitude toward structure. Judgment type people like closure and task completion. They tend to establish deadlines and take them seriously, expecting others to do the same. Perceiving types prefer to keep things open and flexible. They regard deadlines more as a signal to start rather than complete a project and do not feel that work must be done before play or rest begins. People are generally split evenly between these two preferences.

There are 16 MBTI categories based on combinations of the four dimensions. For example, one MBTI category is ESTJ, another is INFP, and another is ENTP. Project managers can often benefit from knowing their team members' MBTI profiles by

260

adjusting their management styles for each individual. For example, if the project manager is a strong N and one of the team members is a strong S, the project manager should take the time to provide more concrete, detailed explanations when discussing that person's task assignments. Project managers might also want to make sure that they have a variety of personality types on their team. For example, if all team members are strong introverts, it might be difficult for them to work well with other stakeholders who are often extroverts.

Many organizations use Wilson Learning's Social Styles Profile in team-building activities. Psychologist David Merril, who helped develop the Social Skills Profile, categorizes four approximate behavioral profiles, or zones. People are perceived as behaving primarily in one of four zones, based on their assertiveness and responsiveness:

- "Drivers" are proactive and task oriented. They are firmly rooted in the present, and they strive for action. Adjectives to describe drivers include pushy, severe, tough, dominating, harsh, strong-willed, independent, practical, decisive, and efficient.

- "Expressives" are proactive and people oriented. They are future oriented and use their intuition to look for fresh perspectives on the world around them. Adjectives to describe expressives include manipulating, excitable, undisciplined, reacting, egotistical, ambitious, stimulating, wacky, enthusiastic, dramatic, and friendly.

- "Analyticals" are reactive and task oriented. They are past oriented and strong thinkers. Adjectives to describe analyticals include critical, indecisive, stuffy, picky, moralistic, industrious, persistent, serious, expecting, and orderly.

- "Amiables" are reactive and people oriented. Their time orientation varies depending on whom they are with at the time, and they strongly value relationships. Adjectives to describe amiables include conforming, unsure, ingratiating, dependent, awkward, supportive, respectful, willing, dependable, and agreeable.

Figure 6-10 shows these four social styles and how they relate to assertiveness and responsiveness. Note that the main determinants of the social style are levels of assertiveness—if you are more likely to tell people what to do or ask what should be done—and how you respond to tasks—by focusing on the task itself or on the people involved in performing the task. For example, a driver is assertive in telling other people what to do and focuses on completing tasks. An amiable prefers to ask others what to do and focuses on pleasing people versus completing tasks.

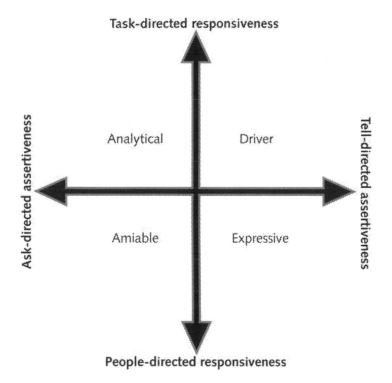

Figure 6-10. Social styles of Wilson Learning (Schwalbe, Information Technology Project Management, Sixth Edition, 2010)

Knowing the social styles of project stakeholders can help project managers understand why certain people may have problems working together. For example, drivers are often very impatient working with amiables, and analyticals often have difficulties understanding expressives. Project managers can use their facilitation skills to help all types of people communicate better with each other and focus on meeting project goals.

An Introduction to Project Management, Third Edition

Reward and Recognition Systems

Another important tool for promoting team development is the use of team-based reward and recognition systems. If management rewards teamwork, it promotes or reinforces people to work more effectively in teams. Some organizations offer bonuses, trips, or other rewards to workers who meet or exceed company or project goals. In a project setting, project managers can recognize and reward people who willingly work overtime to meet an aggressive schedule objective or go out of their way to help a teammate. If teamwork is the essential goal, project managers should not reward people who work overtime just to get extra pay or because of their own poor work or planning. They should, however, recognize individuals who volunteer to put in additional time to meet a deadline or show other exemplary behavior.

Project managers must continually assess their team's performance. When they identify weaknesses in individuals or in the entire team, it's their job to find the best way to develop their people and improve performance.

Sample Team Performance Assessment

Project managers assess team performance in several different ways. As mentioned earlier, Kristin believed in management by wandering around, and she liked to have many short, informal discussions with various stakeholders, especially her project team members. She also observed them working alone and as a team, and assessed the quality of deliverables they produced. Kristin and other project managers at Global Construction also filled out performance appraisals for each team member once a year or when a project was completed. These performance appraisals can be addressed in the team contract during project planning or discussed in early team meetings.

Kristin also felt that it was important for people to assess their own performance and the performance of their teammates. She talked to each team member individually and the team as a group about this assessment because she knew that some people felt uncomfortable evaluating themselves or other people. She stressed that she had successfully used this approach in the past, and she would keep the information confidential. Her main goal was to help everyone work well together on the project. Figure 6-11 is a sample of an informal questionnaire that Kristin periodically asked her project team members to fill out to assist in performance assessment. Kristin would discuss each person's assessment and take corrective actions as needed.

Team Performance Assessment

August 1

Project Name: Just-In-Time Training Project

Individual's Name: _____   **Project Manager:** <u>Kristin Maur</u>

Date: _____

1. Using a scale of 0-100, assess how you think **the project team** is performing: ___

2. Explain the rationale behind the above score.

3. Using a scale of 0-100, assess how **you** are performing on this project: _____

4. Explain the rationale behind the above score. What are your roles and responsibilities, and how well have you performed them?

5. Briefly assess each team member's performance. If you had to give each person a score between 0-100, what would it be?

6. To compare individual contributions, if you had 100 points to allocate to your team, how would you allocate them?

7. What suggestions do you have for improving team performance?

Figure 6-11. Sample team performance assessment

Managing the Project Team

Another human resource management task performed as part of executing a project is managing the project team, which, of course, is no small task. After assessing team performance and related information, the project manager must decide if changes to the project should be requested or if updates need to be made to enterprise environmental factors, organizational process assets, or the project management plan. Project managers also must use their soft skills to find the best way to motivate and manage each team member, as described earlier in this chapter. The following sections describe tools and techniques to help manage project teams and offer general advice on managing teams.

Tools and Techniques for Managing Project Teams

Several tools and techniques are available to assist in managing project teams:

- *Observation and conversation:* It is hard to assess how your team members are performing or how they are feeling about their work if you seldom watch and evaluate their performance or discuss these issues with them. Many project managers, like Kristin, like to physically see and hear their team members at work. Informal or formal conversations about how a project is going can provide crucial information. For virtual workers, project managers can still observe and discuss work and personal issues via e-mail, telephone, or other communications media.

- *Project performance appraisals:* Just as general managers provide performance appraisals for their workers, so can project managers. The need for and type of project performance appraisals varies depending on the length of the project, the complexity of the project, organizational policies, contract requirements, and related communications. Even if a project manager does not provide official project performance appraisals for team members, it is still important to provide timely performance feedback. If a team member hands in sloppy or late work, the project manager should determine the reason for this behavior and take appropriate action. Perhaps the team member had a death in the family and could not concentrate. Perhaps the team member was planning to leave the project. The reasons for the behavior would have a strong impact on the action the project manager would take.

- *Conflict management:* Few projects are completed without any conflict. Some types of conflict are actually desirable on projects, but many are not. As described previously in this chapter, there are several ways to handle conflicts. It's important for project managers to understand strategies for handling conflicts and to proactively manage them.

- *Issue logs:* Many project managers keep an **issue log** to document, monitor, and track issues that need to be resolved for effective work to take place. An **issue** is a matter under question or dispute that could impede project success. Issues could include situations in which people disagree, situations that need more clarification or investigation, or general concerns that need to be addressed. It is important to acknowledge issues that can hurt team performance and take action to resolve them. The project manager should assign someone to resolve each issue and assign a target date for resolution.

Sample Issue Log

Figure 6-12 shows part of an early issue log that Kristin and her team used to help document and manage the resolution of issues on their project. The issue log includes columns for the issue number, the issue description, the impact of the issue on the project, the date the issue was reported, who reported the issue, who the issue resolution was assigned to, the priority of the issue (High, Medium, or Low), the due date to report back on the issue, the status of the issue, and comments related to the issue. Project managers can tailor the format of issue logs as needed. The project management software that Kristin's team used for the Just-In-Time Training project included an online issue log that could be sorted and filtered various ways. For example, Kristin always sorted issues by priority so that she could focus on high priorities. She also sorted them by who reported the issue and who was assigned to each issue to make sure that the appropriate people were making progress.

Issue
Log
Oct. 1

Issue #	Issue Description	Impact on Project	Date Reported	Reported By	Assigned To	Priority (H/M/L)	Due Date	Status	Comments
1	Key project team member is not working out	Can severely hurt project since Jamie is our supplier management expert	Aug 2	Kristin	Kristin	H	Sep 2	Open	Working with Jamie and appropriate managers to find a replacement
2	IT staff that is performing survey is over allocated	Delaying the survey will delay the entire project since it is a critical task	Sep 26	Mohamed	Kristin	H	Aug 5	Closed	Paid overtime was approved
Etc.									

Figure 6-12. Sample issue log

General Advice on Managing Teams

Effective project managers must be good team leaders. Suggestions for ensuring that teams are productive include the following:

- Be patient and kind with your team. Assume the best about people; do not assume that your team members are lazy and careless.

- Fix the problem instead of blaming people. Help people work out problems by focusing on behaviors.

- Establish regular, effective meetings. Focus on meeting project objectives and producing positive results.

- Allow time for teams to go through the basic team-building stages of forming, storming, norming, performing, and adjourning, as described previously in this chapter. Do not expect teams to work at the highest performance level from the start; moreover, not all teams will even reach the performing level.

- Limit the size of work teams to three to seven members to enhance communications.

- Plan some social activities to help project team members and other stakeholders become acquainted. Make the social events fun and not mandatory.

- Stress team identity. Create traditions that team members enjoy.

- Nurture team members and encourage them to help each other. Identify and provide training that will help individuals and the team as a whole become more effective.

- Acknowledge individual and group accomplishments.

- Take the additional actions necessary to work with virtual team members. If possible, have a face-to-face or phone meeting at the start of a virtual project or when introducing a virtual team member. Screen people carefully to make sure they can work effectively in a virtual environment. Clarify how virtual team members will communicate.

EXECUTING TASKS FOR PROJECT COMMUNICATIONS MANAGEMENT

Good communications management is also crucial to project execution. Distributing information and managing stakeholder expectations are the main communications management tasks performed during project execution. The main outputs of these tasks are change requests and updating organizational process assets, the project management plan, and project documents.

Important Project Communications Concepts

Because communications is a crucial part of executing projects, it is important to address important concepts related to improving project communications. Key concepts include formal and informal communications, nonverbal communications, using the appropriate communications medium, understanding individual and group communication needs, and the impact of team size on project communications.

Formal and Informal Communications

It is not enough for project team members to submit formal status reports to their project managers and other stakeholders and assume that everyone who needs to know that information will read the reports. In fact, many people may prefer to have a two-way conversation about project information rather than reading detailed reports, e-mails, or Web pages to try to find pertinent information. These people may want to know the people working on their projects and develop a trusting relationship with them, and so they use informal discussions about the project to develop these relationships. Therefore, project managers must be good at nurturing relationships through good communication. Many experts believe that the difference between good project managers and excellent project managers is their ability to nurture relationships and use empathic listening skills, as described earlier.

Nonverbal Communications

People make or break projects, and people like to interact with each other to get a true feeling for how a project is going. Research poses the theory that in a face-to-face interaction, 58 percent of communication is through body language, 35 percent through how the words are said, and a mere 7 percent through the content or words that are spoken. The author of this information (see *Silent Messages* by Albert Mehrabian, 1980) was careful to note that these percentages were specific findings for a specific set of variables. Even if the actual percentages are different in verbal project communications today, it is safe to say that it is important to pay attention to more than just the actual words someone is saying. Nonverbal communications, such as a person's tone of voice and body language, are often more important than the words being used.

Using the Appropriate Communications Medium

Figure 6-13 provides guidelines from Practical Communications, Inc., a communications consulting firm, about how well different types of media—such as hard copy, phone calls, voice mail, e-mail, face-to-face meetings, and Web sites—are suited to different communication needs. For example, if you were trying to assess commitment of project stakeholders, a meeting would be the most appropriate medium to use. A phone call would be adequate, but the other media would not be appropriate. Project managers must assess the needs of the organization, the project, and individuals in determining which communication medium to use, and when.

Key: 1= Excellent   2 = Adequate   3 = Inappropriate

HOW WELL MEDIUM IS SUITED TO:	Hard Copy	Phone Call	Voice Mail	E-mail	Meeting	Web Site
Assessing commitment	3	2	3	3	1	3
Building consensus	3	2	3	3	1	3
Mediating a conflict	3	2	3	3	1	3
Resolving a misunderstanding	3	1	3	3	2	3
Addressing negative behavior	3	2	3	2	1	3
Expressing support/appreciation	1	2	2	1	2	3
Encouraging creative thinking	2	3	3	1	3	3
Making an ironic statement	3	2	2	3	1	3
Conveying a reference document	1	3	3	3	3	2
Reinforcing one's authority	1	2	3	3	1	1
Providing a permanent record	1	3	3	1	3	3
Maintaining confidentiality	2	1	2	3	1	3
Conveying simple information	3	1	1	1	2	3
Asking an informational question	3	1	1	1	3	3
Making a simple request	3	1	1	1	3	3
Giving complex instructions	3	3	2	2	1	2
Addressing many people	2	3 or 1*	2	2	3	1

Galati, Tess. *Email Composition and Communication (EmC2)*. Practical Communications, Inc. (*www.praccom.com*) (2001).   *Depends on system functionality

Figure 6-13. Media choice table

Additional media not included in this table include the use of Web logs or blogs, instant messaging, Webcasts, and live or delayed video. Global Construction was just starting to use several of these newer media.

Media Snapshot

Although most projects do not use live video as a medium for sending project information, the technology is becoming more available and less expensive. You can reach many people at once using live video, and viewers can see and hear important information.

For example, Microsoft had been experimenting with its new conferencing product, Livemeeting. Anoop Gupta, a vice president of Microsoft's real-time collaboration group, says that one in every five face-to-face meetings can be replaced with Web conferencing tools, and Microsoft estimates that it will save $70 million in reduced travel for organizations worldwide in one year alone.[3] Web-based meeting tools can also help the environment. For example, in May 2007, WebEx, the leading provider of on-demand web collaboration applications, kicked off the WebEx Experience Online Forum. They say they saved over one million pounds of carbon dioxide by not requiring the more than 650 attendees to travel to participate in sessions.[4]

However, any live communication broadcast can also backfire, especially if millions of people are watching. In fact, one event, Janet Jackson's "wardrobe malfunction" during the 2004 Super Bowl in the United States, had a major impact on the entire broadcasting industry, causing television and radio stations to use several second delays to prevent offensive video or audio from reaching the airwaves. Reuters reported on September 22, 2004, that the Federal Communications Commission had officially voted to fine each of the 20 stations owned by the CBS television network $27,500 for violating indecency rules. The fine was the maximum allowed by law at the time, and Congress is considering legislation to increase the fine to as much as $500,000 per incident.[5]

Understanding Individual and Group Communication Needs

Many top managers think they can remediate project delays simply by adding people to a project. Unfortunately, this approach often causes setbacks because of the increased complexity of communications. In his popular book *The Mythical Man-Month,* Frederick Brooks illustrates this concept very clearly. People are not interchangeable parts. You cannot assume that a task originally scheduled to take two months of one person's time can be done in one month by two people. A popular analogy is that you cannot take nine women and produce a baby in one month![6]

In addition to understanding that people are not interchangeable, it is also important to understand individuals' personal preferences for communications. People have different personality traits, which often affect their communication preferences. For example, if you want to praise a project team member for doing a good job, an introvert might be more comfortable receiving that praise in private, whereas an extrovert might like everyone to hear about his or her good work. An intuitive person might want to understand how something fits into the big picture, whereas a sensing person might prefer to have more focused, step-by-step details. A strong thinker might want to know the logic behind information, whereas a feeling person might want to know how the information affects him or her personally, as well as other people. Someone who is a judging person might be very driven to meet deadlines with few reminders, whereas a perceiving person might need more assistance in developing and following plans.

Geographic location and cultural backgrounds also add to the complexity of project communications. For example, if project stakeholders are in different countries, it is often difficult or impossible to schedule times for two-way communication during normal working hours. Language barriers can also cause communication problems—for example, the same word may have very different meanings in different languages. Times, dates, and other units of measure are also interpreted differently. People from some cultures also prefer to communicate in ways that may be uncomfortable to others. For example, managers in some countries still do not allow workers of lower ranks or women to give formal presentations.

The Impact of Team Size on Project Communications

Another important aspect of information distribution is the number of people involved in a project. As the number of people involved increases, the complexity of communications increases because there are more communications channels, or pathways, through which people can communicate. The number of communications channels in relation to the number of people involved can be calculated as follows:

number of communications channels = n(n-1)/2

where n is the number of people involved.

For example, two people have one communications channel: $(2(2-1))/2 = 1$. Three people have three channels: $3(3-1))/2 = 3$. Four people have six channels, five people have 10, and so on. You can see that as the number of people communicating increases, the number of communications channels increases rapidly. The lesson is a simple one: If you want to enhance communications, you must consider the interactions among different project team members and stakeholders. It is often helpful to form several smaller teams within a large project team to help improve project communications.

As you can see, information distribution involves more than creating and sending status reports or holding periodic meetings. Many good project managers know their personal strengths and weaknesses in this area and surround themselves with people who complement their skills. It is good practice to share the responsibility for project communications management with the entire project team.

Distributing Information and Updating Business Processes

Getting project information to the right people at the right time and in a useful format is just as important as developing the information in the first place. The communications management plan prepared during project planning serves as a good starting point for information distribution. During execution, project teams must address important considerations for information distribution, as described previously. The main output of distributing information is organizational process asset updates, such as improving business processes.

Sample Updates to Business Processes

Organizations have many different assets to help them improve business processes. Examples of these assets include various policies and procedures, guidelines, information systems, financial systems, management systems, lessons learned, and historical documents that help people understand, follow, and improve business processes.

As part of the Just-In-Time Training project, Kristin's team followed several existing business processes and provided new information to update some of them. For example, they used several communications media already well established at Global Construction, such as e-mail and project Web sites. Kristin's team also used several new technologies to enhance project communications and processes. Examples of these updated business processes include the following:

- Kristin and her team used instant messaging on a regular basis both within their team and with suppliers. Several of the people working on the project were in various parts of the world, so they found it very useful to use instant messaging.

- Several suppliers used Webcasts to communicate information in a more dynamic way without incurring travel expenses. The Webcasts included visuals, such as PowerPoint slides, along with audio and animation to point to and write in key information. There were several other interactive features available in the Webcasts, such as polling the audience and letting other people add their audio input.

- The Web-based courses that suppliers were developing for the project included discussion threads and an "Ask the Expert" feature, in which learners could ask specific questions of the instructor or experts within the company on various topics related to the course. The questions and their answers were automatically added to a database that future learners could access.

- Kristin kept her own personal project blog to document important events and lessons she was learning while managing the project. She had used blogs for personal communications in the past, such as documenting her last trip to Europe, but she had never used one in a work setting before. She found it very useful for personal reflection and knew it would help her write her final lessons-learned document for the project.

The project steering committee—pleased and fascinated with the success of these new communications media—asked Kristin to prepare guidelines on using them that employees could access on the corporate intranet after the project was completed. Kristin was glad to do so.

EXECUTING TASKS FOR PROJECT PROCUREMENT MANAGEMENT

Many projects include work performed by outside sources. The main executing task performed as part of project procurement is conducting procurements. Key outputs include selected sellers, procurement contract awards, resource calendars, change requests, and updates to the project management plan and project documents.

Conducting Procurements

After planning for procurements, the next procurement management process involves conducting procurements, which involves obtaining seller responses to proposals or bids, selecting sellers, and awarding contracts. Prospective sellers do most of the work in this process by preparing their proposals and bids, normally at no cost to the buyer. The buying organization is responsible for deciding how to approach sellers and providing required procurement documents. These documents generally include a summary letter, a request for proposal or quote, and a contract statement of work, as described in Chapter 5. Documents created as part of conducting procurements include a qualified sellers list and contracts.

Organizations can use several different methods to approach and select qualified sellers or suppliers:

- *Approaching a preferred supplier:* Sometimes, a specific supplier might be the number-one choice for the buyer. In this case, the buyer gives procurement information to just that company. If the preferred supplier responds favorably, the organizations proceed to work together. Many organizations have formed good working relationships with certain suppliers, so they want to continue working with them.

- *Approaching several qualified suppliers:* In many cases, several suppliers could meet an organization's procurement needs. The buying organization can send procurement information to those potential sellers and then evaluate the results. If it does not get the desired response, the buyer can either expand its list of potential sellers until it gets the desired response or revise its procurement plans.

- *Advertising to many potential suppliers:* In many cases, several suppliers may be qualified to provide the goods and services, and the buyer may not know who they are in advance. Advertising the procurement (on a Web site, in a trade journal, or by other means) and receiving proposals and bids from multiple sources often takes advantage of the competitive business environment. Increased globalization and virtual project teams have increased tremendously as organizations find suitable sellers around the globe. As a result of pursuing a competitive bidding strategy, the buyer can receive better goods and services than expected at a lower price.

Sample Qualified Seller List

The Just-In-Time Training project required goods and services from several different suppliers. Recall that the project involved training in four different areas: supplier management, negotiating skills, project management, and software application. The training also had to be provided in various delivery formats—instructor-led, Web-based, and CD-ROM. Kristin and her team used their knowledge of current training suppliers and researched additional ones. They were not sure if they should have different suppliers for each course or have a different supplier based on each delivery method.

As described in Chapter 5, because Global Construction was new to the concept of just-in-time training, the company decided to hire a consulting firm that both specialized in just-in-time training and worked with all types of training suppliers. The consulting firm then developed a qualified sellers list containing 30 potential sellers, as provided in Figure 6-14. In addition to the list, the firm also provided a report with information on each seller, such as relevant products and services, backgrounds of senior management, and current customers. It also provided recommendations for developing partnerships with each seller. See Chapter 5 for the RFP and contract statement of work for this procurement.

Qualified Sellers List
September 9

Project Name: Just-In-Time Training Project

Seller Name/ Web Site	Areas of Expertise	Full-Time Staff	Reputation
Company A www.coA.com	Construction industry, supplier management, project management	40	One of few training firms that specializes in training for the construction industry
Company B www.coB.com	E-learning, custom course development	100	Has many partnerships with other companies, reasonable prices
Company C www.coC.com	Project management, negotiating skills	10	Small firm but well respected, does instructor-led and e-learning
Etc.			

Figure 6-14. Sample qualified sellers list

After buyers receive proposals or bids, organizations can select a supplier or decide to cancel the procurement. Selecting suppliers or sellers, often called source selection, involves evaluating proposals or bids from sellers, choosing the best one, negotiating the contract, and awarding the contract. Several stakeholders in the procurement process should be involved in selecting the best suppliers for the project. Often, teams of people are responsible for evaluating various sections of the proposals. There might be a technical team, a management team, and a cost team to focus on each of those major areas. Often, buyers develop a **short list** of the top three to five suppliers to reduce the work involved in selecting a source. Reviewers often follow a more detailed proposal evaluation process for sellers who make the short list, often checking their references, requesting special presentations, or having them provide sample products. Recall from Chapter 5 that a weighted scoring model is often used to help select sellers.

It is customary to conduct contract negotiations during the source selection process. Sellers on the short list are often asked to prepare a best and final offer (BAFO). Expert negotiators often conduct these negotiations, especially for contracts involving large amounts of money. In addition, senior managers from both buying and selling organizations often meet before making final decisions. The final output of the seller selection process is a contract. It is also appropriate on some projects to prepare a contract management plan to describe details about how the contract will be managed.

Sample Contract

As mentioned in Chapter 5, a contract is a mutually binding agreement that obligates the seller to provide the specified products or services, and obligates the buyer to pay for them. Chapter 5 also described the different types of contracts and provided sample clauses that can be included to address risks. The Just-In-Time Training project would include contracts with several different suppliers. Some might be short, fixed-price contracts, such as one for the consulting firm to develop a list of qualified sellers. Others might be much longer and involve fixed-price, cost-reimbursable, and unit-pricing aspects, such as a contract to develop and deliver several training courses in different formats.

Figure 6-15 provides a sample of part of a contract or service agreement, as some contracts are called, that could be used to produce a qualified sellers list. Note the reference to exhibit A, the statement of work. (A sample was provided in Chapter 5 and sent out to prospective sellers as part of the procurement package.) This document should be modified based on the selected seller's proposal. There is also a reference to a schedule for the work, which the seller also prepared as part of the proposal. It is good practice to include a detailed statement of work and schedule as part of the contract to clarify exactly what work the seller will perform and when.

Global Construction, Inc.

Service Agreement

August 10

Title of Work: Qualified Sellers List and Report

This is an Agreement made as of _____ by ABC Training Consultants, 2255 River Road, Boston, MA (the "Seller"), and Global Construction, Inc., 5000 Industrial Drive, Minneapolis, MN (the "Buyer").

THE SELLER AND THE BUYER AGREE THAT:

1. The Work: The Seller will create the Work as set forth in Exhibit A hereto. The Buyer will provide the Seller with the format and specifications in which each element of the Work is to be submitted. The Seller agrees to conform to such format and specifications.

2. Delivery of the Work: The Seller agrees to deliver to the Buyer the Work in form and content acceptable to the Buyer on or before the dates outlined in Exhibit B of this Agreement, time being of the essence to the Buyer.

---

3. Right to Terminate: If the Seller materially departs from the agreed-upon schedule or if the Work is not satisfactory to the Buyer (based on reviews of drafts, market conditions, and/or other criteria as determined by the Buyer), the Buyer may at its option:

    A. Allow the Seller to finish, correct, or improve the Work by a date specified by the Buyer;

    B. Terminate this Agreement by giving written notice to the Seller.

4. Payments: The Buyer will pay the Seller a fixed price of $5,000 upon accepted completion of the Work.

5. Exhibit: The following Exhibit is hereby incorporated by reference into this Agreement:

    Exhibit A: Statement of Work

    Exhibit B: Schedule

IN WITNESS WHEREOF,   THE PARTIES HERETO HAVE EXECUTED THIS Agreement as a sealed instrument as of the date first above written.

    Global Construction, Inc.   ABC Training Consultants

By: _____   _____

Date   _____   _____

Figure 6-15. Sample contract

CASE WRAP-UP

Kristin did her best to lead the team in executing the Just-In-Time Training project. Like most project managers, however, she faced several challenges. It was hard for Kristin to confront Jamie, a key project team member, about her poor performance. Kristin knew that it was best to address problems head on and come up with the best possible solution. Kristin and her team also had to determine how to address poor ratings for the prototype supplier management course. She was proud of the way they worked together to find the root cause of problems and take corrective actions. Understanding important quality, motivation, and communications concepts and using several tools and techniques helped ensure successful project execution.

CHAPTER SUMMARY

Good execution is crucial to project success. Without it, the products, services, and results planned from the project cannot materialize. This chapter summarizes the executing tasks and key outputs for project integration, quality, human resource, communications, and procurement management.

Executing outputs related to integration management include deliverables, implemented solutions to problems, work performance information, change requests, project management plan updates, project document updates. Sample outputs are provided for the Just-In-Time Training project.

Executing outputs related to quality management change requests, organizational process assets updates, project management plan updates, and project document updates. Quality assurance techniques include benchmarking, quality audits, and cause and effect diagrams. A sample cause and effect diagram is provided for the Just-In-Time Training project.

The human resource management processes project managers perform during execution include acquiring, developing, and managing the project team. Key outputs include project staff assignments, resource calendars, team performance assessment, change requests, and updates to the project management plan organizational process assets. Sample outputs are provided for the Just-In-Time Training project. Project managers must also apply concepts related to motivation, influence, effectiveness, resource loading, and resource leveling to lead people during project execution.

Executing outputs related to communications management include organizational process assets updates, change requests, project management plan updates, and project document updates. Samples of organizational process assets updates (updating business processes) are provided for the Just-In-Time Training project. Project managers must apply important concepts related to communications, such as formal and informal communications, nonverbal communications, the appropriate communications medium, individual and group communication needs, and the impact of team size on project communications.

Executing outputs related to procurement management include selected sellers, procurement contract award, resource calendars, change requests, project management plan updates, and project document updates. Sample outputs are provided for the Just-In-Time Training project.

QUICK QUIZ

1.   *Fortune* magazine summarized research showing that the main reason CEOs failed was due to _____.

     A. poor planning

     B. poor execution

     C. global competition

     D. low stock prices

2.   Which of the following is not an example of a soft skill?

     A. leadership

     B. motivation

     C. team building

     D. financial analysis

3.   Most project sponsors would say that the most important output of any project is _____.

     A. a satisfied customer/sponsor

     B. good financial results

     C. its deliverables

     D. good plans

4.   Which of the following conflict handling modes do successful project managers use most often?

     A. confrontation

     B. compromise

     C. smoothing

     D. forcing

5.   _____ includes all of the activities related to satisfying the relevant quality standards for a project.

     A. Quality assurance

     B. Quality control

     C. Customer satisfaction

     D. ISO certification

6. _____ diagrams can assist in ensuring and improving quality by finding the root causes of quality problems.

   A. Pareto

   B. Mind map

   C. Fishbone or Ishikawa

   D. Social styles

7. Which of the following statements is false?

   A. The highest need in Maslow's pyramid is called self-actualization.

   B. Most people today prefer managers who follow Theory X versus Theory Y.

   C. Herzberg distinguished between motivating and hygiene factors.

   D. Projects are more likely to succeed when project managers influence team members by using work challenge and expertise.

8. Some project managers like to assess team performance by using a technique known as MBWA, which stands for _____.

   A. management by wondering aloud

   B. management by wandering around

   C. measuring by work areas

   D. measuring by watching alertly

9. If a project team goes from three people to six, how many more communications channels are there?

   A. 3

   B. 6

   C. 9

   D. 12

10. Buyers often develop a _____ of the top three to five suppliers to reduce the work involved in selecting a source.

    A. short list

    B. weighted decision matrix

    C. qualified sellers list

    D. BAFO

Quick Quiz Answers

1. B; 2. D; 3. C; 4. A; 5. A; 6. C; 7. B; 8. B; 9. D; 10. A

DISCUSSION QUESTIONS

1. Describe practices that should be followed in directing and managing project execution. Why are deliverables such an important output of project execution? What are some of the typical problems that project teams face during project execution?

2. What is quality assurance, and how does it affect project execution? What are tools and techniques used in performing quality assurance? How did Kristin's team use one of these tools to help improve quality?

3. Why is human resource management so important during project execution? How does Maslow's hierarchy of needs affect motivation? What are some examples of motivators and hygiene factors, according to Herzberg? What are the three main categories in McClelland's acquired-needs theory? What is the difference between Theory X and Theory Y? What are the five steps in Tuckman's team-building model?

4. What are the advantages of resource leveling?

5. Why is communications management so important during project execution? What is the difference between formal and informal communications? Why are nonverbal communications so important?

6. Why do communications become more complicated when team size increases?

7. What is involved in conducting procurements? How do project teams develop a list of qualified sellers? What are some of the main topics addressed in a contract or service agreement?

EXERCISES

1. Find an example of a large project that took more than a year to complete, such as a major construction project. You can ask people at your college, university, or work about a recent project, such as a major fund raising campaign, information systems installation, or building project. You can also find information about projects online such as the Big Dig in Boston (www.masspike.com/bigdig), the Patronas Twin Towers in Malaysia, and many other building projects (www.greatbuildings.com). Describe some of the tasks performed to execute the integration, quality, human resource, communications, and procurement aspects of the project. Write a one-page paper or prepare a short presentation summarizing your findings.

2. Assume that you are working on a one-year project that involves about 20 team members and many different stakeholders working across the globe. Even though your team created a communications management plan and you have all types of communication technologies available, everyone knows that communications is a problem. Using Figure 6-4 as a guide, create a cause and effect diagram to identify potential root causes of the communications problems. You can use the

cause and effect diagram template or create the diagram by hand or using other software. Be creative in your response.

3. Take the Myers-Briggs Type Indicator (MBTI) test and research information on this tool. There are several Web sites that have different versions of the test available free, such as *www.humanmetrics.com*, *www.personalitytype.com*, and *www.keirsey.com*. Write a two-page paper describing your MBTI type and what you think about this test as a team-building tool.

4. Review the following scenarios, and then write a paragraph for each one describing what media you think would be most appropriate to use, and why. See Figure 6-13 for suggestions.

   a. Many of the technical staff on the project come in between 9:30 and 10:00 a.m., while the business users always come in before 9:00 a.m. The business users have been making comments. The project manager wants the technical staff to come in by 9:00 a.m., although many of them leave late.

   b. Your company is bidding on a project for the entertainment industry. You know that you need new ideas on how to put together the proposal and communicate your approach in a way that will impress the customer.

   c. Your business has been growing successfully, but you are becoming inundated with phone calls and e-mails asking similar types of questions.

   d. You need to make a general announcement to a large group of people and want to make sure they get the information.

5. Develop your own scenarios for when it would be appropriate to use each of the six conflict-handling modes discussed in this chapter (confrontation, compromise, smoothing, forcing, withdrawal, and collaborating). Document your ideas in a one- to two-page paper.

TEAM PROJECTS

1. Your organization initiated a project to raise money for an important charity. Assume that there are 1,000 people in your organization. Also, assume that you have six months to raise as much money as possible, with a goal of $100,000. List three problems that could arise while executing the project. Describe each problem in detail, and then develop realistic approaches to solving them in a two- to three-page paper or a 15-minute presentation. Be creative in your responses, and reference ideas discussed in this chapter. Remember that this project is run solely by volunteers.

2. You are part of a team in charge of a project to help people in your company (500 people) lose weight. This project is part of a competition, and the top "losers" will be featured in a popular television show. Assume that you have six months to complete the project and a budget of $10,000. You are halfway through the project, and morale is very low. People are also complaining about a lack of

communication and support on the project. Although many people have been participating and have lost weight, many have plateaued or started gaining weight back. Identify four strategies you can implement to improve morale and communications, referencing some of the theories discussed in this chapter. Document your responses in a two- to three-page paper or a 15-minute presentation.

3. Using the information you developed in Team Project 1 or 2, role-play a meeting to brainstorm and develop strategies for solving problems with key stakeholders. Determine who will play what role (project manager, team member from a certain department, senior managers, and so on). Be creative in displaying different personalities (a senior manager who questions the importance of the project to the organization, a team member who is very shy or obnoxious).

4. Perform the executing tasks for one of the case studies provided in Appendix C. (Note: Your instructor might select just a few of these tasks as they can be very time-consuming.) If you are working on a real team project, perform the applicable executing tasks for that project. Remember to address common problems, focus on deliverables, and practice good soft skills.

5. As you are executing your team project, document the top three problems you have experienced and how you are dealing with them. Document your results in a one- to two-page paper or short presentation.

COMPANION WEB SITE

Visit the free companion Web site for this text at **www.intropm.com** to access template files, online quizzes, Jeopardy-like games, Microsoft Project files, links to sites mentioned in the text, and other information to help you learn more about this important field. Instructors must contact the author at schwalbe@augsburg.edu to gain access to the instructor site. Anyone can access the student site.

KEY TERMS

benchmarking — The process of generating ideas for quality improvements by comparing specific project practices or product characteristics to those of other projects or products within or outside of the performing organization.

cause-and-effect diagrams — Also called fishbone or Ishikawa diagrams, these diagrams can assist in ensuring and improving quality by finding the root causes of quality problems.

collaborating mode — The conflict-handling mode where decision makers incorporate different viewpoints and insights to develop consensus and commitment.

compromise mode — The conflict-handling mode that uses a give-and-take approach to resolve conflicts.

confrontation mode — The conflict-handling mode that involves directly facing a conflict using a problem-solving approach that allows affected parties to work through their disagreements.

empathic listening — The process of listening with the intent to understand by putting yourself in the shoes of the other person.

extrinsic motivation — A motivation that causes people to do something for a reward or to avoid a penalty.

forcing mode — The conflict-handling mode that involves exerting one's viewpoint at the potential expense of another viewpoint.

groupthink — The conformance to the values or ethical standards of a group.

intrinsic motivation — A motivation that causes people to participate in an activity for their own enjoyment.

issue — a matter under question or dispute that could impede project success.

issue log — a tool used to document, monitor, and track issues that need to be resolved for effective work to take place.

Maslow's hierarchy of needs — A hierarchy that states that people's behaviors are guided or motivated by a sequence of needs (physiological, safety, social, esteem, and self-actualization).

mirroring — The matching of certain behaviors of the other person.

Myers-Briggs Type Indicator (MBTI) — A popular tool for determining personality preferences.

overallocation — When more resources than are available are assigned to perform work at a given time.

quality assurance — The activities related to satisfying the relevant quality standards for a project.

quality audit — A structured review of specific quality management activities that helps identify lessons learned, which could improve performance on current or future projects.

rapport — A relationship of harmony, conformity, accord, or affinity.

resource leveling — A technique for resolving resource conflicts by delaying tasks.

resource loading — The amount of individual resources an existing schedule requires during specific time periods.

short list — A list of the top three to five suppliers created to reduce the work involved in selecting a source.

smoothing mode — The conflict-handling mode that de-emphasizes or avoids areas of differences and emphasizes areas of agreement.

synergy — The concept that the whole is equal to more than the sum of its parts.

Tuckman model — A model that describes five stages of team development (forming, storming, norming, performing, and adjourning).

withdrawal mode — The conflict-handling mode that involves retreating or withdrawing from an actual or potential disagreement.

END NOTES

[1] Shadi Rahimi, "Bush Embarks on Tour to Survey Damage," *The New York Times* (September 2, 2005).

[2] Great Place to Work Institute, Best Companies Lists, (*www.greatplacetowork.com*) (June 2005).

[3] Steve Lohr, "Ambitious Package to Raise Productivity (and Microsoft's Profit)," *The New York Times* (August 16, 2004).

[4] Colin Smith, "WebEx Experience Online Forum Saves Over 1 Million Pounds of Carbon Dioxide Emissions in First Week," (*www.webex.com*) (May 22, 2007).

[5] Reuters, "TV Stations Fined for Janet Jackson Breast Flash," *http://www.reuters.com/* (September 22, 2004).

[6] Frederick Brooks, *The Mythical Man-Month,* Addison-Wesley Professional (1995).

Chapter 7
Monitoring and Controlling Projects

LEARNING OBJECTIVES

After reading this chapter, you will be able to:

- List several tasks and outputs of project monitoring and controlling, and describe outputs common to all knowledge areas
- Discuss monitoring and controlling project work and performing integration change control as part of project integration management and how to use earned value management
- Explain the importance of verifying and controlling scope
- Describe the schedule control process and schedule performance measurement tools, such as tracking Gantt charts
- Discuss tools and techniques to assist in cost control
- List the Seven Basic Tools of Quality, and provide examples of how they assist in performing quality control
- Summarize methods for reporting performance as part of project communications management
- Describe the process of monitoring and controlling risks
- Explain how to monitor and control projects through good procurement administration

INTRODUCTION

Monitoring and controlling involves regularly measuring progress to ensure that the project is meeting its objectives and addressing current business needs. The project manager and other staff monitor progress against plans and take corrective action when necessary. This chapter summarizes the main tasks involved in monitoring and controlling projects and provides examples of key outputs from this process group for the Just-In-Time Training project.

SUMMARY OF MONITORING AND CONTROLLING OUTPUTS

Figure 7-1 summarizes processes and outputs of project monitoring and controlling by knowledge area, based on the *PMBOK® Guide, Fourth Edition*. Notice that every knowledge area except project human resource management is included. Also note that several knowledge areas include similar outputs that have been discussed in earlier chapters, such as change requests and updates to the project management plan, project documents, and organizational process assets.

Knowledge area	Monitoring and controlling process	Outputs
Project integration management	Monitor and control project work	Change requests
		Project management plan updates
		Project document updates
	Perform integrated change control	Change request status updates
		Project management plan updates
		Project document updates
Project scope management	Verify scope	Accepted deliverables
		Change requests
		Project document updates
	Control scope	Work performance measurements
		Organizational process assets updates
		Change requests
		Project management plan updates
		Project document updates
Project time management	Control schedule	Work performance measurements
		Organizational process assets updates
		Change requests
		Project management plan updates
		Project document updates
Project cost management	Control cost	Work performance measurements
		Budget forecasts
		Organizational process assets updates
		Change requests
		Project management plan updates
		Project document updates
Project quality management	Perform quality control	Quality control measurements
		Validated deliverables
		Organizational process assets updates
		Change requests
		Project management plan updates
		Project document updates
Project communications management	Report performance	Performance reports
		Organizational process assets updates
		Change requests

Project risk management	Monitor and control risks	Risk register updates
		Organizational process assets updates
		Change requests
		Project management plan updates
		Project document updates
Project procurement management	Administer procurements	Procurement documentation
		Organizational process assets updates
		Change requests
		Project management plan updates

Figure 7-1. Monitoring and controlling processes and outputs

MONITORING AND CONTROLLING TASKS FOR PROJECT INTEGRATION MANAGEMENT

The main monitoring and controlling tasks performed as part of project integration management include monitoring and controlling project work and performing integrated change control. These are crucial tasks that must be done well to ensure project success.

Monitoring and Controlling Project Work

Project changes are inevitable, so it is important to develop and follow a process to monitor and control them. Monitoring and controlling project work includes collecting, measuring, and disseminating performance information. It also involves assessing measurements and analyzing trends to determine what process improvements can be made. The project team should continuously monitor project performance to assess the overall health of the project and identify areas that require special attention.

The project management plan, performance reports, enterprise environmental factors, and organizational process assets are all important inputs for monitoring and controlling project work. The main tool and technique for monitoring and controlling project work is expert judgment. Although it is listed in the *PMBOK® Guide, Fourth Edition* as a technique for controlling cost, earned value management is a powerful tool for monitoring and controlling overall project performance.

Forecasting with Earned Value Management

Earned value management (EVM) is a project performance measurement technique that integrates scope, time, and cost data. Given a baseline, project managers and their teams can determine how well the project is meeting scope, time, and cost goals by entering actual information and then comparing it to the baseline. As defined in Chapter 4, a baseline is a starting point, a measurement, or an observation that is documented so that it can be used for future comparison.

An Introduction to Project Management, Third Edition

In earned value management, a baseline includes the following:

- Scope (WBS tasks)

- Time (start and finish estimates for each task)

- Cost information (cost estimates for each task)

Actual information includes whether or not a WBS was completed or approximately how much of the work was completed; when the work actually started and ended; and how much it actually cost to do the completed work. Some project teams do not define work using a WBS or have cost estimates for each task. Some project teams do not periodically enter actuals for scope, time, and cost information. If you do not have a good baseline or actual information, you cannot use earned value management.

In the past, earned value management was primarily used on large government projects. Today, however, more and more companies are realizing the value of using this tool to help control projects. Most project management software products, including Microsoft Project 2010, provide tables and reports for entering and viewing earned value information. See Appendix A for detailed instructions on using this software for earned value management.

Earned value management involves calculating three values for each activity or summary activity from a project's WBS.

1. The **planned value (PV)** is that portion of the approved total cost estimate planned to be spent on an activity during a given period. The cost baseline for the Just-In-Time Training project included $5,000 to be spent on course development for supplier management training. If the activity involved delivering a detailed course outline to be finished in one week for $5,000, then the planned value (PV) for that activity that week would be $5,000.

2. The **actual cost (AC)** is the total direct and indirect costs incurred in accomplishing work on an activity during a given period. For example, suppose it actually took one week and cost $6,000 to create the detailed course outline because the hourly rate for the person doing the work was higher than planned. The actual cost (AC) for the activity would therefore be $6,000.

3. The **earned value (EV)** is an estimate of the value of the physical work actually completed. It is based on the original planned costs for the activity and the rate at which the team is completing work on the activity to date. The **rate of performance (RP)** is the percentage of actual work completed divided by the percentage of work planned to have been completed at any given time. For example, suppose an activity is only half completed by the end of the week, when it should have been totally completed. The rate of performance for that activity that week would be 50%. In this example, the activity to develop a detailed course outline was totally completed at the end

of the week, so the RP was 100%. Because the PV was $5,000, the EV would also be $5,000.

Figure 7-2 summarizes the general formulas used in earned value management. Note that the formulas for variances and indexes start with EV, the earned value. Variances are calculated by subtracting the actual cost or planned value from EV, and indexes are calculated by dividing EV by the actual cost or planned value. You can use the indexes to forecast what the project will cost when completed (the Estimate at Completion or EAC) and when the project will finish, the Estimated Time to Complete.

Term	Formula
Earned Value (EV)	EV = PV to date × RP
Rate of Performance RP)	RP = Percentage of actual work completed/percentage of work planned to have been completed
Cost Variance (CV)	CV = EV – AC
Schedule Variance (SV)	SV = EV – PV
Cost Performance Index (CPI)	CPI = EV/AC
Schedule Performance Index (SPI)	SPI = EV/PV
Estimate at Completion (EAC)	EAC = Budget at Completion (BAC)/CPI
Estimated Time to Complete	Original time estimate/SPI

Figure 7-2. Earned value formulas (Schwalbe, Information Technology Project Management, Sixth Edition, 2010)

Note: In general, *negative numbers for cost and schedule variance indicate problems in those areas.* Negative numbers mean the project is costing more than planned or taking longer than planned. Likewise, *CPI and SPI less than one or less than 100% indicate problems.*

You can use earned value management at either a detailed or a summary level. In other words, you can use a detailed WBS and its associated time and cost data (using level four, five, or whatever is the most detailed), or you can apply earned value at a higher WBS level, such as level two or three.

Figure 7-3 summarizes the earned value information and also computes the cost and schedule variance and the cost and schedule performance indexes for the Just-In-Time Training project task for course development for supplier management training discussed earlier.

Term or Calculation	Amount
Earned Value (EV)	$5,000
Planned Value (PV)	$5,000
Actual Cost (AC)	$6,000
Cost Variance (CV)	–$1,000
Schedule Variance (SV)	0
Cost Performance Index (CPI)	83.33%
Schedule Performance Index (SPI)	100%

Figure 7-3. Earned value calculations for one activity after one week

The earned value calculations in Figure 7-3 are carried out as follows:

$$EV = \$5,000 \times 100\% = \$5,000$$

$$CV = \$5,000 - \$6,000 = -\$1,000$$

$$SV = \$5,000 - \$5,000 = 0$$

$$CPI = \$5,000/\$6,000 = 83.33\%$$

$$SPI = \$5,000/\$5,000 = 100\%$$

Earned value calculations for all project activities (or summary level activities) are required to estimate the earned value for the entire project. Some activities may be over budget or behind schedule, whereas others may be under budget and ahead of schedule. By adding all of the earned values for all project activities, you can determine how the project as a whole is performing and forecast both when it will be completed and how much it will cost at completion.

The **budget at completion (BAC)**, or the approved total budget for the project, can be divided by the cost performance index to calculate the **estimate at completion (EAC)**, which is a forecast of how much the project will cost upon completion. Likewise, the approved time estimate for the project can be divided by the schedule performance index to calculate when the project will be completed. Earned value, therefore, provides an excellent way to monitor project performance and provide forecasts based on performance to date.

Sample Forecast Using an Earned Value Chart

You can graph earned value information to track project performance and to forecast when a project will be completed and for how much. Figure 7-4 shows an earned value chart for a project that has larger and simpler variances than the Just-In-Time Training project to make the chart easier to read. The budget at completion is $1.2 million for this one-year project. The BAC point on the chart, therefore, is at 12 months and $1.2 million. Based on data for months one through six, an earned value chart was created. In this example, the planned value is $100,000 for each month, so the cumulative planned value at month 6 is $600,000. The earned value is $150,000 each month, with the cumulative earned value at month 6 of $900,000. The actual cost is $200,000 each month, with the cumulative actual cost at month 6 of $1,200,000.

> **Note:** The detailed numbers used to create an earned value chart for the Just-In-Time Training project are provided in the Excel file named JIT-earned-value on the companion Web site.

You can also forecast when the project will be completed and what its final cost will be based on this information.

$$CPI = EV/AC = \$900,000/\$1,200,000 = .75$$

$$SPI = EV/PV = \$900,000/\$600,000 = 1.5$$

$$EAC = BAC/CPI = \$1,200,000/.75 = \$1,600,000$$

$$\text{New time estimate} = \text{Original time estimate} / SPI$$

$$= 12 \text{ months}/1.5 = 8 \text{ months}$$

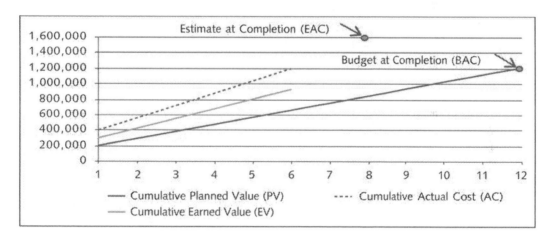

Figure 7-4. Sample earned value chart

Notice that the EAC point is provided on the chart in Figure 7-4 at 8 months and at the cost of $1,600,000. Viewing earned value information in chart form helps you visualize how the project has been performing and forecasts both the end date and the total cost. For example, you can see the planned performance by looking at the planned value line. If the project goes exactly as planned, it will finish in 12 months and cost $1,200,000, as represented by the BAC point. Notice in the example that the actual cost line is always above the earned value line. When the actual cost line is above the earned value line, costs are more than planned. The planned value line in this example is always below the earned value line. This relationship means that the project has been ahead of schedule the first six months. The forecasted completion date, therefore, is earlier than planned while the forecasted total cost is higher than planned.

If there are serious cost and schedule performance problems, management may decide to terminate projects or take other corrective action. The estimate at completion (EAC) is an important input to budget decisions, especially if total funds are limited. Earned value management is an important technique because when used effectively, it helps in evaluating progress and making sound management decisions.

Integrated Change Control

Integrated change control involves identifying, evaluating, and managing changes throughout the project's life cycle. The three main objectives of integrated change control are as follows:

1. *Influencing the factors that cause changes to ensure that changes are beneficial*: Changes can often be good for a project, so it is important to let everyone know that and focus on promoting changes that are beneficial. For example, changes that improve quality, reduce costs, save time, or improve stakeholder relationships are beneficial.

2. *Determining that a change has occurred*: To determine that a change has occurred, project managers must know the status of key project areas at all times. In addition, they must communicate significant changes to senior management and key stakeholders, who normally do not like surprises—especially unpleasant ones.

3. *Managing actual changes as they occur*: Managing change is a key role of project managers and their teams. It is important that project managers exercise discipline in managing the project to help control the number of changes that occur. Managers should focus on achieving project goals rather than putting out fires.

The project management plan provides the baseline for identifying and controlling project changes as follows:

- A section of the plan describes the work to be performed on a project, including key deliverables for the project and quality requirements.

- The schedule section of the plan lists the planned dates for completing key deliverables.

- The budget section provides the planned cost for these deliverables.

The project team must focus on delivering the work as planned. If the project team or someone else causes significant changes during project execution, project managers must formally revise the project management plan and have it approved by the project sponsor.

MONITORING AND CONTROLLING TASKS FOR PROJECT SCOPE MANAGEMENT

The main monitoring and controlling tasks performed as part of project scope management are verifying scope and controlling scope. Key outputs are deliverables that are accepted by the customer and work performance measurements. It is difficult to create a good project scope statement and WBS. It is often even more difficult to verify the project scope and minimize scope changes. Some project teams know from the start that the scope is very unclear and that they must work closely with the project customer to design and produce various deliverables. The project team must develop a process for scope verification that meets unique project needs. Careful procedures must be developed to ensure that customers are getting what they want and that the project team has enough time and money to produce the desired products and services.

Even when the project scope is fairly well defined, many projects suffer from scope creep, as discussed in Chapter 4. There are many horror stories about projects failing due to scope creep. Even for fairly simple projects, people have a tendency to want more. How many people do you know, for example, who said they wanted a simple wedding or a basic new house constructed, only to end up with many more extras than they initially planned? In contrast, some projects also suffer from *not* delivering the minimum scope due to time or cost issues. A couple may have planned to go on a luxurious honeymoon until they saw how much the wedding cost, or a new homeowner may have settled for an unfinished basement in order to move in on time. These scenarios are similar to those faced by a project manager who must constantly cope with the triple constraint of balancing scope, time, and cost.

Verifying Scope

Scope verification involves formal acceptance of the completed project scope by the project customer or designated stakeholders. This acceptance is often achieved through customer inspection and then sign-off on key deliverables. To receive formal acceptance of the project scope, the project team must develop clear documentation of the project's products and procedures, which the appropriate stakeholders can then evaluate for completion and their satisfaction with the results. For example, part of the scope of Kristin's project was to develop a survey to help assess training needs. As part of scope verification, the project steering committee would need to approve the survey before it could be sent out. Scope planning documents, such as the WBS dictionary for that task (see Figure 4-11) would define the scope verification required.

The project management plan, requirements documentation, requirements traceability matrix, and validated deliverables are the main inputs for scope verification. A **validated deliverable** has been completed and checked for correctness as part of quality control. The main tool for performing scope verification is inspection. The customer inspects the work after it is delivered to decide if it is acceptable.

Sample of Accepted and Unaccepted Deliverables

The Just-In-Time Training project included many deliverables. Kristin, the project sponsor, the project steering committee, and other stakeholders—including employees taking the training courses—were all involved in verifying that deliverables were acceptable. Kristin worked closely with her project team and suppliers to make sure that deliverables were being developed correctly along the way. She knew that working closely with key stakeholders and reviewing progress was often the best way to ensure that final deliverables would be acceptable. Kristin knew from experience that foregoing draft reviews and delaying consultation with stakeholders until the final deliverable was ready often resulted in disaster.

Because Global Construction often worked with suppliers on projects, they had a formal process for verifying deliverables produced by suppliers. The project manager was responsible for signing off on their acceptance, as was the project sponsor. Figure 7-5 provides a sample deliverable acceptance form. In this example, Kristin and Lucy, the project sponsor, document the fact that they do not accept the deliverable and provide feedback on what must be done to make it acceptable. Kristin did talk to the supplier about the changes required before accepting this particular deliverable—the course materials for the introductory supplier management course—but the supplier still did not deliver what was expected. The deliverable acceptance form provides formal documentation to ensure that deliverables meet project needs. In this case, because the particular deliverable was part of a contract, the supplier would not be paid until the deliverable was accepted.

Deliverable Acceptance Form			
Project Name:	Just-In-Time Training Project		
Deliverable Name:	Course materials for introductory supplier management course		
Project Manager:	Kristin Maur		
Project Sponsor:	Lucy Camerena		
Date:	November 12		

(We), the undersigned, acknowledge and accept delivery of the work completed for this deliverable on behalf of our organization. My (Our) signature(s) attest(s) to agreement that this deliverable has been completed. No further work should be done on this deliverable. If the deliverable is not acceptable, reasons are stated and corrective actions are described.

Name	Title	Signature	Date

1. Was this deliverable completed to your satisfaction?　　　Yes_____No _X_

2. Please provide the main reasons for your satisfaction or dissatisfaction with this deliverable.

As stated in the contract statement of work, the course materials are not completed until all constructive feedback from the prototype course has been incorporated or the supplier has provided strong rationale as to why the feedback should not be incorporated. We requested that a new section be added to the course to cover issues related to working with suppliers in virtual settings. The final materials delivered did not include this new section or discuss why it was not added. We believe it was an oversight that can be corrected with a minimal amount of additional work.

3. If the deliverable is not acceptable, describe in detail what additional work must be done to complete it.

The supplier will add a new section to the course on working with suppliers in a virtual setting. This section should take about thirty minutes of class time in a face-to-face or e-learning setting. This new section will follow the format and review process used for other topics in the course. We request delivery of the draft of this new section within one week and the final delivery within two weeks.

Contact's signature for resubmission of deliverable if found unacceptable:

Kristin Maur

Figure 7-5. Sample deliverable acceptance form

Controlling Scope

You cannot control the scope of a project unless you have first clearly defined the scope and set a scope verification process in place. You also need to develop a process for soliciting and monitoring changes to project scope. Stakeholders should be encouraged to suggest beneficial changes and discouraged from suggesting unnecessary changes.

Best Practice

An example of successfully controlling scope comes from Northwest Airlines (based on a cases study written by the author several years ago). The company developed a new reservation system in the late 1990s that took several years and millions of dollars to develop. They knew that users would request changes and enhancements to the system, so they built in a special function key for submitting change requests. They also allocated resources for specifically handling change requests by assigning three full-time programmers to work exclusively on them. Users made over 11,000 enhancement requests the first year the system was in use, which was much more than the three programmers could handle. The managers who sponsored the four main software applications had to prioritize the software enhancement requests and decide as a group what changes to approve. Given the time they had, the three programmers then implemented as many items as they could, in priority order. Although they only implemented 38% of the requested enhancements, these were the most important, and users were very satisfied with the system and process.

Another example of scope control is a practice some parents follow when their children get married. The parents provide a fixed budget for the wedding and honeymoon and let the young couple decide how to spend it. If the couple minimizes and controls the scope of the wedding, they can have extra money to pay off other debts or save for a down payment on a home. If they suffer from scope creep, they may not have any money for a honeymoon or become further in debt. This practice can be adapted to most business projects by providing incentives for workers to deliver the work as planned within time and budget constraints.

MONITORING AND CONTROLLING TASKS FOR PROJECT TIME MANAGEMENT

The main monitoring and controlling task performed as part of project time management is controlling the schedule or schedule control. Project managers often cite delivering projects on time (schedule control) as one of their biggest challenges, because schedule problems often cause more conflict than other issues. During project initiation, priorities and procedures are often most important, but as the project proceeds, especially during the middle and latter stages of a project, schedule issues become the predominant source of conflict.

Perhaps part of the reason schedule problems are so common is that time is easily and simply measured. After a project schedule is set, anyone can quickly estimate schedule performance by subtracting the original time estimate from the time actually expended. People often compare planned and actual project-completion times without taking into account the approved project changes. Time is also the variable with the least amount of flexibility. Time passes no matter what happens on a project.

Individual work styles and cultural differences may also cause schedule conflicts. For example, one dimension of the Myers-Briggs team-building tool that was described in Chapter 6 (Judgment/Perception, or J/P) deals with peoples' attitudes toward structure and deadlines. Some people (J's) prefer detailed schedules and focus on task completion. Others (P's) prefer to keep things open and flexible. Different cultures and even entire countries have different attitudes about schedules. For example, some countries close businesses for several hours every afternoon so workers can take naps. Others observe religious or secular holidays during which little work is accomplished. Cultures may also have different perceptions of work ethic—some may value hard work and strict schedules, whereas others may value the ability to remain relaxed and flexible.

Media Snapshot

Planning and scheduling varied greatly for the 2002 Olympic Winter Games in Salt Lake City (see the Media Snapshot of Chapter 4) and the 2004 Olympic Summer Games in Athens, Greece. Many articles were written before the opening ceremonies of the Athens Games predicting that the facilities would not be ready in time. "With just 162 days to go to the opening of the Athens Olympics, the Greek capital is still not ready for the expected onslaught....By now 22 of the 30 Olympic projects were supposed to be finished. This week the Athens Olympic Committee proudly announced 19 venues would be finished by the end of next month. That's a long way off target."[1]

However, many people were pleasantly surprised by the amazing opening ceremonies, beautiful new buildings, and state-of-the-art security and transportation systems in Athens. For example, traffic flow, considered a major pre-Games hurdle, was superb. One spectator at the Games commented on the prediction that the facilities would not be ready in time, "Athens proved them all wrong....It has never looked better."[2] There were, however, several last-minute changes and many extra hours worked in the last few months before the games began. Costs exceeded $12 billion—*more than double the original budget.*[3] Many project managers and team members would have been more comfortable if the original plans had been followed, but Greek workers take pride in putting in major efforts near a deadline. The Greeks even made fun of critics by having construction workers pretend to still be working as the ceremonies began.

The goal of schedule control is to know the status of the schedule, influence the factors that cause schedule changes, determine whether the schedule has changed, and manage changes when they occur. A key output of schedule control is work performance measurements.

Sample Work Performance Measurements

Earned value management, as described earlier, is a key tool for measuring scope, time, and cost performance. Given the earned value and planned value, you can see how well the project team is meeting schedule goals and forecast when the project will be completed based on past schedule performance. Additional ways to measure schedule performance include:

- *Indicators:* Many senior managers like to focus on high-level color indicators of performance, such as green (on target), yellow (fair), and red (poor). They will oversee projects or tasks with red or yellow indicators much more closely than those with green indicators. Project management software offers color indicators as well as numerous reports to show schedule performance information. For example, Microsoft Project 2010 includes activity reports to show "should have started tasks" and "slipping tasks" to quickly identify problem areas. See the *Brief Guide to Microsoft Project 2010* in Appendix A for more information.

- *Milestone completion:* Experienced managers and buyers know that it is not enough to merely review indicators; they like to see the planned and actual completion dates of project milestones *and* the physical evidence that the work was actually completed. (See Chapter 4 for information on milestones.) For example, people having a house built often check on the physical progress to make sure work is completed on schedule. Even though the contractor reports that key milestones are being completed, the buyer wants to see and review the work in person.

- *Worker morale and discipline:* Reviewing morale and work behavior is also a good way to measure schedule performance. If project team members are always working extra hours, the schedule might not be realistic. The project manager might need to negotiate a new schedule or request more resources. On the other hand, if workers are coming in late and leaving early while still producing quality work on time, the schedule might not be challenging enough. Project managers must empower team members to be responsible for completing work on time, yet they often have to use discipline to keep things on track and do what is in the best interest of the organization. (See Chapter 6 for information on motivating workers.)

- *Performance review meetings and tracking Gantt charts:* Another way to control project schedules is by holding periodic performance review meetings with the project sponsor or appropriate stakeholders. The project steering committee for the Just-In-Time Training project held weekly meetings to make sure the project was meeting schedule and other goals. Project managers often illustrate schedule progress at these meetings with a **tracking Gantt chart**—a Gantt chart that compares planned and actual project schedule information. Many project managers believe that tracking Gantt charts are an excellent tool for tracking project schedule performance and reporting that information to stakeholders. Figure 7-6 provides a sample tracking Gantt chart created in Appendix A. The tracking Gantt chart shows bars for both planned and actual start and finish dates for each task as well as the percent of work completed. See the *Brief Guide to Microsoft Project 2010* in Appendix A for information on creating a tracking Gantt chart and other types of performance reports.

		Task Name	Duration	Start	Finish	Predecessors
0		trackinggantt	36 days	Mon 1/5/09	Mon 2/23/09	
1	✓	Main task 1	15 days	Mon 1/5/09	Fri 1/23/09	
2	✓	Subtask 1	1 wk	Mon 1/5/09	Fri 1/9/09	
3	✓	Subtask 2	1 wk	Mon 1/12/09	Fri 1/16/09	2
4	✓	Subtask 3	1 wk	Mon 1/19/09	Fri 1/23/09	3
5		Main task 2	21 days	Mon 1/26/09	Mon 2/23/09	
6	✓	Subtask 1	2.2 wks	Mon 1/26/09	Mon 2/9/09	4
7		Subtask 2	1 wk	Tue 2/10/09	Mon 2/16/09	6
8		Subtask 3	1 wk	Tue 2/17/09	Mon 2/23/09	7
9		Subtask 4	2 wks	Mon 1/26/09	Fri 2/6/09	4

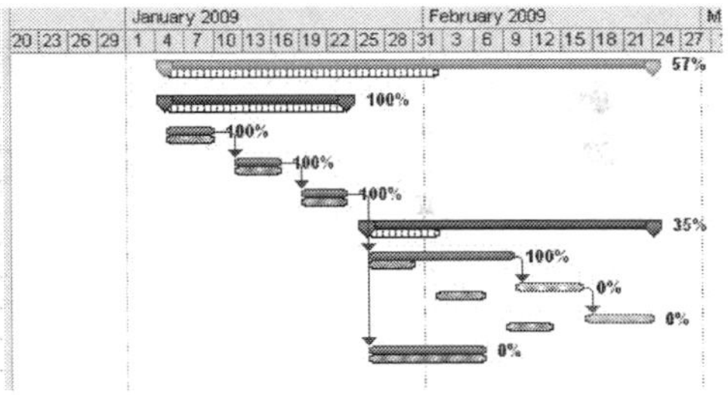

Figure 7-6. Sample schedule performance measurement using a tracking Gantt chart

To serve as a schedule performance measurement tool, a tracking Gantt chart uses a few additional symbols not found on a normal Gantt chart:

- Notice that the tracking Gantt chart in Figure 7-6 often shows two horizontal bars for tasks. The top horizontal bar represents the planned or baseline duration for each task. The bar below it represents the actual duration. If the top and bottom bars are the same length and start and end on the same date, the actual schedule was the same as the planned schedule for that task. If the bars do not start and end on the same date, the actual schedule differed from the planned or baseline schedule. If the top horizontal bar is shorter than the bottom one, the task took longer than planned. If the top horizontal bar is longer than the bottom one, the task took less time than planned. A striped horizontal bar represents the planned duration for summary tasks. Recall from Chapter 4 that summary tasks are tasks that are decomposed into smaller tasks. The black bar adjoining the striped horizontal bar shows the progress for summary tasks.

- A white diamond on the tracking Gantt chart represents a slipped milestone. A **slipped milestone** refers to a milestone activity that was actually completed later than originally planned.

- Percentages to the right of the horizontal bars display the percentage of work completed for each task. For example, 100% indicates that the task is finished, whereas 50% indicates that the task is still in progress and is 50% completed.

- In the columns to the left of the tracking Gantt chart, you can display baseline and actual start and finish dates. See Appendix A for more information on tracking Gantt charts.

What Went Right?

Canadian Imperial Bank of Commerce (CIBC) provides an excellent example of successfully controlling the schedule for a large information technology project in the banking industry. CIBC transformed 20,000 workstations in 1,200 different financial branches in just one year. It created a Web-based tool to enable large geographically dispersed teams to access information simultaneously. Each of the 1,200 sites had 75 milestones to track, including the baseline, latest plan, and actual finish dates, resulting in 90,000 data points. According to Jack Newhouse, the company's director of application support, CIBC's Web-based tracking tool "was a critical component to success....Accurate, timely data was an invaluable management tool."[4]

Project sponsors hate surprises, so the project manager must be clear and honest in communicating project status. By no means should project managers create the illusion that the project is going fine when, in fact, serious problems have emerged. When conflicts arise that could affect the project schedule, the project manager must alert the project sponsor and other stakeholders and work with them to resolve the conflicts. Recall from Chapter 5 that the communications management plan should describe escalation procedures for resolving issues.

MONITORING AND CONTROLLING TASKS FOR PROJECT COST MANAGEMENT

The main monitoring and controlling task performed as part of project cost management is controlling cost. Cost control includes monitoring cost performance, ensuring that only appropriate project changes are included in a revised cost baseline, and informing project stakeholders of authorized changes to the project that will affect costs. The cost performance baseline, performance reports, change requests, and project funding requirements are inputs to the cost-control process. Outputs of cost control include work performance measurements, budget forecasts, change requests, project management plan updates, project document updates, and updates to organizational process assets, such as lessons-learned documents.

Several tools and techniques assist in project cost control:

- *Earned value:* An important tool for cost control is earned value management, as described earlier.

- *Forecasting:* It is very useful to predict or forecast future costs based on past performance.

- **To-complete performance index (TCPI)**: This index is the cost performance that must be achieved on the remaining work in order to meet a specified goal, such as the BAC or EAC. If the BAC can no longer be met, forecasts are based on the EAC. The formula for the TCPI based on the BAC is (BAC-EV)/(BAC-AC), and based on the EAC the formula is (BAC-EV)/(EAC-AC).

- *Project status performance reviews:* These reviews, often done as part of review meetings, can be a powerful aid for controlling project costs, just as they are for controlling schedules. People often perform better when they know they must report on their progress and are held accountable for their performance.

- *Variance analysis:* Cost performance measurements like the CV and CPI show the degree of cost variance. It is important to analyze cost variance and determine if corrective action is needed.

- *Project management software:* Software packages, such as Microsoft Project 2010, have many cost-management features to help you enter budgeted costs, set a baseline, enter actuals, calculate variances, and run various cost reports.

Some projects leaders who encounter major problems, especially quality problems, blame those problems on poor cost control, as described in the "What Went Wrong?" passage.

What Went Wrong?

Many people have heard about the problems with Boston's Big Dig project. Newspapers and Web sites showed the many leaks in the eight- to 10-lane underground expressway that took over 14 years and $14 billion to build. Did the project overseers cut corners to save time and money?

Representative Stephen F. Lynch believes the answer to that question is yes, and that at some point, pressure to get the project done distracted Bechtel/Parsons Brinckerhoff from getting the project done right. "Under the pressure and scrutiny of a lot of people, they went back to look at areas where they could reduce cost in areas of material and time," said Lynch, a South Boston Democrat, in the aftermath of the Big Dig congressional hearing he brought to Boston on April 22, 2005. Pressure to finally speed up the costly, long-running project may explain why the new Artery tunnel is plagued by leaks. "As a casual observer, I am forced to conclude that the focus on the cost overrun and the schedule distracted attention from quality control issues on the Central Artery project," declared George J. Tamaro in written testimony to the Congressional Committee on Government Reform. [5]

MONITORING AND CONTROLLING TASKS FOR PROJECT QUALITY MANAGEMENT

The main project quality management task for monitoring and controlling is performing quality control. Key outputs include quality-control measurements, validated changes, validated deliverables, organizational process asset updates, change requests, project management plan updates, and project document updates. Although one of the main goals of quality control is to ensure and improve quality, the main outcomes of this process are acceptance decisions, rework, and process adjustments.

- Acceptance decisions determine if the products or services produced as part of the project will be accepted or rejected. If they are accepted, they are considered to be validated deliverables. If project stakeholders reject some of the products or services produced as part of the project, there must be rework.

- Rework is action taken to bring rejected items into compliance with product requirements or specifications or other stakeholder expectations. Rework can be very expensive, so the project manager who excels at quality planning and quality assurance can reduce the need for rework.

- Process adjustments correct or prevent further quality problems. Based on the implementation of quality-control measurements, process adjustments often result in updates to the quality baseline, organizational process assets, and the project management plan.

Sample Quality-Control Measurements

Many different tools and techniques for performing quality control and developing control measurements are available. Some of these tools and techniques are also used for quality planning and assurance. The following seven tools are known as the Seven Basic Tools of Quality:

1. *Cause-and-effect diagram*: As described in Chapter 6, cause-and-effect diagrams help you find the root cause of quality problems. Figure 6-4, repeated in this chapter as Figure 7-7, provides a sample cause-and-effect diagram that can be used to find the root cause of low course ratings for the Just-In-Time Training project.

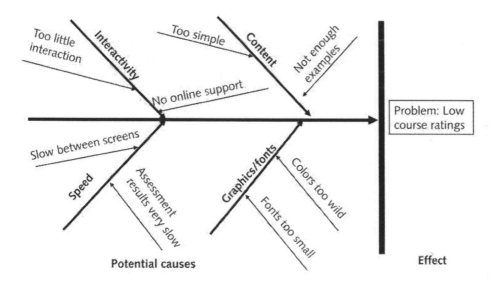

Figure 7-7. Sample cause-and-effect diagram

2. *Control chart:* A **control chart** is a graphical display of data that illustrates the results of a process over time. Control charts allow you to determine whether a process is in control or out of control. When a process is in control, any variations in the results of the process are created by random events. Processes that are in control do not need to be adjusted. When a process is out of control, variations in the results of the process are caused by nonrandom events. When a process is out of control, you need to identify the causes of those nonrandom events and adjust the process to correct or eliminate them. Figure 7-8 provides an example of a control chart for a process that manufactures 12-inch rulers. Assume that these are wooden rulers created by machines on an assembly line. Each point on the chart represents a length measurement for a ruler that comes off the assembly line. The scale on the vertical axis

An Introduction to Project Management, Third Edition

goes from 11.90 to 12.10. These numbers represent the lower and upper specification limits for the ruler. In this case, this would mean that the customer has specified that all rulers purchased must be between 11.90 and 12.10 inches long, or 12 inches plus or minus 0.10 inches. The lower and upper control limits on the control chart are 11.91 and 12.09 inches, respectively. This means the manufacturing process is designed to produce rulers between 11.91 and 12.09 inches long. Looking for and analyzing patterns in process data is an important part of quality control. You can use control charts and the seven run rule to look for patterns in data. The seven run rule states that if seven data points in a row are all below the mean, above the mean, increasing, or decreasing, then the process needs to be examined for nonrandom problems. In Figure 7-8, data points that violate the seven run rule are starred. The first starred point has seven data points in a row that are all below the mean. The second one has seven data points in a row that are all decreasing. Note that you include the first point in a series of points that are all increasing or decreasing. In the ruler-manufacturing process, these data points may indicate that a calibration device may need adjustment. For example, the machine that cuts the wood for the rulers might need to be adjusted, or the blade on the machine might need to be replaced.

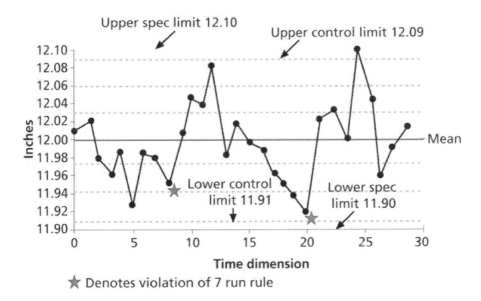

Figure 7-8. Sample control chart (Schwalbe, Information Technology Project Management, Sixth Edition, 2010)

3. *Run charts:* A **run chart** displays the history and pattern of variation of a process over time. It is a line chart that shows data points plotted in the order in which they occur. You can use run charts to perform trend analysis to forecast future outcomes based on historical results. For

example, trend analysis can help you analyze how many defects have been identified over time to determine if there are trends. Figure 7-9 shows a sample run chart, charting the number of defects each day for three different types of defects. Notice that you can easily see the patterns of Defect 1 continuing to decrease over time, Defect 2 increasing over time, and Defect 3 fluctuating each month.

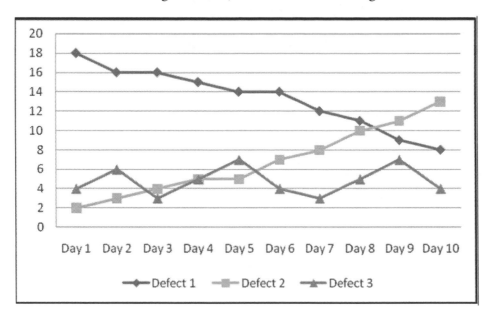

Figure 7-9. Sample run chart

4. *Scatter diagram:* A **scatter diagram** helps show if there is a relationship between two variables. The closer data points are to a diagonal line, the more closely the two variables are related. Figure 7-10 provides a sample scatter diagram that the Just-In-Time Training project team might create to compare training participants' course evaluation ratings with their ages to see if there is a relationship between those two variables. They might find that younger workers prefer the Web-based courses, for example, and make decisions based on that finding.

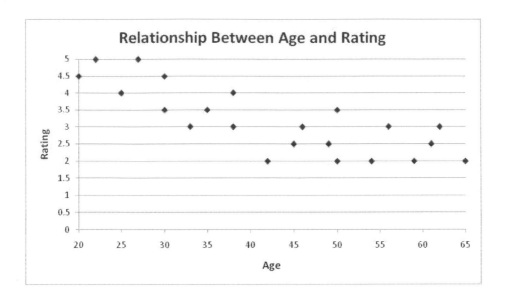

Figure 7-10. Sample scatter diagram

5. *Histograms:* A **histogram** is a bar graph of a distribution of variables. Each bar represents an attribute or a characteristic of a problem or situation, and the height of the bar represents its frequency. Chapter 5 provides a sample resource histogram, showing the number of people required for a project over time. The Just-In-Time Training project team created a histogram to show how many total complaints they received each month related to the project. Figure 7-11 shows the sample histogram.

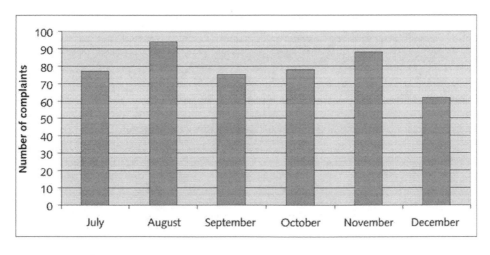

Figure 7-11. Sample histogram

6. *Pareto charts:* A **Pareto chart** is a histogram that can help you identify and prioritize problem areas. The variables described by the histogram are ordered by frequency of occurrence in a column chart, and a line chart is added to show cumulative percentage on the right of the chart. Pareto charts help you identify the vital few contributors that account for most quality problems in a system. Pareto analysis is sometimes referred to as the 80/20 rule, meaning that 80% of problems are often due to 20% of the causes. Figure 7-12 is a sample Pareto chart that the Just-In-Time Training project team developed. They used it to help improve the quality of the information they provided about training courses on the corporate intranet. It shows the number of times people complained about the information on the intranet by category of complaint. Notice that the first two complaints account for a large percentage of the problems, so the team should focus on improving those areas to improve quality. Note that Pareto charts work best when the problem areas are of equal importance. For example, if a life-threatening problem was reported, it should be considered before less important problems.

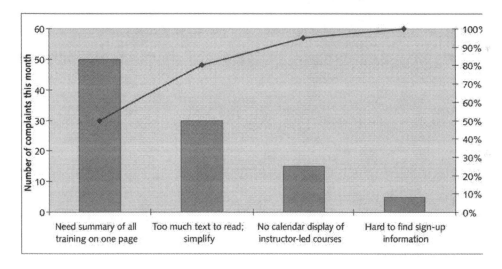

Figure 7-12. Sample Pareto chart

7. *Flowcharts:* **Flowcharts** are graphical displays of the logic and flow of processes that help you analyze how problems occur and how processes can be improved. They show activities (using the square symbol), decision points (using the diamond symbol), and the order of how information is processed (using arrow symbols). Figure 7-13 provides a simple example of a flowchart that shows the process Kristin's team used for accepting or rejecting deliverables.

310

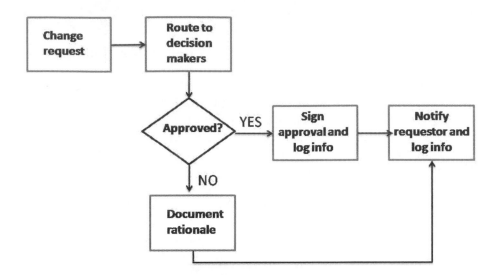

Figure 7-13. Sample flowchart

Figure 7-14 provides a humorous example of using math and statistics to demonstrate quality in a personal relationship.

Figure 7-14. A statistically significant relationship (www.xkcd.com)

MONITORING AND CONTROLLING TASKS FOR PROJECT COMMUNICATIONS MANAGEMENT

The main communications management task performed as part of monitoring and controlling is reporting performance. Key outputs include performance reports, organizational process assets updates, and change requests.

Reporting Performance

Reporting performance keeps stakeholders informed about how resources are being used to achieve project objectives. The project management plan, work performance data and measurements, and organizational process assets are all important inputs to performance reporting. Outputs of performance reporting are performance reports, organizational process assets updates, and change requests. Performance reports are normally provided as status reports or progress reports. Many people use the two terms interchangeably, but some people distinguish between them as follows. A third type of report often used is a forecast:

- **Status reports** describe where the project stands at a specific point in time. Recall the importance of the triple constraint. Status reports address where the project stands in terms of meeting scope, time, and cost goals. Is work being accomplished as planned? How long did it take to do certain tasks? How much money has been spent to date? Status reports can take various formats depending on the stakeholders' needs.

- **Progress reports** describe what the project team has accomplished during a certain period. In many projects, each team member prepares a weekly or monthly progress report. Team leaders often create consolidated progress reports based on the information received from team members.

- **Forecasts** predict future project status and progress based on past information and trends. How long will it take to finish the project based on how things are going? How much more money will be needed to complete the project? Project managers can also use earned value management, as described earlier in this chapter, to answer these questions by estimating the budget at completion and the projected completion date based on how the project is progressing.

Stakeholders often review project performance information at status review meetings, such as the ones Kristin has with the project steering committee. Status review meetings are a good way to highlight important information, empower people to be accountable for their work, and have face-to-face discussions about key project issues. Many project managers also hold periodic status review meetings with their own team members to exchange important project information and motivate people to make progress on their parts of the project. Likewise, many senior managers, who are often part of a review board or oversight committee, hold status review meetings. At these meetings, several program and project managers must report overall status information to keep everyone abreast of important events and to learn from each other as well.

Sample Performance Report

Figure 7-15 provides a sample progress report that Kristin gave at a performance review meeting with the Just-In-Time Training project steering committee. Notice that the report references an earned value chart, similar to the one shown in Figure 7-4. Also notice the use of metrics that are of key interest to senior managers, such as the number of people trained to date and registered for courses. Also note the issues and suggestions and the project changes sections of the report. Performance review meetings should focus on addressing these items to ensure that projects succeed.

Progress Report

Project Name: Just-In-Time Training Project

Project Manager Name: Kristin Maur

Date: February 3

Reporting Period: January 1 – February 1

Work completed this reporting period:

- Held first negotiating skills course (instructor-led) with 20 participants

- Held first supplier management executive course (instructor-led) with 17 participants

- Held second supplier management introductory course (instructor-led) with 20 participants

- Had 32 people begin the Web-based introductory supplier management course

- Continued developing other Web-based courses

- Prepared evaluations of all courses held to date

Work to complete next reporting period:

- Hold first advanced supplier management course

- Hold first project management course

- Hold first software applications course

What's going well and why:

- Participation in all courses is good. Every instructor-led course was full, except the supplier management executive course. All of the courses were advertised well, and we had more than enough people sign-up for the classes. We put several people on the list for later courses after courses were filled in the registration system.

- The average course ratings were above 3.8 on a 5.0 scale. Comments were generally very positive.

- More people than expected started the first Web-based course. Development of new Web-based courses is going well.

What's not going well and why:

- We did not fill the supplier management executive course as planned. Three people could not attend at the last minute, and it was too late to get replacements. We will work on a policy to help prevent this problem in the future for all instructor-led classes.

- We were surprised that so many people started the Web-based introductory supplier management course. We can handle the numbers, but we could have done a better job at forecasting demand.

Suggestions/Issues:

- Develop a policy to handle people not being able to attend instructor-led courses at the last minute.

- Try to do a better job at forecasting demand for Web-based courses.

Project changes:

No major changes to report. The earned value chart in Attachment 1 shows planned value, actual cost, and earned value information to date. We are very close to our plans, running slightly ahead of schedule and a bit over budget.

Figure 7-15. Sample performance report

MONITORING AND CONTROLLING TASKS FOR PROJECT RISK MANAGEMENT

Monitoring and controlling risks involves executing the risk management processes to respond to risk events. Recall from Chapter 5 that a risk event is a specific, uncertain event that may occur to the detriment or enhancement of the project. Executing the risk management processes means ensuring that risk awareness is an ongoing activity performed by the entire project team throughout the project. Project risk management does not stop with the initial risk analysis. Identified risk events may not materialize, or their probabilities of occurrence or impact may diminish or increase. Similarly, new risk events are normally identified as the project progresses. Newly identified risk events need to go through the same process of analysis and control as those identified during the initial risk assessment. A redistribution of resources devoted to risk management may be necessary because of relative changes in risk exposure.

Carrying out individual risk management plans involves monitoring risks based on defined milestones and making decisions regarding risks and their response strategies. It might be necessary to alter a strategy if it becomes ineffective, implement planned contingency activities, or eliminate a risk event from the list of potential risks. Project teams sometimes use **workarounds**—unplanned responses to risk events—when they do not have contingency plans in place.

Risk reassessment, risk audits, variance and trend analysis, technical performance measurement, reserve analysis, and status meetings are all tools and techniques for performing risk monitoring and control. Outputs of this process include risk register updates, organizational process assets updates, change requests, project management plan updates, and project document updates.

Sample Risk Register Updates

Recall from Chapter 5 that the number one risk event in the risk register for the Just-In-Time Training project at that time was a poor survey response. Because the project was now halfway completed, the risk register would have to change significantly. New risks would be identified and potential responses would change based on the current situation. Status of all risks would also be updated.

For example, halfway through the project, senior management informed Kristin that the company, Global Construction, Inc., was growing faster than expected, and they thought the number of people needing training would be higher than expected. This information resulted in the identification of several new risks related to the difficulty of accommodating this growth in trainees. For example, although the Web-based courses were the most popular and adding participants to them would be less expensive than adding to any other type of course, there was a risk that the discussion board would become unmanageable. People might waste time reading through hundreds of messages or just ignore this part of the course altogether. Kristin and her team, including suppliers for the Web-based courses, would need to develop potential responses to this risk and take action if it did occur. Another risk related to employee growth might be the need to offer more instructor-led classes, which would result in increased costs to the project. As you can see, the risk register must be constantly updated as part of project monitoring and control.

MONITORING AND CONTROLLING TASKS FOR PROJECT PROCUREMENT MANAGEMENT

The main procurement management task performed to monitor and control projects is administering procurements, also called contract administration. Administering procurements ensures that the seller's performance meets contractual requirements. The contractual relationship is a legal relationship and, as such, is subject to state and federal contract laws. It is very important that appropriate legal and contracting professionals be involved in writing and administering contracts.

Several tools and techniques can help in contract administration:

- Contract change-control system
- Procurement performance reviews
- Inspections and audits
- Performance reporting
- Payment systems
- Claims administration
- Records management system

In addition to organizational process assets updates, change requests, and project management plan updates, a key output of contract administration is procurement documentation. Procurement documentation would include the contract itself along with requested unapproved contract changes and approved change requests. It is very important to document all changes to the contract and communicate those changes to all affected stakeholders. For example, if a supplier developing a course for the Just-In-Time Training project agreed to add a topic to the course at no extra cost, that agreement must be added to the contract to make it legal. Likewise, if Global Construction decided to add more than the agreed on number of instructor-led courses, it would need to update that information in the contract as well. Updates are often made by having both parties—the buyer and the seller—sign an addendum to the contract.

Project team members must be aware of the potential legal problems of their not understanding a contract. Changes must be handled properly for items under contract. Without understanding the provisions of the contract, a project manager might not realize that she is authorizing the contractor to do additional work at additional cost. Therefore, change control is an important part of the contract administration process.

An Introduction to Project Management, Third Edition

It is critical that project managers and team members watch for constructive change orders. **Constructive change orders** are oral or written acts or omissions by someone with actual or apparent authority that can be construed to have the same effect as a written change order. For example, if a member of Kristin's project team has met with a supplier or contractor on a weekly basis for three months to provide guidelines for performing work, he can be viewed as an apparent authority. If he tells the contractor to redo part of a report that has already been delivered and accepted by the project manager, that action can be viewed as a constructive change order and the contractor can legally bill the buyer for the additional work. Likewise, if this apparent authority tells the contractor to skip parts of a critical review meeting in the interests of time, it would not be the contractor's fault if he missed important information.

Suggestions for Administering Procurements

The following suggestions help ensure adequate change control and good contract administration:

- Changes to any part of the project need to be reviewed, approved, and documented by the same people in the same way that the original part of the plan was approved.

- Evaluation of any change should include an impact analysis. How will the change affect the scope, time, cost, and quality of the goods or services being provided? There must also be a baseline against which to compare and analyze changes.

- Changes must be documented in writing. Project team members should document all important meetings and telephone calls.

- Project managers and their teams must stay closely involved with suppliers to make sure that their deliverables meet business needs and work in the organization's environment. Do not assume that work will run smoothly because you hired a reputable supplier. The buying organization needs to provide expertise as well.

- Have backup plans in case the procurement does not produce the desired results.

CASE WRAP-UP

The project steering committee kept a watchful eye on the Just-In-Time Training project. They were impressed with Kristin's leadership abilities and the way she handled inevitable changes on the project. They especially liked the detailed, honest progress reports Kristin provided to them. They enjoyed brainstorming ideas on solving some of the issues presented to them at review meetings, and Kristin was always very open to their suggestions. Everyone was confident the project could be completed successfully.

CHAPTER SUMMARY

Monitoring and controlling involves regularly measuring progress to ensure that the project is meeting its objectives and addressing current business needs. The project manager and other staff monitor progress against plans and take corrective action when necessary. This chapter summarizes the monitoring and controlling tasks and key outputs for all nine knowledge areas.

Every knowledge area except project human resource management includes tasks and outputs to help monitor and control projects. Outputs common to several knowledge areas include change requests, work performance information, organizational process assets updates, project management plan updates, and project document updates.

Earned value management is a project performance measurement technique that integrates scope, time, and cost data. You can use it to forecast when a project will be completed and how much it will cost given past performance data.

Monitoring and controlling tasks related to scope management include verifying scope verification and controlling scope, and its unique output includes accepted deliverables. A sample form for verifying acceptance of deliverables is provided for the Just-In-Time Training project.

Controlling the schedule cost are the monitoring and controlling tasks of project time and cost management. Earned value management is an important tool for monitoring and controlling scope, time, and cost performance.

Unique outputs of performing quality control include quality-control measurements and validated deliverables. There are seven basic tools of quality to assist in performing quality control. Sample outputs are provided for the Just-In-Time Training project.

A unique monitoring and controlling output related to communications management is performance reports, which can include progress reports, status reports, and forecasts. A sample performance report is provided for the Just-In-Time Training project.

The main monitoring and controlling output related to risk management is risk register updates. Sample updates are provided for the Just-In-Time Training project.

An important monitoring and controlling output related to procurement management is procurement documentation. Suggestions are provided for administering procurements.

QUICK QUIZ

1. Which knowledge areas include tasks related to monitoring and controlling?

    A. project scope, time, cost, and quality management

    B. project integration, scope, time, cost, and quality management

    C. project human resource, communications, risk, and procurement management

    D. all nine knowledge areas except project human resource management

2. _____ is a project performance measurement technique that integrates scope, time, and cost data.

    A. Integrated change control

    B. Flowcharting

    C. Earned value management

    D. Forecasting

3. _____ involves formal acceptance of the completed project scope by the stakeholders.

    A. Scope creep

    B. Scope verification

    C. Deliverable acceptance

    D. Customer sign-off

4. _____ issues cause the most conflict over the life of projects.

    A. Change control

    B. Scope creep

    C. Cost

    D. Schedule

5. A _____ chart is a histogram that can help you identify and prioritize problem areas.

    A. Pareto

    B. control

    C. run

    D. scatter

320

6. When a process is out of control, variations in the results of the process are caused by _____ events.

   A. random

   B. nonrandom

   C. planned

   D. unplanned

7. Which of the following is not a tool or technique for managing project teams?

   A. observation and conversation

   B. issue logs

   C. performance appraisals

   D. control charts

8. _____ predict future project status and progress based on past information and trends.

   A. Forecasts

   B. Status reports

   C. Progress reports

   D. Histograms

9. _____ are unplanned responses to risk events.

   A. Contingencies

   B. Reserves

   C. Workarounds

   D. Overallocations

10. _____ change orders are oral or written acts or omissions by someone with actual or apparent authority that can be construed to have the same effect as a written change order.

    A. Constructive

    B. Contract

    C. Procurement

    D. Controlled

Quick Quiz Answers

1. D; 2. C; 3. B; 4. D; 5. A; 6. B; 7. D; 8. A; 9. C; 10. A

DISCUSSION QUESTIONS

1. What is involved in monitoring and controlling projects? What outputs of monitoring and controlling are common to all knowledge areas?

2. Explain how earned value management helps you monitor project performance and forecast future cost and schedule information. What do you need to do to use earned value management?

3. What are the three main objectives of integrated change control?

4. What is the difference between scope verification and scope control? Why are both important to project success?

5. What are some of the tools and techniques for performing time, cost, and quality control? What are the Seven Basic Tools of Quality?

6. Why is it important to keep the risk register up to date?

7. Why is it important to document contract changes? Why should project teams be watchful for constructive change orders?

EXERCISES

1. Find an example of a large project that took more than one year to complete, such as a major construction project. You can ask people at your college, university, or work about a recent project, such as a major fund raising campaign, information systems installation, or building project. You can also find information about projects online such as the Big Dig in Boston (*www.masspike.com/bigdig*), the Patronas Twin Towers in Malaysia, and many other building projects (*www.greatbuildings.com*). Describe some of the tasks performed to monitor and control the project. Write a one-page paper or prepare a short presentation summarizing your findings.

2. Given the following information for a one-year project, answer the following questions. Assume you have actual and earned value data at the end of the second month. Recall that PV is the planned value, EV is the earned value, AC is the actual cost, and BAC is the budget at completion.

> PV = $23,000
>
> EV = $20,000
>
> AC = $25,000
>
> BAC = $120,000

    a.   What is the cost variance, schedule variance, cost performance index (CPI), and schedule performance index (SPI) for the project?

    b.   How is the project progressing? Is it ahead of schedule or behind schedule? Is it under budget or over budget?

    c.   Use the CPI to calculate the estimate at completion (EAC) for this project.

    d.   Use the SPI to estimate how long it will take to finish this project.

    e.   Sketch the earned value chart for this project, using Figure 7-4 as a guide. Assume the data for month 1 is half of the values given for PV, EV, and AC at the end of month 2.

3.   Follow the steps for using Microsoft Project 2010 provided in the *Brief Guide to Microsoft Project 2010* in Appendix A through the section on earned value management. Open the data files as directed and then establish a baseline plan, create a tracking Gantt chart, and implement earned value management using this software.

4.   Assume you are working on a project to improve customer service. Create a Pareto chart based on the information in the following table. Use the Pareto chart template from the companion Web site or sketch the chart by hand so that your resulting chart looks similar to Figure 7-12.

Customer complaints	Frequency/week
Customer is on hold too long	90
Customer gets transferred to wrong area or cut off	20
Service rep cannot answer customer's questions	120
Service rep does not follow through as promised	40

5.   If you purchased the Fissure simulation software (available at www.ichapters.com for about $12), follow the detailed instructions on the companion Web site to run the Fissure simulation software. See more information about this simulation in Appendix C.

TEAM PROJECTS

1. Your organization initiated a project to raise money for an important charity. Assume that there are 1,000 people in your organization. Also, assume that you have six months to raise as much money as possible, with a goal of $100,000. List three problems that could arise while monitoring and controlling the project. Describe each problem in detail, and then develop realistic approaches to solving them in a two- to three-page paper or a 15-minute presentation. Be creative in your responses, and use at least one quality-control tool in your analysis. Remember that this project is run solely by volunteers.

2. You are part of a team in charge of a project to help people in your company (500 people) lose weight. This project is part of a competition, and the top "losers" will be featured in a popular television show. Assume that you have six months to complete the project and a budget of $10,000. You are halfway through the project, and morale is very low. People are also complaining about a lack of communication and support on the project. Although many people have been participating and have lost weight, many have plateaued or started gaining weight back. Create an issue log to document these and related issues. Also create a new entry for the risk register for this project. Document your responses in a two- to three-page paper or a 15-minute presentation.

3. Using the information you developed in Team Project 1 or 2, role-play a meeting to brainstorm and develop strategies for solving problems with key stakeholders. Determine who will play what role (project manager, team member from a certain department, senior managers, and so on). Be creative in displaying different personalities (a senior manager who questions the importance of the project to the organization, a team member who is very shy or obnoxious).

4. Brainstorm two different quality related problems that you are aware of at your college or organization. Then review the charts found in the section of this chapter on the seven basic tools of quality and create two charts to help analyze the quality problems. Prepare a one- to two-page paper or short presentation describing the problems and how the charts help to visualize them.

5. Perform the monitoring and controlling tasks for one of the case studies provided in Appendix C. If you are working on a real team project, create relevant monitoring and controlling documents, such as performance reports or quality assurance-related charts using the templates and samples in this chapter as guides. Present your results to the class.

COMPANION WEB SITE

Visit the free companion Web site for this text at **www.intropm.com** to access template files, online quizzes, Jeopardy-like games, Microsoft Project files, links to sites mentioned in the text, and other information to help you learn more about this important field. Instructors must contact the author at schwalbe@augsburg.edu to gain access to the instructor site. Anyone can access the student site.

KEY TERMS

actual cost (AC) — The total direct and indirect costs incurred in accomplishing work on an activity during a given period.

budget at completion (BAC) — The approved total budget for the project.

constructive change orders — Oral or written acts or omissions by someone with actual or apparent authority that can be construed to have the same effect as a written change order.

control chart — A graphical display of data that illustrates the results of a process over time.

earned value (EV) — An estimate of the value of the physical work actually completed.

earned value management (EVM) — A project performance measurement technique that integrates scope, time, and cost data.

estimate at completion (EAC) — A forecast of how much the project will cost upon completion.

flowcharts — The graphic displays of the logic and flow of processes that help you analyze how problems occur and how processes can be improved.

forecasts — The reports that predict future project status and progress based on past information and trends.

histogram — A bar graph of a distribution of variables.

integrated change control — The process of identifying, evaluating, and managing changes throughout the project's life cycle.

Pareto chart — A histogram that can help you identify and prioritize problem areas.

planned value (PV) — That portion of the approved total cost estimate planned to be spent on an activity during a given period.

progress reports — The reports that describe what the project team has accomplished during a certain period.

rate of performance (RP) — The percentage of actual work completed divided by the percentage of work planned to have been completed at any given time.

run chart — A chart that displays the history and pattern of variation of a process over time.

scatter diagram — A diagram that helps show if there is a relationship between two variables.

scope verification — The formal acceptance of the completed project scope by the customer or designated stakeholders.

slipped milestone — A milestone activity that was actually completed later than originally planned.

status reports — The reports that describe where the project stands at a specific point in time.

to-complete performance index (TCPI) — The cost performance that must be achieved on the remaining work in order to meet a specified goal, such as the BAC or EAC.

tracking Gantt chart — A Gantt chart that compares planned and actual project schedule information.

validated deliverable — A deliverable that has been completed and checked for correctness as part of quality control.

workarounds — The unplanned responses to risk events.

END NOTES

[1]Fran Kelly, "The World Today—Olympic Planning Schedule behind Time," *ABC Online* (March 4, 2004).

[2]Jay Weiner and Rachel Blount, "Olympics Are Safe but Crowds Are Sparse," *Minneapolis Star Tribune* (August 22, 2004), A9.

[3]Reuters, "Olympics Bill Reportedly Passes $12 Billion," *MSNBC.com* (August 25, 2004).

[4]Tom Chaduri and David Schlotzhauer, "So Many Projects, So Little Time," *PM Network* (October 2003), 58.

[5]Joan Vennochi, "Time, Money, and the Big Dig," *Boston Globe* (April 26, 2005).

Chapter 8
Closing Projects

LEARNING OBJECTIVES

After reading this chapter, you will be able to:

- List several tasks and outputs of project closing
- Discuss the process of closing a project or phase performed as part of project integration management, explain the importance of a project close-out meeting and knowledge transfer, and describe the contents of a customer acceptance/project completion form, final project report, and lessons-learned report
- Explain the process of closing procurements performed as part of project procurement management, and describe the contents of a written notice of a closed contract
- Read advice on closing projects

OPENING CASE

The Just-In-Time Training project was almost finished. Twenty instructor-led courses had been conducted over the past year, and a majority of Global Construction's employees took at least one Just-In-Time course, most using the Web-based delivery option. Some senior managers were surprised at how quickly workers took to the Web-based courses and were also pleased that many employees took the courses on their own time. Participants liked the interactive feedback and started networking more internally to improve productivity and collaboration. Employees provided excellent feedback on the new approach to training and suggested several new topics to be added to the list of training subjects. The project steering committee was looking forward to Kristin's final report and presentation on the project.

INTRODUCTION

Closing activities for phases and projects involves gaining stakeholder and customer acceptance of the final products and services, and bringing the phase or project to an orderly end. It includes verifying that all of the deliverables are complete, and often includes a final presentation and report. For both projects that are completed and those that are canceled before completion, it is important to formally close the project and reflect on what can be learned to improve future projects. As philosopher George Santayana said, "Those who cannot remember the past are condemned to repeat it."

For example, many companies canceled projects due to the poor economy in 2008-2009. Even Google, the "number one" company to work for in America, canceled several projects. They evaluated how popular development projects were with customers and employees, how big a problem they addressed, and whether they were meeting internal performance targets. If they didn't meet those criteria, they were closed. "There's no single equation that describes us, but we try to use data wherever possible," said Jeff Huber, Google's senior vice president of engineering. "What products have found an audience? Which ones are growing?"[1]

It is also important to plan for and execute a smooth transition of the project into the normal operations of the company. Most projects produce results that are integrated into the existing organizational structure. For example, Global Construction's Just-In-Time Training project will require staff to coordinate future training after the project is completed. Recall from Chapter 3 that the life-cycle cost estimate for the project included $400,000 each year for three years for work to be done after the project was completed. Before ending the project, Kristin and her team created a transition plan as part of the final report to integrate the new training into the firm's standard operations.

SUMMARY OF CLOSING OUTPUTS

Figure 8-1 summarizes key outputs of project closing by knowledge area, based on the *PMBOK® Guide, Fourth Edition*. Procedures for administrative and contract closure are part of organizational process assets. Every project should have procedures to guide closure. Samples of closing procedures and other outputs produced in closing the Just-In-Time Training project are provided in this chapter.

Knowledge area	Closing process	Outputs
Project integration management	Close project or phase	Final product, service, or result transition Organizational process assets updates
Project procurement management	Close procurements	Closed procurements Organizational process assets updates

Figure 8-1. Closing processes and outputs

CLOSING TASKS FOR PROJECT INTEGRATION MANAGEMENT

The last process in project integration management is closing the phase or project. To close a project or phase of a project, you must finalize all activities and transfer the completed or canceled work to the appropriate people. The main outputs of closing a project or phase are as follows:

- *Final product, service, or result transition:* Project sponsors are usually most interested in making sure that the final products, services, or results are delivered and transitioned to the appropriate part of the organization. A final project report and presentation are also commonly used during project closing. A sample table of contents from the Just-In-Time Training project's final report is provided in the next section, as well as part of the transition plan produced as part of the final report. The section of the final report summarizing project results should also address how well the project met key project metrics. It is important for project teams to set aside time to prepare a good final report and presentation, as these items often receive high visibility.

- *Updates to organizational process assets:* Recall that organizational process assets help people understand, follow, and improve business processes. Examples of organizational process assets include policies and procedures, guidelines, information systems, financial systems, management systems, lessons learned, and historical information. During closing, the project team should update appropriate process assets, especially lessons learned. At the end of the Just-In-Time Training project, Kristin's team prepared a lessons-learned report, which will serve as a tremendous asset for future projects.

In addition to these two outputs, it is also good practice to hold a close-out meeting and celebrate completion of the project or phase. In closing the Just-In-Time Training project, Kristin and her team prepared a customer acceptance/project completion form, a final report and presentation, a transition plan (provided as part of the final report), and a lessons-learned report. They also held a project close-out meeting to help transfer knowledge to other people in the organization. Kristin also organized a project closure luncheon for the project team right after the final project presentation. She used the luncheon to celebrate a job well done.

Sample Customer Acceptance/Project Completion Form

As part of project closing, Global Construction had the project sponsor complete a customer acceptance/project completion form. Even if the project had been terminated, the sponsor would still have completed the form to signify the end of the project. Figure 8-2 shows the form that was filled out for the Just-In-Time Training project. Note that this form refers to completion of the entire project, not just a specific deliverable. It should be completed and signed by the project sponsor.

Customer Acceptance/Project Completion Form

June 30

Project Name: **Just-In-Time Training Project**
Project Manager: **Kristin Maur**

I (We), the undersigned, acknowledge and accept delivery of the work completed for this project on behalf of our organization. My (Our) signature(s) attest(s) to my (our) agreement that this project has been completed. No further work should be done on this project.

Name	Title	Signature	Date
Lucy Camerena	Training Director	Lucy Camerena	June 30

1. Was this project completed to your satisfaction?   __X__ Yes   _____ No

2. Please provide the main reasons for your satisfaction or dissatisfaction with this project. The project met and exceeded my expectations. In my 15 years with this company, I have never seen workers so interested in training courses. Kristin effectively coordinated all of the people who worked on this project. We worked with a number of new suppliers, and everything went very smoothly.

3. Please provide suggestions on how our organization could improve its project delivery capability in the future.
One suggestion would be to try to improve our estimating and forecasting abilities. The project costs were slightly over budget, even with some reserve built in. The schedule buffer prevented the project from finishing late. We also need to improve the way we forecast the number of people who want to take courses. The demand for the Web-based courses was much higher than expected. Even though that was a pleasant surprise, it was still poor forecasting and caused extra work for project and support staff.

Thank you for your inputs.

Figure 8-2. Sample customer acceptance/project completion form

Sample Final Report

Figure 8-3 is the table of contents for the final project report for the Just-In-Time Training project (the cover page of the report included the project title, date, and team member names). Notice that the report includes a transition plan and a plan to analyze the benefits of the training each year. Also notice that the final report includes attachments for all the project management and product-related documents. Kristin knew the importance of providing complete final documentation on projects and that the project steering committee would expect a comprehensive final report on such an important project. The project team produced a hard copy of the final documentation for the project sponsor and each steering committee member, and placed an electronic copy on the corporate intranet with the other project archives. Kristin also led the team in giving a final project presentation, which summarized key information in the final project report.

Final Project Report
June 20

Project Name: Just-In-Time Training Project
1. Project Objectives
2. Summary of Project Results
3. Original and Actual Scope
4. Original and Actual Schedule
5. Original and Actual Budget
6. Project Assessment
7. Transition Plan
8. Training Benefits Plan

Attachments:
A. Key Project Management Documentation
   - Business case
   - Project charter
   - Project management plan
   - Performance Reports
B. Product-Related Documentation
   - Survey and results
   - Summary of user inputs
   - Report on research of existing training
   - Partnership agreements
   - Course materials
   - Intranet site training information
   - Summary of course evaluations

Figure 8-3. Sample table of contents for a final project report

Sample Transition Plan

As mentioned earlier, the life-cycle cost estimate for Global Construction's Just-In-Time Training project included $400,000 each year for three years for work to be done after the project was completed. The transition plan included information related to what work had to be done, by whom, and when. When developing a transition plan, the project team should work with managers in affected operating departments, and the contents of the plan should be tailored to fit the support needs of the project. Figure 8-4 provides part of the transition plan for the Just-In-Time Training project.

Transition Plan
June 20

Project Name: Just-In-Time Training Project

Introduction

The main goal of this project was to develop a new training program at Global Construction to provide just-in-time training to employees on key topics, including supplier management, negotiating skills, project management, and software applications. New courses were developed and offered in instructor-led, CD-ROM, and Web-based formats. These courses will continue to be offered at Global Construction for the next several years. This transition plan describes the work required to support these courses.

Assumptions

- Support for the just-in-time training will be handled by staff in affected operational departments, including the training, IT, HR, and contract departments.

- Funding for the required support is budgeted at $400,000 per year for three years. These funds will be used to pay staff in the operational departments supporting this project, experts providing information for courses, and suppliers providing training materials and courses.

- New course topics will be developed under a new project and are not part of this transition plan.

Organization

The Training Director, Lucy Camerena, will lead all efforts to support the Just-In-Time Training courses. Staff from the training, IT, HR, and contract departments will provide support as required. See the organizational chart provided in Attachment 1.

Work Required

The main work required to support the training developed from this project includes:

- Maintaining related information on the intranet site
- Handling course registration
- Determining the number of courses offered each year and when they will be offered
- Providing classrooms for the instructor-led training
- Coordinating with suppliers for all training courses

- Planning and managing the internal experts who provide some of the training and expert support for the courses
- Collecting course evaluation information and suggestions for changing the content or format of courses
- Reporting information to senior management on a monthly basis

See the Attachment 2 for detailed information on the work required.

Schedule

See Attachment 3 for a draft schedule of work to be performed in the next year. The Training Director is responsible for scheduling and managing the work required to support the Just-In-Time training.

Figure 8-4. Sample transition plan

Sample Lessons-Learned Report

Instead of asking each member of the Just-In-Time Training project team and the project managers from the major supplier organizations to write individual lessons-learned reports, Kristin decided to use a technique she had read about in an article in which key stakeholders held a sticky-note party to document lessons learned. Instead of writing lessons learned in a traditional way, key stakeholders met, wrote down all of the lessons they had learned on sticky notes, and then posted them to the wall. It was an enjoyable way for everyone to get together and share what they had learned from the project. After they finished, Kristin summarized the inputs in a list that everyone could access on the project Web site. She also used the corporate template to prepare a short lessons-learned report for inclusion in the final documentation for the project, as shown in Figure 8-5. Notice the question-and-answer format of the report, which is part of the lessons-learned template used for all projects done at Global Construction, Inc. Also notice that the lessons-learned report was finished 10 days before the project ended.

Lessons-Learned Report

June 20

Project Name:	Just-In-Time Training Project
Project Sponsor:	Lucy Camerena
Project Manager:	Kristin Maur
Project Dates:	July 1 – June 30
Final Budget:	$1, 072,000

1. Did the project meet scope, time, and cost goals?

We did meet scope and time goals, but we had to request an additional $72,000, which the sponsor approved. We actually exceeded scope goals by having more people take training courses than planned, primarily the Web-based courses.

2. What was the success criteria listed in the project scope statement?

The following statement outlined the project scope and success criteria:

"Our sponsor has stated that the project will be a success if the new training courses are all available within one year, if the average course evaluations are at least 3.0 on a 1-5 scale, and if the company recoups the cost of the project in reduced training costs within two years after project completion."

3. Reflect on whether or not you met the project success criteria.

All of the new training courses were offered within a year, and the course evaluations averaged 3.4 on a 5-point scale. The number of people who took the Web-based training courses far exceeded our expectations. Because the Web-based training is more cost-effective than the instructor-led training, we are confident that the cost of the project will be recouped in less than two years.

4. In terms of managing the project, what were the main lessons your team learned from this project?

The main lessons we learned include the following:

- Having good communications was instrumental to project success. We had a separate item in the WBS for stakeholder communications, which was very important. Moving from traditional to primarily Web-based training was a big change for Global Construction, so strong communications was crucial. The intranet site information was excellent, thanks to support from the IT department. It was also very effective to have different departments create project description posters to hang in their work areas. They showed creativity and team spirit.

- Teamwork and supplier partnerships were essential. It was extremely helpful to take time to develop and follow a team contract for the project team and to focus on developing good partnerships with suppliers. Everyone was very supportive of each other.

- Good planning paid off in when plans were executed. We spent a fair amount of time developing a good project charter, scope statement, WBS, schedules, and so on. Everyone worked together to develop these planning documents, and there was strong buy-in. We kept the plans up-to-date and made key project information available for everyone on a secure Web site.

- Creativity and innovation are infectious: Many creative and innovative ideas were used on this project. After departments had so much fun making their posters in their work areas, people picked up on the idea of being creative and innovative throughout the project. Everyone realized that training and learning could be enjoyable.

- The project steering committee was very effective. It was extremely helpful to meet regularly with the project steering committee. Having members from different departments in the company was very important and helped in promoting the training created as part of this project.

5. Describe one example of what went right on this project.

We were skeptical about hiring an outside consultant to help us develop a short list of potential suppliers for the training courses, but it was well worth the money. We gained a good deal of useful information very quickly, and the consultant made excellent recommendations and helped us develop partnerships that benefited suppliers and us.

6. Describe one example of what went wrong on this project.

The senior supplier management specialist assigned to the team at the beginning of the project was not a good fit. The project manager should have more involvement in selecting project team members.

7. What will you do differently on the next project based on your experience working on this project?

For future training projects it would be helpful to line up experts and mentors further in advance. We underestimated the number of people who would take the Web-based courses, and participants liked the interactive features, such as getting expert advice and having a list of people willing to mentor them on various topics. We were scrambling to get people and had to figure out how to organize them in an effective manner.

Figure 8-5. Project lessons-learned report

Another format for preparing a lessons-learned report is available from Microsoft. Figure 8-6 on the following two pages shows this Word template, available from www.microsoft.com when searching for "project lessons learned template."

[Project Name]

Project Lessons Learned

Department: **Document Owner:**

Focus Area: **Project or Organization Role:**

Product or Process:

Version	Date	Author	Change Description

LESSONS LEARNED PURPOSE AND OBJECTIVES

Throughout each project life cycle, lessons are learned and opportunities for improvement are discovered. As part of a continuous improvement process, documenting lessons learned helps the project team discover the root causes of problems that occurred and avoid those problems in later project stages or future projects. Data for this report was gathered by using Project Lessons Learned Record sheets and is summarized in the table.

The objective of this report is gathering all relevant information for better planning of later project stages and future projects, improving implementation of new projects, and preventing or minimizing risks for future projects.

Lessons learned questions

- What worked well—or didn't work well—either for this project or for the project team?
- What needs to be done over or differently?
- What surprises did the team have to deal with?
- What project circumstances were not anticipated?
- Were the project goals attained? If not, what changes need to be made to meet goals in the future?

Project Highlights

Top 3 Significant Project Successes

Project Success	Factors That Supported Success

Other Notable Project Successes

Project Success	Factors That Supported Success

Project Shortcomings and Solutions

Project Shortcoming	Recommended Solutions

Approvals

Prepared by:_____

Project Manager

Approved by: _____

Project Sponsor

_____

Executive Sponsor

_____

Client Sponsor

Figure 8-6. Microsoft lessons-learned template

Media Snapshot

When President-elect Obama gave his victory speech on November 8, 2008, he was quick to give credit to what he called "the best campaign team ever assembled in the history of politics." To help understand lessons learned from this successful project, 60 Minutes correspondent Steve Kroft interviewed campaign leaders right after Obama's acceptance speech in Chicago.

David Axelrod was Obama's chief strategist, and David Plouffe was the campaign manager who led the 22-month project. Senior aide Robert Gib and Anita Dunn, who handled communications, research, and policy, also shared their thoughts with Kroft. When asked how they took a little-known senator with almost no national experience and got him elected as the 44th president of the United States, they had many insights. In a nutshell, "they did it by recruiting and vesting millions of volunteers in the outcome, by raising more money than any campaign in history, and by largely ignoring that their candidate happened to be a black man."[2]

Project Close-Out Meeting and Knowledge Transfer

It is good practice to hold a close-out meeting as a project nears completion or termination. At this meeting, like the kick-off meeting, you should invite key project stakeholders. Some people call this close-out meeting a **post-mortem** since it is normally held after the project has died or been put to rest. The project champion should start off the meeting, and the project manager and his/her team should review information like the following:

- The scope, time, and cost goals and outcomes
- The success criteria and results in achieving them
- Main changes that occurred during the project and how they were addressed
- The main lessons learned on the project
- A summary of the transition plan

The project team should also ask for comments and questions from stakeholders. It's important to get other perspectives on how things went. If there are still any issues that need to be addressed, the project manager should follow through on them to successfully close them out.

It is also important to take time to transfer knowledge learned while working on the project. In particular, people who will take over products or results produced as part of the project would need to spend time with project team members so they understand what is involved in detail. In this example, people from the training, IT, HR, and contract departments would gain from knowledge transfer from the Just-In-Time Training project.

Of course, these people could read the final report, transition plan, and lessons learned, but most people also want face-to-face interaction to really benefit from knowledge transfer. For example, since Kristin would move on to another project after completing this one, she should meet with the person from the training department who would handle many of the management tasks involved in planning and implementing future training courses. She should offer to mentor this person and be available as needed to answer questions. Likewise, the IT person who developed the intranet materials related to the project should also meet with whoever will take over that work and share his/her expertise as well. If it makes sense to provide further documentation, the person who knows the most about the work should take the time to write it.

Many organizations are working hard to improve the knowledge transfer process, since employee knowledge or human capital is one of their key assets. It is crucial, therefore to make project knowledge transfer a priority, especially if the benefits of a project are not achieved immediately. For example, one of the success criteria for the Just-In-Time Training project was to recoup the cost of the project in reduced training costs within two years after project completion. The business case stated that a goal was to reduce training costs per employee by 10 percent each year or about $100 per employee per year. Kristin should work with the people taking over the training to ensure that they measure training costs and work to achieve their goals.

Best Practice

Kent Greenes is an expert and consultant on knowledge management. Blogger Dale Arseneault captured the following useful ideas from one of Kent's presentations on best practices in knowledge transfer:
1. "Best" or "better" practices are not adopted; they're adapted.
2. As Jack Welch said, "You don't have a better or best practice until someone else is using it."
3. The learner is important, and making learning easy is critical or people will recreate "good enough."
4. Focus on general, broadly applicable practices first, rather than choosing highly specialized practices.
5. Do something, see what works, then broaden the scope.
6. Peer assistance is a critical tool to begin, and even conclude, the process.
7. Uncover success stories, communicate the stories, and assist the learning and adaption processes.
8. Facilitation is critical to the process - both the role and the capability.
9. Documentation/video/audio artifacts are the starting point for discovery and productive conversation; it is vital to put the people with the learning needs and the people who have the experience together to enable transfer.
10. To facilitate discovery of best practices, leverage communities wherever possible.[3]

CLOSING TASKS FOR PROJECT PROCUREMENT MANAGEMENT

The final process in project procurement management is closing the procurement, which involves completion and settlement of procurements/contracts, and resolution of any open items. The project team should determine if all work required in each contract was completed correctly and satisfactorily. The team should also update records to reflect final results and archive information for future use.

Tools to assist in closing procurements include:

- *Procurement audits*: **Procurement audits** are often performed to identify lessons learned in the entire procurement process. Organizations should strive to improve all their business processes, including procurement management.

- *Negotiated settlements*: Ideally, any disagreements during procurement will be settled by negotiating between the buyer and seller. Sometimes other methods are required, such mediation, arbitration, or litigation.

- A *records management system*: A **records management system** provides the ability to easily organize, find, and archive documents, such as those related to procurement. It is often an automated system, or at least partially automated, because there can be a large amount of information related to project procurement.

Outputs from closing procurements include closed procurements (such as closed contracts) and updates to organizational process assets. Just as with closing the project or phase, updating organizational process assets includes documentation, historical information, and lessons learned. To close contracts, the buying organization often provides the seller with formal written notice that the contract has been completed. Buyers might also consider the final payment to the seller as the contract closeout. The contract itself should include requirements for formal acceptance and closure.

Sample Written Notice of a Closed Contract

Figure 8-7 provides an example of a formal letter that Global Construction sent to one of its sellers, ABC Training Consultants, to formally close out their contract. The contract, a service agreement in this case, included a clause stating that written notice would be provided to formally close the contract. The seller in this particular example also requested that the buyer provide a short performance assessment as part of the closure letter. (See Chapter 6 to review the service agreement and Chapter 5 for the contract statement of work. Recall that the work had to be completed by September 9 for this contract.)

Global Construction, Inc. Contract Closure Notice

September 16

As described in our service agreement, this letter provides formal notice that the work you were contracted to perform for Global Construction has been completed. ABC Training developed a qualified sellers list containing thirty potential sellers and a report with one-page of key information on each seller. Payment is being processed based on the invoice provided by ABC Training.

Kristin Maur, the project manager, has provided the following performance assessment for the work provided:

"We were very pleased with the work of ABC Training. Members of the firm were professional, knowledgeable, and easy to work with. Global Construction depended on ABC Training to develop a qualified sellers list for this important project, and we were extremely happy with the results. On a scale of 1 to 10, you earned a 10!"

Lawrence Scheller

By: Lawrence Scheller, Contract Specialist
Date   September 16

Figure 8-7. Sample contract closure notice

What Went Wrong?

Everyone seems to agree that it is important to document and share project lessons learned, yet a survey of 961 experienced project managers found that although 62 percent had formal procedures for learning lessons from projects, only 12 percent adhered closely to them.

The Project Management (PM) Perspective research team wanted to discover how organizations capture lessons learned and apply them to new projects. Their findings were very discouraging. Although many tools and processes were in place for capturing lessons-learned information at the end of a project, few organizations bothered to use them.

"End-of-project post-mortems were infrequently and inadequately performed. Project managers cited the usual problems: a lack of time, key people not available, a culture of blame. And, as one interviewee noted, 'Most projects don't have enough budget to support any good closure.'"[4]

ADVICE ON CLOSING PROJECTS

Although project teams do not typically spend much time on closing projects, it is important to do it well. Below are a few words of advice on quickly and successfully closing projects, whether they were successful or not:

- It is important to plan for project closing. There should be tasks in the WBS and resources allocated to perform project closing. For example, someone should be assigned the task of reviewing lessons learned and creating one final lessons-learned report. Resources should be assigned to prepare the final project report, presentation, and some type of celebration.

- It will be much easier to close a project if the project team captures lessons learned and other important information required for closing as soon as possible. For example, the project team should have some type of log where everyone can document lessons learned as they occur. A simple blog would work well for this purpose, or team members could document lessons learned as part of progress reports.

- Project managers should take time to thank their team and other project stakeholders and have some type of closing celebration. Just having a team lunch or informal gathering with refreshments might be appropriate. If it was a big, highly successful project, a more formal celebration and rewards would be appropriate. See the examples in the following What Went Right? passage.

What Went Right?

Many project teams go all out to celebrate the closing of their projects, whether the project went well or not. A quick search on www.youtube.com and similar sites shows many videos of project closing celebrations. Below are a few examples:

- Popular television shows likes American Idol and Britain's Got Talent have great closing shows. For example, on May 19, 2009, several famous celebrities performed with contestants before ending American Idol's season and announcing the new winner, Kris Allen. Both Kris and the runner-up, Adam Lambert, received free cars from Ford. Of course the winner got additional rewards. You can find several video clips of this and other final talent-related shows on the Internet.
- Many viewers get tears in their eyes watching the last few minutes of Extreme Home Makeover episodes. Ty Pennington and his team of designers, builders, volunteers, friends, family, and neighbors gather to see the new home built quickly for a family in need. Everyone enjoys the tradition of shouting, "Move that bus!"
- On a smaller scale, Allegheny College put together a five minute video of their senior project celebration. Many colleges require senior projects, so why not have a formal celebration when the projects are completed and document the event in a video?

Of course this chapter would not be complete without a cartoon about closing projects (Figure 8-8). May you never have nightmares from not finishing your projects!

Figure 8-8. Bad dreams about not finishing projects (www.xkcd.com)

CASE WRAP-UP

Kristin Maur stood in front of the project steering committee. She invited her entire team to give the final presentation as a group effort. Of course they had several challenges along the way, but overall, the project was a success. All the new training courses were offered within a year, and the course evaluations averaged 3.4 on a 5.0 scale, which exceeded the committee's goal of 3.0. More people took training courses than planned, primarily the Web-based courses. Because the Web-based training was more cost-effective than the instructor-led training, the team was confident that the costs of the Just-In-Time Training project would be recouped in less than two years, as projected. Kristin watched each team member summarize key project results, and she sensed the pride that everyone felt in a job well done. She also felt good knowing that she helped her team members get assigned to even more challenging projects, and she was ready to start her next project as well.

CHAPTER SUMMARY

Closing phases or projects involves gaining stakeholder and customer acceptance of the final products and services, and bringing the phase or project to an orderly end. It includes verifying that all of the deliverables are complete. This chapter summarizes the closing tasks and key outputs for project integration and procurement management.

Closing outputs related to integration management include final products, services, or result transition and updates to organizational process assets. Sample closing documents for the Just-In-Time Training project include a final project report, lessons-learned report, and customer acceptance/project completion form. It is also good practice to hold a close-out meeting and hold some type of celebration when a project ends.

Closing outputs related to procurement management include closed procurements and updates to organizational process assets. A sample written contract closure notice is provided for the Just-In-Time Training project.

Helpful advice for closing projects includes planning for closure, documenting lessons learned and other important information as soon as possible, and celebrating project closure.

QUICK QUIZ

1. Which knowledge areas include tasks related to closing?

   A. project scope, time, cost, and quality management

   B. project integration, scope, time, cost, and quality management

   C. project integration and procurement management

   D. all nine knowledge areas

2. Which of the following statements is false?

   A. Even though many projects are canceled before completion, it is still important to formally close any project.

   B. Closing includes verifying that all of the deliverables are complete.

   C. Closing often includes a final presentation and report.

   D. Closing does not include developing a transition plan.

3. Updating documentation and historical information produced by the project in a useful format is part of _____.

   A. updating organizational process assets

   B. archival

   C. closing procurements

   D. lessons learned

4. Answering questions such as, "What will you do differently on the next project based on your experience working on this project?" is part of a _____.

   A. lessons-learned report

   B. customer acceptance/project completion form

   C. written notice of contract closure

   D. transition plan

5. Contract closure involves completion and settlement of contracts and resolution of _____.

   A. payments

   B. any open items

   C. performance issues

   D. legal matters

6. The _____ should include requirements for formal acceptance and closure of contracts.

   A. project management plan

   B. procurement management plan

   C. contract itself

   D. contract management plan

7. A _____ is another name for a project close-out meeting

   A. celebration

   B. post project

   C. final review

   D. post mortem

8. _____ are reviews often performed during contract closure to identify lessons learned in the entire procurement process

   A. Procurement audits

   B. Post mortems

   C. Lessons learned

   D. Knowledge transfers

9. Which of the following was not a lesson learned from the Just-In-Time Training project?

   A. good communications was instrumental to project success

   B. supplier partnerships were not very effective

   C. good planning paid off in execution

   D. the project steering committee was very helpful

10. Which of the following is not advice for closing projects or phases?

    A. You don't need to celebrate completing a project, especially if it did not go well.

    B. You should capture lessons learned as soon as possible, not just at the end of a project

    C. You should include tasks in the WBS for project closing

    D. You should assign resources to specific project closing tasks

Quick Quiz Answers

1. C; 2. D; 3. A; 4. A; 5. B; 6. C; 7. D; 8. A; 9. B; 10. A

DISCUSSION QUESTIONS

1. What is involved in closing projects? Why should all projects be formally closed?

2. What are the main closing outputs created as part of integration management? Why is it important to create a final project report, presentation, and lessons-learned report?

3. What are the main topics included in a lessons-learned report?

4. What is a post-mortem?

5. What are the main closing outputs created as part of procurement management?

6. What advice about project closing is most useful to you? What other advice would you add?

EXERCISES

1. Find an example of a large project that took more than a year to complete, such as a major construction project. You can ask people at your college, university, or work about a recent project, such as a major fund raising campaign, information systems installation, or building project. You can also find information about projects online such as the Big Dig in Boston (*www.masspike.com/bigdig*), the Patronas Twin Towers in Malaysia, and many other building projects (*www.greatbuildings.com*). Describe some of the tasks performed to close the project. Write a one-page paper or prepare a short presentation summarizing your findings.

2. Using the lessons-learned template on the companion Web site or the one available from Microsoft as shown in Figure 8-6, write a lessons-learned report for a project you worked on. If you cannot think of one, interview someone who recently completed a project and write a lessons-learned report on that project.

3. Compare the lessons-learned template on the companion Web site and the one available from Microsoft as shown in Figure 8-6. Search for at least one other example of lessons-learned report or template. Summarize their similarities and differences in a one-page paper, citing your references.

4. Find an article or video that provides a good example of closing a project. See the What Went Right? passage for ideas, but find your own unique example. Document your findings in a one-page paper, citing your references.

TEAM PROJECTS

1. Your organization is about to complete a project to raise money for an important charity. Assume that there are 1,000 people in your organization. Also, assume that you had six months to raise as much money as possible, with a goal of $100,000. With just one week to go, you have raised $92,000. You did experience several problems with the project, which you described in Chapter 7. Using that information and information you prepared in other chapters related to this project, prepare a two- to three-page paper or 15-minute final presentation for the project. Be creative in your responses.

2. You are part of a team in charge of a project to help people in your company (500 people) lose weight. This project is part of a competition, and the top "losers" will be featured in a popular television show. Assume that you had six months to complete the project and a budget of $10,000. The project will end in one week, so you and your team are busy closing out the project. Prepare a lessons-learned report for the project, using information from your responses to this exercise in previous chapters as well as your creativity to determine what the final outcome was for the project.

3. Using the information you developed in Team Project 1 or 2, role-play the final project meeting, at which you present the final project presentation to key stakeholders. Determine who will play what role (project manager, team member from a certain department, senior managers, and so on). Be creative in displaying different personalities (a senior manager who questions the importance of the project to the organization, a team member who is very shy or obnoxious).

4. Perform the closing tasks for one of the case studies provided in Appendix C. If you are working on a real team project, create relevant closing documents, such as a final project report and lessons-learned report, using the templates and samples in this chapter as guides. Present your results to the class.

COMPANION WEB SITE

Visit the free companion Web site for this text at **www.intropm.com** to access template files, online quizzes, Jeopardy-like games, Microsoft Project files, links to sites mentioned in the text, and other information to help you learn more about this important field. Instructors must contact the author at schwalbe@augsburg.edu to gain access to the instructor site. Anyone can access the student site.

KEY TERMS

post-mortem — A term sometimes used for a project close-out meeting since it is held after the project has died or been put to rest.

procurement audits — Reviews often performed during contract closure to identify lessons learned in the entire procurement process.

records management system — A tool that provides the ability to easily organize, find, and archive documents.

END NOTES

[1]Vindu Goel, "How Google Decides to Pull the Plug," The New York Times (February 14, 2009).

[2]L. Franklin Devine, Michael Radutzky and Andy Court, "Obama's Inner Circle Shares Inside Story," CBSNews.com, (November 9, 2008).

[3]Dale Arseneault, "Best Practice Knowledge Transfer – Practical Ideas," Reflections on Knowledge Management and Organizational Innovation (January 15, 2008).

[4]Blaize Reich, "Lessons Not Learned," Projects @ Work, (October 9, 2008).

Chapter 9
Best Practices in Project Management

LEARNING OBJECTIVES

After reading this chapter, you will be able to:

- Define best practices in general and best practices in project management for organizations
- Summarize best practices in project management for individuals
- Explain how improving project management maturity can improve project and organizational performance
- Describe research on project management maturity
- Discuss best practices described in this text
- Read final advice about project management

OPENING CASE

After completing the Just-In-Time Training project, Kristin was asked to join a special task force to work with the company's Program Management Office (PMO). Their purpose was to create a repository of best practice information and make recommendations on specific best practices most useful for Global Construction. The PMO Director, Marie Scott, led the task force. Other members included representatives from each department in the company as well as three other members of the PMO. They were expected to complete their work within two months, and Kristin was asked to spend about ten hours per week on this task force. She had a good experience as project manager on the Just-In-Time Training project, but she knew that she had a lot to learn about improving her skills. She was excited to be a part of this team and looked forward to improving the company's project management capabilities.

INTRODUCTION

Many organizations understand the value of project management, yet they struggle to implement it well. There is great value to learning about best practices in project management on a case by case basis, but you can also learn a lot by looking at larger studies of best practices. This chapter defines project management best practices and provides information on best practices for organizations and individuals. It also describes how increasing an organization's project management maturity level can improve project and organizational performance.

What Went Right?

It may seem surprising to know that many famous corporations still do not follow very basic project management processes or have just recently adopted them. Below are a few examples of how organizations have benefited from following best practices in project management:

- One of the world's largest rental-car companies, Hertz, just established project management offices in 2007 and developed standard processes for their organization. For example, in order to optimize bus service for customers at Heathrow Airport in London, bus drivers defined project goals and outcomes, analyzed information, established simple milestones, and performed measurements of the scope, time, cost, and customer satisfaction goals of the project. This simple process helped Hertz to greatly improve bus services. "Project management is changing the face of Hertz. It's the toolbox the company has never had before, and it's changing who we are."[1]

- The board of Siemens recently launched a worldwide initiative to improve its project management. The German electronics group had worked out that half its turnover came from project-like work, and it calculated that if it could complete all of these projects on time and to budget, it would add EURO3 billion ($3.7 billion U.S. dollars) to its bottom line over three years. A key element of the scheme was the introduction of project managers to the company's sales teams to try and temper their more extravagant promises, a move that requires a careful balance between reining them in and killing the deal. [2]

- Some companies have changed their whole business philosophy to become more project-oriented. Project management has become an important competitive tool or core competence. For example, "Nike now manages footwear projects instead of just making and selling shoes. Coca-Cola has people called "orchestrators" who manage a collection of projects since most of the company's bottling and marketing of its drinks is outsourced to others. Germany's BMW treats each new car platform as a separate project. BP's converted its exploration division, BPX, into a portfolio of projects, and profits soared after project managers were given more autonomy and had to build their own self-sufficient teams."[3]

DEFINING PROJECT MANAGEMENT BEST PRACTICES

In order to benefit from best practices in project management, it is important to first define what best practices are. Below are two general definitions of best practices:

- Webster's Dictionary (2007) defines a best practice as "a practice which is most appropriate under the circumstances, especially as considered acceptable or regulated in business; a technique or methodology that, through experience and research, has reliably led to a desired or optimum result"
- Wikipedia (2009) defines a best practice as "the most efficient (least amount of effort) and effective (best results) way of accomplishing a task, based on repeatable procedures that have proven themselves over time for large numbers of people…. The idea is that with proper processes, checks, and testing, a desired outcome can be delivered with fewer problems and unforeseen complications."

For example, if you are reading this text as part of a course, you should know about best practices for studying and getting good grades in college. There are general best practices that most people might agree on, such as showing up for and paying attention in class, doing homework on time, setting aside time to study and get a good night's rest before exams, and so on. For individual students, however, there might be other best practices that are more effective. Perhaps you need to be part of study group to do well on homework assignments and exams. Perhaps you need to study alone in a very quiet location. Perhaps a particular course requires a lot of online participation to get a good grade. Some general best practices might apply, but there are also some that are unique to each person or course.

The following sections describe PMI's view of best practices in project management as well as information from a popular business text on the subject.

The Project Management Institute's Definition of Best Practices

The Project Management Institute (PMI) Standards Development Program published the first version of the Organizational Project Management Maturity Model (OPM3) in December 2003 to address the need to bridge the gap between organizational strategy and successful projects. (Maturity models are described in more detail later in this chapter.) OPM3® is a standard developed to provide a way for organizations to measure their organizational project management maturity against a comprehensive set of best practices. The second edition of this document was published in 2008.

OPM3®, Second Edition defines **best practices** as "optimal methods, currently recognized within a given industry or discipline, to achieve a goal or objective."[4] It lists hundreds of best practices, which PMI says are achieved through developing and consistently demonstrating their supporting capabilities, as observed through measurable outcomes. **Capabilities** are incremental steps leading up to one or more best practices, and **outcomes** are the tangible or intangible results of applying capabilities. A **key performance indicator (KPI)** is a criterion used to determine the degree to which an outcome is achieved.

The first edition of OPM3® provides the following example to illustrate a best practice, capability, outcome, and key performance indicator:

- *Best practice:* Establish internal project management communities

- *Capability (one of four for this best practice):* Facilitate project management activities

- *Outcome:* Local initiatives, meaning the organization develops pockets of consensus around areas of special interest

- *Key performance indicator:* Community addresses local issues

Best practices are organized into three levels: project, program, and portfolio. Within each of those categories, best practices are categorized by four stages of process improvement: standardize, measure, control, and improve. For example, the list that follows contains several best practices listed in OPM3:

- Project best practices:

    o *Project initiation process standardization*—Project initiation process standards are established.

    o *Project plan development process measurement*—Project plan development process measures are established, assembled, and analyzed.

    o *Project scope planning process control*—Project scope planning process controls are established and executed to control the stability of the process.

    o *Project scope definition process improvement*—Project scope definition process problem areas are assessed, process improvement recommendations are collected, and process improvements are implemented.

- Program best practices:

    o *Program activity definition process standardization*—Program activity definition process standards are established.

    o *Program activity sequencing process measurement*—Program activity sequencing process measures are established, assembled, and analyzed.

    o *Program activity duration estimating process control*—Program activity duration estimating process controls are established and executed to control the stability of the process.

- o *Program schedule development process improvement*—Program schedule development process problem areas are assessed, process improvement recommendations are collected, and process improvements are implemented.

- Portfolio best practices:

  - o *Portfolio resource planning process standardization*—Portfolio resource planning process standards are established.

  - o *Portfolio cost estimating process measurement*—Portfolio cost estimating process measures are established, assembled, and analyzed.

  - o *Portfolio cost budgeting process control*—Portfolio cost budgeting process controls are established and executed to control the stability of the process.

  - o *Portfolio risk management planning process improvement*—Portfolio risk management planning process problem areas are assessed, process improvement recommendations are collected, and process improvements are implemented.

For more information, consult PMI's OPM3® standards, first and second edition.

Media Snapshot

After reviewing many nominations in 2007, the Project Management Institute published a list of twenty-four organizations from around the world that are considered to be outstanding in project management. These organizations apply project management best practices that are fully supported by the entire organizations and have a significant impact on the bottom line. Project management is a core component of their business. Below is an alphabetical list of these organizations and their countries:

- AgênciaClick (Brazil)
- Airports Company South Africa (South Africa)
- Beijing Organizing Committee for the Olympic Games (China)
- Central Federal Lands Highway Division (United States)
- Commonwealth Scientific and Industrial Research Organisation (Australia)
- Fluor Corp. (United States)
- IBM (United States)
- Indra Sistemas S.A. (Spain)
- Infosys Technologies (India)
- Intel Corp. (United States)
- MD Anderson Cancer Center (United States)
- Memphis Managed Care Corp. (United States)
- Missouri State Government (United States)
- Mutual of Omaha (United States)
- National Aeronautics and Space Administration (United States)
- Petrobras (Brazil)
- Saudi Aramco (Saudi Arabia)
- Serasa (Brazil)
- Shell (Netherlands)
- Stork NV (Netherlands)
- Suncorp (Australia)
- TV Guide Interactive (United States)
- Wipro Technologies (India)Workplace Technology Services (Canada)[5]

Ultimate Business Library Best Practices

In 2003, the Ultimate Business Library published a book called *Best Practice: Ideas and Insights from the World's Foremost Business Thinkers*. This book includes articles by well-known business leaders such as Warren Bennis (author of over 30 books on leadership, including *On Becoming a Leader*), Daniel Goleman (author of *Emotional Intelligence* and other popular books), and Thomas Stewart (editor of the *Harvard Business Review* and author of *Intellectual Capital: The New Wealth of Organizations*).

In the book's introduction, Rosabeth Moss Kanter, a professor at Harvard Business School and a well-known author and consultant, says that visionary leaders know "the best practice secret: Stretching to learn from the best of the best in any sector can make a big vision more likely to succeed."[6] Kanter also emphasizes the need to have measurable standards for best practices. Organizations can measure performance against their own past; against peers; and, even better, against potential. Kanter suggests that organizations need to continue to reach for higher standards. She suggests the following exercise regimen for business leaders who want to intelligently adapt best practices to help their own organizations:

- Reach high. Stretch. Raise standards and aspirations. Find the best of the best and then use it as inspiration for reaching full potential.

- Help everyone in your organization become a professional. Empower people to manage themselves through benchmarks and standards based on best practice exchange.

- Look everywhere. Go far afield. Think of the whole world as your laboratory for learning.[7]

In addition, Robert Butrick, author of *The Project Workout,* wrote an article on best practices in project management for the Ultimate Business Library book. He suggests that organizations need to follow these basic principles of project management:

- Make sure your projects are driven by your strategy. Be able to demonstrate how each project you undertake fits your business strategy, and screen out unwanted projects as soon as possible.

- Use a staged approach. You can rarely plan a project in its entirety. Use progressive steps or stages to project planning, and use the same generic stages for all types of projects. Have gate reviews before starting each stage to revalidate a project and before committing more resources and funding for the project. Place high emphasis on the early stages of a project to reduce risks and decrease time to market.

- Engage your stakeholders. Ignoring stakeholders often leads to project failure. Be sure to engage stakeholders at all stages of a project, and encourage teamwork and commitment at all times.

- Ensure success by planning for it. To help projects succeed, the balance of power often needs to be tipped toward the project and away from line management.

- Monitor against the plan. Everyone working on projects must have guidance, training, and support in creating plans and making project-related decisions. Organizations must develop and follow control techniques for managing risks, issues, scope changes, schedule, costs, and project reviews. Monitoring and forecasting against a plan ensure that everyone is on the same page and prevent unwanted surprises.

358

- Manage the project control cycle. Monitoring should focus more on the future than on the past. Project managers must continuously check that the project plan is still fit for the purpose of the project and likely to deliver the business benefits on time. Project changes must be managed to ensure that only those enabling project benefits to be realized are accepted. Avoid the dangers of scope creep, and let stakeholders know that project benefits drive the scope.

- Formally close the project: Every project should be closed to make sure that all work ceases, that lessons are learned, and that remaining resources are released for other purposes.[8]

BEST PRACTICES OF INDIVIDUAL PROJECT MANAGERS

Andy Crowe, founder and CEO of Velociteach, wrote a book in 2006 called *Alpha Project Managers: What the Top 2% Know That Everyone Else Does Not*. As the title suggests, an alpha project manager is defined as one who falls in the top two percent of project managers in terms of performance. Project managers were rated by their customers, senior managers, and team members based on their performance in the following areas:

- Setting expectations

- Communicating efficiently and effectively

- Managing issues

- Identifying and managing risks

- Leading the project team

- Meeting the scope, quality, time, and budget baselines for the project

- Managing the procurement process

- Managing changes to the project

- Balancing competing stakeholder needs

- Delivering a product, service, or result that met expectations

For this study, Crowe surveyed 860 project managers who had all been clients/students at Velociteach. Although this was not a scientific study, the aggregate results provide interesting information that can help define best practices for project managers. The 860 project managers, their senior managers, customers, and project team members all answered numerous survey questions. The general format of the questions was as follows: Mark the degree with which you agree with the following statement: Strongly disagree (0%), Somewhat disagree (20%), Neutral (50%), Somewhat agree

(75%), Strongly agree (100%). For some questions, the scale was based on the degree of importance, with 100% being the most important.

The 18 people identified as alpha project managers varied most from the other project managers in the following ways:

- *They enjoy their work more than their counterparts.* When asked to mark the degree to which they agreed with the statement: "On the whole, I generally love my job," the alpha average response was 67% while the non-alpha average was only 32%. They also view their jobs more as a career and took 19% more job-related training than the non-alphas (45.1 hours vs. 38.0 hours in the past three years).

- *They believe they have more authority than their counterparts.* When asked to mark the degree to which they agreed with the statement: "I have adequate authority to manage the projects for which I am responsible," the alpha average response was 89% while the non-alpha average was only 47%. It is interesting to note that from senior management's point of view, the alphas and non-alphas had about the same level of organizational authority at about 87%.

- *They believe they can have a personal impact on project success.* When asked to mark the degree to which they agreed with the statement: "What is the importance of your role on your current project," the alpha average response was 96% while the non-alpha average was only 70%. It is interesting to note that the senior managers' response to this question was very close to the project managers for both groups.

- *They are more efficient and effective communicators.* When project managers' customers, senior managers, and team members were asked, "How would you rank this project manager's overall responsiveness to your project-related requests?" (from very ineffective to very effective) the alphas' stakeholders' average response was 88% while the non-alpha average was only 49%. It is also interesting to note that alpha project managers send *fewer* e-mails per day and spend *less* time in meetings than the non-alphas. They know how to prioritize work and focus on what is most important. When the alphas were probed in interviews to understand more about their communication best practices, key traits emerged:

    - *They talk to stakeholders very early in the project and tailor communication to meet their needs.*

    - *They create a communication schedule and stick to it.*

    - *They communicate their messages quickly in a clear and concise manner.*

    - *They create an open communication channel and talk with stakeholders regularly about the topic of communication itself.*

- o *They know that on many projects, communication is the only deliverable stakeholders will receive until the product or service is completed.*

- *They allocate about twice as much time toward project planning.* Alpha project managers spend more time in every process group than their counterparts except for execution, as follows:

  - o *Initiating:* 2% vs. 1%

  - o *Planning:* 21% vs. 11%

  - o *Executing:* 69% vs. 82%

  - o *Controlling:* 5% vs. 4%

  - o *Closing:* 3% vs. 2%

- *They think it is important for the project manager to be a hands-on manager and a domain expert.* When asked to "Rank the importance of the project manager being a domain expert as a contributor to overall project success," the average alpha response was 94% vs. 68% for the non-alphas.

- *They can get consensus and handle conflicts.* When senior managers and customers were asked "How would you rate this project manager's ability to identify, understand, and satisfy your individual goals for the project," the average alpha response was 92% vs. 64%. When asked a similar question about conflict resolution, the alpha average was 61% vs. 46%.

- *They are managing more strategic projects and understand strategic goals.* When asked "Is your primary project considered highly strategic to your organization," the average alpha response was 60% vs. 41%. When asked, "Can you state your organization's top (three) strategic goals," the average alpha response was 60% vs. 23%.

The results of this study can be interpreted in several ways, especially if you analyze the interview responses, as Crowe does in his book. Some of the areas where alpha project managers are different from non-alpha project managers are based on their attitudes and beliefs, such as enjoying their work, believing they have authority, and believing they can have a personal impact on a project. Most of the other areas, however, are based on best practices which *can be learned*, such as being a good communicator, spending more time on project planning, being a hands-on project manager and a domain expert, being able to get consensus and handle conflict, and understanding and supporting strategic goals.[9]

What Went Wrong?

Many people are "thrown" into the role of project manager. For example, Nick Carson (his name is disguised) was an outstanding technical specialist on a large biotech project. He was working on a crucial project for his small company when the project manager quit. Senior management asked Nick to take over. Nick had never led a project, and he made the mistake of trying to still do his old job while also managing the project.

Nick worked lots of overtime and did actually complete the project, but his senior managers were not happy. Nick never gave them a detailed schedule or understandable status reports. Whenever he talked to them, they could not understand all of the technical detail he focused on. Nick thought he did a great job, so he was amazed when he was offered a severance package to leave the company. He decided he never wanted to manage a project again.

This true story illustrates the fact that many organizations do not do a good job of selecting, training, or mentoring their project managers.

PROJECT MANAGEMENT MATURITY

In addition to following best practices, organizations can improve project management performance by using **maturity models**, which are frameworks for helping organizations improve their processes and systems. Maturity models describe an evolutionary path of increasingly organized and systematically more mature processes. Many maturity models have four to six levels, with the first level describing characteristics of the least organized or least mature organizations, and the highest level describing the characteristics of the most organized and mature organizations.

Capability Maturity Model Integration

A popular maturity model is in continuous development at the Software Engineering Institute at Carnegie Mellon University. The Software Engineering Institute (SEI) is a federally funded research and development center established in 1984 by the U.S. Department of Defense with a broad mandate to address the transition of software engineering technology. The **Capability Maturity Model Integration** (CMMI) is "a process improvement approach that provides organizations with the essential elements of effective processes. It can be used to guide process improvement across a project, a division, or an entire organization. CMMI helps integrate traditionally separate organizational functions, set process improvement goals and priorities, provide guidance for quality processes, and provide a point of reference for appraising current processes."[10] Many companies that want to work in the government market have realized that they will not get many opportunities even to bid on projects unless they have a CMMI Level 3.

The capability levels of the CMMI, numbered zero through five, are:

0. *Incomplete*: At this level, a process is either not performed or partially performed. No generic goals exist for this level, and one or more of the specific goals of the process area are not satisfied.

1. *Performed*: A performed process satisfies the specific goals of the process area and supports and enables the work needed to produce work products. Although this capability level can result in improvements, those improvements can be lost over time if they are not institutionalized.

2. *Managed*: At this level, a process has the basic infrastructure in place to support it. The process is planned and executed based on policies and employs skilled people who have adequate resources to produce controlled outputs. The process discipline reflected by this level ensures that existing practices are retained during times of stress.

3. *Defined*: At this maturity level, a process is rigorously defined and the standards, process descriptions, and procedures for a project are tailored from the organization's set of standard processes to suit that particular project.

4. *Quantitatively Managed*: At this level, a process is controlled using statistical and other quantitative techniques. The organization establishes quantitative objectives for quality and process performance that are used as criteria in managing the process.

5. *Optimizing*: An optimizing process is improved based on an understanding of the common causes of variation inherent in the process. The focus is on continually improving the range of process performance through incremental and innovative improvements.[11]

Project Management Maturity Models

In the late 1990s, several organizations began developing project management maturity models based on the Capability Maturity Model (CMM), an earlier version of CMMI. Just as organizations realized the need to improve their software development processes and systems, they also realized the need to enhance their project management processes and systems for all types of projects. A few of these maturity models include:

- PMI's OPM3, as mentioned earlier, which includes four process improvement stages or levels:

    1. Standardize
    2. Measure
    3. Control
    4. Continuously improve

- The International Institute for Learning, Inc. uses Kerzner's model, with five levels of project management maturity:

An Introduction to Project Management, Third Edition

1. Common language

2. Common processes

3. Singular methodology

4. Benchmarking

5. Continuous improvement

- ESI International's ProjectFRAMEWORK™ is a five-level model:

  1. Ad-hoc

  2. Consistent

  3. Integrated

  4. Comprehensive

  5. Optimizing

- Berkeley's Project Management Process Maturity (PM) model includes these five levels:

  1. Ad-hoc: No project management processes or practices are consistently available, and data is not consistently collected or analyzed

  2. Planned: Project management processes, problem areas, and data are informally defined, identified, collected

  3. Managed: Formal project planning and control systems and data are managed

  4. Integrated: Program management is used, and project management data and processes are integrated and quantitatively analyzed, measured, and stored

  5. Sustained: Project management processes are continuously improved and are fully understood, and data is optimized and sustained

Figure 9-1 provides an illustration of the Berkeley model. Each project management maturity model shows a progression from the least mature to most mature level, although the number and title of levels vary somewhat.

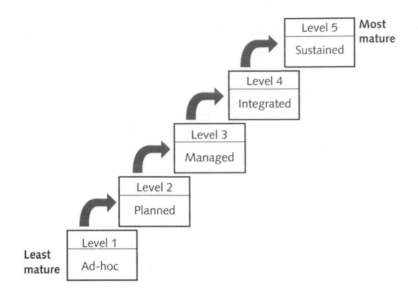

Figure 9-1. Berkeley project management process maturity model

Research on Project Management Maturity

Regardless of the project management maturity model followed, the goal is clear: organizations want to improve their ability to manage projects. Many organizations are assessing where they stand in terms of project management maturity, just as they did for software development maturity with the CMMI maturity model. Organizations are recognizing that they must make a commitment to the discipline of project management to improve project quality and organizational performance.

Ibbs' The Value of Project Management Research

Several studies have proven the value of improving project management maturity to organizations. William Ibbs, a Professor at the University of California at Berkeley, led a PMI-sponsored research study published in 2002 called "The Value of Project Management." After assessing project management maturity using Berkeley's model and reviewing data from 52 companies in the U.S., the researchers made the following conclusions:

- *Companies with more mature project management practices have better project performance.* They deliver projects on time and on budget more often. Less mature companies often miss their schedule targets by 40 percent and their cost targets by 20 percent.

- *Project management maturity is strongly correlated with more predictable project schedule and cost performance.* More mature companies have a schedule performance index (SPI) variation of 0.08 and a cost performance index (CPI) variation of 0.11. Less mature companies have indexes of 0.16

for SPI and CPI. For a $10 million project, this translates into a $1.6 million cost variation.

- *High project management maturity results in lower direct costs of project management.* Companies with a high maturity level spend 6–7 percent of total project costs on project management. Companies with low maturity spent about 11 percent.[12]

Thomas and Mullaly Research on Project Management Value

PMI sponsored a more recent study entitled "Researching the Value of Project Management," which was published in 2008. This 400+-page report summarizes research on 65 organizations. In general, most of the organizations did see value in project management. The researchers stated that they were "extremely comfortable stating unequivocally that project management delivers value to organizations."[13]

It is interesting to note that in this study, unlike the earlier one led by Ibbs, the researchers found that most organizations did not try to quantify the value of project management. They said that measuring ROI "proved extremely elusive." [14] In this study, value focused on measuring project management and satisfaction, alignment, process outcomes, and business outcomes. The authors of this study also found that project management value appears to increase in proportion to the maturity level of the organization. Organizations with a higher level of maturity reported greater levels of intangible value.

This study, as well as the Ibbs' study and many others sponsored by PMI are available for free for PMI members at *www.pmi.org*. You can also keep up-to-date on new developments on the topic of project management value by visiting the Web site *www.valueofpm.com*.

Interthink Consulting's Organizational Project Management Study

Interthink Consulting Incorporated developed the Organizational Project Management (OPM) Baseline Study, which provides a comprehensive overview of project management practices in organizations and industries worldwide, with over 600 participants. Based on the 2004 study, there were definite relationships between maturity and project delivery. The study provides detailed results in several areas, such as maturity level, meeting budgets, schedules, customer satisfaction, and project goal attainment.

Figure 9-2 provides a graph from Interthink's 2004 OPM Baseline Study that compares project management process maturity with project goal attainment. Note that maturity is broken down into several categories, such as program initiation, project initiation, and project tracking.

366

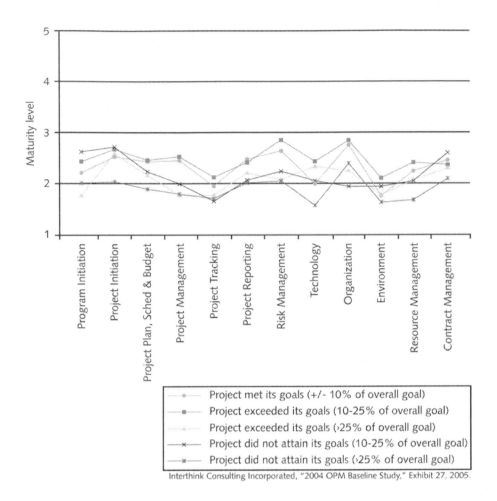

Figure 9-2. Process maturity and project goal attainment

"For projects that met their goals or exceeded them by a factor of 10% to 25% there is a slight but clear increase in overall maturity through the majority of the process capability areas. For the organizational capability areas, the increase in maturity is most clear in the areas of Risk Management and Organization. For projects that failed to exceed their goals, the indicated maturity in the majority of the process capability areas are relatively lower."[15]

PriceWaterhouse Coopers' Study on Boosting Business Performance

As mentioned in Chapter 1, PriceWaterhouse Coopers surveyed 200 companies from 30 different countries about their project management maturity and found that *over half of all projects fail*. They also found that only 2.5% of corporations consistently meet their targets for scope, time, and cost goals for all types of projects. The survey's main objective, however, was to investigate whether a higher maturity level would provide a higher project performance level. The following conclusions were made by the survey authors:

An Introduction to Project Management, Third Edition

- *A higher maturity level for an organization enhances overall project performance, not in just one project, but in the overall portfolio of projects.*

- *Most organizations are not satisfied with their current maturity level.* The total average for survey participants was 2.5 on a 5.0 scale, meaning the organizations use informal processes that are not yet institutionalized. This low maturity level contributes to the high project failure rate.

- *Project failures are often a consequence of organizational aspects over which project managers have little influence.* The top reasons cited for project failure included bad estimates, missed deadlines, scope changes, change in environment, insufficient resources, and change in strategy. Poor quality of deliverables and not adequately defining stakeholders were the least prevalent reasons for project failure.

- *Organizational structure has a big impact on overall project performance.* The higher the alignment between structure and business requirements, the higher the overall project performance. The optimal structure should be based on industry, location, and business objectives. The highest performing companies in terms of project results had a project-oriented or strong matrix structure, giving project managers the most authority and control over resources.

- *Staff development and professional certification enhance overall project performance.* However, more than 60% of the companies surveyed do not regularly offer a development program to their project managers. Investments in project management certification do pay off, and the organizational benefits exceed the costs.

- *A systematic approach to change management is fundamental for superior project performance.* The majority of the best performing and most mature organizations always or frequently apply change management to their projects.

- *Staffing projects with a majority of internal resources as opposed to external resources is a better guarantee of success.* External resources add value when employed in moderation. The highest performance was achieved by using 25% external resources and 75% internal resources.

- *The extent to which project management software is used is correlated to maturity levels.* The lower the maturity level, the more difficulties the organization will have in implementing software. Processes must be established for the software to provide benefits.[16]

Best Practice

As mentioned in the report by PriceWaterhouse Coopers described earlier, staff development and professional certification enhance overall project performance. A company well-known for developing its project managers is IBM.

After launching an initiative in 1996 to better meet customer needs and ensure a consistent approach to project management, nearly 10,000 IBM employees earned the PMP credential. The company developed the IBM Project Management Center of Excellence to advocate five fundamental steps for every project:

1. Define the scope
2. Ensure top-level sponsorship
3. Establish a vision
4. Manage as a program
5. Communicate successes and lessons learned throughout the organization

The company created a worldwide project management method designed to be the single, common method for IBM projects and program worldwide. They provide a collection of processes, templates, and tools for all types of project. IBM also provides a nurturing project management community to help employees find mentors, network, develop relationships, and share knowledge. "Through such initiatives, IBM project managers have the ability to take the same training and pursue certification. They use the same terminology, tools and methodology, customized for their own business unit needs," according to Deborah Dell, PMP, operations and support manager at the Project Management Center of Excellence.[17]

SUMMARY OF BEST PRACTICES MENTIONED IN THIS TEXT

As you can see, understanding and applying best practices can help improve the management of projects, programs, portfolios, and entire companies. Several best practices were described throughout this text. Following is a brief summary of some of them:

- Determine how project, program, and portfolio management will work best in your own organization.

- Involve key stakeholders—including shareholders, customers, and employees—in making major decisions.

- Develop and follow a formal project selection process to ensure projects support business needs.

- Lay the groundwork for projects before they officially start.

- Separate projects by phases, such as a study phase project, when it makes sense to do so.

- Designate a project champion to provide high-level support and participate in key meetings.

- Assign a project manager from operations to lead projects that affect operations.

- Form a steering committee with key managers from various departments for projects that will cause major organizational change.

- Provide mentoring and training for project managers and other stakeholders.

- Document action items at meetings, and set the next meeting time.

- Document meeting with minutes, focusing on key decisions and action items, and send them out quickly.

- Use more than one approach for creating cost estimates.

- Use formal supplier evaluation procedures to help select sellers.

- Include a detailed statement of work and schedule in contracts.

- Develop and follow a formal change-control process.

- Work with suppliers to ensure that deliverables are produced properly.

- Follow a deliverable acceptance process to verify project scope.

- Be clear and honest in communicating project status information, and share the responsibility for project communications with the entire project team.

- Formally close projects and share lessons learned.

FINAL ADVICE ON PROJECT MANAGEMENT

Now that you have read this text and discussed project management with others, I hope that you have matured to see project management as a valuable skill for you as an individual and for all types of organizations. The number of projects and their complexity will continue to increase, so it is important to understand, apply, and improve the state of project management.

The knowledge and experience I have gained working on and managing projects continues to help me in my career and my personal life. I was fortunate to step into a project management role very early in my career as a U.S. Air Force officer. My first real job at the age of 22 was as a project manager, and we followed a very disciplined approach to project, program, and portfolio management. I have held several job titles at different organizations since then—systems analyst, senior engineer, technical specialist, information technology management consultant, independent consultant, college professor, and now author. All of these jobs included working on or managing projects.

An Introduction to Project Management, Third Edition

As a wife and mother of three, I can also attest to the fact that project management skills help in planning and executing personal activities (weddings, birthday parties, vacations, moves, fundraisers, and so on) and in dealing with the joys and challenges of everyday life. When people ask me how I can do so much and still seem so relaxed, I have to say that using good project management definitely helps.

This book would not be complete without one final cartoon, as shown in Figure 9-3. In project management and life in general, it helps to keep a sense of humor.

Figure 9-3. What really matters! (www.xkcd.com)

CASE WRAP-UP

Kristin Maur learned a lot about her company and best practices in project, program, and portfolio management working on the best practices task force. She loved being paid to read books and articles on the subject, and the whole team worked well together. They developed a new section on the corporate Intranet with project management best practice information. As more workers and customers were using smart phones, they also developed a free application people could download to their phones to access key information.

Marie Scott encouraged Kristin to share some of the task force's findings as well as lessons learned on the Just-In-Time Training project in an article and presentation at a large, international conference. Marie even offered to pay for Kristin's trip to the conference out of the PMO's budget. Kristin was honored and excited for this new challenge since she had never done anything like it before.

CHAPTER SUMMARY

Many organizations study and apply best practices to improve their ability to manage projects, programs, and portfolios. PMI developed the Organizational Project Management Maturity Model (OPM3) to help organizations assess and improve their organizational project management maturity. OPM3® lists hundreds of best practices organized by project, program, and portfolio management. The Ultimate Business Library published *Best Practices,* which provides advice on best practices to follow for managing projects and organizations in general.

Individual project managers can also use best practices to improve their performance. Andy Crowe did a study to help understand best practices of alpha project managers, or the top 2%. A few findings include the fact that alpha project managers spend much more time on planning and enjoy their jobs more than other project managers.

A maturity model is a framework for helping organizations improve their processes and systems. Several organizations are using project management maturity models to help improve their project management processes and systems. Several studies, including those by Ibbs, Thomas and Mullaly, Interthink Consulting, and PriceWaterhouse Coopers, show the benefits of improving project management maturity.

This text also describes several best practices in managing projects, programs, and portfolios. A summary list is provided in this chapter.

Project management is a valuable skill for individuals and organizations. As the number of projects and their complexity continue to increase, it is important to understand, apply, and improve the discipline of project management.

QUICK QUIZ

1.	_____ are optimal methods, currently recognized within a given industry or discipline, to achieve a goal or objective

	A. Benchmarks

	B. Key performance indicators

	C. Capabilities

	D. Best practices

2.	The Project Management Institute initially published the _____ in December 2003 to address the need to bridge the gap between organizational strategy and successful projects.

	A. Organizational Project Management Maturity Model (OPM3)

	B. Best Practices Report

	C. Alpha Project Managers Guide

	D. Project Management Process Maturity $(PM)^2$ model

3.	The Project Management Institute defines best practices in each of the following areas except _____.

	A. projects

	B. programs

	C. project personnel

	D. portfolios

4.	Organizations can measure performance against their own past; against peers; and, even better, against _____.

	A. profits

	B. potential

	C. revenues

	D. the future

5.   Alpha project managers represent the top _____ .of project managers based on performance.

   A. 1%

   B. 2%

   C. 5%

   D. 10%

6.   Which of the following is a trait of alpha project managers?

   A. They spend more time on execution than other project managers.

   B. They spend more time in meetings than other project managers.

   C. They send fewer emails than other project managers.

   D. They make more money than other project managers.

7.   Which of the following is true regarding studies on the value of project management and project management maturity?

   A. The PMI-sponsored study by Ibbs (2002) found that companies with a high maturity level spend less money on project management than companies with a low maturity.

   B. The PMI-sponsored study by Thomas and Mullaly (2008) found that companies focus even more on measuring the ROI or tangible benefits of project management.

   C. Interthink Consulting found that there was no statistically significant difference between process maturity level and project goal attainment.

   D. The PriceWaterhouse Coopers study found that the higher the maturity level, the more difficulties the organization will have in implementing software.

8.   What was the average maturity level (with a high of 5) reported by survey participants in the study by PriceWaterhouse Coopers?

   A. 1.5

   B. 2.5

   C. 3.5

   D. 4.5

9.   Which of the following is not a best practice listed in this text?

   A. Determine how project, program, and portfolio management will work best in your own organization.

   B. Involve key stakeholders—including shareholders, customers, and employees—in making major decisions.

   C. Develop and follow a formal project selection process to ensure projects support business needs.

   D. Don't spend time or money on projects before they officially start.

10.   What is the main message of the final cartoon in this chapter in the section on final advice on project management?

   A. No matter how challenging your projects may be, never lose your sense of humor.

   B. Don't invest too much in the stock market.

   C. Always back up your hard drive.

   D. Marry for love, not money.

Quick Quiz Answers

1. D; 2. A; 3. C; 4. B; 5. B; 6. C; 7. A; 8. B; 9. D; 10. A

DISCUSSION QUESTIONS

1.   What is a best practice in general? Give examples of best practices in an area unrelated to project management, such as nutrition, exercise, or child rearing.

2.   Why should organizations identify and use best practices? What are the main categories of best practices developed as part of OPM3?

3.   What are some of the things that alpha project managers do differently from other project managers?

4.   What is a project management maturity model? What is CMMI? What benefits have studies shown from increasing project management maturity levels in organizations?

5.   Do you believe that developing and applying project management skills can help most individuals and organizations? Justify your response.

EXERCISES

1.   Review the project management best practices presented in this chapter or describe several used in an organization you are familiar with. Select any two of them and write a one- to two-page paper describing how each practice could help improve project management. Develop examples of how they could be applied to real project situations.

2.   Read information from one of the studies references in this chapter on project management maturity models or best practices. Summarize your findings in a one- to two-page paper.

3.   Skim PMI's latest version of OPM3. Summarize key information in this document and your opinion of it in a one-to-two-page paper.

4.   Interview an experienced project manager about best practices he or she has used on an individual and organizational level. Document your findings in a one-to two-page paper.

TEAM PROJECTS

1.   Read one of the reports or books listed in the Endnotes. Summarize key information in this document and your opinions of it in a two-to-three-page paper. Also prepare a short (10-15 minute presentation) on the topic.

2.   Research two or three different project management maturity models in more detail, such as those described in this chapter. Several include a sample or free assessment you can take to determine your organization's maturity level. Summarize the results as well as other information about the maturity models in a two- to three-page paper and a short presentation.

3.   Based on your team's experiences on your class project and your work experiences, write a detailed paper describing best practices for project management. Summarize the results as well as other information about the maturity models in a two- to three-page paper and a short presentation. Be sure to include specific examples that fit the best practices you include.

COMPANION WEB SITE

Visit the free companion Web site for this text at **www.intropm.com** to access template files, online quizzes, Jeopardy-like games, Microsoft Project files, links to sites mentioned in the text, and other information to help you learn more about this important field. Instructors must contact the author at schwalbe@augsburg.edu to gain access to the instructor site. Anyone can access the student site.

KEY TERMS

best practices — Optimal methods, currently recognized within a given industry or discipline, to achieve a goal or objective.

capabilities — The incremental steps leading up to one or more best practices.

key performance indicator (KPI) — A criterion used to determine the degree to which an outcome is achieved.

maturity model — A framework for helping organizations improve their processes and systems.

outcomes — The tangible or intangible results of applying capabilities.

END NOTES

[1]Boyd. L. (2008, June) Switching Gears, PM Network (June, 2008).

[2]Mary Evans, "Overdue and Over Budget, Over and Over Again," Economist.com (just 9, 2005).

[3]Ibid.

[4]Project Management Institute, Inc., Organizational Project Management Maturity Model (OPM3) Knowledge Foundation, Second Edition (2008), p 39.

[5]Sarah Fister Gale, "Outstanding Organizations 2007," PM Network (October 2007).

[6]Ultimate Business Library, *Best Practice: Ideas and Insights from the World's Foremost Business Thinkers.* Cambridge, MA: Perseus Publishing (2003), p. 1.

[7]Ibid., p. 8.

[8]Ibid.

[9]Andy Crowe. Alpha Project Managers: What the Top 2% Know That Everyone Else Does Not, Velociteach press, Atlanta, GA (2006).

[10]Software Engineering Institute, "What is CMMI," Carnegie Mellon (*http://www.sei.cmu.edu/cmmi/general/general.html*) (January 2007).

[11]CMMI Product Team, "CMMI® for Development, Version 1.2," CMU/SEI-2006-TR-008ESC-TR-2006-008 (August 2006).

[12]William Ibbs, and Justin Reginato, "Quantifying the Value of Project Management," Project Management Institute (2002).

[13]Janice Thomas and Mark Mullaly, "Researching the Value of Project Management," PMI, (2008), p. 349.

[14]Ibid., p. 246.

[15]Mark E. Mullaly, "2004 Organizational Project Management Baseline Study Results Overview," (*http://www.interthink.ca*) (2005).

[16]PriceWaterhouseCoopers, "Boosting Business Performance through Programme and Project Management," (June 2004).

[17]Sarah Fister Gale, "Outstanding Organizations 2007," PM Network (October 2007), p. 12.

APPENDIX A:

Project Management Software:

Brief Guide to Microsoft Project 2010

Note: This guide was written using the Beta release of Project 2010 and Windows XP. Your screens may appear slightly different. You can download a free trial of Project 2010 from www.microsoft.com/project. You can access the older version of this guide based on Project 2007 on the companion Web site at www.intropm.com. Students who purchased an older version of this text (*An Introduction to Project Management, Third Edition*, by Kathy Schwalbe) can purchase just this new Appendix from www.intropm.com. Instructors can access the latest guide based on Project 2010 on the instructor site.

INTRODUCTION

There are hundreds of project management software products on the market today. Unfortunately, many people who own the software have no idea how to use it. It is important to understand basic concepts of project management, such as creating a work breakdown structure, determining task dependencies, and so on before making effective use of this software. Many project teams still use spreadsheets or other familiar software to help manage projects. However, if you can master a good project management software tool, it can really help in managing projects. This appendix summarizes basic information on project management software in general. It also provides a brief guide to using Microsoft Office Project 2010 (often referred to as Project 2010), the latest version of the most widely used product. Appendix B provides a brief summary of @task, the most popular totally online tool.

PROJECT MANAGEMENT SOFTWARE REVIEWS

Figure A-1 provides a screen shot showing the top ten project management software products based on a June 2009 review by TopTenREVIEWS™. The products listed in the top ten include:

1. Microsoft Project

2. MindView

3. Project KickStart

4. RationalPlan Multi Project

5. FastTrack Schedule

6. Service Desktop Pro

7. Milestones

8. MinuteMan

9. FusionDesk Professional

10. VIP Team To Do List

Notice that Microsoft Project is number one on the list. Also notice its steep price of over $500 for a single user. Remember that students can purchase Microsoft Project and other software at greatly reduced rates from sites such as www.journeyed.com (only $69.98 for Project 2007 Standard in July 2009). You can also normally download free trials of Project and other software products.

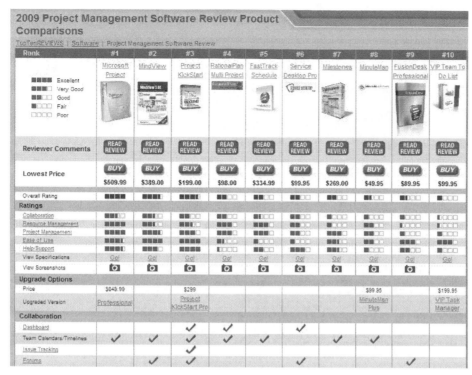

Figure A-1. Top ten project management software product comparisons

Below are descriptions of the criteria for comparing the software products:

- **Collaboration:** How information and issues are communicated with project team members, including email, conference calls, meetings, web-based locations and more. Collaboration should be easy to use.
- **Resource Management: Project management software should** manage and control the resources needed to run a project, such as people, money, time and equipment.
- **Project Management:** The process, practice and activities needed to perform continuous evaluation, prioritization, budgeting and selection of investments are key. Proper project management capabilities provide the greatest value and contribution to the strategic interest of your company.
- **Ease of Use:** All project management software has a learning curve, but the best have functions that are easy to find and simple enough for anyone to use from Day 1, Project 1.
- **Help/Support:** Project management software should offer a comprehensive user guide and help system. The manufacturer should provide email addresses or telephone numbers for direct answers to technical questions.[1]

In addition to reviewing project management software in general, TopTenREVIEWS™ also compared online products in a separate category. These products require an Internet connection for use. Figure A-2 lists the top ten results. The top fourteen products listed include:

1. @task
2. Daptiv PPM
3. Clarizen
4. Project Insight
5. Celoxis
6. Intervals
7. Projecturf
8. Central Desktop
9. Easy Projects NET
10. eStudio
11. Project Office.net
12. Copper
13. Smooth Projects
14. Zoho Projects

@task took the number one spot. Like most tools in this category, @task provides the ability to create Gantt charts, numerous reports and views, project dashboards, and it provides integration with Microsoft Project files. One of its unique features is its support of iPhones. See End Note 1 or visit the Web sites for any of these products and use a free trial version. See Appendix B for more information on using @task.

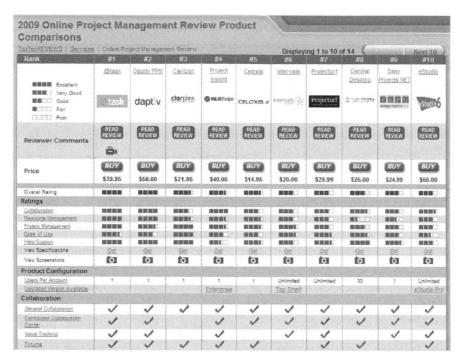

Figure A-2. Top ten online project management product comparisons

BASIC FEATURES OF PROJECT MANAGEMENT SOFTWARE

What makes project management software different from other software tools? Why not just use a spreadsheet or database to help manage projects?

You can do a lot of project management planning and tracking using non-project management software. You could use a simple word processor to list tasks, resources, dates, and so on. If you put that information into a spreadsheet, you can easily sort it, graph it, and perform other functions. A relational database tool could provide even more manipulation of data. You can use email and other tools to collaborate with others. However, project management software is designed specifically for managing projects, so it normally includes several distinct and important features not found in other software products:

- *Creating work breakdown structures, Gantt charts, and network diagrams*: As mentioned in this text, a fundamental concept of project management is breaking down the scope of the project into a work breakdown structure (WBS). The WBS is the basis for creating the project schedule, normally shown as a Gantt chant. The Gantt chart shows start and end dates of tasks as well as dependencies between tasks, which are more clearly shown in a network diagram. Project management software makes it easy to create a WBS, Gantt chart, and network diagram. These features help the project manager and team visualize the project at various levels of detail.

- *Integrating scope, time, and cost data*: The WBS is a key tool for summarizing the scope of a project, and the Gantt chart summarizes the time or schedule for a project. Project management software allows you to assign cost and other resources to tasks on the WBS, which are tied to the schedule. This allows you to create a cost baseline and use earned value management to track project performance in terms of scope, time, and cost in an integrated fashion.

- *Setting a baseline and tracking progress*: Another important concept of project management is preparing a plan and measuring progress against the plan. Project management software lets you track progress for each task. The tracking Gantt chart is a nice tool for easily seeing the planned and actual schedule, and other views and reports show progress in other areas.

- *Providing other advanced project management features*: Project management software often provides other advanced features, such as setting up different types of scheduling dependencies, determining the critical path and slack for tasks, working with multiple projects, and leveling resources. For example, you can easily set up a task to start when its predecessor is halfway finished. After entering task dependencies, the software should easily show you the critical path and slack for each task. You can also set up multiple projects in a program and perform portfolio management analysis with some products. Many project management software products also allow you to easily adjust resources within their slack allowances to create a smoother resource distribution. These advanced features unique to project management are rarely found in other software tools.

As you can see, there are several important features that are unique to project management software that make them worth using. Next you'll learn what's new in Project 2010 and how to use basic features of Project 2010 Standard.

WHAT'S NEW IN PROJECT 2010

Project 2010 is not just a run-of-the-mill update. Microsoft really listened to users and has revised Project to meet user needs. Learning some of the new features might seem like a chore, but it is well worth the effort.

If you are familiar with Project 2007, it may be helpful to review some of the new features in Project 2010.

- *Improved user interface:* Project 2010 now includes the "ribbon" interface instead of using the old menus and toolbars similar to Office 2003. Commands are organized in logical groups under tabs, such as File, Task, Resource, Project, View, and Format. The File tab takes you to the new Backstage feature, a one-stop graphical destination for opening, saving, and printing your files. You can also now right-click on different items, like a table cell or chart, to bring up commonly used commands quickly.

- *New viewing options:* Project 2010 includes several new views. A timeline view is automatically displayed above other views to show you a concise overview of the entire project schedule. You can easily add tasks to the timeline, print it, or paste it into an e-mail. The new team planner view lets you quickly see what your team members are working on, and you can move tasks from one person to another using this view. For example, if a resource is overallocated, you can drag a task to another resource to remove the overallocation. You can also add new columns quickly and use the new zoom slider at the lower right of the screen to zoom your schedule in and out. Also, the tab for viewing and printing reports is easier to navigate with more options for visual reports.

- *Manual scheduling:* Unlike previous versions of Project where tasks were automatically scheduled, Project 2010 uses manual schedule as its default. In past versions of Project, summary tasks were automatically calculated based on their subtasks. Resources were also adjusted automatically. With Project 2010, this is no longer the case. For example, you might want to enter durations for summary tasks and then fill in the detailed information for their subtasks later. When you open a new file, Project reminds you that new tasks are manually scheduled and lets you easily switch to automatic scheduling, if desired. You can also use the new compare versions to see Gantt bars to more clearly see how one version of a project differs from another version.

- *Improved collaboration:* Project 2010 is able to provide an interface with the most popular portals used in industry. Project now uses SharePoint instead of Project Web Access for collaboration. Project Server 2010 also provides integration with Microsoft Exchange 2010 to enable team members to manage and report on tasks directly from Microsoft Outlook. Remember that Project Standard does not include these collaboration features. You must have Project Professional and Project Server to use the enterprise features of Project.

Next, you will learn some basic information about Project 2010 and explore the main screen elements and Help facility.

USING PROJECT 2010

Before you can use Project 2010 or any project management software effectively, you must understand the fundamental concepts of project management, such as creating work breakdown structures (WBS), linking tasks, entering duration estimates, assigning resources, and so on. Make sure you read most of this text before using Project 2010 so you understand these concepts. This text provides instructions for using the stand-alone version of Project 2010 known as Project Standard. Project Professional and the Enterprise version of Project require special server software to perform online and collaborative functions. Consult Microsoft's Web site for detailed information on other products.

Before You Begin

This appendix assumes you are using Project 2010 with Windows XP, Vista, or Windows 7 and are familiar with other Windows-based applications. Check your work by reviewing the many screen shots included in the steps, or by using the solution files that are available for download from the companion Web site for this text or from your instructor.

> **NOTE**: *You need to be running Windows XP, Vista, or Windows 7 to use Project 2010.* It does not run on Macintosh computers or other operating systems. Most organizations have Project 2010 as part of their license if they have Office 2010. You can download a free trial from www.microsoft.com/project. Students can purchase a full version of Project Standard from sites like www.journeyed.com for around $69.

This appendix uses a fictitious project—Project A+—to illustrate how to use the software. The WBS for Project A+ uses the five project management process groups as level 2 items (initiating, planning, executing, monitoring and controlling, and closing). Standard deliverables under each of those process groups are included, as described in this text. Each section of the appendix includes hands-on activities for you to perform.

> **NOTE:** To complete the hands-on activities in the appendix, you will need to download files from the companion Web site for this text (*www.intropm.com*) to your computer. When you begin each set of steps, make sure you are using the correct file. Before you begin your work you should have Customer Feedback.mpp file. Save the files you create yourself in a different folder so you do not write over the ones you download.

In addition, you will create the following files from scratch as you work through the steps:

- wbs.mpp
- schedule.mpp

You will also use the following file to create a hyperlink:

- stakeholder_register.doc

Next you will learn how to start Project 2010, review the Help facility and a template file, and begin to plan Project A+.

Overview of Project 2010

The first step to mastering Project 2010 is to become familiar with the major screen elements and the Help facility. This section describes each of these features.

Starting Project 2010 and Understanding the Main Screen Elements

To start Project 2010:

1. *Open Project 2010.* Click the **Start** button on the taskbar, point to **All Programs** in Windows XP or **Programs** in Vista or Windows 7, point to **Microsoft Office**, and then click **Microsoft Office Project 2010**. Alternatively, a shortcut or icon might be available on the desktop; in this case, double-click the icon to start the software.

2. *Maximize Project 2010.* If the Project 2010 window does not fill the entire screen as shown in Figure A-3, click the **Maximize** button in the upper-right corner of the window.

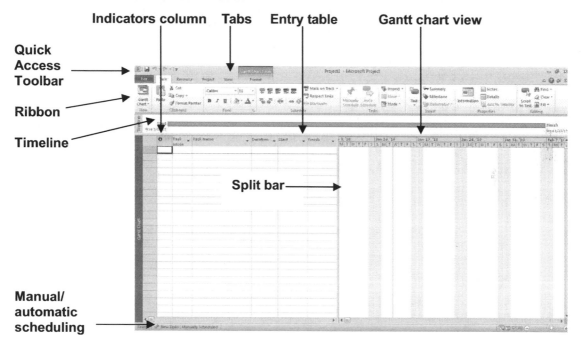

Figure A-3. Project 2010 main screen

Project 2010 is now running and ready to use. Look at some of the elements of the screen.

- The Ribbon, tabs, and Quick Access toolbar are similar to other Office 2007 or 2010 applications.

- The timeline view is displayed below the ribbon.

- The default manual scheduling for new tasks is on the lower left of the screen. You can click that option to switch to automatic scheduling.

- The default view is the Gantt chart view, which shows tasks and other information as well as a calendar display. You can access other views by clicking the View command button on the far left side of the ribbon.

- The areas where you enter information in a spreadsheet-like table are part of the Entry table. For example, you can see entry areas for Task Name, Duration, Start, and Finish.

- You can make the Entry table more or less wide by using the Split bar. When you move the mouse over the split bar, your cursor changes to the resize pointer. Clicking and dragging the split bar to the right reveals other task information in the Entry table, including Predecessors, Resource Names, and Add New columns.

- The column to the left of the Task Name column in the Entry table is the Indicators column. The Indicators column displays indicators or symbols related to items associated with each task, such as task notes or hyperlinks to other files.

Notice that when Project 2010 starts, it opens a new file named Project1, as shown in the title bar. If you open a second file, the name will be Project2, and so on, until you save and rename the file.

Using Project Help and the Project Web Site

You can access information to help you learn how to use Project 2010. Figure A-4 shows the detailed list of topics available from Project Help. You can access help by Pressing F1 or clicking on the question mark/help icon on upper right side of the ribbon. Remember this feature requires an Internet connection.

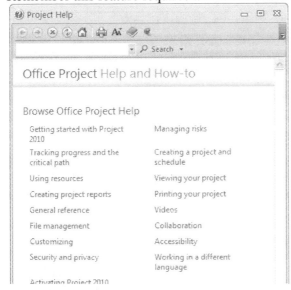

Figure A-4. Topics under Project help

Microsoft provides a number of resources on its Web site to help you learn how to use Project 2010. They provide product information, help and how-to guides on various versions of Project, training information, and templates. Microsoft's Web site for Project 2010 (*www.microsoft.com/project*) provides files for users to download, case studies, articles, and other useful materials. Figure A-5 shows a screen shot of this Web site from March 2010. See the companion Web site for this text for updated information on Project and other resources.

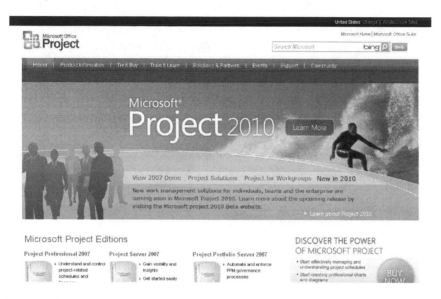

Figure A-5. Microsoft Office Project web site (www.microsoft.com/project)

Many features in Project 2010 are similar to ones in other Windows programs. For example, to collapse or expand tasks, click the appropriate symbols to the left of the task name. To access shortcut items, right-click in either the Entry table area or the Gantt chart. Many of the Entry table operations in Project 2010 are very similar to operations in Excel. For example, to adjust a column width, click and drag or double-click between the column heading titles.

Next, you will get some hands-on experience by opening an existing file to explore various screen elements. Project 2010 comes with several template files, and you can also access templates from Microsoft Office Online or other Web sites.

EXPLORING PROJECT 2010 USING AN EXISTING FILE

To open a file and adjust Project 2010 screen elements:

1. Open an existing file. Click the **File tab**, then select **Open**, and browse to find the file named **Customer Feedback.mpp** that you copied from the companion Web site for this text (www.intropm.com), and then **double-click** the filename to open the file. (This file is a template file that comes with Project 2007 where it is called Customer Feedback Monitoring.) Your screen should resemble Figure A-6.

Task Note Need to widen column   Split Bar

Indicator

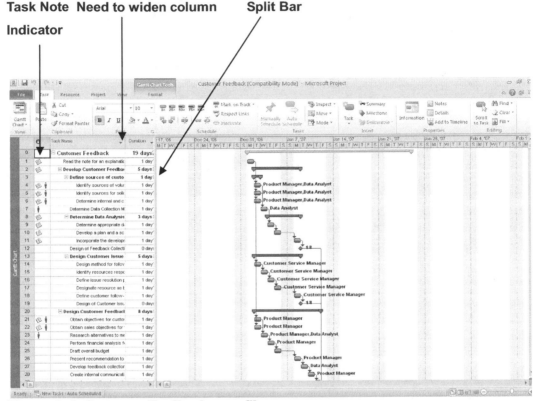

Figure A-6. Customer Feedback.mpp file

2. *Widen the Task Name column*. Move the **cursor** between the Task Name and Duration column, then **double-click** to widen the Task Name column so all of the text shows.

3. *Move the Split Bar*. Move the **Split Bar** to the right so only the entire Task Name column is visible.

4. *View the first Note*. Move your mouse over the yellow **Notes symbol** in the Indicators column for Task 2and read its contents. It is a good idea to provide a short note describing the purpose of project files.

5. *Add the Timeline and a task to it*. Check the **Timeline** box under the View tab, Split View group. If you cannot see the entire project schedule, as shown in Figure A-7, click the **Zoom** button or **Zoom slider** to make adjustments. Click on the Task Name for **Task 12**, click the **Task** tab, and then click the **Add to Timeline** button under the Properties group.

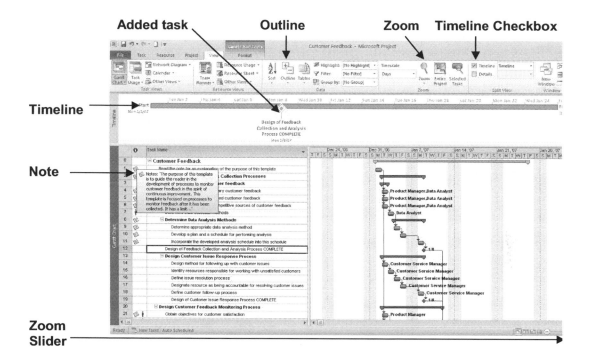

Figure A-7. Adjusted Customer Feedback.mpp file

To show different WBS levels:

1. *Select Outline Level 1 to display WBS level 2 tasks*. Click the **Outline** button's list arrow, and then click **Outline Level 1**. Notice that only the level 2 WBS items display in the Entry table. The black bars on the Gantt chart represent the summary tasks. Recall that the entire project is normally referred to as WBS level 1, and the next highest level is called level 2. This view of the file also shows one milestone task in row 45 indicating when the project was completed. Recall that the black diamond symbol on a Gantt chart shows milestones.

2. *Expand a task*. Click the **expand symbol** (the plus sign) to the left of Task 2, Develop Customer Feedback Collection Processes, to see its subtasks. Your screen should resemble Figure A-8. Click the **collapse symbol** (the minus sign) to hide its subtasks. Experiment with expanding and collapsing other tasks and resizing other columns.

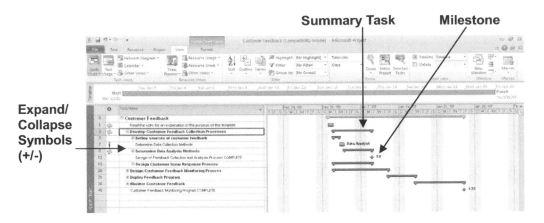

Summary Task   **Milestone**

**Expand/
Collapse
Symbols
(+/-)**

Figure A-8. Showing part of the WBS on the Gantt chart

3. *Close the file without saving.* Click the **Close icon** in the upper right of the window and select **No** when prompted to save the file.

Project 2010 Views

Project 2010 provides many ways to display or view project information. In addition to the default Gantt chart, you can view the network diagram, calendar, and task usage views, to name a few. These views allow you to analyze project information in different ways. The View tab also provides access to different tables that display information in various ways. In addition to the default Entry table view, you can access tables that focus on data related to areas such as the Schedule, Cost, Tracking, and Earned Value.

To access and explore different views:

1. *Explore the Network Diagram view in the Customer* Feedback file. Open the Customer Feedback file again. Click the **Network Diagram** button under the View tab, and then move the **Zoom slider** on the lower right of the screen all the way to the left. Your screen should resemble Figure A-9.

Network Diagram View   **Zoom Slider**

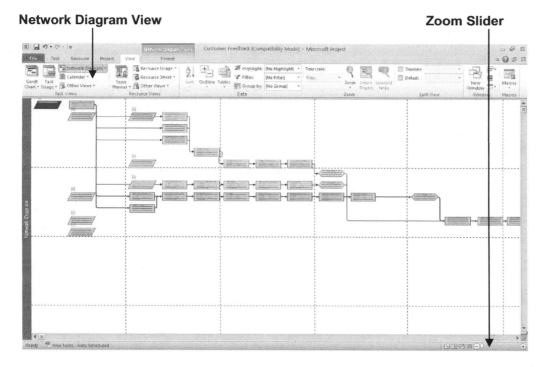

Figure A-9. Network diagram view of customer feedback file

2. Explore the Calendar view. Click the **Calendar** button (under the Network Diagram button). Notice that the screen lists tasks each day in a calendar format.

3. Examine columns in the Entry table. Click the **Gantt Chart** button, move the split bar to the right to see all of the available columns, and review the information provided in each column of the Entry table.

4. Change the table view. Click the **Tables** button under the View tab, and then click **Schedule**. Figure A-10 shows the table view options.

Figure A-10. Table view options

5. *Examine the Table: Schedule and other views.* Notice that the columns in the table to the left of the Gantt chart, as shown in Figure A-11, now display more detailed schedule information, such as Task Mode, Task Name, Start, Finish, Late Start, Late Finish, Free Slack, and Total Slack. Also notice that all of the text in the Task Name column is not visible. Remember that you can widen the column by double-clicking the resize pointer to the right of that column. You can also move the split bar to reveal more or fewer columns. Experiment with other table views, then **return to the Table: Entry view**.

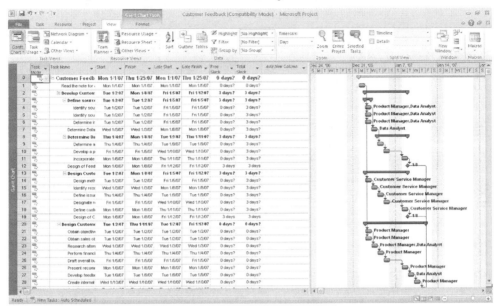

Figure A-11. Schedule table view

Project 2010 Reports

Project 2010 provides many ways to report project information as well. In addition to traditional reports, you can also prepare visual reports, with both available under the Project tab. Note that the visual reports often require that you have other Microsoft application software, such as Excel and Visio. Project 2010 automatically formats reports for ease of printing.

To access and explore different reports:

1. *Explore the Reports feature.* Click the **Project** tab, and then click the **Reports** button. The Reports dialog box displays, as shown in Figure A-12.

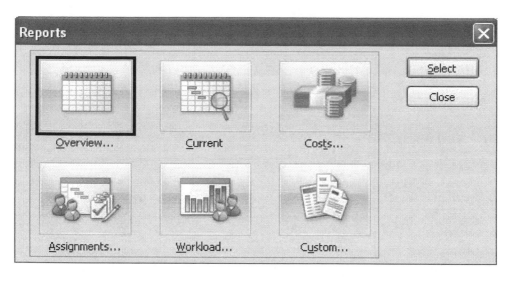

Figure A-12. Reports dialog box

2. *View the Project Summary report.* Double-click **Overview** from the Reports dialog box, and then double-click **Project Summary** in the Overview Reports dialog box. Notice that Project 2010 switches to the Backstage (File tab) to make it easy for you to print or share your report, as shown in Figure A-13.

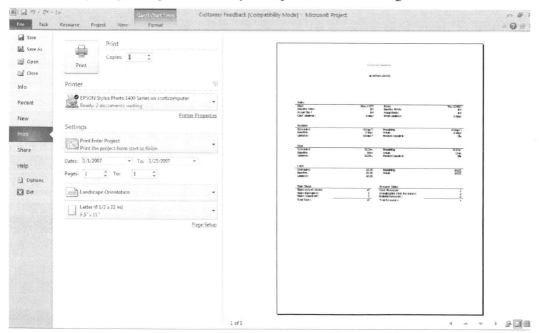

Figure A-13. Previewing the Project Summary report in the Backstage

3. *Examine the report and experiment with others.* Move the mouse to the right side of the screen to exam the report more closely. Notice that the insertion point

now resembles a magnifying glass. Click inside the report to zoom in or zoom out. Click the **Project** tab again, and then experiment with viewing other reports. You will use several reports and other views later in this appendix.

4.   *Close the Reports feature*. Click **Project** tab to return to the Gantt chart view. You can close the file without saving it if you wish to take a break.

Project 2010 Filters

Project 2010 uses a relational database to filter, sort, store, and display information. Filtering project information is very useful. For example, if a project includes thousands of tasks, you might want to view only summary or milestone tasks to get a high-level view of the project by using the Milestones or Summary Tasks filter from the Filter list. You can select a filter that shows only tasks on the critical path if that is what you want to see. Other filters include Completed Tasks, Late/Overbudget Tasks, and Date Range, which displays tasks based on dates you provide. As shown earlier, you can also click the Show button on the toolbar to display different levels in the WBS quickly.

To explore Project 2010 filters:

1.   *Access filters*. Click the **View** tab, if necessary, and make sure the Customer Feedback file is in the Gantt Chart: Table Entry view. Click the **Filter list arrow** (under the Data group), as shown in Figure A-14. The default filter is No Filter, which shows all tasks.

Filter list arrow

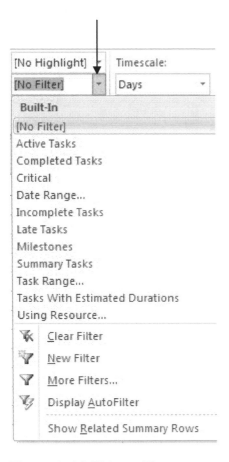

Figure A-14. Using a filter

2. *Filter to show critical tasks.* Click **Critical** in the list of filters. Widen the Task Names column, if needed, and move the split bar to see only that column. Notice that the Gantt chart only shows the critical tasks for the project. Your screen should resemble Figure A-15. Recall that the critical tasks are what drive the schedule completion date.

An Introduction to Project Management, Third Edition

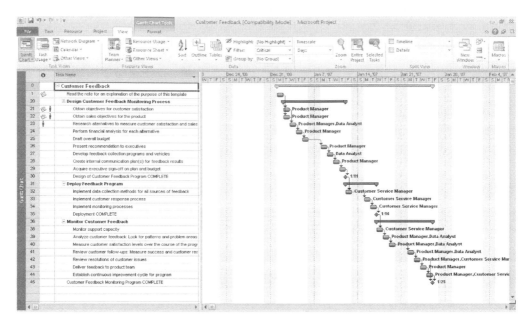

Figure A-15. Critical tasks filter applied

3. *Show summary tasks*. Select **No Filter** from the Filter list box to reveal all the tasks in the WBS again. Click the **Filter** list arrow, and then click **Summary Tasks**. Now only the summary tasks appear in the WBS. Experiment with other filters.

4. *Close the file*. When you are finished reviewing the Customer Feedback file, click **Close** from the File menu or click the **Close** button. Click **No** when asked if you want to save changes.

5. *Exit Project 2010*. Select **Exit** from the File tab or click the **Close** button for Project 2010.

Now that you are familiar with the main screen elements, views, reports, and filters, you will learn how to use Project 2010 to create a new file.

CREATING A NEW FILE AND ENTERING TASKS IN A WORK BREAKDOWN STRUCTURE

To create a new Project 2010 file, you must first name the project, enter the start date, and then enter the tasks. The list of tasks and their hierarchy is the work breakdown structure (WBS). The file you create could be used for a class project which lasts approximately three months. It uses the project management process groups to organize tasks and includes several deliverables described in this text. You could also modify this file to meet your specific needs.

Creating a New Project File

To create a new project file:

1. *Create a blank project.* Open Project 2010. A blank project file automatically opens. The default filenames are Project1, Project2, and so on. (If Project 2010 is already open and you want to open a new file, click the **File** tab and select a **Blank Project**.)

2. *Open the Project Information dialog box.* Click the **Project** tab, and then click **Project Information** to display the Project Information dialog box, as shown in Figure A-16. This dialog box enables you to set dates for the project, select the calendar to use, and view project statistics. The project start date will default to the current date. Note that in Figure A-16 the file was created on 2/24/10 and a Start date of 2/1/10 was entered.

NOTE: All dates are entered in month/day/year or American format. You can change the date format by selecting Options from the File tab. Click the date format you want to use in the Date Format box under the General settings. You can also customize the Ribbon, change default currencies in the display, and so on under Project Options.

**Start
date
text box**

**Current
date**

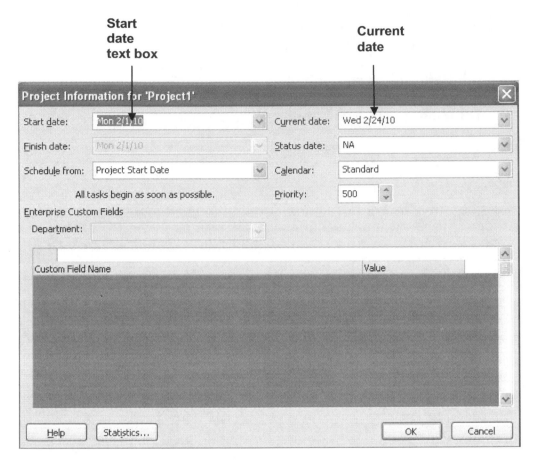

Figure A-16. Project information dialog box

3.   *Enter the project start date.* In the Start date text box, enter **2/01/10**. Setting your project start date to 2/01/10 will ensure that your work matches the results that appear in this appendix. Leave the Finish date, Current date, and other information at the default settings. Click **OK** or press Enter.

4.   *Access advanced project properties.* Click the **File** tab, and then click **Info**. Click Project Information on the right side of the screen to access Advanced Properties, as shown in Figure A-17.

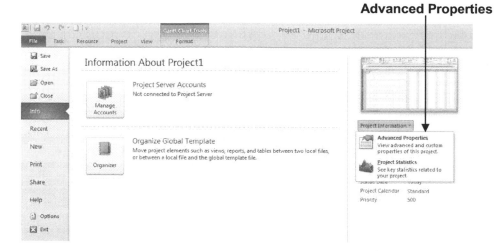

Figure A-17. Accessing advanced project properties

5. *Enter advanced project properties* Type **Project A+** in the Title text box, type **Your Name** in the Author text box, as shown in Figure A-18, and then click **OK**. You may have some default information entered in the Project Properties dialog box, such as your company's name. Click the **Task** tab so you can see the Entry table and Gantt chart view. Keep this file open for the next set of steps.

Figure A-18. Project properties dialog box

Creating a Work Breakdown Structure Hierarchy

As mentioned in Chapter 4 of this text, a work breakdown structure (WBS) is a fundamental part of project management. Developing a good WBS takes time, and it will make entering tasks into the Entry table easier if you develop the WBS first. For this example, you will use the project management process groups and some key processes and deliverables to create the WBS. You will use the information in Figure A-19 to enter tasks.

1. Initiating	16. Work on deliverable 2
2. Identify stakeholders	17. Work on deliverable 3
3. Stakeholder register completed	18. Deliverable 1 completed
4. Stakeholder management strategy completed	19. Deliverable 2 completed
5. Prepare project charter	20. Deliverable 3 completed
6. Project charter completed	21. Monitoring and Controlling
7. Prepare for kickoff meeting	22. Track actual hours
8. Kickoff meeting completed	23. Update project documents
9. Planning	24. Progress report 1
10. Prepare draft schedule	25. Progress report 2
11. Gantt chart completed	26. Hold meetings
12. Prepare scope statement	27. Closing
13. Initial scope statement completed	28. Prepare final project report
14. Executing	29. Prepare final presentation
15. Work on deliverable 1	30. Project completed

Figure A-19. Task list for Project A+

To develop a WBS for the project:

1. Enter task names. Enter the 30 tasks in Figure A-19 into the Task Name column in the order shown. Do not worry about durations or any other information at this time. Type the name of each task into the Task Name column of the Entry table, beginning with the first row. Press **Enter** or the **down arrow** key on your keyboard to move to the next row.

HELP: If you accidentally skip a task, highlight the task row, right-click, and select Insert Task. To edit a task entry, click the text for that task, and either type over the old text or edit the existing text.

An Introduction to Project Management, Third Edition

2. *Adjust the Task Name column width as needed.* To make all the text display in the Task Name column, move the mouse over the right-column gridline in the **Task Name** column heading until you see the resize pointer , and then click the **left mouse** button and drag the line to the right to make the column wider, or double-click to adjust the column width automatically.

This WBS separates tasks according to the project management process groups of initiating, planning, executing, controlling, and closing. These tasks will be the level 2 items in the WBS for this project. (Remember the whole project is level 1.) It is a good idea to include all of these process groups because there are important tasks that must be done under each of them. Recall that the WBS should include *all* of the work required for the project. In the Project A+ WBS, the tasks will be purposefully left at a high WBS level (level 3). You will create these levels, or the WBS hierarchy, next when you create summary tasks. For a real project, you would usually break the WBS into even more levels to provide more details to describe all the work involved in the project. For example, each deliverable would probably have several levels and tasks under it.

Creating Summary Tasks

After entering the WBS tasks listed in Figure A-19 into the Entry table, the next step is to show the WBS levels by creating summary tasks. The summary tasks in this example are Tasks 1 (initiating), 9 (planning), 14 (executing), 21 (monitoring and controlling), and 27 (closing). You create summary tasks by highlighting and indenting their respective subtasks.

To create the summary tasks:

1. *Select lower level or subtasks.* Highlight **Tasks 2** through **8** by clicking the cell for Task 2 and dragging the mouse through the cells to Task 8.

2. *Indent subtasks.* Click the **Indent Tasks** button on the Ribbon under the Schedule group of the Task tab (or press Alt + Shift + right arrow) so your screen resembles Figure A-19. After the subtasks (Tasks 2 through 8) are indented, notice that Task 1 automatically becomes boldface, which indicates that it is a summary task. A collapse symbol appears to the left of the new summary task name. Clicking the collapse symbol (minus sign) will collapse the summary task and hide the subtasks beneath it. When subtasks are hidden, an expand symbol (plus sign) appears to the left of the summary task name. Clicking the expand symbol will expand the summary task. Also, notice that the symbol for the summary task on the Gantt chart has changed from a blue to a black line with arrows indicating the start and end dates. The Task Mode has also changed to make this task Automatically scheduled. You'll learn more about this feature later. For now, focus on entering and indenting the tasks to create the WBS.

**Expand or collapse symbols by
Summary tasks**

Indent Task

Summary task symbol

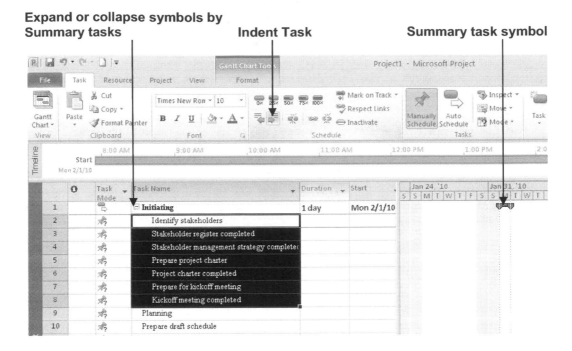

Figure A-19. Indenting tasks to create the WBS hierarchy

3. *Create other summary tasks and subtasks.* Create subtasks and summary tasks for the other process groups by following the same steps. Indent **Tasks 10** through **13** to make Task 9 a summary task. Indent **Tasks 15** through **20** to make Task 14 a summary task. Indent **Tasks 22** through **26** to make Task 21 a summary task. Indent **Tasks 28** through **30** to make Task 27 a summary task. Widen the Task Name column to see all of your text, as needed.

TIP: To change a task from a subtask to a summary task or to change its level in the WBS, you can "outdent" the task. To outdent the task, click the cell of the task or tasks you want to change, and then click the Outdent Task button (the button just to the left of the Indent Task button). You can also press Alt + Shift + Right Arrow to indent tasks and Alt + Shift + Left Arrow to outdent tasks.

Numbering Tasks

To display automatic numbering of tasks using the standard tabular numbering system for a WBS:

1. *Show outline numbers.* Click the **Format** tab, and then click the **Outline Number checkbox** under the Show/Hide group. Project 2010 adds the appropriate WBS numbering to the task names.

2. *Show project summary task.* Click the Project Summary checkbox just below the Outline Number checkbox. Scroll to the top of the file to see that a new task has been added under row 0.

3. *Adjust the file.* Widen the Task Name column and move the split bar so only that column displays. Your file should resemble Figure A-20.

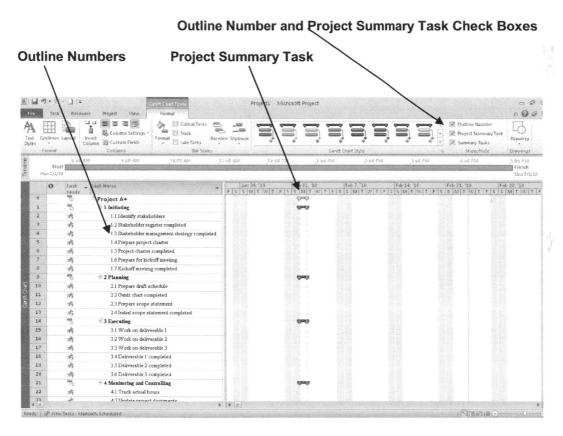

Figure A-20. Adding automatic outline numbers and a project summary task

Saving Project Files Without a Baseline

An important part of project management is tracking performance against a baseline, or approved plan. It is important to wait until you are ready to save your file with a baseline because Project 2010 will show changes against a baseline. Since you are still developing your project file for the Project A+ project, you want to save the file without a baseline, which is the default way to save a file. Later in this appendix, you will save the file with a baseline. You will then enter actual information to compare planned and actual performance data.

To save a file without a baseline:

1. *Save your file*. Click the **File** tab and then click **Save**, or click the **Save** button on the Quick Access toolbar.

2. *Enter a filename*. In the Save dialog box, type **wbs** in the File name text box. Browse to the location in which you want to save the file, and then click **Save**. Your Project 2010 file should look like Figure A-21. Remember that you can move the Split bar to show more or fewer columns.

3. *Close Project 2010*. Click the Close icon to exit Project 2010.

HELP: If you want to download the Project 2010 file wbs.mpp to check your work or continue to the next section, a copy is available on the companion Web site for this text, the author's Web site, or from your instructor.

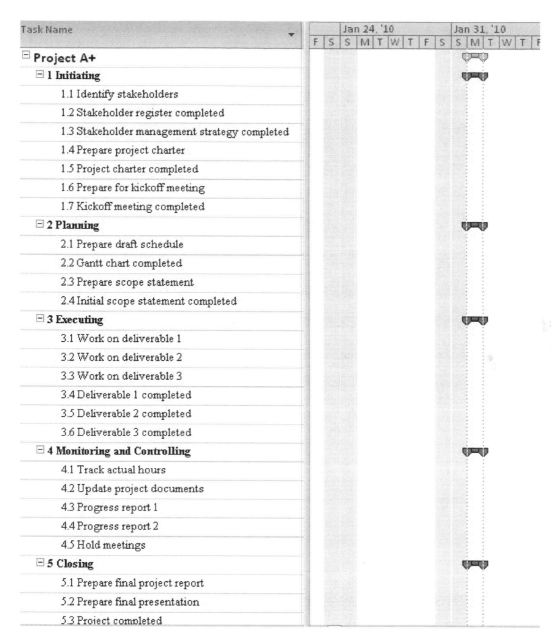

Figure A-21. Project 2010 WBS file

DEVELOPING THE SCHEDULE

Many people use Project 2010 for its scheduling features. The first step in using these features, after inputting the WBS for the project, is to change calendars, if needed, and then enter durations for tasks or specific dates when tasks will occur. You must also enter task dependencies in order for schedules to adjust automatically and to do critical path analysis. After entering durations and task dependencies, you can view the network diagram, critical path, and slack information.

Calendars

The standard Project 2010 calendar assumes that working hours are Monday through Friday, from 8:00 a.m. to 5:00 p.m., with an hour for lunch from noon until 1:00 p.m. In addition to the standard calendar, Project 2010 also includes a 24 Hours calendar and Night Shift calendar. The 24 Hours calendar assumes resources can work any hour and any day of the week. The Night Shift calendar assumes working hours are Monday through Saturday, from 12:00 a.m. to 3:00 a.m., 4:00 a.m. 8 a.m., and 11 p.m. to 12 a.m. You can create a different base calendar to meet your unique project requirements.

To create a new base calendar:

1. *Open a new file and access the Change Working Time dialog box*. With Project 2010 open, click the **Project** tab, and then click the **Change Working Time** button under the Properties group. The Change Working Time dialog box opens, as shown in Figure A-22.

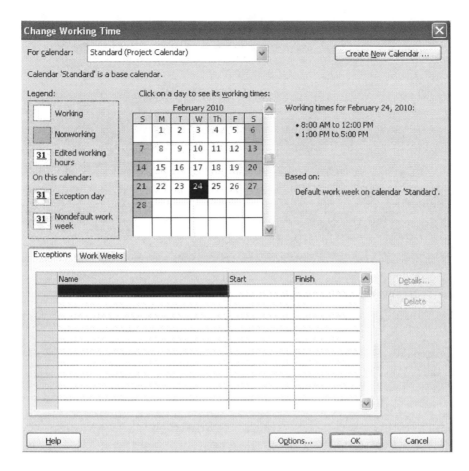

Figure A-22. Change Working Time dialog box

2. *Name the new base calendar.* In the Change Working Time dialog box, click **Create New Calendar**. The Create New Base Calendar dialog box opens. Click the **Create new base calendar** radio button, type **Project A+** as the name of the new calendar in the **Name** text box, and then click **OK**.

3. *Change the fiscal year start.* In the Change Working Time dialog box, click **Options** at the bottom of the screen. Change the **fiscal year** to start in **October** instead of January. Review other options in this screen, and then click **OK twice**.

You can use this new calendar for the whole project, or you can assign it to specific resources on the project.

To assign the new calendar to the whole project:

1. *Open the Project Information dialog box.* Click the **Project** tab, and then click the **Change Working Time** button.

2. *Select a new calendar*. Click the **For calendar** list arrow to display a list of available calendars. Select your new calendar named **Project A+** from this list, and then click **OK**.

To assign a specific calendar to a specific resource:

1. *Assign a new calendar*. Click the **View** tab, and then click the **Resource Sheet** button under the Resource Views group. Type **Adam** in the Resource Name column, press **Enter**, and then select the word **Adam**.

2. *Select the calendar*. Click the **Base Calendar** cell on the right part of the screen for Adam. If the Base Calendar column is not visible, click the horizontal scroll bar to view more columns. Click the **Base Calendar** list arrow to display the options, and then select **Project A+**, as shown in Figure A-23.

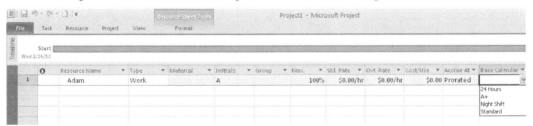

Figure A-23. Changing calendars for specific resources

3. *Block off vacation time*. Double-click the resource name **Adam** to display the Resource Information dialog box, and then click the **Change Working Time** button, located on the General tab in the Resource Information dialog box. You can block off vacation time for people by selecting the appropriate days on the calendar and marking them as nonworking days. Click **OK** to accept your changes, and then click **OK** to close the Resource Information dialog box.

4. *Close the file without saving it*. Click the **Close** box, and then click **No** when you are prompted to save the file.

Entering Task Durations

Recall that duration includes the actual amount of time spent working on a task plus elapsed time. Duration does not equal effort. For example, you might have a task that you estimate will take one person 40 hours of effort to complete, but you allow two weeks on a calendar for its duration. You can simply enter 2w (for two weeks) in the Duration column for that task

Manual and Automatic Scheduling

If you have used earlier versions of Project, you probably noticed that when you entered a task, it was automatically assigned a duration of one day, and Start and Finish dates were also automatically entered. This is still the case in Project 2010 if you use automatic scheduling for a task. If you use manual scheduling, no durations or dates are automatically entered. The other big change with manual scheduling is that summary task durations are not automatically calculated based on their subtasks when they are set up as manually scheduled tasks. Figure A-24 illustrates these differences. Notice that the Manual subtask 1 had no information entered for its duration, start, or finish dates. Also note that the duration for Manual summary task 1's duration is not dependent on the durations of its subtasks. For the automatic summary task, its duration is dependent on its summary tasks, and information is entered for all of the durations, start, and end dates. You can switch between automatic and manual scheduling for tasks in the same file, as desired, by changing the Task Mode.

Task Mode	Task Name	Duration	Start	Finish	February 21	March 7	March 21
	⊟ Manual summary task 1	4 wks	Thu 2/25/10	Wed 3/24/10			
	Manual subtask 1						
	Manual subtask 2	2 wks					
	⊟ Automatic summary task 1	15 days	Thu 2/25/10	Wed 3/17/10			
	Automatic subtask 1	1 wk	Thu 2/25/10	Wed 3/3/10			
	Automatic subtask 2	2 wks	Thu 3/4/10	Wed 3/17/10			

Figure A-24. Manual versus automatic scheduling

When you move your mouse over the Task Mode column (shown in the far left in Figure A-24) Project 2010 displays the following information:
- A task can be with Manually Scheduled or Automatically Scheduled.
- Manually Scheduled tasks have user-defined Start, Finish and Duration values. Project will never change their dates, but may warn you if there are potential issues with the entered values.
- Automatically Scheduled tasks have Start, Finish and Duration values calculated by Project based on dependencies, constraints, calendars, and other factors.

Project Help provides the following example of using both manual and automatic scheduling. You set up a preliminary project plan that's still in the proposal stage. You have a vague idea of major milestone dates but not much detail on other dates in various phases of the project. You build tasks and milestones using the Manually Scheduled task mode. The proposal is accepted and the tasks and deliverable dates become more defined. You continue to manually schedule those tasks and dates for a while, but as certain phases become well-defined, you decide to switch the tasks in those phases to the Automatically Scheduled task mode. By letting Project 2010 handle the complexities of scheduling, you can focus your attention on those phases that are still under development.

Duration Units and Guidelines for Entering Durations

To indicate the length of a task's duration, you normally type both a number and an appropriate duration symbol. If you type only a number, Project 2010 automatically enters days as the duration unit. Duration unit symbols include:

- d = days (default)

- w = weeks

- m = minutes

- h = hours

- mo or mon = months

- ed = elapsed days

- ew = elapsed weeks

For example, to enter two weeks for a task's duration, type 2w in the Duration column. (You can also type wk, wks, week, or weeks, instead of just w.) To enter four days for a task's duration, type 4 or 4d in the Duration column. You can also enter elapsed times in the Duration column. For example, 3ed means three elapsed days, and 2ew means two elapsed weeks.

You would use an elapsed duration for a task like "Allow cement to dry." The cement will dry in exactly the same amount of time regardless of whether it is a workday, a weekend, or a holiday. Project's default calendar does not assume that work is done on weekends. You will learn to change the calendar later in this appendix.

It is important to follow a few important rules when entering durations:

- To mark a task as a milestone, enter 0 for the duration. You can also mark tasks that have a non-zero duration as milestones by checking the "Mark task as milestone" option in the Task Information dialog box on the Advanced tab. You simply double-click a task to access this dialog box. The milestone symbol for those tasks will appear at their start date.

- You can enter the exact start and finish dates for activities instead of entering durations in the automatic scheduling mode. To enter start and finish dates, move the split bar to the right to reveal the Start and Finish columns. You normally only enter start and finish dates in this mode when those dates are certain.

- If you want task dates to adjust according to any other task dates, do not enter exact start and finish dates. Instead, enter durations and then establish dependencies to related tasks.

- To enter recurring tasks, such as weekly meetings, select Recurring Task from the Task button under the Task tab, Insert group. Enter the task name, the duration, and when the task occurs. Project 2010 will automatically insert appropriate subtasks based on the length of the project and the number of tasks required for the recurring task.

- Project 2010 uses a default calendar with standard workdays and hours. Remember to change the default calendar if needed, as shown earlier.

An Introduction to Project Management, Third Edition

Next, you will set task durations in the **Project A+** file that you created and saved in the previous section. If you did not create the file named wbs.mpp, you can download it from the companion Web site for this text.

Use the information in Figure A-25 to enter durations. The Project 2010 row number is shown to the left of each task name in the table.

Task Row	Task Name	Duration
2	Identify stakeholders	1w
3	Stakeholder register completed	0
4	Stakeholder management strategy completed	0
5	Prepare project charter	1w
6	Project charter completed	0
7	Prepare for kickoff meeting	3d
8	Kickoff meeting completed	0
10	Prepare draft schedule	5d
11	Gantt chart completed	0
12	Prepare scope statement	8d
13	Initial scope statement completed	0
15	Work on deliverable 1	3w
16	Work on deliverable 2	5w
17	Work on deliverable 3	6w
18	Deliverable 1 completed	0
19	Deliverable 2 completed	0
20	Deliverable 3 completed	0
24	Progress report 1	0
25	Progress report 2	0
28	Prepare final project report	4d
29	Prepare final presentation	4d
30	Project completed	0

Figure A-25. Task durations for Project A+

Entering Task Durations

To enter task durations:

1. *Enter the duration for Task 2.* Open the wbs file, and move the split bar to the right, if needed, to reveal the Duration, Start, and Finish columns. Click the **Duration** column for row 2, Identify stakeholders, type **1w**, and then press **Enter**. Notice that the duration for the first task, Initiating, also changed since it is a summary task and is an Automatically scheduled task, as shown in the Task Mode column. When you created summary tasks earlier, Project changed their scheduling mode to Automatic. Also notice that the Start and Finish date for Task 2 remain blank, since that task is a Manually scheduled task.

2. *Enter the duration for Task 3* In the **Duration** column for row 3, Stakeholder register completed, type **0**, then press **Enter**. Remember that a task with zero duration is a milestone. Notice the milestone or black diamond symbol that appears on the Gantt chart, as shown in Figure A-26

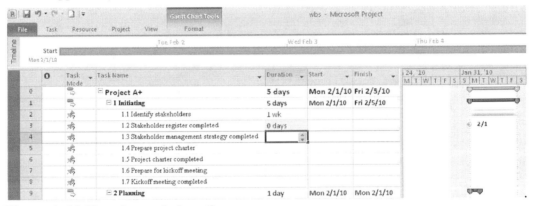

Figure A-26. Entering task durations

3. *Make all tasks Automatically scheduled tasks.* To save time since you do want most of the tasks to be automatically scheduled, select all of the tasks by clicking the **Task Name** column heading, and then click the **Auto Schedule** button under the **Task** tab, Tasks group.

4. *Enter remaining task durations.* Continue to enter the durations using the information in Figure A-25. Do not enter durations for tasks not listed in the figure. Notice that the Planning Wizard dialog box displays when you make the same entry several times in a row, such as after task 20. Click OK to close the dialog box.

5. *Insert a recurring task above Task 26, Hold meetings.* Click **Hold meetings** (Task 26) in the Task Name column to select that task. Click the **Task** tab, and click the **Task** button drop-down box under the Insert group, and then click **Recurring Task**. The Recurring Task Information dialog box opens.

6. *Enter task and duration information for the recurring task.* Type **Hold meetings** as the task title in the Task Name text box. Type **30min** in the Duration text box. Select the **Weekly** radio button under Recurrence pattern. Make sure that **1** is entered in the **Recur every** list box. Select the **Thursday** check box. In the Range of recurrence section, type **2/1/10** in the Start text box, click the **End by** radio button, and then type **4/29/10** in the End by text box, as shown in Figure A-27. The new recurring task will appear above Task 26, Hold meetings, when you are finished. **Delete task 40**, Hold meetings, by right clicking anywhere in row 40 and selecting Delete Task.

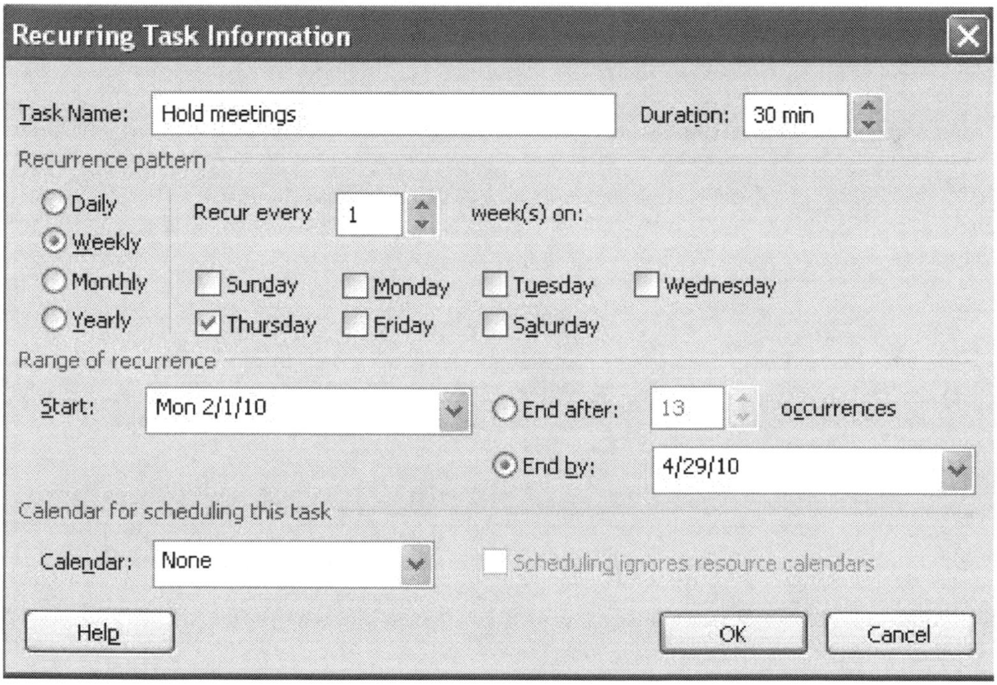

Figure A-27. Recurring task information dialog box

TIP: You can also enter a number of occurrences instead of an End by date for a recurring task. You might need to adjust the End by date after you enter all of your task durations and dependencies. Remember, the date on your computer determines the date listed as Today in the calendar.

7. *View the new summary task and its subtasks.* Click **OK**. Project 2010 inserts a new Hold meetings subtask in the Task Name column. Expand the new subtask

by clicking the **expand symbol** to the left of Hold meetings. To collapse the recurring task, click the **collapse symbol.** Move your mouse over the Recurring Task symbol in the Indicator column for row 26. Notice that the recurring task appears on the appropriate dates on the Gantt chart.

8. *Adjust the columns displayed and the timescale*. Move the **split bar** so that only the Task Name and Duration columns are visible. If needed, increase the Duration column's width so all of the text is visible. Click the **Zoom Out** button on the Zoom slider in the lower left of the screen to display all of the symbols in the Gantt chart. Your screen should resemble Figure A-28.

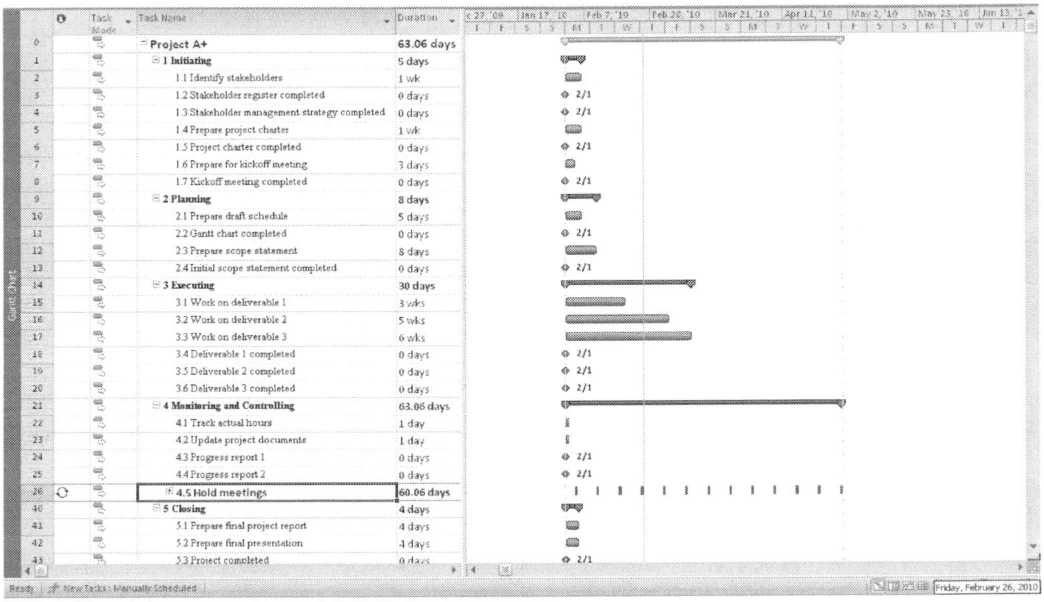

Figure A-28. All task durations and recurring task entered

9. *Save your file and name it*. Click **File** on the Menu bar, and then click **Save As**. Enter **schedule** as the filename, and then save the file to the desired location on your computer or network. Notice that all of the tasks still begin on February 1. This will change when you add task dependencies. Keep this file open for the next set of steps.

Establishing Task Dependencies

To use Project 2010 to adjust schedules automatically and perform critical path analysis, you *must* determine the dependencies or relationships among tasks. There are several different methods for creating task dependencies: using the Link Tasks button, using the Predecessors column of the Entry table or the Predecessors tab in the Task Information dialog box, or clicking and dragging the Gantt chart symbols for tasks with dependencies. You will use the first two methods in the following steps.

To create dependencies using the Link Tasks button, highlight tasks that are related and then click the Link Tasks button under the Task tab, Schedule group. For example, to create a finish-to-start (FS) dependency between Task 1 and Task 2, click any cell in row 1, drag down to row 2, and then click the Link Tasks button. The default type of link is finish-to-start. In the Project A+ file, you will also set up some other types of dependencies and use the lag option to set up overlaps between dependent tasks.

> **TIP:** To select adjacent tasks, click and drag the mouse to highlight them. You can also click the first task, hold down the Shift key, and then click the last task. To select nonadjacent tasks, hold down the Control (Ctrl) key as you click tasks in order of their dependencies.

When you use the Predecessors column of the Entry table to create dependencies, you must manually enter the information. To create dependencies manually, type the task row number of the preceding task in the Predecessors column of the Entry table. For example, Task 3 has Task 2 as a predecessor, which can be entered in the Predecessors column, meaning that Task 3 cannot start until Task 2 is finished. To see the Predecessors column of the Entry table, move the split bar to the right. You can also double-click on the task, click the Predecessors tab in the Task Information dialog box, and enter the predecessors there.

Next, you will use information from Figure A-29 to enter the predecessors for tasks as indicated. You will create some dependencies by manually typing the predecessors in the Predecessors column, some by using the Link Tasks button, and the remaining dependencies by using whichever method you prefer.

To link tasks or establish dependencies for Project A+:

1. Display the Predecessors column in the Entry table. Move the split bar to the right to reveal the full Predecessors column in the schedule.mpp file you saved in the previous section. Widen the Task Name or other columns, if needed.

2. Highlight the cell where you want to enter a predecessor, and then type the task number for its predecessor task. Click the **Predecessors cell for Task 3**, Stakeholder register completed, type **2**, and press **Enter**. Notice that as you enter task dependencies, the Gantt chart changes to reflect the new schedule. Also notice that several cells become highlighted, showing the Visual Change Highlights feature of Project 2010.

3. Enter predecessors for Task 4. Click the **Predecessors cell** for Task 4, type **2**, and press **Enter**.

4. Establish dependencies using the Link Tasks button. To link Tasks 5 and 6, click the task name for Task 5 in the Task Name column and drag down through Task 6. Then, click the Task Tab, and click the **Link Tasks** button (looks like a chain link) under the Schedule group. Notice that the result is the same as typing 5 in the Predecessors column for Task 6.

5. *Enter dependencies and lag time using the Task Information dialog box.*
Double-click on the **Task Name** for **task 5**, Prepare project charter, and then
click on the **Predecessors tab** in the Task Information dialog box. Click in the
cell under Task Name, and then click the **Task Name** down arrow and select
Identify stakeholders. Click the **Type** drop down arrow to see the various types
of dependencies. For this task, you will keep the default type of finish-to-start.
Click the **Lag drop down arrow**, then **type -50%** and press **Enter**. (Lag means
there is a gap between tasks, and lead or negative lag means there is an overlap).
Your screen should resemble Figure A-29. Click **OK** to close the dialog box.
Notice that the Predecessor column for task 5 displays 2FS-50%, meaning there
is a finish-to-start relationship with task 2 and a lag of -50%, meaning the task
can start when task 2 is 50% completed.

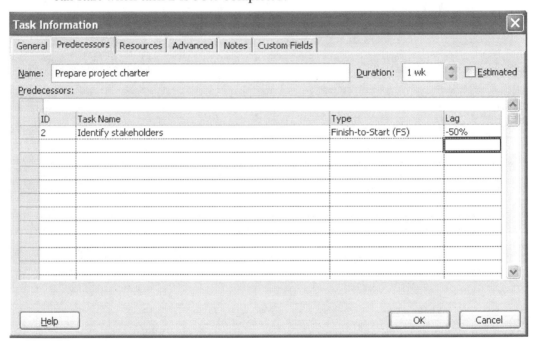

Figure A-29. Entering predecessor information using the task information dialog box

6. *Enter remaining dependencies.* **Link the other tasks** by either manually
entering the predecessors into the Predecessors column, by using the Link Tasks
button, or using the Task Information dialog box. Use the information in Figure
A-30 to make your entries. If you have entered all data correctly, the project
should end on 4/30, or April 30, 2010. (Note that you could manually enter a
Start date for tasks 22 and 23 to make those dates more realistic. The current
dependency shows them both ending one day before the project ends.)

Task Row	Task Name	Predecessors
3	Stakeholder register completed	2
4	Stakeholder management strategy completed	2
5	Prepare project charter	2FS-50%
6	Project charter completed	5
7	Prepare for kickoff meeting	2,6
8	Kickoff meeting completed	6,7
10	Prepare draft schedule	5,12FS-50%
11	Gantt chart completed	10
12	Prepare scope statement	5
13	Initial scope statement completed	12
15	Work on deliverable 1	12
16	Work on deliverable 2	18
17	Work on deliverable 3	18
18	Deliverable 1 completed	15
19	Deliverable 2 completed	16
20	Deliverable 3 completed	17
22	Track actual hours	43FF-1 day,2
23	Update project documents	43FF-1 day,3
41	Prepare final project report	18,19,20
42	Prepare final presentation	18,19,20
43	Project completed	41,42

Figure A-30. Predecessor information for Project A+

7. *Review the file.* If needed, click the **Zoom Out** button on the Zoom slider to adjust the timescale so all of the information shows on your screen. When you finish, your screen should resemble Figure A-31. Double-check your screen to make sure you entered the dependencies correctly.

	Task Mode	Task Name	Duration	Start	Finish	Predecessors
0		Project A+	64.5 days	Mon 2/1/10	Fri 4/30/10	
1		1 Initiating	10.5 days	Mon 2/1/10	Mon 2/15/10	
2		1.1 Identify stakeholders	1 wk	Mon 2/1/10	Fri 2/5/10	
3		1.2 Stakeholder register completed	0 days	Fri 2/5/10	Fri 2/5/10	2
4		1.3 Stakeholder management strategy completed	0 days	Fri 2/5/10	Fri 2/5/10	2
5		1.4 Prepare project charter	1 wk	Wed 2/3/10	Wed 2/10/10	2FS-50%
6		1.5 Project charter completed	0 days	Wed 2/10/10	Wed 2/10/10	5
7		1.6 Prepare for kickoff meeting	3 days	Wed 2/10/10	Mon 2/15/10	2,6
8		1.7 Kickoff meeting completed	0 days	Mon 2/15/10	Mon 2/15/10	6,7
9		2 Planning	9 days	Wed 2/10/10	Tue 2/23/10	
10		2.1 Prepare draft schedule	5 days	Tue 2/16/10	Tue 2/23/10	5,12FS-50%
11		2.2 Gantt chart completed	0 days	Tue 2/23/10	Tue 2/23/10	10
12		2.3 Prepare scope statement	8 days	Wed 2/10/10	Mon 2/22/10	5
13		2.4 Initial scope statement completed	0 days	Mon 2/22/10	Mon 2/22/10	12
14		3 Executing	45 days	Mon 2/22/10	Mon 4/26/10	
15		3.1 Work on deliverable 1	3 wks	Mon 2/22/10	Mon 3/15/10	12
16		3.2 Work on deliverable 2	5 wks	Mon 3/15/10	Mon 4/19/10	18
17		3.3 Work on deliverable 3	6 wks	Mon 3/15/10	Mon 4/26/10	18
18		3.4 Deliverable 1 completed	0 days	Mon 3/15/10	Mon 3/15/10	15
19		3.5 Deliverable 2 completed	0 days	Mon 4/19/10	Mon 4/19/10	16
20		3.6 Deliverable 3 completed	0 days	Mon 4/26/10	Mon 4/26/10	17
21		4 Monitoring and Controlling	63.5 days	Mon 2/1/10	Thu 4/29/10	
22		4.1 Track actual hours	1 day	Wed 4/28/10	Thu 4/29/10	43FF-1 day,2
23		4.2 Update project documents	1 day	Wed 4/28/10	Thu 4/29/10	43FF-1 day,3
24		4.3 Progress report 1	0 days	Mon 2/1/10	Mon 2/1/10	
25		4.4 Progress report 2	0 days	Mon 2/1/10	Mon 2/1/10	
26		4.5 Hold meetings	60.86 days	Thu 2/4/10	Thu 4/29/10	
40		5 Closing	4 days	Mon 4/26/10	Fri 4/30/10	
41		5.1 Prepare final project report	4 days	Mon 4/26/10	Fri 4/30/10	18,19,20
42		5.2 Prepare final presentation	4 days	Mon 4/26/10	Fri 4/30/10	18,19,20
43		5.3 Project completed	0 days	Fri 4/30/10	Fri 4/30/10	41,42

Figure A-31. Project A+ file with durations and dependencies entered

8. *Preview and save your file.* Click the **File** tab, and then select **Print** to preview and print your file, if desired. Make adjustments as needed back in the Task tab, and preview the file until it looks correct. When you are finished, **save** your schedule file again. Keep the file open for the next set of steps.

Gantt Charts, Network Diagrams, and Critical Path Analysis

Project 2010 shows a Gantt chart as the default view to the right of the Entry table. As described earlier in this text, network diagrams are often used to show task dependencies. This section explains important information about Gantt charts and network diagrams and describes how to make critical path information more visible in the Gantt Chart view.

Because you have already created task dependencies, you can now find the critical path for Project A+. You can view the critical tasks by changing the color of those items in the Gantt Chart view. Tasks on the critical path will automatically be red in the Network Diagram view. You can also view critical path information in the Schedule table or by using the Critical Tasks report.

To make the text for the critical path tasks appear in red on the Gantt chart:

1.   Change the critical tasks format. Using the schedule.mpp file you previously saved, click the **Format** tab, and then click the Critical Tasks check box in the Bar Styles group, as shown in Figure A-32. Notice that the critical tasks display in red in the Gantt chart.

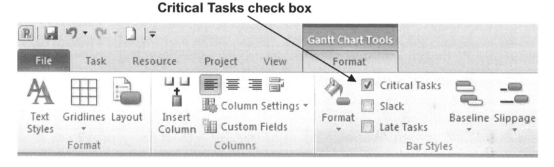

Figure A-32. Formatting critical tasks

2.   View the network diagram. Click the View tab, and then click the **Network Diagram** button under the Task Views group Click the **Zoom Out** button on the Zoom slider several times and watch the view change. Figure A-30 shows all of the tasks in the Project A+ network diagram. Note that milestone tasks, such as Stakeholder management strategy completed, the fourth box on the top, appear as pointed rectangular boxes, while other tasks appear as rectangles. Move your mouse over that box to see it in a larger view. Notice that tasks on the critical path automatically appear in red. A dashed line on a network diagram represents a page break. You often need to change some of the default settings for the Network Diagram view before printing it. As you can see, network diagrams can be messy, so you might prefer to highlight critical tasks on the Gantt chart as you did earlier for easier viewing.

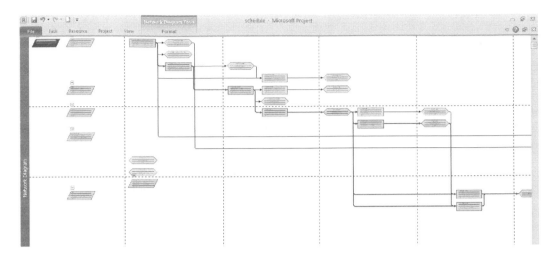

Figure A-34. Network diagram view

3.   *View the schedule table.* Click the **Gantt Chart** button under the **View** tab to return to Gantt Chart view. Right-click the **Select All** button to the left of the Task Mode column heading and select **Schedule**. Alternatively, you can click the **View** tab and click the **Tables** button under the Data group and then select **Schedule**. The Schedule table replaces the Entry table to the left of the Gantt Chart. Your screen should resemble Figure A-35. This view shows the start and finish (meaning the early start and early finish) and late start and late finish dates for each task, as well as free and total slack. Right-click the **Select All** button and select **Entry** to return to the Entry table view.

Select All button   **Schedule table**

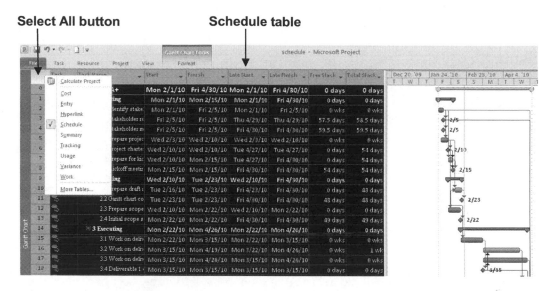

Figure A-35. Schedule table view

4. *Open the Reports dialog box.* Click the **Project** tab, and then click the **Reports** button under the Reports group. Double-click **Overview** to open the Overview Reports dialog box, and then double-click **Critical Tasks**. A Critical Tasks report as of today's date is displayed.

5. *Close the report and save your file.* When you are finished examining the Critical Tasks report, click the **Tasks**. Click the **Save** button on the Quick Access toolbar to save your final schedule.mpp file, showing the Entry table and Gantt chart view. Close Project 2010 if you are not continuing to the next section.

HELP: If you want to download the Project 2010 file schedule.mpp to check your work or continue to the next section, a copy is available on the companion Web site for this text at www.intropm.com.

Next you will explore some of the cost and resource management features of Project 2010.

PROJECT COST AND RESOURCE MANAGEMENT

Many people do not use Project 2010 for cost or resource management. Most organizations have more established cost management software products and procedures in place, and many people simply do not know how to use the cost or resource management features of Project 2010. However, these features make it possible to integrate total project information more easily. This section offers brief instructions for entering fixed and variable cost estimates, assigning resources to tasks, viewing resource histograms, and entering actual cost and schedule information after establishing a baseline plan. It also explains how to use Project 2010 for earned value management.

More details on these features are available in Project Help, online tutorials, or other texts. See other chapters of this text for information on some of these concepts.

Entering Fixed and Variable Cost Estimates

You can enter costs as fixed or variable. Fixed costs include costs like a specific quantity of materials or consultants hired at a fixed cost. Variable costs vary based on the amount of materials or hours people work. On many projects, human resource costs are the largest percentage of total project costs.

Entering Fixed Costs in the Cost Table

The Cost table allows you to easily enter fixed costs related to each task. You will enter a fixed cost of $200 related to Task 15, Work on deliverable 1.

To enter a fixed cost:

1. Display the Cost Table view. Open your Project 2010 file schedule.mpp, if necessary. Right-click the **Select All** button to the left of the Task Mode column heading and select **Cost**. The Cost table replaces the Entry table to the left of the Gantt chart. Widen the Task Name column and move the **split bar** to the right, as needed, until you see the entire Cost table. **Widen** the Task Name column to reveal all of the text in that column.

2. Enter a fixed cost. In the **Fixed Cost column for Task 15,** Work on deliverable 1, type **200** and press **Enter**. Notice that the Total Cost and Remaining Cost columns reflect this entry, and changes are made to the summary task, Executing, as well. Your screen should resemble Figure A-36

Select All button   **Fixed Cost column of cost table**

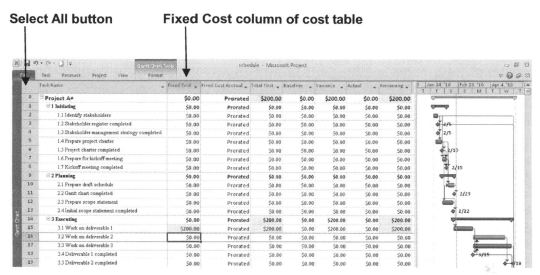

Figure A-36. Entering a fixed cost

Entering Resource Information and Cost Estimates

Several methods are available for entering resource information in Project 2010. The Resource Sheet allows you to enter the resource name, initials, resource group, maximum units, standard rate, overtime rate, cost/use, accrual method, base calendar, and code. Once you have established resources in the Resource Sheet, you can assign those resources to tasks in the Entry table with the list arrow that appears when you click a cell in the Resource Names column. The Resource Names column is the last column of the Entry table. You can also use other methods for assigning resources, such as using the Assign Resources button or using the split window, which is the recommended approach to have the most control over how resources are assigned because Project 2010 makes several assumptions about resources assignments that might mess up your schedule or costs. Next, you will enter information for three people working on Project A+ and assign them to a few tasks using various methods.

To enter basic information about each person into the Resource Sheet and assign them to tasks using the Entry table and toolbar:

1. *Display the Resource Sheet view*. Click the **View** tab, and then click the **Resource Sheet** button under the Resource Views group.

2. *Enter resource information*. Enter the information from Figure A-37 into the Resource Sheet. The three resources names are **Kathy, Dan, and Scott**. The Std. Rate and Ovt. Rate for Kathy is **40**, and the Std. and Ovt. Rates for Dan and Scott are **30**. Type the information as shown and press the **Tab** key to move to the next field. When you type the standard and overtime rates, you can just type the number, such as 40, and Project 2010 will automatically enter $40.00/hr. The

An Introduction to Project Management, Third Edition

426

standard and overtime rates entered are based on hourly rates. You can also enter annual salaries by typing the annual salary number followed by /y for "per year." Your screen should resemble Figure A-37 when you are finished entering the resource data.

Resource Name	Type	Material	Initials	Group	Max	Std. Rate	Ovt. Rate	Cost/Use	Accrue At	Base Calendar
Kathy	Work		K		100%	$40.00/hr	$40.00/hr	$0.00	Prorated	Standard
Dan	Work		D		100%	$30.00/hr	$30.00/hr	$0.00	Prorated	Standard
Scott	Work		S		100%	$30.00/hr	$30.00/hr	$0.00	Prorated	Standard

Figure A-37. Resource sheet view with resource data entered

TIP: If you know that some people will be available for a project only part time, enter their percentage of availability in the Max Units column of the Resource Sheet. Project 2010 will then automatically assign those people based on their maximum units. For example, if someone can work only 50% of his or her time on a project throughout most of the project, enter 50% in the Max Units column for that person. When you enter that person as a resource for a task, his or her default number of hours will be 50% of a standard eight-hour workday, or four hours per day. You can also enter the number of hours each person is scheduled to work, as shown later.

3. *Assign resources to tasks*. Click the **View** tab, select the **Gantt Chart** button under the Task Views group, and then click the **Select All** button and switch back to the **Entry** table. Widen the Task Name column and move the split bar to reveal the Resource Names column, if needed.

4. *Assign Kathy to task 2, Identify stakeholders*. Click in the **Resource Names** cell for **row 2**. Click the list arrow, click on the **checkbox** by **Kathy**, and then press **Enter** or click on another cell. Notice that the resource choices are the names you just entered in the Resource Sheet. Also notice that after you select a resource by checking the appropriate checkbox, his or her name appears on the Gantt chart, as shown in Figure A-38. To assign more than one resource to a task using the list arrow, simply select another checkbox. Note that Project 2010 will assume that each resource is assigned full-time to tasks using this method since the task is in automatically schedule mode.

Figure A-38. Resource assigned using the entry table

5. *Assign two resources to a task*. Click in the **Resource Names** cell for **row 5.** Click the **list arrow**, then click on the **checkbox by Dan and Kathy,** and then press **Enter**. Notice that both resource names appear in the Resource Names

An Introduction to Project Management, Third Edition

column and on the Gantt chart for this task, and the task duration remains at 1 week.

6. *Change the resource assignments.* Click in the **Resource Names** cell for **Task 2**, Identify stakeholders, click the **list arrow**, and add **Dan** as another resource. Notice that when you change an original resource assignment, Project prompts you for how you want to handle the change, as shown in Figure A-39. Click the **Exclamation point** symbol to read your options. *This is an important change!* In past versions of Project, resource additions would change schedules automatically unless the user entered them a certain way. Now you have much more control of what happens to your schedule and costs. In this case, we do want to accept the default of keeping the duration constant.

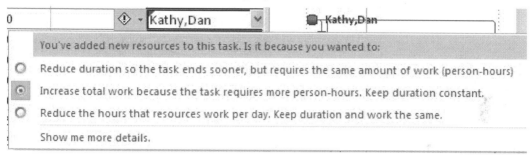

Figure A-39. Options when additional resources are added to tasks

7. *Review the cost table.* Right-click the **Select All** button to the left of the Task Mode column heading and select **Cost**. Notice that costs have been added to the tasks where you added resources. Project assumes that people are assigned full-time to tasks. It is showing a cost of $2,800 each for Task 2 and Task 5. In the next section, you will see how to control resources entries even more.

To control resource and work assignments using the Resource details window:

1. Open the Resource Form. Click the **Resources** tab, and then click on the **Details** button under the Properties group. The Cost Table and Gantt Chart view is displayed at the top of the screen and a Resource Form is displayed at the bottom of the screen, as shown in Figure A-40. Also notice the symbol in the Indicators column showing that resources are overallocated. This is because Project 2010 assumes every task is assigned full-time, so since Kathy is scheduled on two tasks on the same day, it says she is overallocated.

> **TIP:** You can right-click on the lower screen to review see additional forms/views. You can click the Select All button at the top right of the screen to view different tables at the top of the screen. You want to make sure that resource and work hour assignments do not adjust your schedules in ways you did not intend.

2. Make tasks 2 and 5 manually scheduled. Click the **Select All** button and switch to the **Entry table**. Click the drop-down in the **Task Mode** column for Tasks 2 and 5 to make them **manually scheduled**. Notice the symbol in the Indicator column. This symbol means that tasks are currently overallocated. This is because when you assigned resources, Project 2010 assumed they were working full-time or 40 hours per week on each task. Since these two tasks have days that overlap, there is an overallocation.

3. Change the number of Work hours. Select Task 2, **Identify stakeholders** in the top window, and then click the **Work** column in the Resource Form window for Kathy in the lower part of your screen. Type **10h**, press **Enter**, and then click the **OK** button, as shown in Figure A-40.

Overallocation indicator   Manually scheduled task   Changing # work hours

OK button

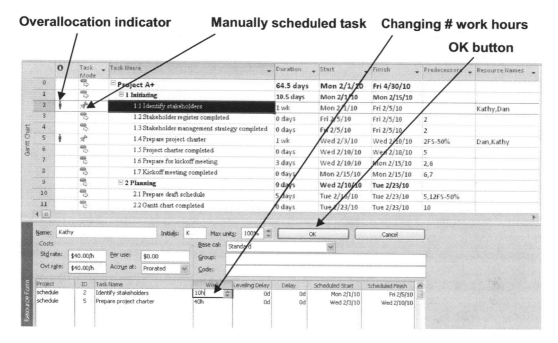

Figure A-40. Changing Work hours for tasks

4. *Enter the work hours and review the Gantt chart.* Click **Next** in the lower window, and change Dan's work hours to 10h for Task 2 as well. Notice in the Gantt chart that the duration for Task 2 is still one week, but there is still an overallocation. Click on **Task 5** in the upper window, and change the **Work** hours for both Dan and Kathy to 10h for this task as well. Note: Click the **Next** or **Previous** buttons in the lower window to access different resources, and click OK when finished. The overallocation indicator should now disappear because the number of hours has been reduced from the default of 8 hours per day, or 40 hours for a 5-day task

5. Examine the new cost information. Click the Select All button, and then click **Cost** to view the Cost table. Tasks 2 and 5 each show only $700 for Total Cost.

6. *Close the file without saving it.* Close the file, but do not save the changes you made.

Using the New Team Planner Feature

Another way to assign resources and reduce overallocations is by using the new Team Planner feature. Assume you have two people assigned to work on a project, Brian and Cindy, as shown in Figure A-41. Notice that Brian is assigned to work on both Task 1 and Task 2 full-time the first week. Therefore, Brian is overallocated. Cindy is scheduled to work on Task 3 full-time the second week, and Task 4, also scheduled for the second week, is not assigned yet.

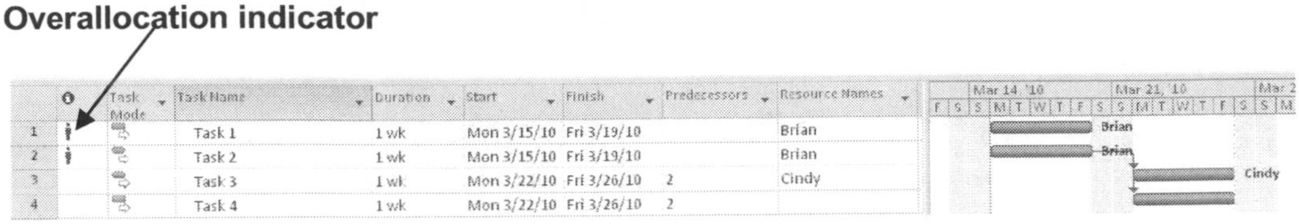

Overallocation indicator

Figure A-41. Overallocated resource

You can click on the Team Planner view under the View tab to see a screen similar to the top section of Figure A-42. Notice that Brian has both Tasks 1 and 2 assigned to him at the same time. These tasks and Brian's name display in red to show the overallocation. Cindy is assigned Task 3 the following week, and Task 4 is unassigned. By simply clicking and dragging Task 4 straight up so it is under Brian in Week 2 and Task 2 straight down so it is under Cindy in Week 1, you can reassign those tasks and remove Brian's overallocation, as shown in the bottom section of Figure A-42. Many people will appreciate the simplicity of this new feature!

Before moving tasks in the Team Planner View:

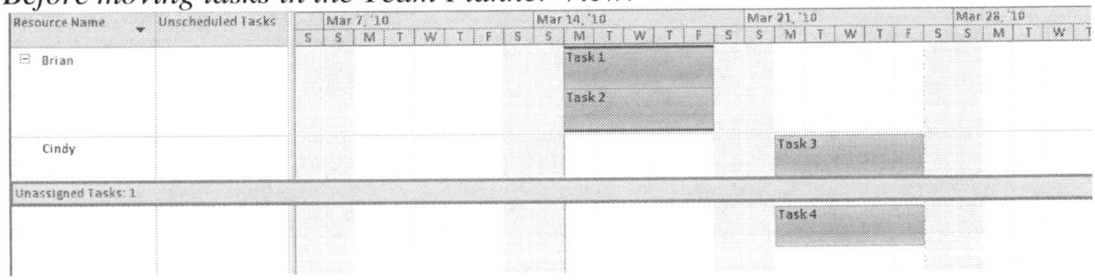

After moving tasks in the Team Planner View:

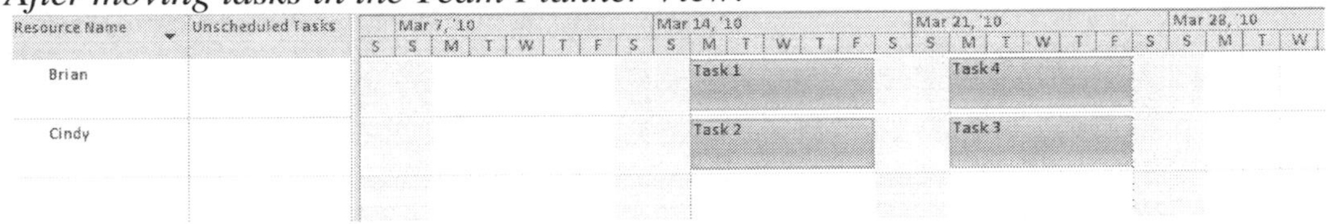

Figure A-42. Adjusting resource assignments using the Team Planner feature

Entering Baseline Plans, Actual Costs, and Actual Times

After entering tasks in a WBS, establishing task durations and dependencies, and assigning costs and resources, you are ready to establish a baseline plan. By comparing the information in your baseline plan to actual progress during the course of the project, you can identify and solve problems. After the project ends, you can use the baseline and actual information to plan similar, future projects more accurately. To use Project 2010 to help control projects and view earned value information, you must establish a baseline plan, enter actual costs, and enter actual durations. In the next series of steps you will use a new file called tracking.mpp that you downloaded from the companion Web site for this text (www.intropm.com).

To save a file as a baseline and enter actual information:

1. *Open the file called tracking.mpp.* Notice that this short project was planned to start on January 5, 2009 and end on February 13, have three resources assigned to it, and cost $11,200. Click the **Project** tab, click the **Set Baseline** button under the Schedule group, and click **Set Baseline**, as shown in Figure A-43.

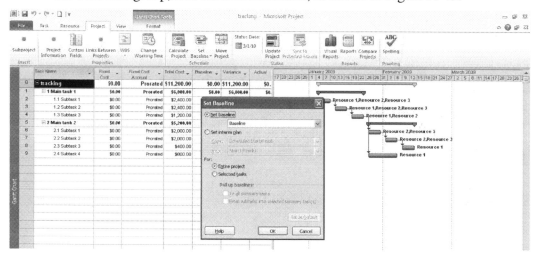

Figure A-43. Saving a baseline

2. *Save the file as a baseline.* Examine the **Set Baseline** dialog box. Click the drop-down arrow to see that you can set up to ten baselines. Accept the default to save the entire project. Click **OK**. Notice that the Baseline column changes to blue.

3. *Display the Tracking table.* Click the **Task** tab, right-click the **Select All** button, and then click **Tracking** to view the tracking table. Move the split bar to the right to reveal all of the columns in the table. Move your mouse over each tracking button in the top line of the Schedule group to see what it does. Your screen should resemble Figure A-44.

432

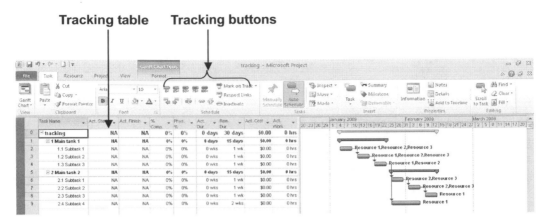

Tracking table   **Tracking buttons**

Figure A-44. Using the tracking table and tracking buttons

4. *Mark Tasks 2 though 4 as 100% complete*. Click the Task Name for Task 2, **Subtask 1 under Main task 1**, and drag down through Task 4 to highlight those tasks. Click the **100% Complete** button on the Ribbon. The columns with dates, durations, and cost information should now contain data instead of the default values, such as NA or 0. The % Comp. column should display 100%. Adjust column widths if needed. Your screen should resemble Figure A-45. Notice that the Gantt chart bars for those three tasks now have a black line through them.

Figure A-45. Tracking table information

5. *Enter actual completion dates for Task 6*. Click the Task Name for Task 6, **Subtask 1 under Main task 2**, click the **Mark on Track drop-down**, and then click **Update Tasks.** The Update Tasks dialog box opens. For Task 6, enter the Actual Start date as **1/26/09** (the same as the Current start date) and the Actual Finish date as **2/9/09** (later than the Current finish date), as shown in Figure A-46. Click **OK**. Notice how the information in the tracking sheet has changed.

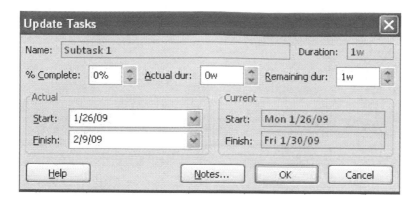

Figure A-46. Update Tasks dialog box

6. *View the Tracking Gantt chart*. Right-click on the far left of the screen where it says Gantt chart, and then click **Tracking Gantt** to quickly switch to that view. Move the **split bar** and adjust column widths as needed. Use the **horizontal scroll bar** in the Gantt chart window to the right (move the slider to the left) to see symbols on the Tracking Gantt chart. Use the Zoom slider on the lower right of the screen to adjust the timescale so you can see all of the symbols. Your screen should resemble Figure A-47. The blue bar for task 6 shows the actual time you just entered. Notice that the delay in this one task on the critical path has caused the planned completion date for the entire project to slip. Also notice the Indicator column to the far left. The check marks show that tasks are completed.

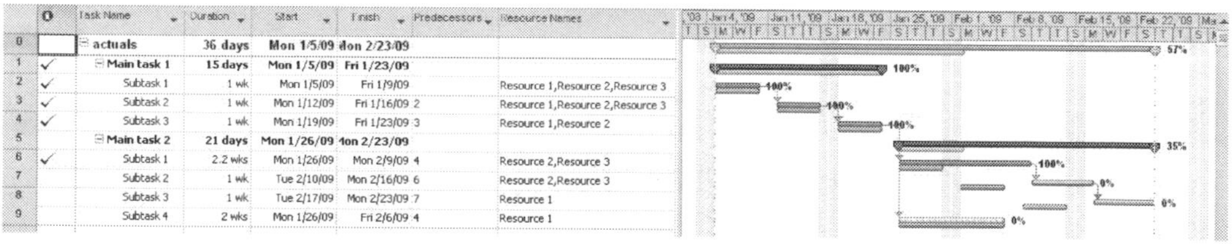

Figure A-47. Tracking Gantt chart view

7. *Save your file as a new file named actuals.mpp.* Click **File** on the Menu bar, and then click **Save As**. Name the file **actuals**, and then click **Save**.

Notice the additional information available on the Tracking Gantt chart. Completed tasks have 100% by their symbols on the Tracking Gantt chart. Tasks that have not started yet display 0%. Tasks in progress, such as Task 5, show the percentage of the work completed (35% in this example). The project summary task bar indicates that the entire project is 57% complete. Viewing the Tracking Gantt chart allows you to easily see your schedule progress against the baseline plan. After you have entered some actuals, you can review earned value information for the initiating tasks of this project.

VIEWING EARNED VALUE MANAGEMENT DATA

Earned value management is an important project management technique for measuring project performance. (See Chapter 7 of this text or other resources for detailed information on earned value management). Because you have entered actual information, you can now view earned value information in Project 2010. You can also view an earned value report using the new visual reports feature.

To view earned value information:

1. *View the Earned Value table.* Using the actual file you just saved (or downloaded from the companion Web site), click the **Select All** button, select **More Tables,** and double-click **Earned Value.** Move the split bar to the right to reveal all of the columns, as shown in Figure A-48. Note that the Earned Value table includes columns for each earned value acronym, such as SV, CV, etc., as explained in this text. Also note that the EAC (Estimate at Completion) is higher than the BAC (Budget at Completion) starting with Task 6, where the task took longer than planned to complete. Task 0 shows a VAC (Variance at Completion) of ($3,360.00), meaning the project is projected to cost $3,360 more than planned at completion. Remember that not all of the actual information has been entered yet. Also note that the date on your computer must be set later than the date of a completed task for the data to calculate properly.

	Task Name	Planned Value - PV (BCWS)	Earned Value - EV (BCWP)	AC (ACWP)	SV	CV	EAC	BAC	VAC
0	actuals	$11,200.00	$8,000.00	$10,400.00	($3,200.00)	($2,400.00)	$14,560.00	$11,200.00	($3,360.00)
1	Main task 1	$6,000.00	$6,000.00	$6,000.00	$0.00	$0.00	$6,000.00	$6,000.00	$0.00
2	Subtask 1	$2,400.00	$2,400.00	$2,400.00	$0.00	$0.00	$2,400.00	$2,400.00	$0.00
3	Subtask 2	$2,400.00	$2,400.00	$2,400.00	$0.00	$0.00	$2,400.00	$2,400.00	$0.00
4	Subtask 3	$1,200.00	$1,200.00	$1,200.00	$0.00	$0.00	$1,200.00	$1,200.00	$0.00
5	Main task 2	$5,200.00	$2,000.00	$4,400.00	($3,200.00)	($2,400.00)	$11,440.00	$5,200.00	($6,240.00)
6	Subtask 1	$2,000.00	$2,000.00	$4,400.00	$0.00	($2,400.00)	$4,400.00	$2,000.00	($2,400.00)
7	Subtask 2	$2,000.00	$0.00	$0.00	($2,000.00)	$0.00	$2,000.00	$2,000.00	$0.00
8	Subtask 3	$400.00	$0.00	$0.00	($400.00)	$0.00	$400.00	$400.00	$0.00
9	Subtask 4	$800.00	$0.00	$0.00	($800.00)	$0.00	$800.00	$800.00	$0.00

Figure A-48. Earned value table

2. *View the earned value chart.* Click the **Project** tab, and then click **Visual Reports** under the Reports group to open the Visual Reports dialog box. Click **Earned Value Over Time Report**, as shown in Figure A-49. Notice the sample of the selected report on the right side of the dialog box. If you have Excel and other necessary software, you could click View to see the resulting report as Project 2010automatically creates Excel data and a chart based on your current file. Click the **Close** button of the Visual Reports dialog box.

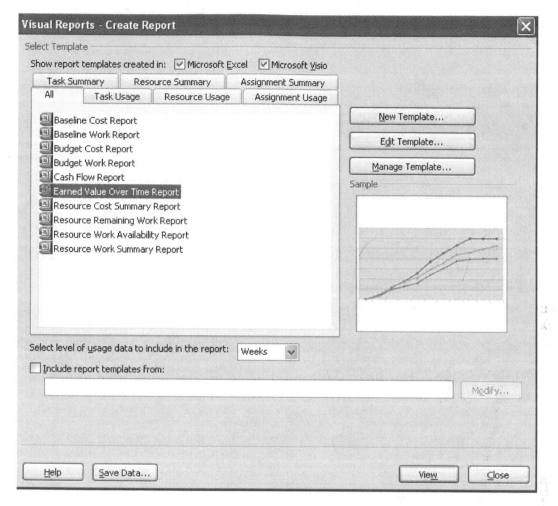

Figure A-49. Visual reports dialog box

3. *Save and close the file.* Click the **Save** button on the Standard toolbar, and then close the file. You can also exit Project 2010 and take a break, if desired.

Next you will use a few more features of Project 2010 to help tie your Project to your other applications.

INTEGRATING PROJECT 2010 WITH OTHER APPLICATIONS

Project 2010 provides many different tables, views, reports, and formatting features to aid in project communications, as you have seen in the previous sections. This section highlights some common reports and views. It also describes how to insert hyperlinks within Project 2010 to other project documents.

Common Reports

As you have seen, you can easily change and print out various table views in Project 2010, such as the Entry Table, Cost Table, Schedule Table, and so on. Many different reports are also available in Project 2010, categorized as follows when clicking the Reports button under the Project tab.

- Overview reports include:

  - Project Summary

  - Top-Level Tasks

  - Critical Tasks

  - Milestones

  - Working Days

- Current reports include:
  - Unstarted Tasks
  - Tasks Starting Soon
  - Tasks In Progress
  - Completed Tasks
  - Should Have Started Tasks
  - Slipping Tasks

- Costs reports include:

  - Cash Flow

  - Budget

  - Overbudget Tasks

  - Overbudget Resources

  - Earned Value

- Assignments reports include:

  - Who Does What

  - Who Does What When

  - To-do List

  - Overallocated Resources

- Workload reports include:
  - Task Usage
  - Resource Usage
- Custom allows you to customize and save your own report formats.

By selecting the Visual Reports button from the Project tab, you can access the following types of reports:

- Baseline Cost Report
- Baseline Work Report
- Budget Cost Report
- Budget Work Report
- Cash Flow Report
- Earned Value Over Time Report
- Resource Cost Summary Report
- Resource Remaining Work Report
- Resource Work Availability Report
- Resource Work Summary Report

Feel free to experiment with the various reports available in Project 2010 or to create your own.

Creating Hyperlinks to Other Files

Some people like to use their Project 2010 file as a main source of information for many different project documents. To do this, you can simply insert a hyperlink to other document files. For example, you can create a hyperlink to the file with the stakeholder register you listed as a milestone in your Task Name column earlier.

To insert a hyperlink within a Project 2010 file:

1. Open the **schedule.mpp** file. Use the file you saved earlier or download it from the companion Web site for this text. The Entry table and Gantt Chart view should display.

2. Select the task in which you want to insert a hyperlink. Click the Task Name for Task 3, **Stakeholder register completed**.

3. Open the Insert Hyperlink dialog box. Right-click, then click **Hyperlink**. The Insert Hyperlink dialog box opens, as shown in Figure A-50. You will have different folders visible based on your computer's directory structure.

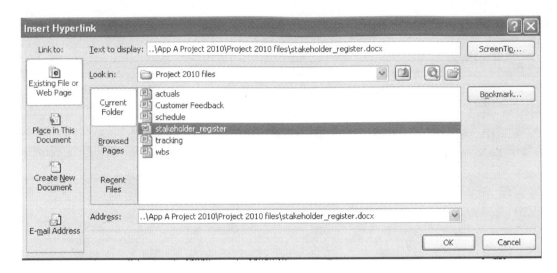

Figure A-50. Insert hyperlink dialog box

4. *Double-click the filename of the hyperlink file.* Change the **Look in:** information until you find where you have saved the files you downloaded for this appendix. Double-click the Word file named **stakeholder_register**, and then click **OK**. A Hyperlink button appears in the Indicators column to the left of the Task Name for Task 3. Move your mouse over the hyperlink button until the mouse pointer changes to the Hand symbol to reveal the name of the hyperlinked file. If you click on it, the file will open.

You have really just touched the surface of Project 2010's powerful features, but you probably know more than most people who have this software! There are several books with more detailed information on using Project 2010 that you can use to learn even more, or you can experiment with the software and Help feature to understand it more.

DISCUSSION QUESTIONS

1. What are some unique features of project management software?

2. What are the new features of Project 2010?

3. How do you create a WBS in Project 2010?

4. How do you enter task durations and establish dependencies between tasks?

5. What is the recommended method for assigning resources to tasks? Why is it the preferred method?

6. How can you use the Team Planner to assign resources and reduce overallocations?

7. How do you establish a baseline in Project 2010 and enter actual information?

8. What type of information do you see in the Earned Value table?

9. What are some of the reports built-in to Project 2010? Which ones do you think are commonly used?

10. How can you access other application files from within Project 2010?

EXERCISES

1. To make sure you understand the information in this appendix, perform the steps yourself. Print out the following screens or send them to your instructor, as directed:
    a. The adjusted Customer Feedback.mpp file as shown in Figure A-7.
    b. The Schedule table view for the Customer Feedback file, similar to Figure A-11.
    c. The Customer Feedback file filtered to show only critical tasks, similar to Figure A-15.
    d. The wbs file, similar to Figure A-21, but without the Closing tasks indented. Also type your first and last name after the word Initiating, the first Task Name.
    e. Create a new Project file called mywbs that shows the WBS for a generic project. Make the main categories phase 1, phase 2, phase 3, and phase 4. Include at least four tasks and one milestone under each of these main categories, using meaningful, fictitious names for them. Enter 0 for the duration of the milestones, but do not enter any durations for the other tasks. Be sure to indent tasks and show the outline numbers before printing.

2. Continue performing the steps in this appendix, starting with the section called Developing the Schedule. Print out the following screens or send them to your instructor, as directed:

   a. The schedule file with durations and dependencies entered, similar to Figure A-27. Type your first and last name after the word Initiating, the first Task Name, before printing or handing in the file.

   b. The earned value table, similar to Figure A-48. Again type your name after the word Initiating, the first Task Name.

   c. Continue performing the steps, even if you do not have to print out more screens. Write a one-to-two page paper describing the capabilities of Project 2010 and your opinion of this software. What do you like and dislike about it?

3. Use some of the information in the body of this text to practice your Project 2010 skills.

   a. Review the sample WBS for the Just-In-Time Training project provided in Chapter 4, Figure 4-10. Enter the WBS into Project 2010. Indent tasks and use the automatic numbering feature. Print or hand in your file.

   b. Use the information in Figure 4-14 for Project X to create a Gantt chart, as shown in Figure 4-18. Also create the network diagram for Project X, as shown in Figure 4-16. Make sure both will print out on one page each, then print or send them to your instructor Assume the start date was 6/9/09, or June 9, 2009.

   c. Make up actual information for Project X. Assume some tasks are completed as planned, some take more time, and some take less time. View and then print out or hand in the tracking Gantt chart.

4. If you are doing a team project as part of your class or for a project at work, use Project 2010 to create a detailed file describing the work you plan to do for the project.

   a. Create a detailed WBS, including several milestones, estimate task durations, link tasks, add tasks to the timeline, enter resources and costs, assign resources, and so on. Save your file as a baseline and print it out send it to your instructor, as desired.

b.   Track your progress on your team project by entering actual cost and schedule information. Create a new baseline file if there have been a lot of changes. View earned value information when you are halfway through the project or course. Continue tracking your progress until the project or course is finished. Print or send your Gantt chart, Project Summary report, Earned Value table, and relevant information to your instructor.

c.   Write a two- to three-page report describing your experience. What did you learn about Project 2010 from this exercise? How do you think Project 2010 helps in managing a project? You may also want to interview people who use Project 2010 for their experiences and suggestions.

COMPANION WEB SITE

Visit the free companion Web site for this text at **www.intropm.com** to access template files, online quizzes, Jeopardy-like games, Microsoft Project files, links to sites mentioned in the text, and other information to help you learn more about this important field. Instructors must contact the author at schwalbe@augsburg.edu to gain access to the instructor site. Anyone can access the student site.

END NOTES

[1]TopTenREVIEWS™, "Project Management Software," (http://project-management-software-review.toptenreviews.com) (accessed June 17, 2009).

Appendix B:

Brief Guide to @task

INTRODUCTION

As mentioned in Chapter 1 and Appendix A, @task is the most popular online project management software tool. As stated on their Web site in July 2009, "Over 1,600 of the world's leading organizations have selected @task to help them validate business initiatives, fully utilize their resources, and enjoy real-time visibility into project status. @task is the world's most popular project and portfolio management software for companies committed to making the most of their resources."[1] Some well-known companies using @task include Google, Boeing, Whirlpool, Toyota, Coca Cola, Walt Disney, Proctor and Gamble, NASA, and Amazon.com. According to Ty Kiisel, AtTask, Inc. Content Manager, the typical company using @task has 500 users.

"AtTask is proving to be the definitive solution for companies wanting tools that effectively focus their workforce on the most relevant activities," says Scott Johnson, CEO of AtTask. "Even in difficult economic times, we are pleased that our product innovation and leadership is resonating with businesses who are pushing for greater success in their own organizations." Gartner analyst Lars Mieritz adds, "Against a backdrop of flat 2009 budgets compared with 2008, the top business priorities revolve around reducing costs and being more effective. As such, the PPM function takes on a pivotal role during tough economic times, when limited resources put a different perspective on analyzing, prioritizing, selecting and delivering projects and programs." [2]

This brief guide summarizes the powerful capabilities of @task. You can follow step-by-step instructions on using @task to create a new project, import a Microsoft Project file, adjust screen elements, and use filters, views, and reports. This appendix also provides brief step-by-step instructions for using some of the portfolio management features of @task.

FEATURES OF @TASK

According to their Web site (www.attask.com), "@task is the only software that provides Management, Collaboration, and Integration tools in a design that is easy to use and full of powerful features that help companies get work done." [3]

Management features of @task fall under the following categories:
- Portfolio Management
- Project Management
- Demand Management
- Resource Management
- Capacity Planning
- Time Management
- Process Improvement
- Auditing
- Collaboration Features

Collaboration features include:

- Task Management & Scheduling
- Reports & Dashboards
- Real-time Projections
- Document Management
- Status Updates
- Notifications
- Notes & Discussions

Integration features include:

- Software Development Kit (SDK)
- Turnkey Integrations
- Partnered Integrations
- Multiple Delivery
- Universal Compatibility
- Customization
- Language Neutral
- Location Neutral
- Technical

You can read more about these features on @task's Web site under Features or in their user manuals.

USING @TASK TO HELP MANAGE INDIVIDUAL PROJECTS

Anyone can use a trial version of @task by visiting their Web site at www.attask.com and speaking to a sales representative. In order to write this tutorial, @task set up an account for me called augcol. You need to use this account to access the sample data used for the portfolio management section of this appendix.

Before You Begin

NOTE: You need to be running a browser, such as Internet Explorer 6/XP or 7+, Firefox 2+, Safari, Chrome, or Camino. You must also go to the companion Web site for this text at www.intropm.com to get a user name and password information as well as any updated instructions for using @task. These instructions were written in July 2009 using Release 11, and @task has frequent updates. Some of the screen shots may vary, so it is best to use the updated information on the companion Web site and view the latest help information. Also be aware that several people may use the same user account, so follow instructions carefully. **If you want to have your own secure evaluation account, fill out a request form at www.attask.com**.

The first step to mastering @task is to become familiar with the major screen elements, help facility, and user manuals. This section describes each of these features.

Starting @task and Understanding the Main Screen Elements

To start @task:

> *1. Access @task.* From your web browser, type **https://augcol.attask-ondemand.com/attask/home.cmd**. Enter your **user name** and **password** (available from the companion Web site for this text)**,** and then click **Submit**. Your screen should resemble Figure B-1. Notice that this screen is showing options from the Home context. You can select different options from either the contextual menu or in the section area.

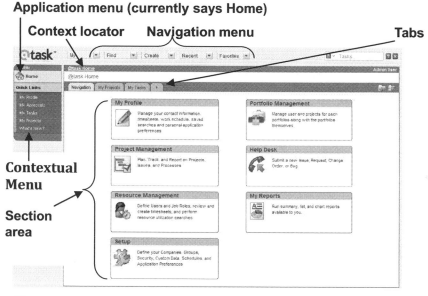

Figure B-1. @task main or home screen

> *2. Access My Profile.* Click the **My** dropdown in the Navigation Menu, and select **My Profile**, or click on My Profile under Quick Links in the contextual menu. Your screen should resemble Figure B-2. Notice that you can access Information, Timesheets, My Dashboards, Personal Time, Saved Searches, and Interfaces.

An Introduction to Project Management, Third Edition

446

Application menu (My Profile)

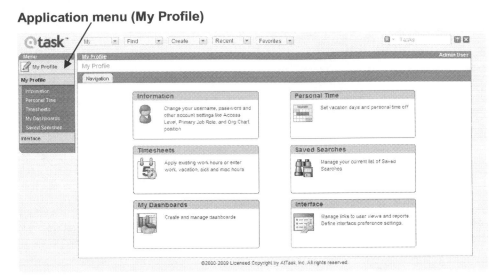

Figure B-2. My profile screen

3. *Access Project Management.* Click the Application menu at the top where it first says **My Profile** so the other application choices are visible, and then click on **Project Management**. Your screen should resemble Figure B-3. Notice the various options available.

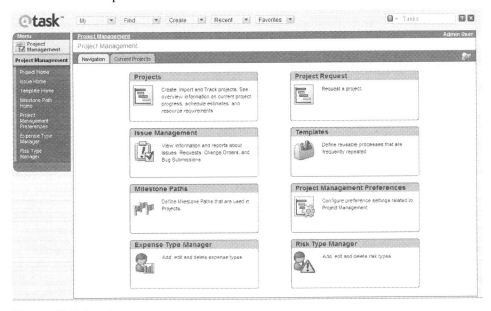

Figure B-3. Project management screen

An Introduction to Project Management, Third Edition

NOTE: You need to be registered for a separate @task community site account to access the User Manuals , Video Tutorials, etc. You will not see these help options using your account unless you login to the community site. See the companion Web site for details if you want to access the community site. **You can just read steps 4 and 5 to know that extensive help is available.**

4. *Access Help.* Click the **Help icon** in the upper right of the screen (question mark icon). Notice the different options available for help, as shown in Figure B-4 (FAQs, Forums, Idea Share, User Manuals, and Video Tutorials).

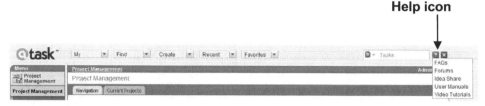

Figure B-4. Help Options in @task

5. *View user manuals.* Click the **User manuals** option, and then click **Quick Start Guide**, as shown in Figure B-5. Review information in this manual. View other user manuals to get familiar with the great information available online about this powerful software. **Close** the Help window to return to the main @task screen.

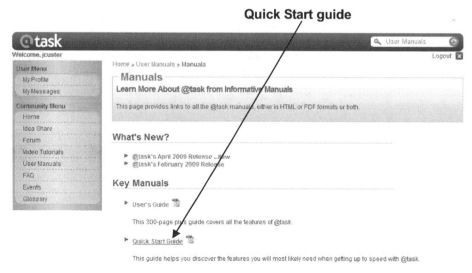

Figure B-5. Accessing the Quick Start guide

An Introduction to Project Management, Third Edition

Creating a New Project in @task

Next, you will create a new project and begin to enter tasks using the Gantt chart, similar to how you entered tasks in Project 2007 or 2010. Note that there are several additional ways to enter tasks, such as entering task details and using the task worksheet. Most people use the Gantt chart to enter task information, as shown below.

> 1. *Access the New Project screen.* From the Project Management screen, click the upper left box in the section area called **Projects**. Your screen should resemble figure B-6.

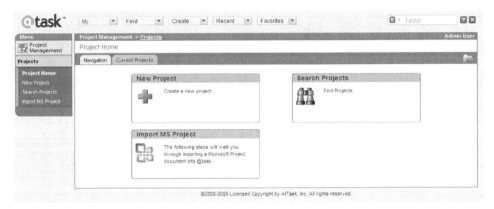

Figure B-6. Project home screen

> 2. *Access the Project Details screen.* Click the upper left box in the section area called **New Project** to access the Project Details screen, as shown in Figure B-7. (Note: You can also click on the Create dropdown, and then select Project as alternatives for steps 1 and 2).

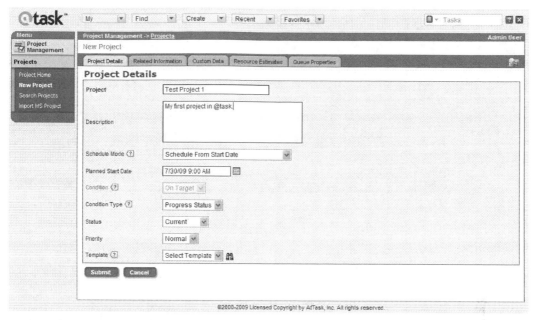

Figure B-7. Project details screen

3. *Enter and review project details.* Type **Test Project 1** in the Project name textbox and **My first project in @task** in the Description textbox, as shown in Figure B-7. Do not change the other information. The Planned Start Date defaults to the current date. Click **Submit**, and then Click on the **Gantt Chart** option. (It may take a few seconds for the Gantt chart to load.) Notice that the Gantt chart looks very similar to one in Project 2007 or 2010.

4. *Enter task names.* Click under the Name column where it says "*+Add Task...*" Click on the resulting Task name and type **Main task 1** in Row 1, and then press **Enter**. Type **Subtask A** in Row 2 and press **Enter**, and then type **Subtask B** in Row 3 and press **Enter twice**. Your screen should resemble Figure B-8.

450

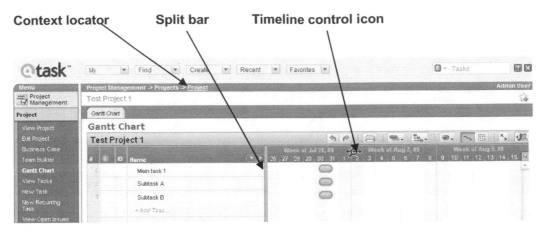

Context locator   **Split bar**   **Timeline control icon**

Figure B-8. Gantt chart for entering task information

5.   *Indent tasks*. Click on **Subtask A,** Click the now visible **Task Edit icon** in the right section of that cell, and then click **Indent Tasks**. Indent Subtask B to make it a subtask as well. You can also right-click on a task row to indent it, outdent it, edit it, mark it as completed, delete it, or perform other operations on it. You can also move the split bar to reveal more of less of the Gantt chart, similar to Project 2007 or 2010. To adjust the timescale, click and drag on the Timeline Control icon.

6.   *Delete the project*. Click **Delete Project** in the lower left part of the screen in the contextual menu, and then click **OK**. If you want to save a file, you would click the Save icon at the bottom left of the screen, and then click OK

7.   *Return to the Projects screen.* Click **Submit** to confirm that you want to delete the project and return to the Project Home screen, as shown in figure B-9.

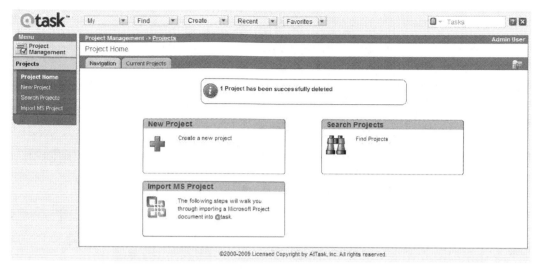

Figure B-9. Project home screen

Importing a Microsoft Project File into @Task

Instead of typing a lot of new information, next you will create a new project by importing the schedule.mpp file you created in Appendix A using Project 2007 or 2010.

HELP: If you have not already done so, download the schedule.mpp file from the companion Web site at www.intropm.com.

1. *Access the Import MS Project screen.* Click the box labeled **Import MS Project**. Your screen should resemble figure B-10, except you have not located the file to import yet.

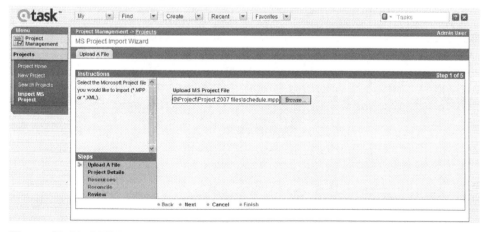

Figure B-10. MS Project import wizard

An Introduction to Project Management, Third Edition

2. *Browse to find the schedule.mpp file.* Click the **Browse** button and navigate to find the schedule.mpp file you downloaded for this text or created yourself in Appendix A. Notice that each step of the MS Project Import Wizard is visible at the lower right of the screen.

3. *Go to the next step.* Click **Next** at the bottom of the screen. Notice that the name of the project, Project A+, and other information appears. The next two steps are valuable when you have other users in @task that you want to map task assignments to, and/or you are merging Microsoft Project changes with an existing @task project. Click **Next** two more times until you are in the Review step of the MS Project Import Wizard, as shown in figure B-11. Review the information in the Project Import Summary.

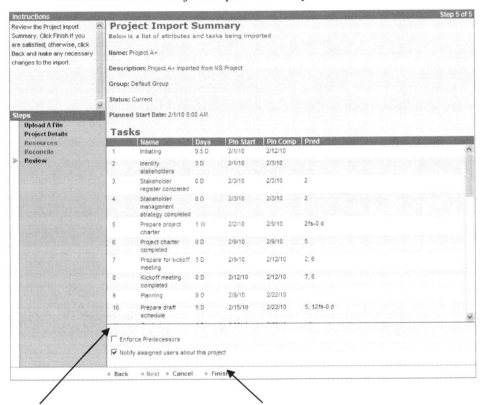

Enforce Predecessors check box   **Finish**

Figure B-11. MS Project import wizard review step

4. *Enforce Predecessors.* Click the **Enforce Predecessors check box** on the bottom of the screen, and then click **Finish** at the lower right of the screen. Your

screen should resemble figure B-12. The top of the screen says "The MS Project file has been successfully imported. To synchronize future changes in MS Project, always use a current export from @task."

Collapse symbol   **Full Screen icon**

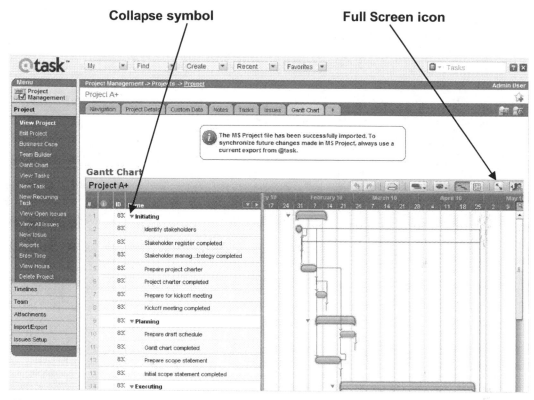

Figure B-12. Successfully imported schedule.mpp file

Adjusting Screen Elements and Accessing Filters, Views, and Reports

1.   Adjust screen elements. Click the **collapse symbols (upside-down triangle)** to the left of the tasks Initiating, Executing, and Hold Meetings. Click the **Full Screen icon**. Your screen should resemble Figure B-13.

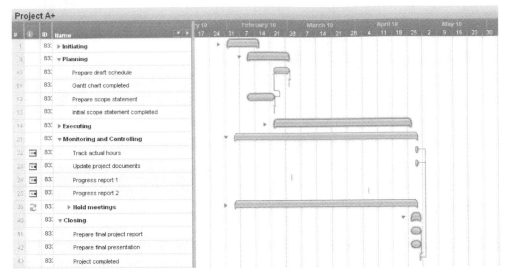

Figure B-13. Full screen view

2. *Access the Tasks tab*. Click the **Full Screen icon** again, and then click on **View Tasks** in the contextual menu. Click the **Filter list arrow**, as shown in Figure B-14.

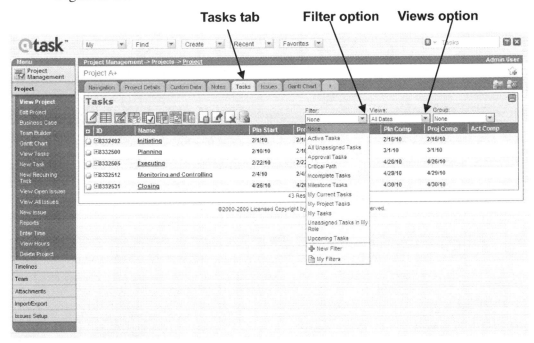

Figure B-14. Task tab

An Introduction to Project Management, Third Edition

3. *Filter information.* Click **Critical Path** in the Filter section. Your screen should resemble Figure B-15. Review the resulting information, and then click **None** for the filter.

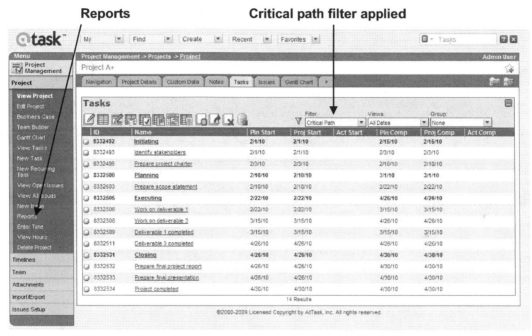

Figure B-15. Critical path filter applied

4. *Access Views.* Click the **Views list arrow**, and then click **Project Outline**. Notice that the level two WBS items display.

5. *Access Report.* Click **Reports** on the left side of the screen. Figure B-16 shows some of the project reports available.

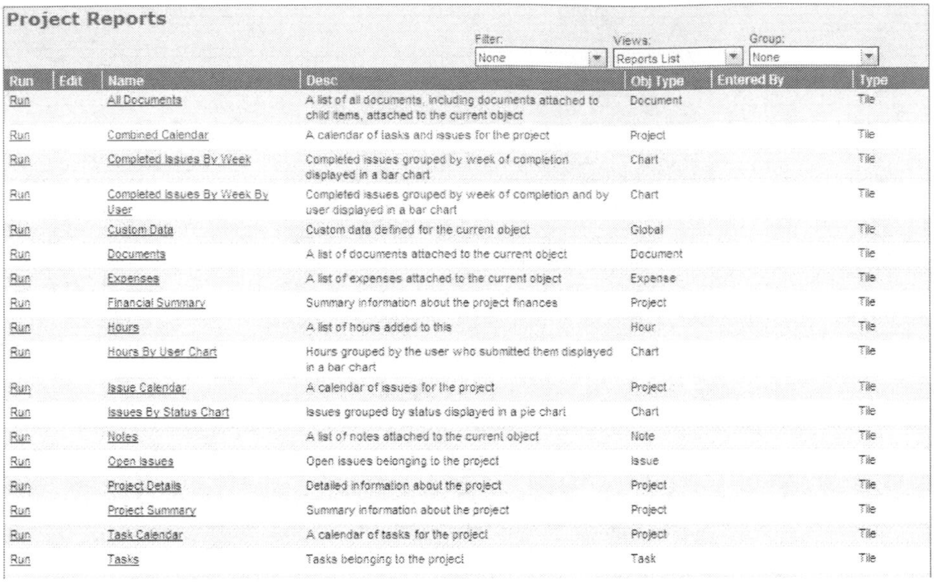

Project Reports

Filter: None | Views: Reports List | Group: None

Run	Edit	Name	Desc	Obj Type	Entered By	Type
Run		All Documents	A list of all documents, including documents attached to child items, attached to the current object	Document		Tile
Run		Combined Calendar	A calendar of tasks and issues for the project	Project		Tile
Run		Completed Issues By Week	Completed issues grouped by week of completion displayed in a bar chart	Chart		Tile
Run		Completed Issues By Week By User	Completed issues grouped by week of completion and by user displayed in a bar chart	Chart		Tile
Run		Custom Data	Custom data defined for the current object	Global		Tile
Run		Documents	A list of documents attached to the current object	Document		Tile
Run		Expenses	A list of expenses attached to the current object	Expense		Tile
Run		Financial Summary	Summary information about the project finances	Project		Tile
Run		Hours	A list of hours added to this	Hour		Tile
Run		Hours By User Chart	Hours grouped by the user who submitted them displayed in a bar chart	Chart		Tile
Run		Issue Calendar	A calendar of issues for the project	Project		Tile
Run		Issues By Status Chart	Issues grouped by status displayed in a pie chart	Chart		Tile
Run		Notes	A list of notes attached to the current object	Note		Tile
Run		Open Issues	Open issues belonging to the project	Issue		Tile
Run		Project Details	Detailed information about the project	Project		Tile
Run		Project Summary	Summary information about the project	Project		Tile
Run		Task Calendar	A calendar of tasks for the project	Project		Tile
Run		Tasks	Tasks belonging to the project	Task		Tile

Figure B-16. Project reports

6. *Run a report*. Click **Run** to the left of the **Project Details** report to run that report. Click Reports to access the full list of project reports again, and experiment with running other reports.

7. *Logout of @task.* Click the small x in the upper right of your screen to logout of @task.

As you can see, @task performs many of the functions you learned in Appendix A using Project 2010. Consult the user manuals for more detailed instructions. The next section focuses on portfolio management features of @task. Note that Microsoft also provides an enterprise version of Project, but it is not easily available online.

USING @TASK FOR PORTFOLIO MANAGEMENT

This section summarizes the project portfolio management process used in @task and then uses sample data to demonstrate some of the portfolio management features.

Project Portfolio Management Process

In the @task User's Guide, Chapter 14, Portfolio Management, typical steps to conducting project portfolio management are listed as follows:

1. Create evaluation criteria for project selection and prioritization
2. Collect project requests
3. Select several requested projects as a portfolio project based on the criteria created
4. Prioritize the selected projects using the same criteria
5. Evaluate the resource availability for carrying out the selected projects
6. Review and evaluate the progress of the projects in the portfolio, and make adjustments if necessary

Figure B-17 provides a high-level overview of the project portfolio management (PPM) process used in @task. A brief description of each step in this process is provided below, based on the User Guide.

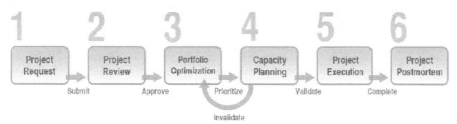

Figure B-17. @task PPM process (@task User Guide, 2009)

1. Project Request: In this phase, project requests are created and submitted for review. The necessary review criteria need to be created prior to the creation of any project requests.
2. Project Review: Once the project requests are submitted, they will be reviewed by an appropriate committee to determine if the requests can be selected in a company project portfolio.
3. Portfolio Optimization: After all portfolio projects were selected, they will be further optimized or prioritized according to the value, alignment, and benefit of the projects.

An Introduction to Project Management, Third Edition

4. Capacity Planning: In the Capacity Planning phase, resource availability for the portfolio projects will be assessed. When enough resources are available (resources are validated), the projects can be executed; however, when the resources are invalidated, the portfolio projects need to go back to the previous phase to be re-prioritized.

5. Project Execution: Projects will be executed in this phase and you will be using @task to manage your projects.

6. Project Postmortem: After the completion of portfolio projects, you can review the success of each project.

Accessing and Reviewing Sample Portfolio and Program Data

The account that @task has set up for this text includes sample data. This data was accessed through the Setup menu under Sample Data. The following section assumes that you are working through this account and have access to this sample data.

1. Access the Portfolio Management menu. Click **Portfolio Management** from the @task Home screen. Your screen should resemble Figure B-18.

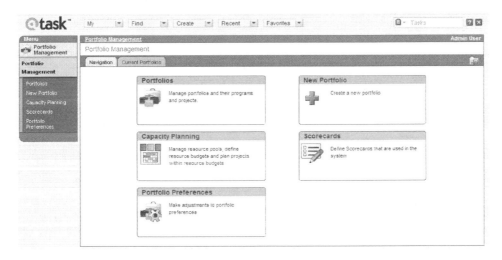

Figure B-18. Portfolio management screen

2. View the current portfolios. Click the **Current Portfolios** tab, click the portfolio called **Information Technology**, and then click **All Projects**. Make sure the selected view is **Business Case Review** Your screen should resemble Figure B-19.

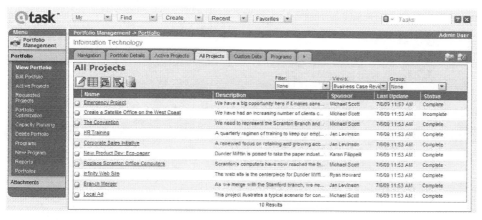

Figure B-19. All projects in the Information Technology portfolio

3. *View individual project information.* Find the project named **Emergency Project** and click on its name. Your screen should resemble Figure B-20, showing the Business Case information for this project. Scroll down to see all of the information entered in the business case.

Figure B-20. Emergency project business case information

4. *Review other project information.* Click the **Project Info** tab and review that information. Do the same for the other tabs labeled Goals, Costs, Alignment, Risks, and Custom Data

5. *Review program information.* Click **Portfolio** on the context locator at the top of the screen, and then click the **Programs tab**, as shown in Figure B-21. Notice that there are two programs in this portfolio. Click on each program to see which projects they include.

An Introduction to Project Management, Third Edition

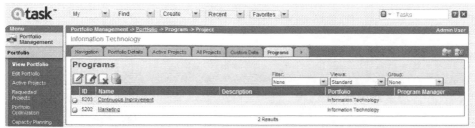

Figure B-21. Programs

Running Portfolio Management Reports

As you can see, the sample data includes detailed information on projects, including estimates of net value, planned cost, potential risk, and alignment. It is important to enter detailed information in order to use the portfolio management features of @task. Next, you will run a few reports to see the power of project portfolio management.

1. *Access Portfolio Management reports.* Click **Reports** on the left side of the screen in the contextual menu. Your screen should resemble Figure B-22.

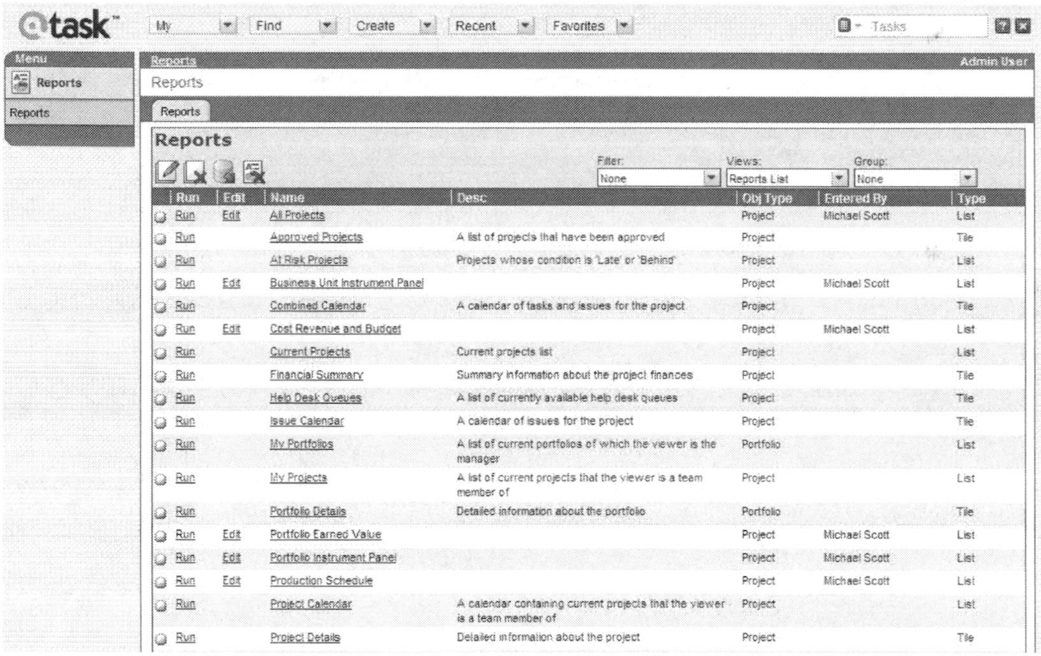

Figure B-22. Reports screen

2. *Access the Current Projects report.* Click **Run** to the left of the **Current Projects** report name. Your screen should resemble Figure B-23. Review the information in this report, such as the Priority and Flags data.

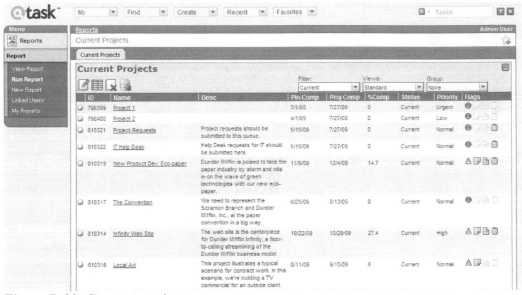

Figure B-23. Current projects report

3. *Filter portfolio information.* Click the **Filter** list box, and then click **Behind Schedule**. Your screen should resemble Figure B-24. Review the information in this filter.

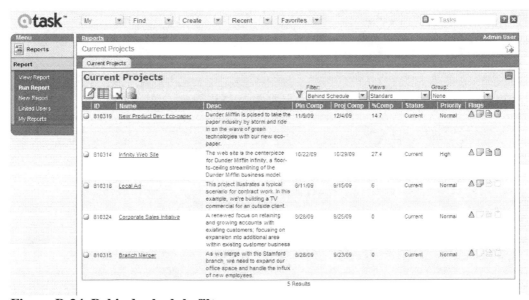

Figure B-24. Behind schedule filter

An Introduction to Project Management, Third Edition

4. *Change views.* Click the **Views** list box, and then click **Earned Value**. Your screen should resemble Figure B-25. Review the information in this filter.

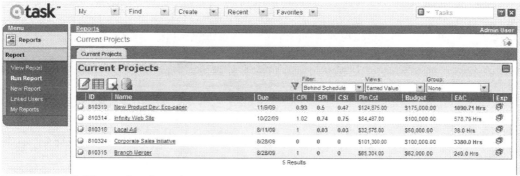

Figure B-25. Earned value view

5. *Remove your changes.* Click the **Views** list box, and then click **None**. Click the **Filter** list box, and then click **None**.

Optimizing Portfolios

Portfolio optimization is a very powerful feature of @task. This feature helps you to compare, prioritize, and select projects for execution.

1. *Access Portfolio Optimization feature.* Click **Reports** in the Application Menu, click **Portfolio Management**, click the **Current Portfolio tab**, and then click **Information Technology**. Your screen should resemble Figure B-26.

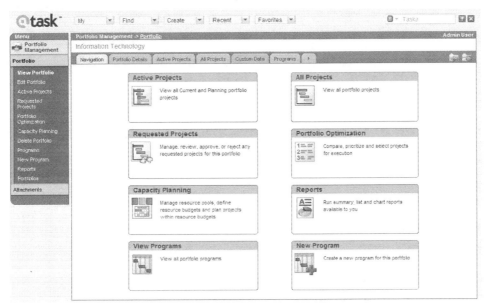

Figure B-26. Accessing the portfolio optimization feature

2. *View Portfolio Optimization screen.* Click **Portfolio Optimization.** Your screen should resemble Figure B-27. Notice the information at the top of the screen, including visual symbols like the Alignment gauge (at 59%) the ROI (at 484.4%), and the Risk to Net Value columns. Also notice the detailed entries made for each project in the portfolio.

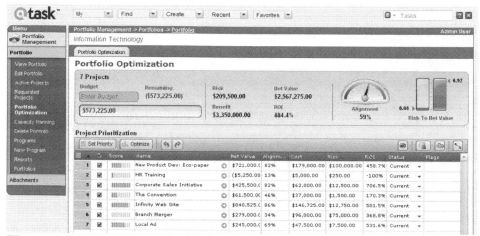

Figure B-27. Portfolio optimization screen

> 2. *Remove a project from the portfolio.* Click the **check box** by **HR Training** to unselect it since its alignment to business strategy was only 13% and it has a negative net value and ROI. Your screen should resemble Figure B-28. Notice how the values and images at the top of the screen have changed, such as the Alignment gauge changing to 67%. Note that you can change the status of a project in a portfolio by changing the Status column, such as changing it from Current to On Hold or Rejected.

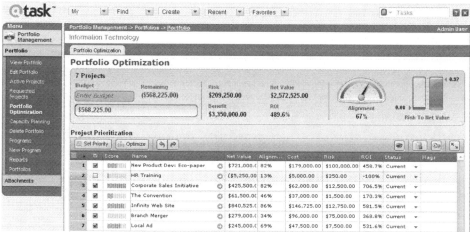

Figure B-28. Adjusting the portfolio optimization entries

> 3. *Set prioritization value.* Click the **Optimize button** under Project Prioritization to view the Optimizer options, as shown in figure B-29.

An Introduction to Project Management, Third Edition

Optimizer button   **Optimizer options**

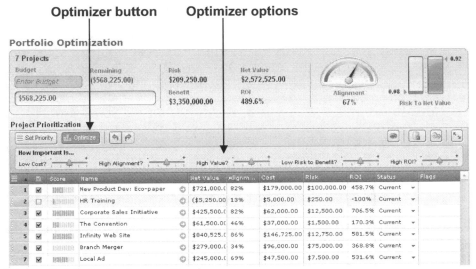

Figure B-29. Optimizer options

4. *Change optimization values.* Slide the **High Alignment** and **High ROI** options to the far right. Notice the score indicators changing by several of the projects. Click the **Set Priority button** to set these new priorities.

5. *Enter budget amount.* Click in the upper left textbox labeled **Enter Budget**, type **500000**, and press **Enter**. Notice the changes on the screen, as shown in Figure B-30. The project named Branch Merger displays in red, suggesting it for possible removal from the portfolio.

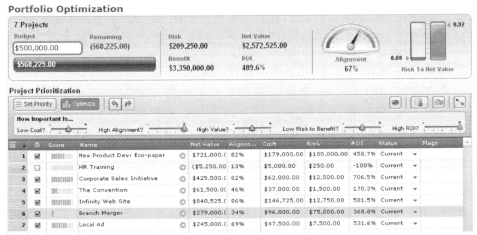

Figure B-30. Entering a budget amount

An Introduction to Project Management, Third Edition

6. *Remove another project.* Click the **checkbox** by the **Branch Merger** project to unselect it. Notice the changes on the screen, as shown in Figure B-31. There is now a positive amount of money remaining in the budget, the alignment gauge is at 73%, and the ROI is 514.1%.

Figure B-31. Updated/optimized portfolio

7. *Cancel your changes.* Click the **Cancel** button at the bottom left of the screen and then click **OK**.
8. *Log out of @task.* Click the **Logout icon** to log out of @task (small x in the upper right of the screen by the question mark.)

> **NOTE:** Because users may be sharing passwords when using the augcol account, some data or entries may vary slightly from these instructions. You should still be able to get a good idea of the capabilities of @task. If you want to have your own secure evaluation account, fill out the information at www.attask.com or contact a sales person.

As you can see the portfolio management features of @task are easy to use and provide valuable information in making important business decisions.

DISCUSSION QUESTIONS

1. What are some unique features of @task software?

2. How do you create a WBS in @task?

3. How do you import a Microsoft Project file in @task?

4. What are some of the reports and filters built-in to @task? Which ones do you think are commonly used?

5. How does the portfolio optimization feature of @task work?

6. How can project portfolio management help you make better business decisions?

EXERCISES

1. To make sure you understand the information in this appendix, perform the steps yourself. Print out the following screens or send them to your instructor, as directed. Note: You might want to use the Print Screen (PrtSc) button on your computer to take screen shots and paste them into another program to get the full screen views.

    a. Gantt chart information, similar to Figure B-8.
    b. Your imported schedule.mpp file, as shown in Figure B-12.
    c. The critical path filter applied, as shown in Figure B-15.
    d. Create a new Project file called mywbs that shows the WBS for a generic project. Make the main categories phase 1, phase 2, phase 3, and phase 4. Include at least four tasks and one milestone under each of these main categories. Enter 0 for the duration of the milestones, but do not enter any durations for the other tasks. Be sure to indent tasks and show the outline numbers before printing.

2.	Continue performing the steps in this appendix, starting with the section called Using @task for Portfolio Management. Print out the following screens or send them to your instructor, as directed:

    a.	Figure B-19. All projects in the Information Technology portfolio

    b.	Figure B-24. Behind schedule filter

    c.	Figure B-31. Updated/optimized portfolio

    d.	Write a one-to-two page paper describing the capabilities of @task and your opinion of this software. What do you like and dislike about it?

3.	Use some of the information in the body of this text to practice your @task skills.

    a.	Review the sample WBS for the Just-In-Time Training project provided in Chapter 4, Figure 4-10. Enter the WBS into @task. Indent tasks and use the automatic numbering feature. Print or hand in your file.

    b.	Use the information in Figure 4-14 for Project X to create a Gantt chart, as shown in Figure 4-18. Print it so it fits on one page or send it to your instructor Assume the start date was 6/9/09, or June 9, 2009.

4.	If you are doing a team project as part of your class or for a project at work, use @task to create a detailed file describing the work you plan to do for the project.

    a.	Create a detailed WBS, including several milestones, estimate task durations, link tasks, enter resources and costs, assign resources, and so on. You can create all of the information in @task or import it from Microsoft Project. Save your file as a baseline and print it out send it to your instructor, as desired.

    b.	Track your progress on your team project by entering actual information. Create a new baseline file if there have been a lot of changes. View earned value information when you are halfway through the project or course. Continue tracking your progress until the project or course is finished. Print or send your Gantt chart, earned value data, and relevant information to your instructor.

    c.	Write a two- to three-page report describing your experience. What did you learn about @task from this exercise? How do you think @task helps in managing a project? You may also want to interview people who use @task for their experiences and suggestions.

An Introduction to Project Management, Third Edition

COMPANION WEB SITE

Visit the free companion Web site for this text at **www.intropm.com** to access template files, online quizzes, Jeopardy-like games, Microsoft Project files, links to sites mentioned in the text, and other information to help you learn more about this important field. Instructors must contact the author at schwalbe@augsburg.edu to gain access to the instructor site. Anyone can access the student site.

END NOTES

[1]AtTask Inc. (www.attask.com) (accessed July 7, 2009).

[2]AtTask Inc., "AtTask Exceeds Projections with 140% Year-Over-Year Increase in Bookings" (www.attask.com) (April 13, 2009).

[3]AtTask Inc. (www.attask.com) (accessed July 7, 2009).

Appendix C

Resources

An Introduction to Project Management, Third Edition

INTRODUCTION

This appendix summarizes resources you can use to expand your understanding of project management. It describes information provided on the companion Web sites, summarizes information about template files, provides detailed case studies, discusses the option to use project management simulation software, and provides information and resources on project management certifications. Feel free to visit my Web site at www.kathyschwalbe.com and contact me at schwalbe@augsburg.edu with any questions or suggestions.

COMPANION WEB SITES

For Students (www.intropm.com)

The student companion Web site for this text is not password-protected. Anyone can access it. The site includes the following:

- Links and sample documents mentioned in each chapter and appendix

- Interactive, multiple-choice quizzes for each chapter where you can test your understanding of key concepts

- Jeopardy games for each chapter created in PowerPoint, another method for testing your understanding of materials

- Template files, as described in the following section

- Microsoft Project information, including necessary data files for performing steps in Appendix A

- Instructions for using Fissure's project management simulation software, as described later in this appendix

- Links to additional resources related to project management

For Instructors (http://groups.google.com/group/teachintropm)

The instructor companion Web site for this text is password-protected. Contact the author at schwalbe@augsburg.edu to verify that you are an instructor using this text to receive the password. In addition to the information on the student site, the instructor site includes the following:

- Lecture slides for each chapter, created in PowerPoint. Note: These slides are copyrighted and must remain on a secure site. Instructors can copy them onto their own school's secure network and make changes as desired as long as the copyright information remains on each slide.

An Introduction to Project Management, Third Edition

- An instructor manual for the text

- A solution manual for the text

- Teaching ideas, including information on using real projects in classes and using other cases, such as those from Harvard Business Review

- Ideas and inputs from other instructors

TEMPLATE FILES

As mentioned throughout this text, using templates can help you prepare various project management documents, spreadsheets, charts, and other files. Figure C-1 lists the template name, the chapter where it is used in the text, and the application software used to create it. Be careful to enter information into the templates carefully, and feel free to modify the templates to meet your particular project needs. You can download the files in one compressed file (intropm3_templates) from the companion Web site or the author's Web site. The files are saved in Office 2003 format.

Template name	Chapter	Application software
Payback period chart	2	Excel
Weighted scoring model	2	Excel
Stakeholder register	3	Word
Stakeholder management strategy	3	Word
Business case	3	Word
Business case financials	3	Excel
Charter	3	Word
Kick-off meeting agenda	3	Word
Team contract	4	Word
Project management plan	4	Word
Project organizational chart	4	Word
Requirements management plan	4	Word
Requirements traceability matrix	4	Word
Scope statement	4	Word
WBS	4	Word
WBS dictionary entry	4	Word
Activity list and attributes	4	Word
Milestone list	4	Word
Activity resource requirements	4	Word

Project schedule	4	Project
Cost estimate	4	Excel
Cost baseline	4	Excel
Quality management plan	5	Word
Quality metrics	5	Word
Quality checklist	5	Word
Project organizational chart	5	PowerPoint
RACI chart	5	Excel
Resource histogram	5	Excel
Human resource plan	5	Word
Communications management plan	5	Word
Project Web site	5	FrontPage
Risk management plan	5	Word
Probability/impact matrix	5	PowerPoint
Risk register	5	Excel
Make-or-buy analysis	5	Word
Procurement management plan	5	Word
Request for proposal	5	Word
Contract statement of work	5	Word
Supplier evaluation matrix	5	Excel
Milestone report	6	Word
Change request	6	Word
Cause-and-effect diagram	6 and 7	PowerPoint
Team roster	6	Word
Team performance assessment	6	Word
Issue log	6	Excel
Qualified sellers list	6	Word
Contract	6	Word
Earned value chart	7	Excel
Deliverable acceptance form	7	Word
Run chart	7	Excel
Scatter diagram	7	Excel
Histogram	7	Excel
Pareto chart	7	Excel

An Introduction to Project Management, Third Edition

Flow chart	7	PowerPoint
Performance report	7	Word
Customer acceptance-project completion form	8	Word
Final project report table of contents	8	Word
Transition plan	8	Word
Lessons-learned report	8	Word
Contract closure notice	8	Word
Potential project	App C	Word

Figure C-1. Templates available for download on the companion Web site

CASE STUDIES

Each chapter of this text includes Exercises and Team Projects, but some instructors like to assign more detailed case studies. This section provides three running case studies: Real Projects, Project Management Videos, and New Business Venture. You can also find further suggestions for using real projects or other case studies, such as those provided by the Harvard Business Review, on the companion Web site for instructors under "Teaching Ideas."

The first running case provides two individual homework assignments to solicit real project ideas from each student and to assess the team project. It then provides detailed instructions on what is required for the real projects. The two other running cases include five parts—initiating, planning, executing, monitoring and controlling, and closing—with scenario-based information and several tasks to complete under each part. Students can refer to the sample documents found in the text to help them complete the tasks. Several of the tasks involve using templates provided on the companion Web site. Anyone can use these cases as long as they mention the source. Feel free to modify them to meet your class needs, and feel free to share additional case studies on the instructor site.

Case Study 1: Real Projects

Note: My personal preference is to use real projects as part of a project management class. It helps students gain real-world experience and practice working with a "real" sponsor and other stakeholders. Projects often produce very useful results for the college, non-profit organizations, businesses, or the students themselves. The information below is based on my personal experience and syllabi instructions for having students work on real projects in a team setting. I give students the option of doing another case study, but the vast majority of students choose to work on a real project.

An important part of coming up with good project ideas is the following required homework assignment, due very early in the course. Each student must do the homework,

An Introduction to Project Management, Third Edition

so as long as you get about one good idea out of every four, you should have enough real projects to work on. I often propose additional project ideas, mostly from suggestions from colleagues or former students.

Individual Homework: Project Proposal (100 points)

*Here's your chance to get some useful work done! Each student will propose a project to be done as part of this class, and hopefully we will do several of them. Even if you want to do a case study, you must still propose a real project. Projects must have a sponsor (can be a student, friend, boss, community leader, etc.), provide a needed service or product, and be a good fit for this class. Each student normally spends between 20-40 hours on the class project. Review my Web site and look at some of the past student projects and the information in the syllabus about the projects. Then write a proposal for a potential project, using the **potential project template**. Talk to the sponsor **before** writing the proposal, and try to come up with a good proposal! Think about projects at work, for community groups, etc. that you could do. If you do not do a real project, you will work on a case study. You still need to propose a real project, though, to get experience doing that!*

It is also important to explain how grades will be determined for these team projects. Below is another individual homework assignment that allows each student to provide inputs on his/her own team project grade and the grade of each team member. They do this assignment for both the real projects and case studies, and it is due the last day of class.

Individual Homework: Self Assessment (100 points)

Write a 1-2-page self-assessment based on the team project, answering the following questions:

1. *If you had to give your team a grade for the project, what would it be? Why?*
2. *What were your roles and responsibilities on the group project? How well do you think you performed on this project?*
3. *Briefly assess each team member's performance. If you had to give each person, including yourself, a grade, what would it be and why? To compare individual contributions, if you had 100 points to allocate to your team, how would you allocate them? If you're an Apprentice fan, what would be the order you would use to fire people from your team?*

Syllabus Description of Team Projects

NOTE: Instructors can find this whole appendix on the instructor site in Microsoft Word for easy editing.

The purpose of the team project is to use a structured approach to project management in a team setting (3-5 students/team). I normally let teams self select and assign people to teams as needed. One person could take the lead on each task, but other team members should provide inputs and edit the work so it is consistent and of high quality and reflects a team effort. Each team member should plan to spend **20-40 hours** total on the team project, including some time in class. If the project is done for someone outside of Augsburg, students can earn the Augsburg Experience credit. **You must have the sponsor call or email me to approve the project after you propose it if you really want to work on it.** If you do not choose to work on a real project, teams will work on one of the case studies in the text (Project Management Videos or New Business Venture). You can substitute a different business idea for the new business venture case study, if you like, with my approval.

Examples of "real" class projects: Two examples are included on my Web site under My Classes, MIS376, called the Tempting Templates Project Web Site (which I sponsored, and which was all done virtually), and the Theatre Past Productions Web Site (which the head of Augsburg's theatre department sponsored.). Other examples of recent class projects include the following, and more are listed on my Web site:

- Organizing and running a fundraising event, like the Hockey Team Fights Cancer project (raised over $5,000 last fall), a benefit for someone with a disease, a game night at Grand Slam, a 5K race for the Make a Wish foundation, or making baby blankets for hurricane victims.
- Creating/updating a Web site for a small business or non-profit organization
- Helping a new pizza shop market its products to college students
- Researching graduate programs in project management (link to results on my site)
- Helping an Augsburg group perform a project, like food services project to change suppliers, career services organizing a special job fair, etc.
- Redesigning one or more rooms of someone's home or rental property

Team Progress Reports:
If you are working on a case study, I'll provide instructions on which tasks you should have completed by the progress report dates and which ones to present. In general, you should have the initiating tasks done for the first progress report and the planning tasks and some of the executing tasks done for the second one. Below are instructions for what is needed for progress reports for the "real" projects. **I also want to be copied on all emails/communications with your sponsor.**

1. Initiate and begin planning how your team will do all of the work required for the project. Present the bulleted items below for your first progress report (about 10-15

An Introduction to Project Management, Third Edition

*minutes for the presentation, given by the project manager), and track progress as the course progresses. **Give me a hard copy of the documents you present before your presentation,** and have the data available on your team Web site or in a team member's public folder. Type all team members' names on the status report and the location of all of these files as well. Items to include:*

- *a one-page progress report (using the template called performance report)*
- *a project charter (using template), signed by all stakeholders, including your sponsor (an email confirmation is okay in place of a signature for now)*
- *a copy of communications so far with your project sponsor (emails or documented meeting minutes)*
- *a preliminary scope statement (using template)*
- *a team contract, emphasizing the communications section (using template)*
- *a draft schedule (using the template in my public folder for this class). It include columns that list each major task by process group, estimated start and end dates for each task, who has the main responsibility for each task, estimated hours for each task by person, and actual hours for each task by person that you'll complete as you have the information. You'll use this data later to create a Gantt chart*
- *a brief summary of your team's MBTI types and how they might affect your team dynamics*

2. *Prepare a second progress report (about 10 -15 minutes for the presentation, given by someone other than the PM). Include the following information, and have copies available electronically:*

- *a one-page progress report (using the template called performance report)*
- *a Gantt chart created in Microsoft Project*
- *a detailed scope statement*
- *a comparison and explanation of estimated versus actual hours to date*
- *a summary/preview of completed deliverables*
- *feedback from your sponsor since the last progress report*

Final Project Notebooks
*By the last day of class, each team will present a **final presentation** and hand in a **project notebook** (stapled pages are fine). If you do a case study, put all of that information together in a notebook. If you do a real project, include the following information. All documentation should also be available in the project manager's AugNet account. Note: Each team member must give part of the 20-30 minute final presentation.*
- *Cover page and detailed table of contents. List the project name, team members, and date on the cover page of the notebook. Be sure to number all*

pages (by hand is fine), which should match the table of contents. You may include tabs or dividers between major sections of the notebook, too.

- *A double-spaced 3-4-page project report. Address the following questions in your report, which should be in the front of your notebook after the table of contents: What did your team produce? Was the project a success or not, and what was your criteria for determining success? (Remember that should be defined in your scope statement early in the project). What project management tools/documents did you use, and did they help? How close was your draft schedule and estimate of hours to the actual schedule and actual hours worked on the project? What went right on the project? What went wrong? What did your team learn by working on this project? How did you select the project manager? Did he/she do a good job at leading your team? Did you work well as a team? What was your project sponsor's final assessment of the project? Include some written feedback from the sponsor in your final report and presentation. See the sample customer acceptance form in your text for an example. **Discuss this information in your final project presentation** and show/summarize the main products produced. **If your project involves some type of event, be sure to show pictures of the event.***

- *Hard copies of all of the products your team produced. Include the project management documents you created (charter, Gantt chart, etc.), communications with your sponsor, and all product-related items.*

Part of the grade for the team project will be based on the team's final presentation and progress reports, and part of grade will be based on the quality of the project and its notebook (one notebook per team, due the last day of class). Team project managers will earn a small amount of extra credit for successfully leading their project teams.

Case Study 2: Project Management Videos

Part 1: Initiating

Background Scenario:

You and several of your classmates are taking a project management class, and your instructor suggested a project to find or create good video clips to illustrate various concepts related to the class. For example, the *Oceans 11, 12,* and *13* movies all include great planning and execution clips. *Apollo 13* provides a great example of scope management and creative problem solving when the team has to figure out how to keep the astronauts alive. *The Office* television show includes many examples of poor motivation techniques. In addition to providing the clips on DVD, you will write a summary of them, including the length and source of the clip, introductions for each clip, discussion questions that you can pose before and after each clip, and suggested answers to those questions. Your instructor has suggested that teams find or create at least two good clips per team member. If several teams in your class work on this project, you will have to coordinate with them to avoid duplicating clips and to share resources. Everything your team creates for the project should fit on one DVD that will run on your instructor's computer. The DVD will be for educational use only, so there should not be any copyright issues.

Work with your teammates and instructor to perform all or just some of the following initiating tasks for this project.

Tasks

1. To become more familiar with finding short video clips, do some preliminary research. Go to sites like *youtube.com* and search for videos related to project management concepts. Also search for articles related to project management in the movies, and visit sites such as *imdb.com* to see movie trailers. Find other sites that have legitimate movie and television clips. Also discuss movies or television shows that you and your teammates are familiar with that could be used for this project. Write a two- to three-page paper (double-spaced) with your findings, citing all references.

2. To become familiar with creating or editing short video clips, research how to take short segments of an existing DVD and put it on a computer. Also research the devices and software needed to create, edit, and post your own videos (such as *theFlip.com* and *youtube.com*). Summarize at least three options, including price information. Write a two- to three-page paper (double-spaced) with your findings, citing all references.

3. Prepare a team contract for this project. Use the team contract template provided on the companion Web site, and review the sample in the text.

4. Prepare a draft project charter for the Project Management Videos Project. Assume the project will be completed by the last day of class, and costs will include an estimate of hours (unpaid) your team will work on this project plus the cost of any necessary hardware/software you would like for the project (such as DVDs, a camcorder, video editing software, etc.). Use the charter template provided on the companion Web site, and review the sample in the text.

5. Prepare a draft schedule for completing all of the tasks for this project. Include columns that list each task by process group; estimated start and end dates for each task; who has the main responsibility for each task; estimated hours for each task by person; and actual hours for each task by person that you'll complete as you have the information.

6. Write a brief summary of your team's MBTI types and how they might affect your team dynamics. You can take a version of the test from *www.humanmetrics.com*.

7. Prepare a 10-minute presentation that summarizes results from the above initiating tasks. Assume the presentation is for a review with your class and instructor. Be sure to document notes of any feedback received during the presentation and hand in hard copies of everything you produced.

Part 2: Planning

Work with your teammates and instructor to perform all or just some of the following planning tasks for this project.

Tasks:

1. Develop a requirements traceability matrix and a scope statement for the project. Use the requirements matrix and scope statement templates provided on the companion Web site, and review the sample in the text. Be as specific as possible in describing product characteristics and requirements, as well as key deliverables. Determine which video clips your team will provide and what resources you think you will need (DVDs, camcorders, etc.). Be sure to coordinate the clips with your instructor and other teams and get feedback before handing in your scope statement.

2. Develop a WBS for the project. Use the wbs template provided on the companion Web site, and review the samples in the text. Print the WBS in list form as a Word file. Be sure the WBS is based on the project charter, scope statement, and other relevant information.

3. Create a milestone list for this project, and include at least ten milestones and estimated completion dates for them. Note that your instructor should have input for several of these milestones and completion dates. Use the milestone_report.doc template.

4. Develop a cost estimate for the project. Estimate hours needed to complete each task (including those already completed) and the costs of any items you would like to purchase for the project. Assume a rate of $10 per hour for all labor. Use the cost estimate template.

An Introduction to Project Management, Third Edition

5. Use the WBS and milestone list you developed in numbers 2 and 3 above to create a Gantt chart and network diagram in Project 2010 for the project. Estimate task durations and enter dependencies, as appropriate. Print the Gantt chart and network diagram.
6. Create a quality checklist for ensuring that the project is completed successfully. Also define at least two quality metrics for the project.
7. Create a RACI chart for the main tasks and deliverables for the project.
8. Develop a communications management plan for the project using the template and sample in the text.
9. Create a probability/impact matrix and list of prioritized risks for the project. Include at least ten risks. Use the template and sample provided in the text.
10. Prepare a ten-minute presentation that you would give to summarize results from the above planning tasks. Assume the presentation is for a review with your class and instructor. Be sure to document notes of any feedback received during the presentation and hand in hard copies of everything you produced. Plan to show one video clip along with the discussion questions to get feedback.

Part 3: Executing

Work with your teammates and instructor to perform all or just some of the following executing tasks for this project.

Tasks:

1. Find or create your video clips and put them on one DVD. Be sure it runs on your instructor's computer or meets other requirements for your class.

2. Write the clip summaries, introductions, discussion questions, and suggested answers to those questions.

3. Document any change requests you have during project execution and get sponsor approval, if needed.

Part 4: Monitoring and Controlling

Work with your teammates and instructor to perform all or just some of the following monitoring and controlling tasks for this project.

Tasks:
1. Review the Seven Basic Tools of Quality. Pick one of these tools and create a chart or diagram to help you solve problems you are facing. Use the available templates and samples provided.
2. Create and update, as required, an issue log. Use the template and sample provided in the text.
3. As described in the last task for the initiating and planning sections, be ready to show progress you have made as part of a project review. Also be sure to document

An Introduction to Project Management, Third Edition

actual hours on each task in the draft schedule you created for Task 5 under Initiating.

Part 5: Closing

Work with your teammates and instructor to perform all or just some of the following closing tasks for this project.

Tasks
1. Prepare a 20-minute final project presentation to summarize the results of the project. Describe the initial project goals, planned versus actual scope, time, and cost information, challenges faced, lessons learned, and key products produced. Be sure to list all of the clips your team found and show at least two of them along with the discussion questions.
2. Prepare a final project report. Include a cover page and detailed table of contents, getting feedback from your instructor on information required. Be sure to include all of the documents and products you have prepared as appendices.
3. Get feedback from your sponsor in the form of a customer acceptance/project completion form (see the template called customer acceptance-project completion form) or in some other fashion. Also get feedback from your classmates.
4. If you are comfortable doing so, send a copy of your final project report and feedback on this case to the author of this text at *schwalbe@augsburg.edu*.

Case Study 3: New Business Venture

This case should be interesting to anyone interested in starting a new business. It involves research, marketing, finance, technology, and personal ethics. Feel free to change the type of business, if desired. The main purpose of this and other cases, however, is to help you practice some of the project management skills you are developing as part of your course. Note: If students want to propose a different business idea, let them!

Part 1: Initiating

Background Scenario:

You and several of your friends have been working for corporations for over five years, but several of you have a desire to start your own business. You have decided that you are ready to pursue your idea of starting a music academy for children ages 3-16. You all enjoy creating music, and you saw the advantages that some children had from participating in special music programs beyond those available in schools. In particular, you see the need for music training in your area for children interested in voice, guitar, keyboard, and percussion so they can perform in their own bands.

This New Business Venture Project would primarily involve you and three of your friends, who were all part of your high school band:

- You are an excellent bass player, and you were the one who organized your band in high school and got the few paid gigs that you had. You can also play keyboard. You continue to play both instruments occasionally, but your full-time job and new spouse take up a lot of your time. Your current full-time job is working as a business analyst for a large retail store. Although your job is going well, you realize that you would be happier working in your own business and with something involving music. Your strengths are your creativity, organization, and analytical skills. Your spouse is employed full-time and supports your idea to start your own business, as long as you have a detailed plan and financial backing.

- Brian, one of your best friends since sixth grade, played lead guitar in your band. He is a natural musician and has little trouble learning to play very complicated songs. Brian is very quiet, but he would love to work for a successful small business and be able to share his passion for guitar with children. He is also a whiz at music technology, having recorded and edited CDs for several years. He works as a software developer for a large consulting firm. He is married and has one young child, and his spouse works part-time. Brian would not give up his full-time job until he knew he could support his family in this new business venture, but he could do a lot of part-time work.

- Nicole, also one of your best friends since sixth grade, was the lead singer in your band. She has a great voice and really knows how to work a crowd, too. She is currently working as a part-time telemarketer, but she doesn't like her job at all and is ready for something new. Her spouse has a great job and supports her in pursuing a new business opportunity. Her strengths are her vocal talent, professional voice training, and sales ability. She also loves working with children and would be willing to work full-time on this new business venture.

- Andres was the last person to join your band in high school, having replaced your original drummer. He currently works as a music teacher at a local middle school. He has a lot of contacts with local schools and is dying to get this new music academy started. He is single and would want to keep his current job, but he could devote a fair amount of time to the business in the evenings, on weekends, and full-time in the summer. His strengths are his drumming expertise, teaching ability, music technology experience, and contacts with school-age children, parents, and school administrators. He currently gives some private lessons and knows other people who do as well, so he has potential clients and instructors that he could bring into the business.

The main goals of the New Business Venture Project are to prepare a business plan, get financial backing, handle legal issues, develop marketing materials, find a rental space for the music academy, purchase/develop curriculum, hire staff, and open for business by one year from now, September 1, to coincide with the school year. Your team has already analyzed the market, and you know you can make this business succeed. Your goal would be to cover your investment costs after two years in business.

Work with your teammates and instructor to perform all or just some of the following initiating tasks for this project.

Tasks

1. To become more familiar with the children's music instruction market, do some preliminary research to find out how big this market is, who the main companies are in the market, what the best-selling services are, pricing and marketing strategies, etc. If you do not want to focus on your own geographic area, pick one to focus on for this and future tasks. Write a two- to three-page paper (double-spaced) with your findings, citing at least two references. For example, the author's son took lessons and performed in rock bands from Virtuosos Music Academy in Plymouth, Minnesota (*www.virtuososonline.com*). You can also include a paragraph or two with your team's personal experience in this area, if applicable.

2. Prepare a stakeholder register and management strategy for the project. Include all project team members and make up names and information for at least one spouse, one potential financial backer, and one local competitor. Assume that you and your three friends are all team members, and you each invest $10,000 into the business.

An Introduction to Project Management, Third Edition

Your mother, a retired business professor, has decided to provide a substantial loan ($30,000), so she will be the sponsor. You still need to figure out how to get an additional $30,000 for the first-year start-up costs. Use the templates provided on the companion Web site, and review the sample stakeholder register and management strategy in the text.

3. Prepare a team contract for this project. Use the template provided on the companion Web site, and review the sample in the text.

4. Prepare a project charter for the New Business Venture Project. Assume the project will take one year to complete and cost about $100,000. Recall that the main project objectives are to prepare a business plan, get financial backing, handle legal issues, develop marketing materials, find a rental place for the music academy, purchase/develop curriculum, hire staff, and open for business by one year from now. Your project team will not get paid for the hours they put into this project, but once the business opens, they will be compensated. You will incorporate the business and hire a lawyer to help with this and other legal issues. Use the template provided on the companion Web site, and review the sample in the text.

5. An important part of starting any business is preparing financial projections. Although you will prepare a more detailed financial analysis when you create your business plan, you still want to do rough projections at this stage. Prepare a spreadsheet that can be used to determine the profit potential of starting this business. Include inputs for the initial investment cost, number of customers in the first month, customer growth rate/quarter, average monthly fee per customer, fixed and variable monthly operating costs, and variable costs per customer. Use the most likely, optimistic, and pessimistic inputs as shown in Figure C-2 to generate results for all three scenarios. For each month (Month 1-24), calculate your revenues (number of customers that month X monthly fee/customer) and expenses (fixed monthly salaries plus fixed monthly operative costs plus variable costs/customer/month X number of customers that month). Then determine the cumulative income each month. For example, the cumulative income in Month 1 is the Monthly Revenues - Monthly Expenses for Month 1. The cumulative income for Month 2 is the Monthly Revenues - Monthly Expenses for Month 2 plus the Cumulative Income for Month 1. The first month for the most likely scenario is filled in for you to check your formulas. Will you be able to recoup your start-up costs within two years in each scenario? If so, in what month? There is no template for this example, but you can use the format in Figure C-2. Print out a sheet with results for each scenario, clearly labeling if/when you recoup your investment.

Financial Projections for New Business Venture				
Assumptions/Inputs:	**Most likely**	**Optimistic**	**Pessimistic**	
Year 0 investment cost:	$100,000	$80,000	$120,000	
Number of customers in month 1	150	200	100	
Quarterly customer growth rate	10%	30%	5%	
Monthly fee/customer	$150	$175	$125	
Fixed monthly salaries	$9,000	$8,000	$10,000	
Fixed monthly operating costs	$5,000	$4,000	$6,000	
Variable costs/customer/month	$80	$70	$100	
		Most likely Solution		
Month	**No. Customers**	**Mo. Income**	**Mo. Expenses**	**Cum. Mo. Income**
1	150	$22,500	$26,000	($3,500)
2				
3				
4				
...24				

Figure C-2. Financial Projections Format

6. Prepare a 10–15 minute presentation that you would give to summarize results from the initiating phase of the project. Assume the presentation is for a management review to decide if the project should move on to the next phase.

Part 2: Planning

Work with your teammates and instructor to perform all or just some of the following planning tasks for this project.

Tasks

1. Develop a requirements traceability matrix and a scope statement for the project. Use the templates provided on the companion Web site, and review the samples in the text. Remember that the main project goals are to prepare a business plan, get financial backing, handle legal issues, develop marketing materials, find a rental space for the music academy, purchase/develop curriculum, and hire staff so you can open for business by one year from now. Be as specific as possible in describing product characteristics and requirements, as well as key deliverables. For example, assume that you need to rent a space for your business that is in a desirable part of town near other businesses and schools, has enough room for a reception area, technology lab with five computers, two larger band rooms that have soundproofing or can be sound proofed, and five small rooms for private lessons.

2. Develop a work breakdown structure (WBS) for the project. Break down the work to what you think is an appropriate level. Use the template provided on the companion Web site, and review the samples in the text. Print the WBS in list form as a Word file. Be sure the WBS is based on the project charter, scope statement, and other relevant information.

An Introduction to Project Management, Third Edition

3. Create a milestone list for this project, and include at least 10 milestones and estimated completion dates for them.

4. Use the WBS and milestone list you developed in numbers 2 and 3 above to create a Gantt chart and network diagram in Project 2010 for the project. Estimate task durations and enter dependencies, as appropriate. Remember that your scheduled goal for the project is one year. Print the Gantt chart and network diagram.

5. Develop a cost estimate for developing just the technology lab for your music academy. Assume that you will purchase five personal computers that can connect to the Internet and run several popular music creation and editing programs. Include the costs of the desks, chairs, microphones, keyboards, soundproofing the room, set-up, testing, etc.

6. Create a quality checklist for ensuring that the business is ready to open its doors. Also define at least two quality metrics for the project. Use the templates and samples provided.

7. Create a RACI chart for the main tasks and deliverables for the project. Use the template and sample provided.

8. Develop a communications management plan for the project. Use the template and sample provided.

9. Create a probability/impact matrix and list of prioritized risks for the project. Include at least 10 risks. Use the template and sample provided.

10. Prepare a request for proposal for the technology lab (including purchasing the hardware, software, installation, soundproofing, testing, and maintenance) for your music academy and describe at least two procurement issues you need to consider for the project.

11. Prepare a 10–15 minute presentation that you would give to summarize results from the planning phase of the project. Assume the presentation is for a management review to decide if the project should move on to the next phase.

Part 3: Executing

Remember that the main project goals are to prepare a business plan, get financial backing, handle legal issues, develop marketing materials, find a rental space for the music academy, purchase/develop curriculum, and hire staff so you can open for business by one year from now.

Work with your teammates and instructor to perform all or just some of the following executing tasks for this project.

Tasks

1. Write a business plan for this project. Review sample business plans. For example, *www.bplans.com/*, *www.score.org*, and Microsoft Office online (select File, New, Microsoft Online, Plans from within Microsoft Word) provide templates and/or guidelines for preparing business plans. Decide on a name for this business, as well. Include, at a minimum, the following sections in a five- to eight-page paper:

   - Executive Summary

   - Company Description

   - Products and Services

   - Marketing Plan

   - Operational Plan

   - Management Summary

   - Financial Plan

2. Research options for getting small business loans. For example, most governments have a small business administration office that offers loans or loan information. (See *www.sba.gov* for U.S. information.) Several colleges provide loans to alumni. You can also go to banks and credit card companies for funds. Develop a list of at least five different, realistic options for getting financial backing for your new business. Recall that you estimate that you will need $100,000 the first year alone, and you are still short $30,000. Include the source of the funds, interest rates, payment arrangements, etc. Document your results in a two- to three-page paper, including a recommendation on which option to pursue.

3. Create a one-page flier for your new business, a home page for a Web site, and a tri-fold brochure listing key services/courses of the business, and any other marketing materials you think you would need for your business.

4. Research options for a rental space for the music academy. Develop at least five alternative sites. Include a picture of the site, if available, square footage, cost, pros and cons, etc. Document the results and make a recommendation for which site to select in a three- to four-page paper.

5. Assume that you decide to have students sign up for weekly individual instruction on a term basis. You will offer a fall, spring, and two summer terms consisting of 12 hours of instruction in each. Half of the hour will be one-on-one with an instructor, and the other half will be in the music technology lab. You will also have several rock band courses with three to five students each that will meet weekly for six weeks, followed by a performance. Research where to purchase curriculum or what is involved in developing it, if needed, for the following courses:

- Basic, intermediate, and advanced keyboard

- Basic, intermediate, and advanced bass

- Basic, intermediate, and advanced guitar

- Basic, intermediate, and advanced percussion/drums

- Basic, intermediate, and advanced voice

- Basic, intermediate, and advanced rock band

6. Include a one-page curriculum sheet for each course and a one-page schedule for all of the courses, including times for performances for the rock band. Also include a performance each term for students taking the individual lessons.

7. Create a plan for hiring staff for your new business. Assume that you will work full-time as the main manager, providing some front-desk coverage, giving some lessons, and managing most of the business. Assume that Nicole will also work full-time, heading up the vocal lessons area, marketing, and providing some front-desk coverage. Brian will lead the music technology lab development, outsourcing a fair amount of the work. He will also teach some of the rock band ensembles in the evenings or on weekends. Andres will help with marketing and give percussion instructions as his schedule allows. You will also need to hire a part-time receptionist to always have front-desk and phone coverage. You also need to hire several part-time instructors for all of the classes provided. Include job descriptions for all of the positions, salary/pay information, and a work schedule. Document your results in a four- to six-page paper.

8. Assume that the following has occurred since the project started: As usual, you ended up taking lead of this team, but you're starting to get burned out. You are four months into the project. You are still working your full-time job, and your spouse has been complaining that you work too much and aren't delegating enough. Nicole quit her telemarketing job to focus on this new business, and she is getting nervous about the business actually opening. Andres promised to get a big list of potential students and instructors to you for the past two months, but he still hasn't delivered it. Brian thinks that he can set up the whole music technology lab instead of outsourcing it, as you planned. Write a two- to three-page paper describing how you would handle these challenges.

Part 4: Monitoring and Controlling

Background Scenario:

You are six months into the project. You completed the business plan and most of the marketing materials. You had planned to have the location for your business selected and additional start-up funds by now, but you are behind schedule. Brian and Nicole seem to disagree on a lot of key decisions, especially the location. Your mother calls at least three times a week asking how things are going. You are happy that she lives 500 miles away, but you know that she needs assurance that the business will actually open. Andres is in charge of purchasing/developing the curriculum, but he has had very little time to work on it since school is in session. You want him to focus on creating a list of potential students and instructors, so you might hire someone else to help with the curriculum.

Work with your teammates and instructor to perform all or just some of the following monitoring and controlling tasks for this project.

Tasks

1. Create a new Gantt chart based on the revised information above, if needed. Briefly describe other plans you have created so far that you think you should update in a one- to two-page paper.

2. Prepare an agenda for a team meeting to discuss several of the issues you are facing. You definitely want to decide on the location at this meeting, since it is down to two and you have to decide soon. Also write a one- to two-page paper summarizing how you will approach particular people during the meeting.

3. Prepare a 10–15 slide presentation to give to potential funders for your business. Use information from your business plan.

4. Write a two- to three-page statement of work to hire someone to help you purchase/develop the curriculum. Use the template and sample provided.

5. Review the Seven Basic Tools of Quality. Based on the current project scenario, pick one of these tools and create a chart/diagram to help you solve problems you are facing. Use the templates and samples provided.

6. Update your list of prioritized risks. Create a risk register entry for two of them. Use the template and sample provided.

Part 5: Closing

Background Scenario:

It is one month before you plan to open your new business. You just got into your leased building, and you are busy starting to get it ready to open. You have hired a small construction firm to put in a few walls, do some painting, etc. You also got a lot of help from family and friends. You quit your job, and Nicole is also working every day now on the new business. She did a great job at marketing, and you are getting calls and e-mails from your new Web site every day. Brian's friend, Tom, built the site for you at no charge after Brian said he could come in and use the technology lab when it wasn't busy. Eric, the person you hired to help with the curriculum, was a fantastic resource, even though it cost you $10,000 you had not planned on spending. He did help you expand your list of potential students and instructors, as well, since he knew the local market very well. You did meet your schedule goal, but you had to borrow another

$10,000 from your mom. She is only charging you 5% interest, starting when your doors open. She is happy with the results and has already booked a flight to visit for your grand opening celebration, where you and your team will be performing. Your mom loves to cook and bake, so she volunteered to handle the food for the opening.

Work with your teammates and instructor to perform all or just some of the following closing tasks for this project.

Tasks

1. You have scheduled a final project presentation two days before your grand opening. Prepare a 10–15 slide presentation to summarize the results of the project. Describe the initial project goals, planned versus actual scope, time, and cost information, challenges faced, and key products produced.

2. Prepare a lessons-learned report for the entire project. Include input from all stakeholders in summarizing the lessons learned. Use the template and sample provided, and be creative in your response.

3. Prepare a final project report, using information from your final project presentation and the template provided. Be sure to include all of the documents you have prepared as appendices.

4. Document your own list of best practices that you think helped or could have helped you on this project in a two- to three-page paper.

FISSURE SIMULATION SOFTWARE

Another way to practice your project management skills is by using simulation software. You can purchase a CD with Fissure's project management simulation software at www.ichapters.com for about $12. Search for Fissure from the site. Fissure's project management simulation software is based on the SimProject Alliance Prototype project. The demo version of the simulation software includes a fairly simple, 11-week project consisting of only seven tasks and ten potential team members. Fissure estimates that it takes about three to four hours to run the demo simulation.

Background Information

To participate in this simulated project, you are expected to read about the company, project, and people available to work on this project. You plan your project and make typical project decisions each week, such as when to assign staff, when to hold meetings, when to send staff to various training opportunities. You run your project a week at a time, analyzing your results each week, referring to your weekly reports, and making your decisions for the next week. As you run the simulation each week, you are presented with communications from people within the company, team members, or other stakeholders related to the project. You choose how to respond to these communications, and all the decisions you make impact how your project progresses.

An Introduction to Project Management, Third Edition

You can close the simulation at any time and save your work, if desired. You can also run the simulation as many times as you like, and the results vary based on your decisions. You can use the software for 120 days.

Assignment

Run the Fissure simulation software at least two different times. Summarize key decisions and results from each week for each run, and print out the final earned value chart as well as any other information you think is valuable. Write a two- to three-page single-spaced report summarizing what you thought about using this simulation software. Be honest, specific, and thorough in your report.

PROJECT MANAGEMENT CERTIFICATIONS

As mentioned in Chapter 1 of this text, many people are interested in certification in project management. I personally earned PMP certification in 1998, before I started writing textbooks, and this book was written to be a resource in earning PMP certification as well as a general textbook in project management.

You can access a 20-page pdf file from my personal Web site at www.kathyschwalbe.com under Test advice (the lower left link on the home page). This document, called *Appendix B: Advice for the Project Management Professional (PMP) Exam and Related Certifications*, describes various certification programs and provides detailed information on PMI's PMP and CompTIA's Project+ certifications, the structure and content of these exams, suggestions on preparing for the exams, tips for taking the exams, sample questions, and information on related certifications. This document is an appendix from my other book, *Information Technology Project Management, Sixth Edition*, and provided on my Web site with publisher permission. My Web site also provides general advice on taking exams and links to free sample PMP exams.

GLOSSARY

activity attributes — Information that provides schedule-related information about each activity, such as predecessors, successors, logical relationships, leads and lags, resource requirements, constraints, imposed dates, and assumptions related to the activity.

activity list — A tabulation of activities to be included on a project schedule.

activity-on-arrow (AOA) approach, or the **arrow diagramming method (ADM)** — A network diagramming technique in which activities are represented by arrows and connected at points called nodes to illustrate the sequence of activities.

actual cost (AC) — The total direct and indirect costs incurred in accomplishing work on an activity during a given period.

agile methodologies — Popular software development methodologies that use an iterative workflow and incremental delivery of software in short iterations.

analogous estimates, or **top-down estimates** — The estimates that use the actual cost of a previous, similar project as the basis for estimating the cost of the current project.

balanced scorecard — A methodology that converts an organization's value drivers to a series of defined metrics.

baseline — A starting point, a measurement, or an observation that is documented so that it can be used for future comparison; also defined as the original project plans plus approved changes.

benchmarking — The process of generating ideas for quality improvements by comparing specific project practices or product characteristics to those of other projects or products within or outside of the performing organization.

best practice — An optimal way recognized by industry to achieve a stated goal or objective.

best practices — Optimal methods, currently recognized within a given industry or discipline, to achieve a goal or objective.

bid — A document prepared by sellers providing pricing for standard items that have been clearly defined by the buyer.

blogs — Easy-to-use journals on the Web that allow users to write entries, create links, and upload pictures, while allowing readers to post comments to particular journal entries.

An Introduction to Project Management, Third Edition

bottom-up estimates — Cost estimates created by estimating individual activities and summing them to get a project total.

budget at completion (BAC) — The approved total budget for the project.

buffer — Additional time to complete a task, added to an estimate to account for various factors.

burst — An occurrence when two or more activities follow a single node on a network diagram.

business case — A document that provides justification for investing in a project.

capabilities — The incremental steps leading up to one or more best practices.

cash flow — Benefits minus costs, or income minus expenses.

cause-and-effect diagrams — Also called fishbone or Ishikawa diagrams, these diagrams can assist in ensuring and improving quality by finding the root causes of quality problems.

champion — A senior manager who acts as a key proponent for a project.

checklist — A list of items to be noted or consulted.

closing processes — The actions that involve formalizing acceptance of the project or phase and bringing it to an orderly end.

collaborating mode — The conflict-handling mode where decision makers incorporate different viewpoints and insights to develop consensus and commitment.

communications management plan — A document that guides project communications.

compromise mode — The conflict-handling mode that uses a give-and-take approach to resolve conflicts.

conformance to requirements — The process of ensuring that the project's processes and products meet written specifications.

confrontation mode — The conflict-handling mode that involves directly facing a conflict using a problem-solving approach that allows affected parties to work through their disagreements.

constructive change orders — Oral or written acts or omissions by someone with actual or apparent authority that can be construed to have the same effect as a written change order.

contingency plans — The predefined actions that the project team will take if an identified risk event occurs.

contingency reserves or **contingency allowances** — The funds held by the project sponsor that can be used to mitigate cost or schedule overruns if unknown risks occur.

contract statement of work (SOW) — A document that describes the goods or services to be purchased.

contracts — The mutually binding agreements that obligate the seller to provide the specified products or services, and obligate the buyer to pay for them.

control chart — A graphical display of data that illustrates the results of a process over time.

cost performance baseline — A time-phased budget that project managers use to measure and monitor cost performance.

cost-reimbursable contract — A contract that involves payment to the seller for direct and indirect actual costs.

crashing — A technique for making cost and schedule trade-offs to obtain the greatest amount of schedule compression for the least incremental cost.

critical chain scheduling — A method of scheduling that takes limited resources into account when creating a project schedule and includes buffers to protect the project completion date.

critical path — The series of activities that determine the *earliest* time by which the project can be completed; it is the *longest* path through the network diagram and has the least amount of slack or float.

critical path method (CPM), or **critical path analysis** — A network diagramming technique used to predict total project duration.

deliverable — A product or service produced or provided as part of a project.

dependency, or **relationship** — The sequencing of project activities or tasks.

directives — The new requirements imposed by management, government, or some external influence.

discount factor — A multiplier for each year based on the discount rate and year.

discount rate — The rate used in discounting future cash flows.

discretionary dependencies — The dependencies that are defined by the project team.

duration — The actual amount of time spent working on an activity *plus* elapsed time.

earned value (EV) — An estimate of the value of the physical work actually completed.

earned value management (EVM) — A project performance measurement technique that integrates scope, time, and cost data.

effort — The number of workdays or work hours required to complete a task.

empathic listening — The process of listening with the intent to understand by putting yourself in the shoes of the other person.

estimate at completion (EAC) — A forecast of how much the project will cost upon completion.

ethics — A set of principles that guide our decision making based on personal values of what is "right" and "wrong".

executing processes — The actions that involve coordinating people and other resources to carry out the project plans and produce the deliverables of the project.

external dependencies — The dependencies that involve relationships between project and non-project activities.

extrinsic motivation — A motivation that causes people to do something for a reward or to avoid a penalty.

fallback plans — The plans that are developed for risks that have a high impact on meeting project objectives, and are put into effect if attempts to reduce the risk are not effective.

fast tracking — A schedule compression technique where you do activities in parallel that you would normally do in sequence.

feeding buffers — Additional time added before tasks on the critical path that are preceded by non-critical-path tasks.

fitness for use — The ability of a product to be used as it was intended.

fixed-price or **lump-sum contract** — A type of contract that involves a fixed price for a well-defined product or service.

flowcharts — The graphic displays of the logic and flow of processes that help you analyze how problems occur and how processes can be improved.

forcing mode — The conflict-handling mode that involves exerting one's viewpoint at the potential expense of another viewpoint.

forecasts — The reports that predict future project status and progress based on past information and trends.

Gantt charts — A standard format for displaying project schedule information by listing project activities and their corresponding start and finish dates in a calendar format.

groupthink — The conformance to the values or ethical standards of a group.

histogram — A bar graph of a distribution of variables.

initiating processes — The actions to begin projects and project phases.

integrated change control — The process of identifying, evaluating, and managing changes throughout the project's life cycle.

internal rate of return (IRR) — The discount rate that results in an NPV of zero for a project.

intrinsic motivation — A motivation that causes people to participate in an activity for their own enjoyment.

issue — a matter under question or dispute that could impede project success.

issue log — a tool used to document, monitor, and track issues that need to be resolved for effective work to take place.

key performance indicator (KPI) — A criterion used to determine the degree to which an outcome is achieved.

kick-off meeting — A meeting held at the beginning of a project so that stakeholders can meet each other, review the goals of the project, and discuss future plans.

leader — A person who focuses on long-term goals and big-picture objectives, while inspiring people to reach those goals.

make-or-buy analysis — The process of estimating the internal costs of providing a product or service and comparing that estimate to the cost of outsourcing.

manager — A person who deals with the day-to-day details of meeting specific goals.

mandatory dependencies — The dependencies that are inherent in the nature of the work being performed on a project.

Maslow's hierarchy of needs — A hierarchy that states that people's behaviors are guided or motivated by a sequence of needs (physiological, safety, social, esteem, and self-actualization).

maturity model — A framework for helping organizations improve their processes and systems.

merge — A situation when two or more nodes precede a single node on a network diagram.

methodology — A plan that describes how things should be done to manage a project.

metric — A standard of measurement.

milestone — A significant event on a project.

mind mapping — A technique that uses branches radiating out from a core idea to structure thoughts and ideas.

mirroring — The matching of certain behaviors of the other person.

monitoring and controlling processes — The actions taken to measure progress toward achieving project goals, monitor deviation from plans, and take corrective action.

multitasking — When a resource works on more than one task at a time.

Murphy's Law — If something can go wrong, it will.

Myers-Briggs Type Indicator (MBTI) — A popular tool for determining personality preferences.

net present value (NPV) analysis — A method of calculating the expected net monetary gain or loss from a project by discounting all expected future cash inflows and outflows to the present point in time.

network diagram — A schematic display of the logical relationships among, or sequencing of, project activities.

node — The starting and ending point of an activity on an activity-on-arrow network diagram.

opportunities — Chances to improve the organization.

opportunity cost of capital — The return available by investing the capital elsewhere.

organizational process assets — Policies and procedures related to project management, past project files, and lessons-learned reports from previous, similar projects.

outcomes — The tangible or intangible results of applying capabilities.

overallocation — When more resources than are available are assigned to perform work at a given time.

parametric modeling — A technique that uses project characteristics (parameters) in a mathematical model to estimate project costs.

Pareto chart — A histogram that can help you identify and prioritize problem areas.

Parkinson's Law — Work expands to fill the time allowed.

payback period — The amount of time it will take to recoup, in the form of net cash inflows, the total dollars invested in a project.

phase — A distinct stage in project development.

planned value (PV) — That portion of the approved total cost estimate planned to be spent on an activity during a given period.

planning processes — The actions that involve devising and maintaining a workable scheme to ensure that the project meets its scope, time, and cost goals as well as organizational needs.

portfolio — A collection of projects or programs and other work that are grouped together to facilitate effective management of that work to meet strategic business objectives.

post-mortem — A term sometimes used for a project close-out meeting since it is held after the project has died or been put to rest.

precedence diagramming method (PDM) — A network diagramming technique in which boxes represent activities.

problems — Undesirable situations that prevent the organization from achieving its goals.

process — A series of actions directed toward a particular result.

procurement audits — Reviews often performed during contract closure to identify lessons learned in the entire procurement process.

program — A group of projects managed in a coordinated way to obtain benefits and control not available from managing them individually.

Program Evaluation and Review Technique (PERT) — A network analysis technique used to estimate project duration when there is a high degree of uncertainty about the individual activity duration estimates.

program manager — A person who provides leadership and direction for the project managers heading the projects within the program.

progress reports — The reports that describe what the project team has accomplished during a certain period.

project — A temporary endeavor undertaken to create a unique product, service, or result.

project buffer — The additional time added before a project's due date to account for unexpected factors.

project charter — A document that formally recognizes the existence of a project and provides a summary of the project's objectives and management.

project dashboard — A graphic screen summarizing key project metrics.

project management — The application of knowledge, skills, tools, and techniques to project activities to meet project requirements.

Project Management Institute (PMI) — International professional society for project managers.

project management knowledge areas — Project integration management, scope, time, cost, quality, human resource, communications, risk, and procurement management.

project management office (PMO) — An organizational entity created to assist project managers in achieving project goals.

project management plan — A document, which is a deliverable for the project integration management knowledge area, used to coordinate all project planning documents and to help guide a project's execution and control.

project management process groups — The progression from initiating activities to planning activities, executing activities, monitoring and controlling activities, and closing activities.

Project Management Professional (PMP) — Certification provided by PMI that requires documenting project experience, agreeing to follow the PMI code of ethics, and passing a comprehensive exam.

project management tools and techniques — Methods available to assist project managers and their teams; some popular tools in the time management knowledge area include Gantt charts, network diagrams, critical path analysis, and project management software.

project manager — The person responsible for working with the project sponsor, the project team, and the other people involved in a project to meet project goals.

project organizational chart — A graphical representation of how authority and responsibility is distributed within the project.

project portfolio management — The grouping and managing of projects and programs as a portfolio of investments that contribute to the entire enterprise's success.

project sponsor — The person who provides the direction and funding for a project.

PRojects IN Controlled Environments (PRINCE2) — A project management methodology with eight process groups developed in the U.K.

proposal — A document in which sellers describe what they will do to meet the requirements of a buyer.

quality — The degree to which a set of inherent characteristics fulfill requirements.

quality assurance — The activities related to satisfying the relevant quality standards for a project.

quality audit — A structured review of specific quality management activities that helps identify lessons learned, which could improve performance on current or future projects.

RACI charts — A type of responsibility assignment matrix that shows **R**esponsibility, **A**ccountability, **C**onsultation, and **I**nformed roles for project stakeholders.

rapport — A relationship of harmony, conformity, accord, or affinity.

rate of performance (RP) — The percentage of actual work completed divided by the percentage of work planned to have been completed at any given time.

Rational Unified Process (RUP) framework — A project management methodology that uses an iterative software development process that focuses on team productivity and delivers software best practices to all team members.

records management system — A tool that provides the ability to easily organize, find, and archive documents.

Request for Proposal (RFP) — A document used to solicit proposals from prospective suppliers.

Request for Quote (RFQ) — A document used to solicit quotes or bids from prospective suppliers.

required rate of return — The minimum acceptable rate of return on an investment.

requirement — A condition or capability that must be met or possessed by a system, product, service, result, or component to satisfy a contract, standard, specification, or other formal document.

requirements management plan — A plan that describes how project requirements will be analyzed, documented and managed.

requirements traceability matrix (RTM) — A table that lists requirements, various attributes of each requirement, and the status of the requirements to ensure that all of them are addressed.

resource histogram — A column chart that shows the number of resources required for or assigned to a project over time.

resource leveling — A technique for resolving resource conflicts by delaying tasks.

resource loading — The amount of individual resources an existing schedule requires during specific time periods.

responsibility assignment matrix (RAM) — A matrix that maps the work of the project as described in the WBS to the people responsible for performing the work.

return on investment (ROI) — (Benefits minus costs) divided by costs.

risk — An uncertainty that can have a negative or positive effect on meeting project objectives.

risk events — The specific, uncertain events that may occur to the detriment or enhancement of the project.

risk register — A document that contains results of various risk management processes, often displayed in a table or spreadsheet format.

root cause — The real or underlying reason a problem occurs.

run chart — A chart that displays the history and pattern of variation of a process over time.

scatter diagram — A diagram that helps show if there is a relationship between two variables.

scope baseline — The approved project scope statement and its associated WBS and WBS dictionary.

scope creep — The tendency for project scope to continually increase.

scope verification — The formal acceptance of the completed project scope by the customer or designated stakeholders.

short list — A list of the top three to five suppliers created to reduce the work involved in selecting a source.

Six Sigma — A comprehensive and flexible system for achieving, sustaining, and maximizing business success; uniquely driven by close understanding of customer needs, disciplined use of facts, data, and statistical analysis, and diligent attention to managing, improving, and reinventing business processes.

slack or **float** — The amount of time an activity may be delayed without delaying a succeeding activity or the project finish date.

slipped milestone — A milestone activity that was actually completed later than originally planned.

smoothing mode — The conflict-handling mode that de-emphasizes or avoids areas of differences and emphasizes areas of agreement.

staffing management plan — A plan that describes when and how people will be added to and taken off of a project.

stakeholder management strategy — An approach to help increase the support of stakeholders throughout the project.

stakeholder register — A document that includes details related to the identified project stakeholders

stakeholders — People involved in or affected by project activities.

standard — A document that describes best practices for what should be done to manage a project.

status reports — The reports that describe where the project stands at a specific point in time.

strategic planning — The process of determining long-term objectives by analyzing the strengths and weaknesses of an organization, studying opportunities and threats in the business environment, predicting future trends, and projecting the need for new products and services.

SWOT analysis — Analyzing Strengths, Weaknesses, Opportunities, and Threats.

synergy — The concept that the whole is equal to more than the sum of its parts.

team contract — A document created to help promote teamwork and clarify team communications.

template — A file with a preset format that serves as a starting point for creating various documents so that the format and structure do not have to be re-created.

Theory of Constraints (TOC) — A management philosophy that states that any complex system at any point in time often has only one aspect or constraint that is limiting its ability to achieve more of its goal.

three-point estimate — An estimate that includes an optimistic, most likely, and pessimistic estimate.

time-and-material contract — A type of contract that is a hybrid of both a fixed-price and cost-reimbursable contract.

to-complete performance index (TCPI) — The cost performance that must be achieved on the remaining work in order to meet a specified goal, such as the BAC or EAC.

tracking Gantt chart — A Gantt chart that compares planned and actual project schedule information.

triggers — The indicators or symptoms of actual risk events.

triple constraint — Balancing scope, time, and cost goals.

Tuckman model — A model that describes five stages of team development (forming, storming, norming, performing, and adjourning).

validated deliverable — A deliverable that has been completed and checked for correctness as part of quality control.

weighted scoring model — A technique that provides a systematic process for basing project selection on numerous criteria.

withdrawal mode — The conflict-handling mode that involves retreating or withdrawing from an actual or potential disagreement.

work breakdown structure (WBS) — A deliverable-oriented grouping of the work involved in a project that defines the total scope of the project.

work breakdown structure (WBS) dictionary — A document that describes detailed information about WBS tasks.

work package — A task at the lowest level of the WBS.

workarounds — The unplanned responses to risk events.

INDEX

508

An Introduction to Project Management, Third Edition

Made in the USA
Charleston, SC
25 February 2012